AF477894

Authority in the Global Political Economy

International Political Economy series

General Editor: **Timothy M. Shaw**, Professor and Director, Institute of International Relations, The University of the West Indies, Trinidad & Tobago

Titles include:

Lucian M. Ashworth and David Long (*editors*)
NEW PERSPECTIVES ON INTERNATIONAL FUNCTIONALISM

Robert W. Cox (*editor*)
THE NEW REALISM
Perspectives on Multilateralism and World Order

Frederick Deyo (*editor*)
GLOBAL CAPITAL, LOCAL LABOUR

Stephen Gill (*editor*)
GLOBALIZATION, DEMOCRATIZATION AND MULTILATERALISM

Björn Hettne, András Inotai and Osvaldo Sunkel (*editors*)
GLOBALISM AND THE NEW REGIONALISM

Christopher C. Meyerson
DOMESTIC POLITICS AND INTERNATIONAL RELATIONS IN US–JAPAN
TRADE POLICYMAKING
The GATT Uruguay Round Agriculture Negotiations

Volker Rittberger and Martin Nettesheim (*editors*)
AUTHORITY IN THE GLOBAL POLITICAL ECONOMY

Justin Robertson (*editor*)
POWER AND POLITICS AFTER FINANCIAL CRISES
Rethinking Foreign Opportunism in Emerging Markets

Michael G, Schechter (*editor*)
FUTURE MULTILATERALISM
The Political and Social Framework

INNOVATION IN MULTILATERALISM

Ben Thirkell-White
THE IMF AND THE POLITICS OF FINANCIAL GLOBALIZATION
From the Asian Crisis to a New International Financial Architecture?

Thomas G. Weiss (*editor*)
BEYOND UN SUBCONTRACTING
Task Sharing with Regional Security Arrangements and Service-Providing NGOs

Robert Wolfe
FARM WARS
The Political Economy of Agriculture and the International Trade Regime

---

International Political Economy Series
Series Standing Order ISBN 0–333–71708–2 hardcover
Series Standing Order ISBN 0–333–71110–6 paperback
(*outside North America only*)

You can receive future titles in this series as they are published by placing a standing order. Please contact your bookseller or, in case of difficultly, write to us at the address below with your name and address, the title of the series and one of the ISBNs quoted above.

Customer Services Department, Macmillan Distribution Ltd, Houndmills, Basingstoke, Hampshire RG21 6XS, England

Authority in the Global Political Economy

Edited by

Volker Rittberger

Professor of Political Science and International Relations and Director of the Centre for International Relations/Peace and Conflict Studies, University of Tübingen, Germany

Martin Nettesheim

Chair for German Public Law, Public International Law, European Law and International Political Theory, University of Tübingen, Germany

and Associate Editor

Carmen Huckel

Research Associate, Centre for International Relations/Peace and Conflict Research, University of Tübingen, Germany

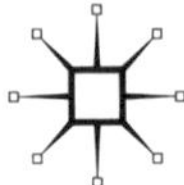

First published 2008 by
PALGRAVE MACMILLAN
Houndmills, Basingstoke, Hampshire RG21 6XS and
175 Fifth Avenue, New York, N.Y. 10010
Companies and representatives throughout the world

PALGRAVE MACMILLAN is the global academic imprint of the Palgrave Macmillan division of St. Martin's Press, LLC and of Palgrave Macmillan Ltd. Macmillan® is a registered trademark in the United States, United Kingdom and other countries. Palgrave is a registered trademark in the European Union and other countries.

ISBN-13: 978–0–230–57389–5   hardback
ISBN-10: 0–230–57389–4   hardback

This book is printed on paper suitable for recycling and made from fully managed and sustained forest sources. Logging, pulping and manufacturing processes are expected to conform to the environmental regulations of the country of origin.

A catalogue record for this book is available from the British Library.

Library of Congress Cataloging-in-Publication Data

Authority in the global political economy / edited by Volker
  Rittberger, Martin Nettesheim, and associate editor, Carmen Huckel.
      p. cm. — (International political economy series)
   Includes bibliographical references and index.
   ISBN 0–230–57389–4 (alk. paper)
  1. International economic relations.   2. Authority.   3.
   International organization.   4. Globalization—Political aspects.
   I. Rittberger, Volker, 1941–   II. Nettesheim, Martin.   III. Huckel,
   Carmen, 1978–
   HF1411.A973 2008
   337.01—dc22
                                                                    2007052980

10   9   8   7   6   5   4   3   2   1
17   16   15   14   13   12   11   10   09   08

Printed and bound in Great Britain by CPI Antony Rowe,
Chippenham and Eastbourne

Contents

Part 4   Business in Global Governance

Part 5   Regulation in Global Governance

List of Tables

List of Figures

Editors' Preface

This volume has been developed from the proceedings of the international conference 'Changing Patterns of Authority in the Global Political Economy' that took place in Tübingen as a project of the postgraduate research programme 'Global Challenges – Transnational and Transcultural Approaches' from 14 to 16 October 2004. The conference had the aim of analysing central questions and different dimensions and characteristics of authority on inter-, trans-, and supranational levels, in particular from international relations and public international law perspectives. The direction and scope of the conference were inspired by the interdisciplinary focus of the postgraduate research programme, which recognizes that emerging global processes, structures and networks transcend state borders and demonstrate more clearly a limited capacity of states to cope effectively with pressing international problems. These global challenges have increased the demand on politics, law, economics and education (fields which have become increasingly intertwined) to provide guidance and solutions.

The postgraduate research programme 'Global Challenges – Transnational and Transcultural Approaches', which has been generously funded by the German Science Association, was formed in 2002 and brings together a multidisciplinary group of professors and young scholars who have been working on projects designed around the three following sub-themes: 1) form and content of responses to globalization in economics, law and politics; 2) ethical and cultural as well as religious aspects of globalization; and 3) cultural diversity and intercultural and inter-religious education. Within the programme, two research units, led by Professors Volker Rittberger and Martin Nettesheim, worked together to organize the conference. With many of the global challenges of the twenty-first century culminating, in one way or another, on the axis of trade, finance and wealth distribution, the conference focused on the global political economy as a core field of activities in which problems and their solutions are continually experienced and tested, and where authority is being exerted more strongly in a global context.

Participants were invited to analyse and discuss the various dimensions of authority beside and beyond the nation-state. The UN Global Compact and the WTO's Dispute Settlement System served as examples of global governance institutions designed to achieve a high level of effectiveness and accountability. The proceedings touched upon expectations directed at institutions of global governance and upon the challenges they currently face. The conference proceedings involved presentations and panel discussions concentrated on the following four general topics:

First: The future of international institutions in the global political economy: Here, general questions on the conference theme were addressed such as: What are the main sources of authority in the global political economy?

Can public international law accommodate the necessary regulatory and institutional infrastructure? What are the implications of the emerging new forms of authority for the theory and doctrine of public international law? Are multilateral treaties to be supplemented by alternative methods of law-making? What role are the states supposed to assume in the emerging framework?

Second: The provision of global public goods: At this panel it was highlighted that, since the beneficiaries of global public goods are diverse and their interests and concerns vary, the production path for global public goods is highly complex. In particular it was asked how global governance institutions can target the problem of conflicting public goods.

Third: Taking stock of civil society involvement in the global political economy: This panel discussed the capacities of civil society organizations (CSOs) as compared to states, international organizations (IGOs), and transnational corporations (TNCs), and how the relationship between CSOs, states, IGOs and TNCs will develop in the future.

Fourth: Legitimacy as a global ordering principle: Here, conference participants reflected upon how rapid changes in the global political economy have raised many new questions about how we are to understand public authority in a global context and which actors have the ability, and may claim the right, to act on a global level. From a normative point of view, the question was raised whether it is necessary to reconceptualize the idea of legitimate transnational and extra-statal governance.

Throughout the conference an eye was kept on new actors, institutions and structures, their performance in terms of provision of public goods, and on new forms of regulation. Participants from several countries debated where authority is to be found in the era of globalization and global governance and how it can be conceptualized and understood.

From the ensuing discussions it became clear that, whereas the state for a long time served as the core institution and its organs, particularly its executive branch of government, as central actors in international governance, new actors, structures and issues have emerged to transform it into global governance. Accordingly, this volume is divided into important sub-themes representing key substantive aspects of changing patterns of authority: *first*, the nature and 'constitution' of institutions for governance in the global political economy; *second*, the definition of (global) public goods, their (under-)supply, and their transformation into private goods (and vice versa); *third*, the contribution of civil society organizations to global governance in general and to the provision of (global) public goods in particular; *fourth*, business actors' contributions to global governance and to the provision of (global) public goods; and *fifth*, the differences between various modes of regulation incorporated in new institutions for global governance.

Which structures emerge, and how can these fulfil the functions that have been formerly performed by the individual state? Is governance beyond the state capable of regulating the global political economy as well as externalities of globalization? How can globalization be governed and by whom? These are the questions behind the chapters that follow and the answers are as surprising as they are challenging to conventional wisdom. Throughout the book, an in-depth look at the changing role of the state as well as non-state actors such as civil society organizations and business actors is presented, examining how these new players are involved in alternative forms of regulation. The number of non-state actors active in agenda-setting, decision-making and policy implementation alone has increased considerably in previous decades and with intensifying emancipation of these new actors they are demanding a greater share in exercising authority in global governance. With this, they attempt to achieve a higher leverage in regulating the global political economy competing with states as well as with other non-state actors. Finally, regulation is addressed as a means to resolve the underlying tension between the emerging patterns of authority and the need to provide global public goods.

Following the successful conference, premier contributions were revised and updated for publication. The editors greatly appreciate the cooperation of all contributors to this volume; they apologize for not having been able to include all papers presented at the conference for a lack of space in a one-volume publication. The editors also wholeheartedly thank scholars and staff of the postgraduate research programme 'Global Challenges – Transnational and Transcultural Approaches', in particular Lothar Rieth and Ralf Reusch for their constructive participation in the planning and organization of the 2004 conference. For their financial support of the conference the editors are also grateful to the Fritz Thyssen Foundation and the Association of the Friends of the University of Tübingen. Further thanks go to Karin Moser von Filseck from the International Centre of the University of Tübingen and to the staff at the host institution, Hohentübingen Castle. The publication would not have been possible without the encouragement and support from Palgrave Macmillan's Philippa Grand and Steven Kennedy.

Special thanks also go to the staff at the Centre for International Relations/Peace and Conflict Research, and the Chair for German Public Law, European Community Law, and Public International Law at the University of Tübingen; especially Rosita Retzlaff and Isolde Zeiler for their helpful assistance during the late stages of the project, and to our associate editor Carmen Huckel for her diligent work on the individual chapters, and general support.

Notes on the Contributors

Helmut K. Anheier is Professor of Public Policy and Social Welfare and Director of the Center for Civil Society, Department of Social Welfare, School of Public Affairs, University of California, Los Angeles, USA.

Wolfgang Benedek is Professor at the Institute of International Law and International Relations, University of Graz, Austria.

Steven Bernstein is Associate Professor at the Department of Political Science, University of Toronto, Canada.

Benjamin Cashore is Professor at the School of Forestry and Environmental Studies, Yale University, New Haven, USA.

A. Claire Cutler is Professor of International Law and Relations, Department of Political Science, University of Victoria, BC, Canada.

Jeffrey L. Dunoff is Charles Klein Professor of Law and Government at the Beasley School of Law, Temple University, Philadelphia, USA.

Thorsten Göbel is a Research Associate at the Centre for International Relations/Peace and Conflict Studies and a member of the postgraduate research programme 'Global Challenges: Transnational and Transcultural Approaches', University of Tübingen, Germany.

Virginia Haufler is Associate Professor at the Department of Government and Politics, University of Maryland, College Park, USA.

Carmen Huckel is a Research Associate at the Centre for International Relations/Peace and Conflict Studies and a member of the postgraduate research programme 'Global Challenges: Transnational and Transcultural Approaches', University of Tübingen, Germany.

Inge Kaul is Director (retd.) of the Office of Development Studies, United Nations Development Programme.

Martin Nettesheim is Professor of German Public Law, Public International Law and European Law, School of Law, University of Tübingen, Germany.

Lothar Rieth is a Research Associate at the Institute of Political Science, Darmstadt University of Technology, Germany.

Volker Rittberger is Professor of Political Science and International Relations and Director of the Centre for International Relations/Peace and Conflict Studies, University of Tübingen, Germany.

Peter-Tobias Stoll is Professor and Director at the Institute of International Law and European Law, School of Law, Göttingen University, Germany.

Nuno S. Themudo is Assistant Professor of International Affairs at the Graduate School of Public and International Affairs, University of Pittsburgh, USA.

Peter Utting is Deputy Director of the United Nations Research Institute for Social Development (UNRISD), Geneva, Switzerland.

Melanie Zimmer is a Research Associate at the Frankfurt Peace Research Institute, Frankfurt/M., Germany.

Introduction: Changing Patterns of Authority

Volker Rittberger, Martin Nettesheim, Carmen Huckel, Thorsten Göbel

The capacity of states to fulfil basic governance functions has become strained in the era of globalization; their authority is under pressure from without and within. The global integration of markets and the increase and spread of direct investments by transnational corporations (TNCs) have limited state control over national societies and economies. The increasing inter-dependence of enterprises in global markets and the growing importance of new cross-border actors and identities undermine the power of the state. Interdependence and new transnational problems (most notably since the mid-1980s environmental problems such as 'acid rain', ozone depletion and climate change) are challenging the authority of the state and promote shifts of authority to new actors and institutions that are better enabled to deal with these issues. This implies that TNCs and other non-state actors are assuming a new role on the international stage.

Policy domains which have been regulated on a purely domestic level, such as environmental and consumer protection, are now increasingly dealt with by competing global, regional and national institutions. In the past, international institutions served as a forum in which national policy processes were coordinated. Today, however, substantive decision-making has emerged within supra-national fora within which decision-making is not dependent on a consensus among participating states. The practice of majority decision-making adds another element to the changing nature of authority in the international system (Nettesheim 2002).

Regardless of where governance powers are finally located, their effectiveness and stability depend on their bearer's ability to exercise authority. In the global political economy, this not only refers to the legal obligations, supranational decision-making, transnational public policy networks, and effective monitoring mechanisms, but also to the more subtle consensus-building procedures and incentive systems now exercised by new institutions for global governance. This books aims to bring together contributions that demonstrate the need for, and assist in the development of, a conceptualization of authority suitable for the globalized age.

The concept of authority requires considerably more attention in international relations and law than currently is devoted to it. In mainstream international relations centred on realist and liberal schools of thought, authority is presumed to be a function of the formal position of an actor or agency. As a result, in the absence of any overarching government and in a consequent state of anarchy, authority is said to be generally absent in the global realm.

However, as demonstrated by the concept of complex interdependence in the 1970s (Keohane and Nye 2001), regime analysis of the 1980s and 1990s (Rittberger 1993, Hasenclever, Mayer et al. 1997) and several key texts on the role of non-state actors during the past ten years (Cutler, Haufler et al. 1999; Anheier, Glasius et al. 2002) it has become increasingly evident that authority must indeed exist on a global level. Furthermore, some authors have pressed for more attention for authority, not just because of new patterns of authority between states and outside of the state, but because the authority *of* the state over internal affairs is also coming under pressure (Strange 1996). In this book we uncover plentiful evidence of authority on the global level and conclude that a broader conceptualization of authority is required to understand various phenomena that can be observed in interactions between states, international organizations, civil society actors and business actors that exist today (Held and McGrew 2002). Authority is therefore found to be dispersed among many actors and exercised through means other than formal position.

Despite several streams of scholarly work progressively touching on the evidence for the existence of authority on the global level, for most the concept of authority remains peripheral rather than central to understanding the global political economy. Wendt notes 'that scholars are just beginning to grapple with how decentralized authority might be understood' (Wendt 1999: 308). For some, authority entails 'institutionalized forms or expressions of power' (Hall and BiersBecker 2002: 4) while others explicitly include the pull to compliance in accordance with beliefs and norms by defining political authority as 'a fusion of power with legitimate social purpose' (Ruggie 1982: 198). The chapters in this volume are aligned along these lines, but also recognize that with dispersing locations of authority new demands on the legitimacy of actors also arise.

In this volume, authority is defined as part of the relationship between the makers of rules and norms and those which are expected to follow them. One can be both an authority and in authority. Authority is then: the ability of an actor or an institution to induce relevant addressees to take note of, and comply with, their norms and rules.

Authority can be based on various grounds: on coercion, interest and legitimacy (Rieth 2004: 182). In *Economy and Society*, Weber already conceptualized different modes of authority, as rational-legal, but also traditional or charismatic. His suggestion that authority can rest on elements such as customs, habits, social structure or 'inspiration' implies that in all settings from familial to domestic to global, apart from coercion or interests, non-material factors can also provide a basis for exercising power that is taken as authoritative

(Weber 1968: 215). This implication has re-emerged in recent studies that explicate several modes of authoritative power based on 'soft factors' such as moral, knowledge-based, reputational, issue-specific and 'affiliative' authority (James Rosenau 2002: 267). Consequently, factors other than material power can underpin habitual patterns of compliance that define authoritative relationships allowing for a relocation of authority from public to quasi-public and to private actors and institutions to take place.

The existence of various locations and modes of authority in the global political economy has significant consequences for international relations and international public law. Two in particular should be noted:

First, recognizing new patterns, locations and modes of exercising authority on the global level has consequences for how the global system as a whole is to be conceptualized. A global system in which structured and well-ordered authoritative relationships exist between various actors on various levels cannot be classified as essentially anarchic. Hurd, for example, notes that '(a)n international system with authoritative institutions cannot be said to be "anarchic," and indeed it displays many of the traits that we usually associate with domestic government. If we accept that some authoritative international institutions exist, by virtue of their being accepted by states as legitimate, then the international system is not an anarchy' (Hurd 1999: 401). In this book, the authors consider this consequence further by addressing possible alternatives to anarchy that better describe the observed reality of the global system today. In chapter one, for instance, Rittberger et al. conclude that the notion of heterarchy better fits the observable realities in the global system than the concept of anarchy used by some observers to study the functioning of international relations in a variety of issue areas.

Second, new modes of exercising authority especially through non-state actors have consequences for legal-ethical issues such as the allocation of responsibilities, and accountability. Cutler, Haufler and Porter, for example, posit that 'in an era when the authority of the state appears to be challenged in so many ways, the existence of alternative sources of authority takes on great significance, especially when that authority is wielded internationally by profit seeking entities' (1999: 4). With various actors exercising authority, who, at first glance, are not subject to same the checks and balances as democratic governments, questions arise as to how their responsibilities are defined and how they are held accountable for their actions. In this book, further consequences of changing patterns of authority in relation to issues of legitimacy and accountability are addressed, for example by Cutler, who takes a critical view of the authority of TNCs, and by Themudo and Anheier, who examine the legitimacy and accountability of NGOs.

The chapters in this book recognize that the international system is characterized by a variety of authority relationships of varying degrees of hierarchy, but also heterarchical relationships, where actors or sets of actors may accept the authority of peers or those representing the wider community. In order to break out of the state-centric lens, a differentiated approach towards examining authority relationships embodied in new institutions of global governance is required. To achieve this, core analytical aspects must be identified that can provide the basis for research. In *Authority in the Global Political Economy*, the chapters concentrate on four different dimensions of global governance analysis: *demand, supply, effect* and *design*. Each of these elements supplement each other and allow for a comprehensive analytical coverage of the most fundamental theoretical issues underlying empirical trends in the global political economy. The advantage of concentrating on these four elements is that it allows for analysis from both institutionalist and critical points of view as well as lends itself to interpretive or rationalist epistemologies.

By focusing on the *demand dimension*, authors have investigated what kinds of new institutional forms are needed at the global level and why. When looking at the *supply dimension*, authors considered actors that are willing and capable to create or sustain institutions that have the capacity to wield global authority. In studying the *effect dimension*, the expected consequences of these new institutions were sought out, as well as which externalities they produce, what tensions exist between some of them, and who their main addressees are. Finally, as many new institutions for global governance have already come into existence, by bringing in the *design dimension* authors also examined how the design of these institutions has influenced their effectiveness and legitimacy.

The interplay between these four themes of analysis deserves some closer attention, as they can provide a basis for future investigations into changing patterns of authority, not only in the realm of global political economy, but with reference to other issue-areas as well.

In terms of *demand*, market failures as well as a lack of legal clarity and societal security have generated a general need for new approaches toward regulating market processes including, where necessary, their reinvigoration. Therefore institutionalized authority is needed to both enable and restrict non-state actors' activities alike. Corporate claims as well as those of civil society actors for control and readjustments often conflict and vary according to the relevant business sector or the geographic place of activity. A *demand* for authority, however, does not necessarily mean a higher level of regulation. Instead, it may also imply a reliable commitment by public and private sector actors to implement a few guiding principles accompanied by institutionalized monitoring.

An inquiry into the *demand* for authority then naturally leads to questions concerning its *supply*. Thus far, neither states nor international organizations have demonstrated sufficient powers to remedy the deficits ('governance gaps') that have led to a demand for alternative forms of authority (Brühl and Rittberger 2001: 19ff; Rittberger/Huckel/Rieth/Zimmer, in this volume). Therefore, either the capacities of international organizations must be enlarged or non-state actors must be legally and politically empowered to provide adequate governance arrangements for global markets.

Societal and environmental pressures have put the effects of global economic integration under public scrutiny. This also applies to the *effects* of new institutions for global governance. Decisions and actions taken in the economic realm often cause unintended consequences in other policy domains such as environmental protection or human rights. The externalities of institutions for global governance are, therefore, another important subject matter for social scientific inquiry. The effectiveness of these institutions varies depending on the actors addressed and the specific goals pursued. Both trade and non-trade issues must be dealt with in the global political economy but the question of how to deal with them without provoking legitimacy concerns among the various stakeholders is still to be resolved.

An examination of the *effects* of global political authority must also take into consideration the possible *design* of institutions for global governance. Even in a multi-layered system of global governance, the state still constitutes in many respects an indispensable participant in the policy-making cycle. Nevertheless, it is widely accepted that traditional patterns of governance must be further developed. The intellectual and political challenge is to devise institutions for global governance which combine effectiveness of policy-making and accountability toward their stakeholders.

While the different chapters in this book focus on each of these *analytical* aspects to varying degrees, this volume is further divided into important sub-themes representing key *substantive* aspects of changing patterns of authority: *first*, the nature and 'constitution' of institutions for governance in the global political economy; *second*, the definition of (global) public goods, their (under-)supply, and their transformation into private goods (and vice versa); *third*, the contribution of civil society organizations to global governance in general and to the provision of (global) public goods in particular; *fourth*, business actors' contributions to global governance and to the provision of (global) public goods; and *fifth*, the differences between various modes of regulation incorporated in new institutions for global governance.

Against the backdrop of the four analytical dimensions of global governance analysis (demand, supply, effect and design) and the five substantive themes just identified, this book is divided into five parts: a) New Institutions for Global Governance: aiming to give an overview of future locations of authority; b) Providing and Managing Global Public Goods: introducing an approach towards global governance that focuses on the demand for and supply of authority; c) Civil Society and Global Governance: focusing on actors and their role in exercising and repositioning authority; d) Business in Global Governance: concentrating on a type of actor still neglected in analysis of critical aspects such as responsibilities and accountability in global governance; e) Regulation in Global Governance, bringing the book full circle by once again looking at concrete issues of compliance within new institutions.

In the following, a short introduction into the topics of each of these five parts of this volume will be given.

New institutions for global governance

The first substantive theme analysed in this volume is the nature and 'constitution' of institutions for global governance. Non-state actors are increasingly present in global governance and are challenging the state as the central actor in international relations. The main questions addressed are: Is there a need for new governing institutions on the global level that give a more prominent role to non-state actors? And what 'constitutional form' should these new institutions take on? The chapters by Volker Rittberger et al. and Jeffrey Dunoff approach this issue from political, normative and legal viewpoints concentrating on the *demand* for, and *supply* of, new institutions on the global level.

Providing and managing global public goods

The contributions by Inge Kaul and Peter-Tobias Stoll take a look at the *demand* for, and *supply* of, new institutions for global governance based on the (global) public goods approach. The mainstream definition of public goods is a good that is nonrival in consumption and nonexcludable. Private goods can be (made) exclusive in consumption, in other words the owner of the good determines how to use it. In general, public goods are those that are provided by the state because markets usually fail to produce them in sufficient quantity and quality, if at all (e.g. national defence, clean environment, public education, economic infrastructure). *Global* public goods are public goods, the benefits of which extend across countries and regions, across rich and poor population groups, and even across generations. In reality, however, certain global public goods such as human rights and free trade are provided neither by the state (or states alone) nor the market, creating a need for new governing institutions beyond the state and the market (e.g. the WTO and the Global Compact) that will contribute to the provision of these goods.

Civil society and global governance

Civil society organizations (CSOs) have been increasingly participating in international affairs. The importance of this phenomenon is demonstrated by a more prominent international political role of CSOs in terms of service (e.g. humanitarian aid) and advocacy (e.g. the International Campaign to Ban Landmines) (see, e.g. Rittberger, Schrade et al. 1999; and Breitmeier and Rittberger 2000). This raises the question of how civil society actors can be integrated into institutions for global governance. The contributions of Helmut Anheier and Nuno Themudo as well as of Wolfgang Benedek deliberate the role of CSOs (referred to by the authors as non-governmental organizations (NGOs)) in the *supply* and *design* of new institutions for global governance. In particular, they address the question of how NGOs can position themselves in order to influence new institutions for global governance most effectively, and which criteria NGOs would have to fulfil in order to play an increased role in global governance.

Business in global governance

Thus far the role of business actors in global governance has received scant attention in academic research. Nonetheless, business actors have been recognized as being able to provide knowledge, expertise, material resources and strategic advantages to institutions for global governance. In practice, business actors are already expanding their scope of influence beyond the provision of marketable goods and services to the provision of public goods such as the protection of the environment, public health and human rights. Contributions in this part by Claire Cutler and Virginia Haufler scrutinize the role of business actors in global governance in terms of *effect* and *design*. Both authors ask to what extent business actors are willing and able to perform functions traditionally reserved for the state (*effect*) and whether they consciously do this via new governing institutions on the global level (*design*).

Regulation in global governance

Regulation in global governance is an issue raised in several contributions in this volume and is a part of global governance, i.e. 'the collective identification of high-potential approaches for solving common problems and the process of transforming them into binding rules of behaviour, monitoring behaviour and, if necessary, adjusting the rules to changes in external conditions' (Rittberger 2003: 181f; Rittberger 2004: 249). Regulation as part of governance, more specifically, refers to 'the formal rules or standards that dictate what is acceptable and required behaviour, putting limits on what is permissible' (Haufler 2001: 8). As there is no world government, forms of regulation that differ from those at the disposal of states domestically must be sought. When discussing regulation, the main questions raised are: Which roles do different actors, and especially states, play in providing regulation? To what degree can and shall regulation take the form of self-regulation and/or to what extent can and shall regulation be monitored by states alone or in cooperation with other public or private sector actors? How can forms of co-regulation, i.e. inclusive decision-making processes and partnerships overcome problems of self- or state regulation?

With the chapters by Benjamin Cashore and Steven Bernstein as well as by Peter Utting on regulation the book comes full circle by means of this highly critical topic in the current debates on changing patterns of authority and one which will surely gain increasing attention. All of the topics analysed – the constitution of institutions for global governance, the roles of civil society and private business, and the challenges of providing global public goods culminating in issues of regulation – raise critical questions of authority, effectiveness and legitimacy. These issues remain at the core of the current debate on changing patterns of authority in the global political economy.

References

Anheier, Helmut, Marlies Glasius and Mary Kaldor (2002): *Global Civil Society Yearbook 2002*. Oxford: Oxford University Press.

Breitmeier, Helmut and Volker Rittberger (2000): Environmental NGOs in an Emerging Global Civil Society. In: Chasek, Pamela (ed.): *The Global Environment in the Twenty-First Century: Prospects for International Cooperation*. Tokyo/New York: United Nations University Press: 130–63.

Brühl, Tanja and Volker Rittberger (2001): From International to Global Governance: Actors, Collective Decision-making, and the United Nations in the World of the Twenty-First Century. In: Rittberger, Volker (ed.): *Global Governance and the United Nations System*. Tokyo/New York: United Nations University Press: 1–47.

Cutler, Claire (1999): Locating 'Authority' in the Global Economy. In: *International Studies Quarterly* 43 (1): 59–81.

Cutler, Claire, Virginia Haufler and Tony Porter (eds.) (1999): *Private Authority and International Affairs*. Albany: State University of New York Press.

Hall, Rodney Bruce and Thomas J. Biersteker (eds.) (2002): *The Emergence of Private Authority in Global Governance*. Cambridge: Cambridge University Press.

Haufler, Virginia (2001): *A Public Role for the Private Sector. Industry Self-Regulation in a Global Economy*. Washington, DC: Carnegie Endowment for International Peace.

Hasenclever, Andreas, Peter Mayer and Volker Rittberger (1997): *Theories of International Regimes*. Cambridge: Cambridge University Press.

Held, David and Anthony G. McGrew (2002): *Governing Globalization: Power, Authority and Global Governance*. Malden, MA: Polity Press.

Hurd, Ian (1999): Legitimacy and Authority in International Politics. In: *International Organisation* 53 (2): 379–408.

Keohane, Robert O. and Joseph S. Nye (2001): *Power and Interdependence: World Politics in Transition* (3rd edition). New York: Longman.

Nettesheim, Martin, (2002): Das kommunitäre Völkerrecht. In: *Juristenzeitung* 57 (12): 569–78.

Rieth, Lothar (2004): Corporate Social Responsibility in Global Economic Governance: A Comparison of the OECD Guidelines and the UN Global Compact. In: Schirm, Stefan A. (ed.) *Public and Private Governance in the World Economy: New Rules for Global Markets*. New York: Palgrave Macmillan: 177–92.

Rittberger, Volker (ed.) (1993): *Regime Theory and International Relations*. Oxford: Clarendon Press.

Rittberger, Volker (2003): Weltregieren: Was kann es leisten? Was muss es leisten? In: Küng, Hans and Dieter Senghaas (eds.): *Friedenspolitik: Ethische Grundlagen Internationaler Beziehungen*. Munich: Zürich: Piper: 177–208.

Rittberger, Volker (2004): Weltregieren zwischen Anarchie und Hierarchie. In: Rittberger, Volker (ed.): *Weltpolitik heute. Grundlagen und Perspektiven*. Baden-Baden: Nomos: 245–70.

Rittberger, Volker, Christina Schrade and Daniela Schwarzer (1999): 'Introduction: Transnational Civil Society and the Quest for Security'. In: Alagappa, Muthiah and Takashi Inoguchi (eds.). *International Security Management and the United Nations: the United Nations System in the 21st Century*. Tokyo/New York, United Nations University Press: 109–38.

Rosenau, James (2002): NGOs and Fragmented Authority in Globalizing Space. In: Yale Ferguson and R. Barry Jones (eds.) *Political Space: Frontiers of Change and Governance in a Globalizing World*. Albany: State University of New York Press: 261–79.

Ruggie, John (1982): International Regimes, Transactions and Change: Embedded Liberalism in the Postwar Economic Order. In: *International Organisation* 36 (2): 379–415.

Weber, Max (1968): *Economy and Society, Vols 1 and 2*. Berkeley: University of California Press.

Wendt, Alexander, (1999): *Social Theory of International Politics*. Cambridge: Cambridge University Press.

Strange, Susan (1996): *The Retreat of the State: the Diffusion of Power in the World Economy*. Cambridge: Cambridge University Press.

Part 1
New Institutions for Global Governance

1
Inclusive Global Institutions for a Global Political Economy

Volker Rittberger, Carmen Huckel, Lothar Rieth,
Melanie Zimmer

Introduction

Our world is changing in many ways which are most commonly described as globalization. Meaning more than just a trend towards economic liberalization and integration, today's 'thick' globalization can be observed in terms of the intensification of economic as well as social and political interactions across borders such as the sharing of knowledge and opinions through new means of communication, the deepening impact that localized events have on global trends, the establishment of worldwide standards in science and technology, and the transnational production of goods and services (Held, McGrew, Goldblatt and Perraton 1999: 21f.; Zürn 1998).[1]

Not surprisingly, the state-based Westphalian system finds itself amidst a process of transition. On the domestic level, the capacity and willingness of states to control what goes on inside their borders and to shield themselves against potentially damaging events outside of their borders have declined considerably. State sovereignty as a normative concept, as well as a functional ordering principle, has therefore found itself weakened, and states are losing their autonomous capacity to effectively govern (Clark 1999: 75).

This decline in states' autonomous capacity has been caused by two parallel developments. First, globalization has led to the emergence of new transsovereign problems and the intensification of existing problems that states and intergovernmental institutions are not able to solve alone (Cusimano 2000). Second, new actors, such as private companies and civil society organizations have become increasingly important as rule makers and 'teachers of norms'. Added to these two developments, the blurring of the policy domains 'security', 'welfare', and 'system of rule', analytically separated in political science (Czempiel 1981: 198), has expanded the scope and reach of political action of non-state actors allowing them to move into policy areas that were previously the exclusive domain of states.

Let us consider just a few examples of recent years. Despite the intergovernmental make up of the WTO, it has almost become the rule that private companies or economic interest groups become intimately involved in the initiation of government complaints. Recent disputes between the EU and the US over the aircraft manufacturing industry are a case in point. Meanwhile, as private companies make use, albeit in an indirect way, of the WTO Dispute Settlement Mechanism, civil society networks are involved in lobbying activities outside of the organization's official bodies.[2] The protests in Seattle in 1999/2000, almost every year at the World Economic Forum's Annual Meetings, and also during the Doha Round trade negotiations have raised awareness of the need to reconcile free trade with social responsibilities. These protests symbolize an increasingly organized civil society movement gaining considerable media attention and popular support (Anheier and Themudo in this volume).

In other areas, the participation of civil society organizations (CSOs) in global governance has been more direct and consequential. Throughout the 1990s, CSOs led a campaign for the banning of landmines, which resulted in the Ottawa Process for the drafting of the Anti-Landmine Treaty. Furthermore, the reliance of states and intergovernmental organizations on CSOs for operational assistance in carrying out relief efforts in situations of acute humanitarian crisis as well as the increasing reliance on private actors for the funding of development programmes, for example through public–private partnerships, contribute to the increased visibility and importance of these new actors. Finally, let us not forget that not all examples of the increasing influence of non-states actors are positive. Terrorist networks and transnational organized crime are another type of non-state actors with obvious negative impacts on global society (Rittberger, Schrade and Schwarzer 1999).

So far, existing international institutions based on intergovernmental cooperation have failed to respond adequately to new global challenges and to the aspirations, influence and scope of non-state actors (Brühl and Rittberger 2001: 1919). Recently, however, new institutions involving non-state actors in particular ways have emerged, which indicate the beginning of a trend towards what we call 'inclusive' global institutions that promise to tackle global problems more adequately. These institutions reflect a new form of global governance that appears to differ in logic and design from that of executive multilateralism.[3] While 'executive multilateralism' is today widely accepted as reflecting the reasoning of states in a complex world, it remains puzzling as to why these new institutions have emerged and what consequences their emergence will have.

The discipline of international relations has now seen a considerable effort to try to better understand the trend towards an increasing influence of non-state actors on global governance. Theoretically, scholars recognize that emerging institutional arrangements seem to float between the 'anarchical' and 'hierarchical' principles of world order. Previous work on institutionalism, regimes and international organizations,[4] will be built upon throughout the chapter. The aim is to give a thorough description of this emerging trend towards the creation of more inclusive global institutions and to lay the groundwork for further research into this new phenomenon. As academic enquiry into this type of institution is still in its infancy, the chapter progresses by probing the following four basic propositions which reflect some the most fundamental questions surrounding the emergence of inclusive global institutions:

1. There is a trend towards the creation of more inclusive global institutions.
2. It is possible to pinpoint certain conditions which give rise to, and shape the creation of, these institutions.
3. These 'inclusive' institutions have the potential to close global governance gaps and thus to reduce input and output legitimacy deficits which plague existing intergovernmental institutions.
4. Inclusive global institutions can be conceived as the underpinnings of an emerging system of heterarchical governance, as opposed to international anarchy or a hierarchical system of world government.

In the next section of this chapter, we will elaborate on the concept of 'inclusiveness', firstly, by describing recent observable changes in institutional structures at the global level and, secondly, by providing a definition of inclusive institutions. These inclusive institutions formally recognize and incorporate both state and non-state actors. The concept of inclusiveness will then be illustrated on the examples of five different institutions: the WTO, the ILO, UNAIDS, the Global Compact and the Global Fund. Section three of the chapter will identify conditions for the emergence of inclusive global institutions including changes in the international system and actors' motivations. In section four, it will be argued that 'inclusiveness' enables global institutions to close certain governance gaps and thereby tackle current transsovereign problems more effectively and more legitimately. Finally, section five will focus on the fourth proposition and the concept of heterarchy will be introduced. It is suggested that heterarchy is the most appropriate term to capture the changes in the international order that are identified in this chapter.

Towards more 'inclusive' global institutions

Government and governance: historical shifts towards global governance[5]

Historically, the sixty years since the end of the Second World War represent a period of unprecedented, rising levels of institutionalization on the inter-, trans-, and supranational level (Zürn 1998: 22f., 171f.; Rittberger 1973: 28–54). During this period, the aims, scope and influence of international institutions have developed through several stages during which new organizational structures have been added to existing ones. The first stage of executive multilateralism was complemented and, to some degree, followed by a second stage in which intergovernmental organizations (IGOs) incrementally increased their openness to non-state actors (advanced executive multilateralism). Today, global governance is moving into its third stage of development where new institutions are established, whose membership is composed of state and non-state actors (inclusive institutions).

Executive multilateralism

As a reaction to new international challenges in the post Second World War era, such as disarmament of nuclear and conventional weapons or market access and liberalization of trade, states established an unprecedented number of international regimes and organizations such as the United Nations, the General Agreement on Tariffs and Trade (GATT) and the International Atomic Energy Agency (IAEA). These institutions were intended to facilitate multilateral cooperation among member states' executive branches of government as a means of collective problem solving. Representatives of the executive branches negotiate behind closed doors and then report their agreements to national legislatures and publics (Keohane and Nye 2000a: 26). These institutions were deliberately separated from public participation. Although some had constitutions that allowed for consultations with non-state actors, CSOs were rarely openly invited to take up formal consultative status;[6] rather, their influence came through informal engagement with government representatives.

A growth in the number of international organizations, many within the United Nations system, came about as a result of a process of rapid denationalization (Zürn 1998: 203f; Rittberger and Zangl 2006: 25–57). *Governance by national governments* became steadily less viable as it became increasingly difficult for them to satisfy societal demands and achieve their goals of governance. As a result, a trend emerged towards *governance with multiple governments* (through intergovernmental organizations (IGOs)) and regimes (Brühl and Rittberger 2001: 5). These institutions are part of a strategy by states to deal with their decreasing ability to manage new international problems on the national level (Zürn 1998) and their loss of autonomy vis-à-vis civil society and economic actors on the domestic level (Wolf 2000: 13). During this stage, states were clearly the dominant actors on the global level, and IGOs were the result of this trend.

Advanced executive multilateralism

Major systemic changes since the end of the cold war, such as globalization and new communication technologies, led to the decreasing ability of both states and their intergovernmental organizations to tackle certain problems such as environmental degradation and humanitarian crises (Simmons and De Jonge Oudraat 2001; Lomborg 2004). Although executive multilateralism has continued to play a significant role in the management of many global issues, as can be seen for example in the continuing importance placed on meetings of the G7/G8,[7] many institutions have begun opening up and fully utilizing avenues allowing for consultation with CSOs (Alger 2002; Martens 2005: 155–6).

The rise in the demands and aspirations of CSOs, especially at the beginning of the 1990s, and their role in voicing global public opinion led organizations such as the United Nations to recognize that CSOs represent a basic form of popular participation and representation (Boutros-Ghali 1996: 7). The UN Economic and Social Council (ECOSOC) and specialized agencies within the UN system increasingly invited CSOs to participate in their deliberations. Major UN sponsored conferences that have taken place since 1990 have served not only as channels for CSOs' participation in global governance, but also as avenues to strengthen their position as vital actors (United Nations 1997; Schechter 2001).

By granting consultative status to all CSOs that participated in UN sponsored world conferences, a dramatic increase in the number of CSOs with access to the UN system occurred during this decade.[8] At the same time, business actors, while rarely engaged in international institutions, were gaining importance and influence through their sheer number, geographical spread and global political and economic activities (UNCTAD 2002). This phenomenon was met with scepticism on behalf of a growing civil society movement. Still, during this stage, states were the main actors determining which non-state actors were given formal access to intergovernmental organizations. This stage of increasing openness of IGOs towards CSOs can be labelled advanced executive multilateralism or 'complex multilateralism' (O'Brien, Goetz, Scholte and Williams 2000: 207).

Inclusive institutions

Around the turn of the twenty-first century, new institutional arrangements for managing global problems have emerged, which vary widely in size, composition, and functional capacity. Some of these institutions have been initiated by business actors, others by CSOs, and still others by states or IGOs (Muldoon 2004: 203) (see Table 1.1).

One of the more recent world conferences, the World Summit on Sustainable Development (WSSD), held in Johannesburg in 2002, is a good example because it produced a critically different outcome than the conferences of the 1990s in terms of the relationship between state and non-state actors. At the WSSD, the bulk of CSOs continued to be active in agenda setting, conference planning, information dissemination, and lobbying (Brühl 2003). In addition, states, IGOs, CSOs and business actors, in particular, negotiated and agreed upon joint programmatic and operational activities, the 'Type 2 Partnership Initiatives'.

Since the 1990s, global public policy networks[9] and public–private partnerships[10] were created as ways of addressing narrowly defined problems.

Table 1.1:   Forms of governance

Forms of governance	Executive multilateralism	Advanced executive multilateralism	Inclusive institutions
Status of non-state actors	Informal access	Consultative status	Membership
Empirical examples	UN Security Council IAEA G7/G8	UN ECOSOC World Bank WTO	UNAIDS UN Global Compact Global Fund

The fight against AIDS, and global public health in general, has been an issue area in which a number of institutions with a multi-actor membership were founded, e.g. The Global Alliance for Vaccines and Immunization, UNAIDS and the Global Fund. In other issue areas, such as environmental protection, human rights, and labour standards, partnerships like the UN Global Compact and the World Commission on Dams were created.

Taking these developments into account, it can be inferred that a new type of institution for global governance, the 'inclusive global institution', based on state and non-state members, has emerged.

Inclusive institutions: a definition

As indicated in the previous section, we posit that there is a general trend in global governance from executive multilateralism towards more inclusive institutions. In contrast to international institutions such as the UN Security Council or the G7/G8 (examples of almost pure executive multilateralism) and the UN ECOSOC or the WTO (examples of advanced executive multilateralism) newly created international organizations, such as UNAIDS, the Global Compact as well as the Global Fund, more often take the form of an inclusive institution.[11]

Inclusiveness is defined as a characteristic of an international institution that (1) provides a variety of actors with the possibility of membership and (2) endows them with certain rights in the policy-making process.

The variety of actors can be divided into four categories: (1) states, (2) intergovernmental organizations, (3) civil society organizations, and (4) business actors. States and IGOs can be termed 'public sector actors', whereas CSOs and business actors are 'private sector actors'. Inclusiveness requires that membership is granted to actors from both sectors, i.e. at least one actor from the public sector and one from the private sector.

If an institution meets this minimum requirement, inclusiveness is further defined by the rights that these members have in the policy-making process of the institution. An inclusive institution allows for membership of both public sector and private sector actors and endows these members with rights in the policy-making process, comprised of agenda-setting, decision-making, implementation, and monitoring.

The focus here will be on decision-making, because it represents the most important part of the policy-making process and is the part from which private sector actors have thus far been excluded. For our analysis, the right to vote in governing bodies is used as the indicator to determine whether actors have decision-making rights.

According to this definition an institution granting membership to all four categories of actors of which all have decision-making rights represents the highest degree of inclusiveness; an institution which just meets the minimum requirements of inclusiveness according to the definition, i.e. membership of at least one public and at least one private sector actor, represents a low degree of inclusiveness.

The following sections will offer short case studies to illustrate the definition of inclusive institutions and provide a number of arguments for the existence of a trend towards inclusive institutions.

Case studies

In order to demonstrate the differences between 'inclusive' institutions and institutions of executive multilateralism we will first provide an introduction to one of the most prominent examples of advanced executive multilateralism, the World Trade Organization (WTO). The International Labour Organization (ILO) is then introduced as an exception to the state-centrism of early international institutions. Thereafter, we provide an overview of three novel institutions which can be considered as approaching the 'inclusive' end of the continuum of public and private sector actors' participation in institutions of global governance, i.e. UNAIDS, the UN Global Compact and the Global Fund.

World Trade Organization

International economic organizations usually exist on the basis of multilateral treaties and agreements. The WTO provides the organizational framework for a large number of such treaties and agreements. In 1995, the World Trade Organization became the successor to the General Agreement on Tariffs and Trade (GATT), including not only the GATT but also encompassing, inter alia, the General Agreement on Trade in Services (GATS) and an agreement on Trade-Related Aspects of Intellectual Property Rights (TRIPS). Seven years of intensive negotiations in the Uruguay Round (1986–1994) gave birth to an international organization with 149 member states[12] with vastly expanded responsibilities for international economic affairs (Sampson 2001a: 1). The WTO deals with the rules of trade between nations. The main goal is to liberalize trade and to provide a set of rules for international trade. At the same time, as stated in the 'Agreement Establishing the World Trade Organization', the goal is to raise standards of living, ensure full employment, a large and steadily growing volume of real income, and to expand the production of, and trade in, goods and services. This is to be achieved through the optimal use of the world's resources in accordance with the objective of sustainable development.

Unlike a number of other international organizations, the WTO permits only representatives of governments and selected international organizations to participate in, or observe, its regular activities in various councils and committees (Sampson 2001b: 11). All decision-making processes are strictly intergovernmental.

The WTO has followed the lead of many international organizations by including a provision for CSOs' access in its constitution. However, additional 'Guidelines for Arrangements on Relations with NGOs', agreed on in 1996, are widely considered to only allow for a 'shallow' inclusion of CSOs and thus entail no significant procedural adaptation (Charnovitz 2001: 270; Stoll and Schorkopf 2002: 24). Nevertheless, CSOs can attend Plenary Sessions of the Ministerial Conferences as observers. Moreover, there are regular briefings for CSOs, informal Secretariat–CSO dialogues and circulation of NGO policy statements to WTO member states. Outreach activities of the Appellate Body of the WTO's Dispute Settlement Mechanism by actively requesting *amicus curiae* briefs in recent disputes have remained ad hoc measures, and they have also been met with resistance by a large share of the organization's membership (Staisch 2003: 23–5; Stoll and Schorkopf 2002: 162–3).

Officially, business actors cannot take any official part in proceedings other than the aforementioned ways for CSOs. However, governments of member states often act as proxies for both powerful business actors and civil society interests (Shaffer 2003).

There are claims that the WTO is neither accountable to a wider public nor responsive to public concerns, and that it should pursue a comprehensive reform agenda for increasing transparency and the participation of private sector actors, in general, and in its dispute settlement processes, in particular (Howse 2001: 362).

Referring back to the definition of inclusiveness, WTO membership is only open to one type of actor, namely states. It only engages with civil society organizations through a restricted consultative status and ad hoc arrangements. Business actors, while increasingly involved behind the scenes in complaint cases, are represented through states. For these reasons, the WTO does not meet the minimum requirement for inclusiveness.

International Labour Organization

The Constitution of the International Labour Organization (ILO) was adopted in 1919 as part of the Treaty of Versailles. It became an autonomous organization within the structure of the League of Nations and in 1946 the first specialized agency of the United Nations. The unique feature of the ILO is the tripartite representation of member states in two of its three principal organs.[13]

The idea of international labour legislation came up in the nineteenth century as a result of the humanitarian, economic and political concerns over the human costs of the industrial revolution (ILO 2004: 4). The ILO constitution recognizes that 'conditions of labor exist involving ... injustice, hardship and privation to large number of people' (ILO Constitution, Preamble). Without improvement in these conditions, political consequences in the form of unrest and even revolution were feared. The economic argument put forward was that a transnational solution to labour issues was necessary to avoid competitive disadvantages for socially progressive states (ILO 2004: 4; Rittberger and Zangl 2006: 36).[14]

Today, the ILO has four strategic objectives. These objectives include (1) the promotion, observance, implementation and realization of 'standards and fundamental principles and rights at work', (2) the creation of greater opportunities for women and men to secure decent employment, (3) the enhancement of coverage and effectiveness of social protection for all as well as (4) the promotion of tripartism on the domestic level and social dialogue (ILO 2001: 3).

The ILO's main activity has been standard setting. Since 1919, 185 Conventions and 195 Recommendations[15] covering a broad range of labour issues have been adopted. Each convention is an independent treaty, i.e. once a convention is adopted by the International Labour Conference it is the responsibility of member states to ratify and implement it.

The tripartite structure of the ILO is often referred to as being unique because two of its principal organs of the ILO, namely the International Labour Conference and the Governing Body, and all of their subsidiary organs and committees are composed of member state delegations consisting of government, employers', and workers' representatives (Altmann and Kulessa 1998: 99). In the International Labour Conference, each of the 178 national delegations consists of two government representatives, one workers' and one employers' representative. However, non-governmental delegates do not primarily represent their countries, but their interest groups (Senti 2002: 13). All delegates have the same rights, and each delegate is free to speak and vote individually on all matters (ILO Constitution, Art. 4; ILO 2001: 2). Workers' and employers' representatives may vote against their governments as well as oppose each other (ILO 2004: 7). The Governing Body of the ILO consists of 28 government representatives,[16] 14 workers' and 14 employers' representatives. Delegates representing employers and workers in the Governing Body are elected by the employers' delegates and the workers' delegates to the International Labour Conference (ILO Constitution, Art. 7).

Due to its tripartite structure, the International Labour Organization (ILO) is often said to be an exception to the state-centricity of early international organizations. The ILO is certainly the first international organization granting equal participation rights to private sector actors relevant to the solution of a certain problem, in this case labour issues (Wolf 2003: 236). Yet, in contrast to today's new inclusive institutions the ILO grants membership only to states.[17] Moreover, states are the main addressees of the ILO because compliance with, and enforcement of, ILO Conventions is the sole responsibility of states. This is still compatible with the '"conventional" state-centric model of international governance' because states can 'adopt or ignore a convention' according to their interests (Hurd 2003: 102). In this respect, the ILO differs from today's inclusive institutions which transfer responsibility for implementation to public as well as private sector actors. For this reason, the ILO must be considered an outlier case. It is a multi-actor based organization but not an inclusive institution, because membership is ultimately granted according to statehood.

UNAIDS

UNAIDS, the Joint United Nations Programme on HIV/AIDS, began operations in 1996 following its formal creation by the UN Economic and Social Council in 1994. The creation of UNAIDS coincided with the closure of the Global Programme on AIDS of the World Health Organization and can be seen as a deliberate step to reinvigorate the fight against AIDS through new forms of cooperation and institutionalization. A large number of state, private sector and United Nations system initiatives targeted at HIV/AIDS already existed by this time, and the decision to create a new organization with the specific task of combating the spread of AIDS was implemented in the form of a *consortium* of existing organizations (Altmann 2003: 38).

UNAIDS took on, as its main objective, the coordination of the many initiatives within the UN system, reducing organizational overlap and acting as the 'main advocate for global action on the epidemic' (UNAIDS 2004b: 4). The main task of UNAIDS is to develop and disseminate policy and coordinate on ground assistance with member, as well as non-member, states and CSOs.

UNAIDS' internal structure deliberately seeks to ensure equal representation from both developed and developing countries and allows for the participation of both public and private sector actors. Aside from the ILO, it is the first UN Organization to formally include CSOs in its governing body, the Programme Coordinating Board (PCB). The PCB decides on all programmatic issues concerning policy, finance, monitoring and evaluation. The PCB has a multi-actor membership comprised of 22 government representatives, 10 co-sponsoring UN organizations, and 5 representatives of CSOs, the latter elected through a system of nomination and voting amongst incumbent CSO representatives rather than through applying to the Board or being invited by member states. The PCB, however, has drawn up qualification guidelines.

Both CSOs' and states' delegates are balanced geographically with CSO delegates coming from Africa, Asia/Pacific, Europe, Latin America and the Caribbean, and North America. However, only states have voting rights in the PCB, and the co-sponsoring UN organizations have more rights in the formal decision-making process than CSOs. CSOs' participation includes a seat at the board table along with the co-sponsoring UN organizations and the member states with the right to participate in debating and drafting (agenda-setting rights) (UNAIDS 1999). The only permanent members of the PBC are the co-sponsoring UN organizations, whereas both states' and CSOs' representatives rotate on a regular basis. Business actors are not directly included in the organizational structure; rather UNAIDS cooperates with business actors within certain projects which may be governed through memoranda of understanding or ad hoc arrangements with, e.g., the Global Business Coalition on HIV/AIDS (UNAIDS 2004a).

In reference to the definition of inclusiveness, UNAIDS allows three types of actors to hold membership, i.e. states, IGOs and CSOs. Although all of them are involved in debating and drafting, voting rights are reserved for representatives of states only. These disparities in decision-making rights mean that UNAIDS only meets the minimum requirements of inclusiveness and therefore ranks as an institution of low inclusiveness.

UN Global Compact

The Global Compact initiative is mostly considered to be an example of a public policy network and a public–private partnership (Kell and Levin 2003: 151; Nelson and United Nations 2002: 135f; Rieth 2004: 154–5). The Global Compact network seeks to contribute to a more equitable and sustainable globalized economy by making its ten (albeit rather general) principles in the areas of human rights, labour standards, environmental protection and prevention of corruption an integral part of business activities everywhere (Hamm 2006; Kell 2003). This public–private partnership initiative was launched by the former UN Secretary-General Kofi Annan in 1999 and has been administered by a small unit within the UN secretariat. Its main addressees are business actors.

The Global Compact offers various engagement opportunities such as the annual 'learning forum', policy dialogues, and partnerships with UN agencies. Through these cooperative ventures, TNCs can live up to principles of corporate social responsibility set out in the Global Compact by integrating social and environmental concerns into their business activities (European Commission 2001: 6). It focuses on the shortcomings of corporate behaviour in key social and ecological issue areas and seeks to promote best practices in order mitigate or overcome these shortcomings.

The Global Compact network comprises several UN agencies, about 2500 businesses, a dozen civil society organizations, some international labour federations, and academic institutions. In addition, it is supported by a large number of (mainly Western) governments. Although states are not formal members of the Global Compact, they occasionally take part in some of the policy discussions and endorse the initiative through the adoption of General Assembly resolutions (Rieth 2004: 165ff). In December 2005, the UN General Assembly again unanimously adopted the Resolution 'Toward Global

Partnership', in which for the first time the Global Compact, as one of the important voluntary initiatives and partnerships, was referred to by name (A/RES/60/215).

It is often stated that the Global Compact is an experiment in learning or a learning network (Ruggie 2002). Its hitherto precarious development has been strengthened by the revision of its governance structure, to include the new Global Compact Board comprising four constituency groups, totalling 20 members: Business (10), International Labour (2) and Business Organizations (2), Civil Society (4), and the executive head of the Global Compact Office as well as the Chair of the Foundation for the Global Compact. The Board has no formal decision-making rights, but will instead provide ongoing strategic and policy advice for the initiative as a whole and make related recommendations to the Global Compact Office, participants and other stakeholders. It is supposed to help ensure the Global Compact's continuity and facilitate its further growth (Annan 2004).[18] Regarding measures such as the misuse of association with the Global Compact, the Global Compact Office reserves the right to make final decisions (United Nations Global Compact Office 2005: 6–7).

In summary, the Global Compact is a voluntary initiative of self-regulation organized as a network of the UN and related agencies, business actors and CSOs. They can take part in all policy discussions through the above mentioned engagement opportunities, and all categories of actors are represented on the Board. However, major strategy decisions, such as the addition of the 10th principle,[19] as well the revision of rules concerning reports on the progress of implementing the Global Compact principles ('Communication on Progress') have been devised through informal consultations mostly between the UN secretariat, on the one side, and business associations and TNCs, on the other.

In short, IGOs, CSOs and business actors are all categories of actors with full membership in the Global Compact. Although all members have participation rights, decision-making realities do not reflect a high level of inclusiveness. For these reasons the Global Compact ranks as an institution with a medium degree of inclusiveness.

Global Fund to Fight AIDS, Tuberculosis and Malaria

In April 2001, UN Secretary-General Kofi Annan called for the creation of the Global Fund to Fight AIDS, Tuberculosis and Malaria (here referred to as the 'Global Fund') in reaction to projections from UNAIDS and the World Health Organization (WHO) that the fight against these diseases will require funds of at least US$10 billion per year and that existing bodies were unable to effectively collect these funds due (in part) to donor fatigue (Smith 2002: 3). Before the Global Fund was formally established in January 2002, commitments to the Fund were made at the General Assembly Special Session on HIV/AIDS in 2001 (UNGASS), through consultations with the G8, and through pledges by states as well as private donors totalling over US$600 million. Leading up to the Fund's creation an exhaustive negotiation process took place concerning the most appropriate governance and management structure. The result was a governing body, in which states, IGOs, CSOs and private donors have membership rights.

The Global Fund's aim is to 'attract and disburse additional resources to prevent and treat AIDS, tuberculosis (TB) and malaria'.[20] The influence that it has gained through its selection of programmes that are eligible for funding has given the Fund considerable leverage to steer the direction of the fight against these diseases globally. Most significantly, the requirement that 'Country Coordinating Mechanisms' be established in order to receive funds has both encouraged cooperation between governments and other organizations when it comes to implementing programmes and caused controversy due to the difficulty of creating effective systems of state–private sector coordination mechanisms in some countries (Global Fund to Fight Aids Tuberculosis and Malaria 2003).

The Global Fund comprises four primary organs: the Partnership Forum, the Foundation Board, the Secretariat and the Technical Review Panel. The Foundation Board is the central governing body; it has the power to determine eligibility criteria for projects and makes funding decisions. Board membership is deliberately divided up between public and private sector actors. All may participate in debating and drafting, but only three categories (states, CSOs and business actors) have voting rights. The twenty voting members comprise seven representatives from developing states (one representative based on each of the six World Health Organization regions and one additional representative from Africa), eight representatives from donor states and five representatives from CSOs and business.[21] There are also four non-voting members representing UNAIDS, WHO, the World Bank, and a Swiss citizen as required by Swiss law on foundations. It is stipulated that the Board will make decisions by consensus; only when negotiations are fully exhausted and no consensus is reached, can any member with voting rights call for a vote as laid out in the Global Fund by-laws.

The Global Fund allows membership for all four categories of actors. While all of them participate in debating and drafting, only CSOs, business actors and states have voting rights (IGOs, however, are the only members that are not subject to rotation). According to our definition of inclusiveness, the Global Fund presents itself as an institution with a high degree of inclusiveness.

Comparing WTO, ILO, UNAIDS, UN Global Compact and the Global Fund

The examples discussed can be placed along a continuum ranging from more state-based towards more inclusive global governance institutions (see Figure 1.1).

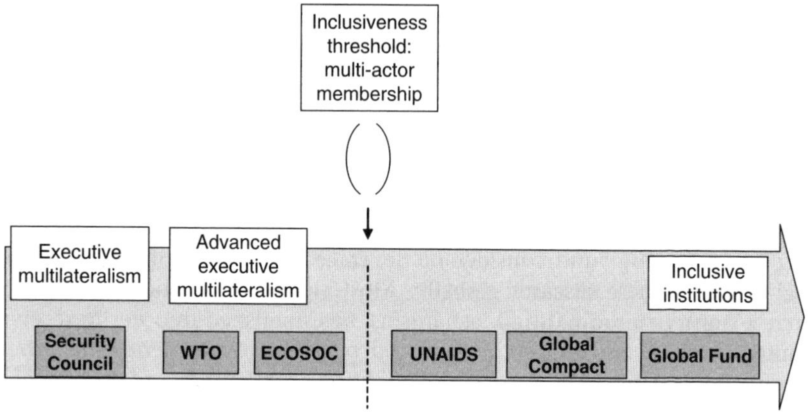

Figure 1.1:   Continuum of governance institutions[22]

It can be concluded that UNAIDS shows a low degree of inclusiveness due to the fact that voting rights are limited to one type of actor. The Global Compact shows a medium degree of inclusiveness because, although three categories of actors have policy-making rights, real decision-making takes place within the Global Compact office in close collaboration with business actors. The Global Fund with voting rights for states, business actors and CSOs is therefore positioned closest to the right end of the spectrum.

All three of these institutions need to be clearly separated from the WTO, which is placed on the left side of the 'inclusiveness threshold'. Although the ILO can be characterized as a multi-actor organization, it differs from today's inclusive institutions in important respects and therefore cannot be classified as an inclusive institution.

A general trend towards inclusive institutions?

Having shown that there are novel institutions of global governance, in the following we want to provide additional arguments to demonstrate that these inclusive institutions are not isolated cases or exceptions but rather may be seen as part of a trend which, although still being in its infancy, can be traced back over a longer period of time.

The trend towards more inclusive global institutions is, firstly and primarily, reflected in the rise of the sheer number of organizations, public–private partnerships, global public-policy networks and programmes in all issue-areas of public policy that meet the requirement of multi-actor membership and shared decision-making rights. While this quantitative growth is a generally accepted fact, exact data on the number and activities of these institutions is missing, because research in the field is still relatively new.

The seminal work of Reinicke et al. from the late 1990s, identified around fifty to sixty global public policy networks in different issue areas such as crime, environment, and health (Reinicke and Deng 2000: 3).

The 'Initiative on Public–Private Partnerships for Health' database (IPPPH 2004), for example, which contains a comprehensive list of health oriented partnerships between private and public actors and their dates of creation, shows that the first such partnership was created in 1974, the Onchocerciasis Control Programme in West Africa.[23] According to this database, the number of such partnerships increased to twelve in 1990 and to 92 in 2003. The large number of IGOs and CSOs included in the governing bodies of these partnerships demonstrates their inclusiveness. The WHO itself is a member in 42 of these partnerships, the World Bank in 17 and UNICEF in 19.

There is a similar number of multi-actor partnerships in the field of environmental protection. The number of partnerships for sustainable development with a global scope increased by at least 100 since the Sustainable Development Summit in 2002 (UNDESA 2004).

In her review of new public finance, Kaul (2006: 222) notes that the number of multi-actor based partnerships with shared decision-making powers has risen from around 50 in the mid-1980s to at least 400 today (cf. Reinicke 1999/2000; Benner, Reinicke and Witte 2004). These observations show a rapid acceleration in the setting-up of public–private partnerships in different issue areas from environment to welfare, and even security.

Prominent examples in the field of security and conflict prevention are the 'Voluntary Principles on Security and Human Rights' (known as the US–UK Voluntary Principles), the Kimberly Process Certification Scheme, and the Chad–Cameroon Pipeline project (Rittberger 2004a: 26–7). The formation of inclusive institutions in the field of security is a rather new development (Böge et al. 2006). It is nevertheless significant since security is usually regarded as the primary responsibility of states and too sensitive to open it up to private sector actors.

The significance of the trend towards inclusiveness can also be underlined by several other observations. *First*, the creation of several organizations or organs, such as the United Nations Fund for International Partnerships (UNFIP) and United Nations Office for Project Services (UNOPS), designed specifically to promote and accommodate such partnerships suggests that inclusive institutions are here to stay. UNFIP with the mission to 'bring together representatives of corporations, foundations, civil society and academia to work together with the United Nations for a common purpose' is one such organization (UNFIP 2004). It supports partnerships between civil society, business actors and UN bodies in the areas of environment, human rights and peace and security based on funds from the United Nations Foundation.

Second, within the UN system several specialized agencies have created secretariat units with the mandate of coordinating and accommodating multi-actor partnerships, such as the Division for Business Partnerships at the United Nations Development Programme, the Division of Technology, Industry and Economics at United Nations Environment Programme and the Business Partnership Programme at United Nations Industrial Development Organization (Nelson and the United Nations 2002: 168f.).

Third, the creation of research institutes and educational programmes with the aim of exploring and supporting 'innovative answers to complex governance challenges bringing together all key players: governments, international organizations, civil society organizations as well as businesses' (Global Public Policy Institute 2004) is another development suggesting the pervasiveness of this new form of governance.

These new developments are also reflected in recent high-level UN reports such as 'We the peoples: Civil Society, the United Nations and Global Governance' ('Cardoso Report') and 'A More Secure World: Our Shared Responsibility'. In the former report it is suggested that the 'UN should emphasize the inclusion of all constituencies relevant to the issue, recognize that the key actors are different for different issues and foster multi-stakeholder partnerships to pioneer solutions and empower a range of global policy networks to innovate and build momentum on policy options' (United Nations 2004b: 16–17). In the latter report the panel emphasizes several times that state and non-state actors should work in a more integrated fashion to improve problem-solving (United Nations 2004a: 27, 30, 31).

The fact that most of these changes are institutional is often seen as further evidence that inclusive institutions are not only a temporary fad, but rather a trend that is not likely to be reversed. For some, this leads to the perspective that the emergence and increasing importance of inclusive institutions is a progressive consequence of changes in the international system, which have given rise to particular governance gaps. However, this understanding of inclusive institutions as a remedy for these governance gaps is by no means generally shared (von Schorlemer 2006: 19). Therefore, in the following section the focus will be on the analysis of the systemic conditions of inclusive institutions' emergence and of actors' reasons for their creation. Following that, in section four, possible solutions and the potential of inclusive institutions will be discussed.

Changes in the international system, actors' responses and the emergence of new governance mechanisms

This section refers to the second proposition (see section one) and analyses the background conditions and triggering factors for change in the international system and the resulting demand for new types of institutions for global governance. To understand the emergence of a trend towards inclusive institutions, it is necessary to look at two phases of change and accordingly different sets of conditions that set the stage for these phases to run their course. The first set of conditions primarily led to institutions of advanced executive multilateralism and was driven by global challenges, i.e. the end of the cold war, technological revolution, and the processes of global economic liberalization and integration. In turn, this laid the foundations for the more recent trend towards inclusive institutions. The second set of conditions further prompting the creation of inclusive institutions is comprised of the emergence of new transsovereign problems, the rising importance of making long-term decisions that span generations, and the increasing occurrence of previously separate issue areas overlapping that lead to conflicts in policy-making. Each of these sets of condition will be detailed below.

To provide a coherent account of the emergence of new, inclusive institutions for global governance, it is necessary to analyse structure and agency in global governance. For this reason the interests and motivations of the different actors that have been identified will also be analysed (Rittberger 2003: 195). Changing interests of, and resources available to, actors and possible changes in actors' perceptions are relevant for establishing inclusive institutions (Benner, Reinicke and Witte 2004: 195). In sum, we will look at how changes in the international system combined with changing interests and motivations of different actors have led to new, inclusive institutions for global governance.

Global challenges in the international system

The first set of conditions, which led to advanced executive multilateralism, but nevertheless laid the foundations for the emergence of the trend towards inclusive institutions, consists of three challenges that contributed to the transformation of the international system in the 1990s.

The first challenge was the end of the cold war which has led to fundamental changes in the relations between states, the rise of civil society organizations and the spread of transnational business (Anheier et al. 2004: 297–309). The main frontlines of conflict with regard to governance institutions as they stood during the cold war period can be summarized as follows: first, unstable cooperation between East and West (at best) and conflict brinkmanship (at worst) and, second, a dramatically reduced capacity for action of most intergovernmental organizations, in particular the UN system (Brühl and Rittberger 2001: 17). After the end of the cold war, the structure of the international system began to change. Most importantly, bipolarity no longer limited international organizations' scope of action, and, as a consequence, they succeeded in gaining greater salience in world politics (Brühl and Rittberger 2001: ibid.). Additionally, a receding urgency of the nuclear threat also contributed to a growing awareness of globalizing non-military problems.

The emergence of a 'world without borders' has given these issues, formerly considered to be a part of 'low politics' (in other words, not vital to the survival of states), a more prominent status. Nye has suggested that world politics today is like playing chess on a three-dimensional chess board.

'The top board of military is unipolar ... but the middle economic board is multipolar ... and the bottom board of transnational relations that cross borders outside the control of governments has a widely dispersed power structure' (Nye 2002: 238).

While Nye points in the right direction, the real linkages between the three 'chess boards' (or policy domains) are in fact more closely related than the metaphor suggests. Military issues, inter-state economic issues and transnational issues such as terrorism or transboundary air pollution are not only all relevant to human survival and well-being, but are, in one way or another, intrinsically intertwined. This can be seen on the example of recent conflicts in Congo or in Sudan where the goals, methods and financing of warfare, as well as the degree to which public sector and private sector actors are involved indicate that the traditional separation of policy domains is no longer applicable. It is particularly on the third chessboard, that of transnational issues, that private sector actors enjoy a rising level of autonomous action and growing influence (Kaldor 1999).

The second challenge contributing to changes in the international system in the 1990s has been the revolution in information, communication and transportation technologies. These technological changes have transformed the international system by the way in which information and knowledge are created, processed and disseminated (Reinicke and Deng 2000: 14). Common limitations in space and time have been progressively overcome thus dramatically enhancing connections between peoples and places (Brühl and Rittberger 2001: 8). This has led to a more integrated world which poses challenges in particular to states and state based institutions. On the one hand, the ability of national governments and intergovernmental organizations to reduce transaction costs and provide better governance services has been enhanced; on the other hand, non-state actors' ability to influence international politics has also increased dramatically. The heightened international political role of international CSOs arising from achievements of the technological revolution has been illustrated using three examples: (1) The International Campaign to Ban Landmines (ICBL), launched in October 1992, which built public awareness and contributed to political resolve necessary to bring about a landmine ban. (2) The NGO Coalition for an International Criminal Court, established in 1995, which advocated the establishment of an effective, just and independent International Criminal Court (ICC). (3) The 'Anti-MAI campaign' (carried forward by more than 600 (I)NGOs from more than 50 states), which defeated an OECD sponsored Multilateral Agreement on Investment. In sum, the technological revolution has helped CSOs to build powerful transnational coalitions (Brühl and Rittberger 2001: 11; Keck and Sikkink 1998).

In addition, international negotiations have undergone profound changes. Although extra resources and information at first glance should ease decision-making, a surplus of information has sometimes actually increased uncertainty, and thus negotiations have been prolonged rather than short-ened. Another result of the technological revolution is that governments have lost control over international negotiations processes because they can no longer take advantage of information exclusivity (Reinicke and Deng 2000: 2). As a direct consequence the role of international organizations as an arena for negotiations has become more salient (Rittberger and Zangl 2006).

The third challenge instigating change in international institutions arises from what is commonly labelled 'globalization.' Although the term is often used in a restrictive sense to mean economic liberalization and integration (e.g. increased foreign direct investments (FDI) and the growing significance of intrafirm trade and interfirm alliances), in this context, it also refers to the extension of cross-border societal exchanges and transactions in a wide range of non-economic areas such as culture, security and environment (Zürn 1998: 141; Beisheim et al. 1999). Globalization challenges international gov-ernance institutions in at least three ways (Brühl and Rittberger 2001: 15–16). First, it tends to contribute to a widening of the gap between rich and poor, which indicates that state-based international governance institutions fail to attain one of the primary goals of governance, i.e. to provide for social welfare. Second, owing to deregulation, economic (which often has gone hand in hand with political) liberalization, and privatization, transboundary market forces are increasingly participating in international affairs. The grow-ing importance of private authority has changed the relationship between business actors and state actors in a significant way, by being increasingly involved in authoritative decision-making that was previously the prerog-ative of state actors (Cutler, Haufler and Porter 1999). Third, civil society actors react to this failure of international governance, and to the changed balance within the triad, by forming alliances and protesting against these developments and other unwelcome effects of globalization. Moreover, civil society organizations have become more attractive for donor organizations (public as well as private) to implement development projects. A new divi-sion of labour has emerged in which CSOs serve as intermediaries, deliverers of services, and consultants (Tussie and Riggirozzi 2001: 164f.).

Although, the factors mentioned above did not lead to the replacement of institutions of executive multilateralism, these new developments in the international system facilitated a trend towards less state-dominated forms of governance. In the new stage of *advanced* executive multilateralism, policy-making has been complemented by private sector actors that were in part granted access to the policy-making process. This laid the foundation for the creation of inclusive institutions, catalysed by transsovereign problems which will be described below.

The rise of transsovereign problems

The challenges to the international system in the 1990s were not superseded by, but rather became even more obvious with, the rise of transsovereign problems and with the negative highlight of the 9/11 terrorist attacks on the World Trade Centre in New York and on the Pentagon in Washington DC. Transsovereign problems, such as terrorism, environmental degradation, refugee flows, but also the increasing negative external effects of economic globalization, are problems which cannot be solved by individual state action alone as they transcend state boundaries in ways that set limits to state interventions. Transsovereign problems have come to dominate foreign affairs and international relations in the post-cold war world, and make a mockery of state-borders and unilateral state responses (Cusimano 2000: 3). However, even in dealing with 'old' problems state-based governance institutions have difficulties in coming to terms with demands by private sector actors to provide, for instance, for environmental protection, respect for human rights and security, and efficient markets (Kaul und Mendoza 2003: 98).

Finding solutions to transsovereign problems is further complicated by temporal asymmetry, i.e. the apparent discrepancy 'between the need in a fast moving environment to make timely decisions that at the same time also take into account an intergenerational perspective of sustainability' (Benner, Reinicke and Witte 2004: 194). Decisions taken today have intergenerational implications going beyond standard political cycles, which are determined, in democracies for instance, by elections (Benner, Reinicke and Witte 2004: 194). This is compounded by a 'mismatch between the time available for making decisions and the time over which our descendants will suffer the consequences' (Reinicke and Deng 2000: 17).

The current situation is aggravated even further in that decisions in one issue area increasingly have implications in another, as for instance trade liberalization may have external effects on the social, ecological or security realm. As a result, the process of policy-making becomes even more complex when governance goals conflict.

Due to the fact that present state-based international governance institutions have difficulties managing transsovereign problems, public sector as well as private sector actors have recognized a perceived lack of appropriate governance institutions.

Actors' interests and resources and the quest for new institutions for global governance

As noted above, simply identifying systemic changes does not provide for a complete explanation of the emergence of inclusive institutions. In this section, it will therefore be analysed whether there is an actual demand on the agency level for the formation of new, inclusive institutions for global governance.

All actors concerned with global governance, states, international organizations, civil society organizations and business actors alike, have a common interest that transsovereign problems are addressed, preferably solved or at least their negative effects mitigated. Following a rationalist approach, all actors are primarily self-interested, goal seeking actors whose behaviour can be accounted for in terms of the maximization of individual utility. Following this assumption the 'contractualist' theory of international institutions argues that, in problematic social situations, actors create and maintain institutions to reduce uncertainty as well as transaction costs while pursuing their individual self-interest (Keohane 1984: ch. 5, 6; Hasenclever, Mayer and Rittberger 1997: 23f., 55f.).

Before and during the cold war, the main actors in international politics were states, and therefore new international institutions were created and maintained by states. After the end of the cold war, the impact of globalization and the rise of transsovereign problems, states acknowledged that some problems cannot be tackled successfully by them alone. This is, first, due to interdependence among all public sector and private sector actors and, second, derives from a lack of resources, available to public sector actors, for pursuing governance goals (Koenig-Archibugi 2002: 47f). Keohane and Nye have called this phenomenon policy interdependence (1974: 600; 2000b: 1). In addition, public sector actors have become increasingly dependent on private sector actors because of their increasing power and influence on world affairs. Interdependence is basically defined as mutual dependence, it refers to situations characterized by reciprocal effects among public and private sector actors (Keohane and Nye 2000b: 7). There are many situations where public and private sector actors are interdependent in order to carry out governance tasks, such as providing public goods. To give an example: While CSOs organize und deliver humanitarian aid in zones of conflict, to which states, and sometimes intergovernmental organizations as well, have no or only limited access, they are, at the same time, dependent on financial support from public actors.

There are various possible explanations for the motivations of states, but also of other actors, to pool resources or transfer them to other actors for the purpose of collective action, most prominently principal–agent and resource dependency or exchange theories. Resource dependency or exchange theory is most commonly explored in respect to the formation of voluntary cooperative relationships between organizations and will therefore be the focus here (Edele 2006: 43).[24]

The policy interdependence of all categories of actors translates into interdependence of resources. Further insights into interdependence of resources can be gained from resource dependency or exchange theory developed within the fields of management studies and organizational theory. It holds that no organization is self-sufficient; therefore, in order to survive, an organization must be capable of acquiring and maintaining resources (Pfeffer and Salancik 1978: 2). The most common solution to this problem inherent in interdependence is to increase the mutual control over each others' resources. Pfeffer and Salancik refer to organizations that seek to gain control over their environment through alliances and other forms of cooperation (Pfeffer and

Salancik 1978: 43f.). There are various strategies available for acquiring additional resources and coordinating the (inter-)dependence between various actors, such as negotiations, treaties, co-optation, etc. (Scott 2003: 114f.).[25]

Bringing the insights from organizational theory to the study of global governance, inclusive institutions are held to be the result of a strategy of public and private actors to exchange or pool resources toward some over-arching governance goal (Nölke 2000: 334f.; Brozus, Take and Wolf 2003: 121f.).[26] To effectively address transsovereign problems an institution for global governance has to be equipped with the necessary regulatory, material, organizational and epistemic resources. A single type of actor does not possess all of these resources, therefore public and private sector actors have to cooperate. All actors are able to contribute resources to the solution of transsovereign problems. Only if all actors participate and place their resources at the disposal for the pursuit of the collective interest can current global challenges be effectively tackled.

In situations where there is an inability to reach intergovernmental solutions, stemming from resource deficiencies, states tend to include private sector actors as instruments for solving global problems. Engaging with private sector actors and leveling with them as partners can pave the way for greater problem-solving capacity, albeit with at least some loss of policy-making autonomy on the part of the state. The motivation of all actors to form inclusive institutions can be traced back to the realization of problems caused by interdependence, which leads them to seek out the pooling or transferring of resources.

The UN Global Compact offers a good example for illustrating the logic of resource dependence or exchange theory. Although the states assembled within the United Nations lack the necessary regulatory power, they allowed Kofi Annan as Secretary General of the United Nations leeway to make wide use of his statutory compentency. Owing to this leeway he himself was able to call upon business actors to engage in a 'Global Compact' (Annan 1999; Ruggie 2003). Business actors, equipped with the necessary material and organizational resources, were willing to participate in the Compact because they have been under increasing pressure and attack by the public and in particular civil society organizations for taking advantage of globalization dynamics (Spar and La Mure 2003). A number of CSOs, although being quite reserved in the beginning, soon realized that a cooperative approach towards companies, such as collaborating in concrete partnership projects, can be more promising than simply following an adversarial mode of interaction, such as campaigning against and seeking to shame companies. As a result, more CSOs have been willing to engage in the Global Compact and thereby contribute their knowledge and moral weight to the process (Winston 2002, Rieth and Göbel 2005). In addition, business associations and trade unions have discovered, next to their conventional function as lobbyists, a new field of activity where they can demonstrate their usefulness to their constituencies.

They contribute certain resources on which the other types of actors can be considered dependent, such as specialist knowledge and linkages with a wider public. All four categories of actors expect advantages from, and contribute resources to, the Global Compact, making it a project capable of addressing and closing certain governance gaps.

Owing to the fact that the UN Global Compact has made serious progress (despite a heavily contested discussion about its (non-)performance) the UN General Assembly has, after a period of six years, for the first time officially acknowledged the work of the Global Compact in the field of corporate social responsibility. It remains to be seen, however, whether the Global Compact is able to meet its objectives and keep the mix of very diverse public and private actors interested in the project. The diversity of Global Compact Board, representing all crucial non-state stakeholder groups, is a further step in reaching these goals. It will be the task of the Global Compact office and the new Secretary-General to continuously balance the effects of resource dependency between the various actors.

Closing governance gaps and reducing legitimacy deficits through inclusive institutions

In this section, the consequences of the trend towards more inclusive institutions for global governance as a whole are analysed. While the conditions contributing to the creation of inclusive institutions were analysed in the preceding section, it is just as important to place 'inclusiveness' in the position of an independent variable and examine its possible effects.

One of the most pressing issues in global governance research today, the legitimacy of governance institutions called into question by the existence of governance gaps, will be the focus of our analysis. It has been claimed that international governance institutions today suffer from legitimacy deficits both in terms of inadequate participation in policy-making and in terms of their shortcomings in efficiency and effectiveness (Coicaud 2001a; 2001b; Keohane and Nye 2003). By taking an in-depth look at two cases, we will explore here whether there is a direct relationship between 'inclusiveness' and the potential to close governance gaps and thus to reduce legitimacy deficits.

Governance gaps

Governance on the global level differs from governance on the national level in that the compulsion exerted to follow rules is not backed up by a legal monopoly of physical violence, and material incentives for securing rule compliance are limited. Any governance institution beyond the state must rely on states, however, to carry out enforcement, or find alternatives. In the absence of coercion or material incentives, it is the rules themselves, and how they are perceived by their addressees, that exert a pull to comply. Rules that are seen as appropriate, right or desirable, and therefore perceived as legitimate, draw compliance. In order to achieve the overarching goals of governance, i.e. security, rule of law, identity and channels of participation, and social welfare (Zürn 2001), global governance institutions therefore have to build up and maintain legitimacy, both in terms of their inputs and their outputs. The existence of deficiencies in public policy-making conceptualized as 'governance gaps' has contributed to the withholding or undermining of this legitimacy by certain actors, most prominently CSOs and developing countries, when it comes to institutions of executive multilateralism.

Analytically, we identify four governance gaps as follows: First, the jurisdictional gap which results from a mismatch between 'transsovereign problems' and predominantly national public policy-making approaches. Second, the operational gap which stems from the discrepancy between the amount of policy-relevant information as well as pertinent policy instruments available to the governance institution and those which are needed to attain its governance goals. Third, the incentive gap which arises from an under-developed operational follow-up of international agreements, such as the inability to provide material incentives or to follow through on sanctions, and the consequent limited willingness to implement such agreements. Fourth, the participatory gap which has opened up because of restricted access of the general public and particular stakeholders, to policy-relevant deliberations and decision-making processes at the global level (Kaul, Grunberg and Stern 1999b: 16; Brühl and Rittberger 2001: 21–3). The existence of these governance gaps refers to the non-attainment of governance goals and thus raises the question of the legitimacy of institutions for global governance.

An empirical-analytical approach to legitimacy (i.e. one that does not presuppose universal values which determine the desirability of a governing authority) takes 'legitimacy' to mean a perception or assumption on the part of relevant stakeholders that an organization and its actions are desirable or appropriate (adapted from Suchman 1995: 574). Institutions for global governance aim to attain this legitimacy in order to effectively govern in their respective fields of jurisdiction or competence.[27]

Problematic at the global level is the identification of the 'relevant stakeholders' or, in other words, of a constituency which collectively determines what is desirable or appropriate (Junne 2001: 193). At the state level, the constituency is readily identifiable; relevant stakeholders are citizens who can express their (dis)satisfaction with policy outcomes or their belief in the value of democratic representation through participation in elections. At the global level, relevant stakeholders are much more varied and diverse (Howse 2001: 362; Huckel, Reusch and Scholtes 2005: 153–5). Stakeholders can be transnational interests groups without state or territorial affiliation; they can be professional associations, indirectly or directly affected individuals or organizations of large scale. Here it is not possible to fully describe and assess the positions of all the relevant stakeholders towards the institutions to be examined.

There are many aspects of an organization's make-up, operations and effects that can contribute to its legitimacy. Generally, however, it is possible to aggregate these aspects into two dimensions, 'inputs' and 'outputs'.

Participatory gap – inputs

On the global level, input legitimacy is called into question if there is a participatory gap. This gap can open up with increasing pooling and delegating of policy-making at the global level and through restricted access of the general public or particular stakeholders to policy-relevant deliberations and political decision-making processes. These attributes have arisen through the transfer of policy-making to the global level in the form of advanced executive multilateralism, and their prevalence has raised doubts about the input legitimacy of global governance institutions.

Input legitimacy can be increased when the institution's decisions are made with the consent of its stakeholders (government 'by' the people) (Scharpf 1999: 14–15; Brühl and Rittberger 2001: 21f.). Foremost, this refers to increasing the number and types of actors who directly participate in decision-making and the extent to which they fairly represent a constituency of individuals or collective bodies claiming the right to participation. A comprehensive assessment of input legitimacy recognizes that consent can also stem from factors other than direct delegation through states. Representation through non-state actors accountable to the public, appropriate procedures and openness to external scrutiny (indicated at least in part through an institution's transparency) also contribute to input legitimacy (Keohane and Nye 2003: 389f.).[28]

Jurisdictional, incentive and operational gaps – outputs

Output legitimacy can be undermined by three governance gaps: the jurisdictional gap, the operational gap, and the incentive gap. Put together, output legitimacy refers foremost to the effectiveness of the institution in ensuring the successful implementation of its policy decisions and the perception that those decisions 'serve the common interest of the constituency' (government "for" the people) (Scharpf 1998: 3). Effectiveness, however, can be disaggregated down into three components: outputs, outcomes and impacts.[29] Outputs refer to formal decisions of governance institutions from which policy programmes in the form of norms and rule emanate, outcomes are called those changes in human or organizational behaviour which occur in response to these norms and rules, and impacts are the actual effects on the problem at hand which derive from the behavioural changes brought about by the norms and rules of the governance institution (Underdal 2002: 6; Young 1999: 110).

By closing jurisdictional, operational and incentive gaps, all three components of effectiveness, inputs, outputs and outcomes can be improved and thereby output legitimacy increased. Addressing transnational problems with a matching jurisdictional reach will allow for more pertinent outputs in terms of norms and rules that address pressing policy problems directly. Closing the operational gap will allow for more accurate information in terms of both problem identification and appropriate rule-making as well as monitoring and compliance. Closing the incentive gap will increase levels of compliance directly linked to effectiveness.

Assessment of cases: WTO and UNAIDS

The institutional designs described in the case studies above (see section two) will now be analysed by asking whether inclusiveness really does help closing governance gaps and thus reduce output and input legitimacy deficits which plague existing intergovernmental institutions. This is the most pressing question to be answered in terms of the real-world consequences of the trend towards inclusiveness. While it is not expected that inclusive institutions will prove to be a panacea for effective global governance, at least some small steps towards closing governance gaps are to be expected. WTO and UNAIDS are two good test cases for examining such a question because of their proximity to the inclusiveness threshold on the continuum for governance institutions (see Figure 1.1 above). The WTO is situated just to the left of the inclusiveness threshold and does not qualify as an inclusive institution (see pp. 19f.). UNAIDS is situated just to the right of the inclusiveness threshold (see pp. 22f.). By comparing these two institutions their potential to close governance gaps will be scrutinized.

Firstly, however, a note about closing the jurisdictional gap. By addressing problems directly on the international (WTO) and the transnational level (UNAIDS) rather than relying on problem solving on the state level, both the WTO and UNAIDS represent advances towards closing jurisdictional gaps. For this reason, looking at this gap provides little added value to a comparison between advanced executive multilateralism and inclusive global institutions; it is therefore excluded from the analysis.

The participatory gap

UNAIDS demonstrates significant advantages over the WTO in closing the participatory gap, despite UNAIDS only having a low level of inclusiveness. This is not just in terms of the most obvious participatory aspects such as who has membership or voting rights but also in terms of the procedural elements of input legitimacy.

In terms of membership, the WTO remains a state-based organization with official but very restrictive 'Guidelines for Arrangements on Relations with NGOs'. Demands by CSOs (including groups such as trade unions, farmers associations, and coalitions from the South) for greater participation in the WTO decision-making processes, which are increasingly being seen as having a direct influence on the welfare of corporations and individuals, has led to an even greater 'imagined' participatory gap. UNAIDS, on the other hand, includes two specific measures to close participatory gaps in its governing body (Programme Coordination Board). First, it includes states, IGOs and CSOs as full members (although only states have voting rights). Second, states and CSOs must represent different geographical regions, with developing countries having the same level of representation as developed states. UNAIDS therefore offers considerably more widely and fairly distributed participatory opportunities than the WTO. By moving beyond the ad hoc nature of partnering with NGOs on specific questions and projects to institutionalized involvement UNAIDS adds weight to private sector involvement.[30]

While some claim that multi-actor networks of this type 'can only be as legitimate as the actors involved' (Benner, Reinicke and Witte 2004: 200), on the global level, it is important to consider that it is the involvement of a plurality of actors representing a plurality of interests and values and accountable to a plurality of constituencies, which offers the best opportunity to close participatory gaps. Therefore, while CSOs and business actors themselves may not always be democratically legitimated their inclusion nonetheless expands the number of interests and values that are represented in the global institution's policy-making process, and thus the participatory gap becomes smaller. This gives inclusive institutions such as UNAIDS an advantage over less inclusive institutions, which rely solely on representation through governments coupled with ad hoc consultations with private sector actors.

In terms of procedures, UNAIDS' inclusion of actors other than states has been introduced with specific formal rules of procedure for the selection of representatives as well as a policy for transparency and reporting. These rules of procedure can pose obstacles to participation, in that not all CSOs meet recommended criteria to be on the Board; however, this is offset by the increased security that they provide in terms of 1) formal participations rights and 2) acceptance of CSO participation on behalf of other members such as states. Once elected to the PCB, CSOs must be in attendance for drafting and debating and are therefore not at risk of missing important deliberations in, and decisions by, the Board.[31] Arrangements that merely allow for CSOs to observe, receive briefings or circulate statements, as is the case within the WTO, does not give this safeguard. Moreover, through the regulated nomination and selection process the sustainability of CSO involvement on the UNAIDS PCB is ensured in that it minimizes possible criticism over the inappropriateness of CSO delegates. Furthermore, UNAIDS publishes the results of its Programme Coordinating Board meetings online which even lists the telephone contact numbers of almost all representatives (UNAIDS 2004c).

In contrast, though there are improvements towards enhancing the dialogue with civil society in the WTO, participatory gaps remain. Despite the day-to-day contact between the WTO Secretariat and CSOs as well as the release of specific WTO information and documents there is a lack of transparency about how, and by whom, decisions are made within the WTO. This adds considerably to its perceived legitimacy deficit. For example, the complexity of the WTO Dispute Settlement Mechanism, which involves several stages of consultation and review and the appointment of a panel of experts to consider a case, has been criticized for being too ad hoc and susceptible to manipulation.

The transparency issue has been raised during discussions on CSO relations at WTO Ministerial Conferences. Summaries of these debates state that 'a large number of delegations emphasized the intergovernmental character of the WTO' and that it should remain the primary responsibility of individual states to keep the public informed (WTO News, 22.11.2000). However, it should be acknowledged that the WTO Secretariat has increasingly made documents available to the broader public, particularly on its website. Within UNAIDS the importance of allowing CSOs access to information is a given. CSOs are after all already formally included as members. In contrast, the strictly intergovernmental make up of the WTO gives the principle of state sovereignty the highest priority. This indicates that UNAIDS, even with only a 'low' level of inclusiveness, allows for a higher priority to be put on procedural fairness and openness as well as on representation of a greater variety of stakeholders. UNAIDS is more successful than the WTO at closing the participatory gap.

The incentive gap

There are two ways through which the incentive gap can be closed, referring to two types of operational follow-up. UNAIDS uses the first type of operational follow-up, i.e. 'active management.' This type of follow-up only becomes relevant once it is clear that any non-compliance is not due to 'a conscious decision to disregard norms and rules, but to the member states' inability to abide by them, as well as from a certain incomprehensibility of the norms and rules themselves' (Brühl and Rittberger 2001: 23f.). UNAIDS seeks compliance with its policy recommendations through engagement with stakeholders, capacity building and the adapting of policies to different circumstances. As an inclusive institution UNAIDS has advantages when it comes to this kind of operational follow-up. Its co-sponsoring UN organizations as well as CSO members bring together a significant body of expertise which contribute to capacity building and information dissemination. For example, once a national ministry of health decides to adopt the UNAIDS' policy approach, experts from other IGOs (predominantly the WHO, but, in principle, all 10 co-sponsoring organizations) can be approached to assist in the development of a viable plan for a nation-wide fight against AIDS.

The WTO relies, by and large, on the second type of operational follow-up, i.e. 'authoritative dispute settlement'. In general, this leads to higher levels of compliance than 'active management'. Disputing states can settle disagreements about whether trade is conducted in accordance with WTO norms and rules. In addition, independent quasi-judicial organs such as the

Panels and the Appellate Body adjudicate on the conformity of state action with WTO law. This legalized element of the WTO's operational follow-up has created strong incentives for states to, first, act in accordance with WTO rules, second, to use the WTO Dispute Settlement Mechanism (rather than act unilaterally), and, third, to seek permission for implementing sanctions against a recalcitrant losing party as a way of enforcement.

While UNAIDS, as an inclusive institution, may have increased its capacity to perform 'active managerial' follow-up, its move away from executive multilateralism means that legalized authoritative dispute settlement is not an option. While both institutions, WTO and UNAIDS, contribute to closing the incentive gap, the WTO has clear advantages.

The operational gap

As noted above, the operational gap stems from the discrepancy between the information and tools needed to attain governance goals and those which are available to the institution. UNAIDS has taken up innovative approaches for coping with any lack of relevant policy information and other deficits in resources required. This is achieved through the inclusion of a variety of actors as members that can provide specialized knowledge and expertise as well as disseminate information to, and coordinate implementation of policies amongst, different types of actors. For example, the member representing communities living with HIV/AIDS considerably shortens the distance between target communities and the governing body, compared with establishing these communication channels through state representatives. Furthermore, through partnerships with the business sector, further informational resources can be gained for policy development and operations can be supplemented.[32]

The WTO, as an example of advanced executive multilateralism, has very different operational capacities at its disposal. As a large organization it mainly incorporates expertise into its internal structure by building specialized departments staffed by professionals and consulting with experts in their individual capacity. It has also taken steps towards closing operational gaps by allowing, on an ad hoc basis, the submission of *amicus curiae* briefs in dispute settlement cases, thereby making use of the expertise of private sector actors. However, during the trade negotiation rounds no allowance is made for formal and transparent engagement with private sector actors.

Thus, when it comes to gaining the required knowledge and instruments to close operational gaps and to better attain governance goals UNAIDS demonstrates considerable advantages over the WTO.

Closing governance gaps: implications for institutional design

By placing the empirical findings into Table 1.2, it is possible to see that inclusive institutions have the potential to close some governance gaps.

Table 1.2: The potential of international institutions for closing governance gaps

	Jurisdictional gap	*Incentive gap*	*Operational gap*	*Participatory gap*
WTO	+	++	+	−
UNAIDS	+	+	++	++

Although the jurisdictional gap is not an appropriate benchmark for assessing differences between executive multilateralism and inclusive institutions we do note that both UNAIDS and the WTO help close the jurisdictional gap in their respective spheres of competence. Importantly, inclusive institutions show an advantage in closing both the operational gap and the participatory gap. This is achieved through deliberate institutional designs, which include members representing a wide range of stakeholders' interests and values relevant for solving specific problems, and by including different categories of actors to obtain more relevant policy information and pertinent policy instruments.

However, while there appears to be a strongly positive correlation between closing the participatory gap and closing the operational gap, we observe an apparent weakly positive, if not negative correlation between closing the participatory gap and closing the incentive gap. A possible explanation for this finding could be that inclusive institutions only have the opportunity to engage in active managerial follow-up, which is generally considered weaker than the legalized approach towards dispute settlement at the disposal of executive multilateralism.

Although inclusive institutions cannot be seen as perfect solutions for the problems of global governance, they do close gaps that plague institutions of executive multilateralism, and the conjecture arises that legitimacy has been increased. Evidence for this increased legitimacy can also be found independently of the closing of the gaps. Increasing participation[33] and high levels of donated funds[34] indicate a high level of support both from peers and the wider public for these still relatively young inclusive institutions for global governance. While these institutions hardly escape criticism, rhetorical support from peers and governments in both the North and South remains relatively high. Inclusive global institutions therefore appear to hold a considerable potential to close governance gaps and gain in legitimacy.

Conclusion: inclusive institutions as part of heterarchical global governance

In this final section the concept of heterarchy will be introduced. It is suggested that heterarchy is the most appropriate concept for making sense of the broader developments that have been identified. The concept of heterarchy, as opposed to anarchy and hierarchy (as the two classical ordering principles of international politics), adequately describes the dense web of international governance institutions created and maintained by public and private sector actors. It captures more adequately the realities of global politics and, thereby, reflects the polycentric nature of today's emerging global authority structure (Rittberger 1973: 49ff.).

Kenneth Waltz, in his now classical analysis, argues that international politics is organized around two fundamental ordering principles: hierarchy and anarchy (Waltz 1979). However, a closer look at current global governance structures reveals an order that is neither hierarchical nor anarchical. According to Waltz, the two terms 'anarchy' and 'hierarchy' create a dichotomy: Anarchy is defined as the absence of hierarchy. The state is then defined in terms of a centralized authority structure (hierarchy). Accordingly, anarchy in international politics can only be overcome through the establishment of a world state (Wendt 1999: 307).

Three different models of governance beyond the nation state can be distinguished which reflect different ordering principles: (1) a world state (hierarchical order), (2) governance under a hegemonic umbrella and (3) horizontal self coordination (both assuming anarchy) (Rittberger 2004b). However, a world state is neither desirable nor feasible in the foreseeable future. In a second model, governance under the hegemonic umbrella, a world state would be substituted by a hegemon as a central authority. The model of hegemonic governance has also proven to be inadequate for understanding international politics. A third model of global governance, horizontal self-coordination, takes the anarchic nature of international politics as a starting point. Nevertheless, it is recognized that the anarchic system may still be governed by institutions, i.e. some kind of normative order does exist (Rosenau and Czempiel 1992; Rittberger 2004b).

All three models of global governance (world state, governance under the hegemonic umbrella, and horizontal self-coordination) are rooted in classical schools of though about international relations and are therefore strongly state-centric. This stands in sharp contrast to the observations made in this chapter, i.e. the increasing incorporation of private sector actors into global politics and the establishment of inclusive governance institutions. Governance tasks are performed, in addition to, or instead of, states, by international organizations, CSOs, and business actors, i.e. they participate on different levels and in different actor constellations in the creation and implementation of norms and rules to manage and solve global problems (Rittberger 2004b).

Like many contemporary IR scholars we conclude that neither anarchy-induced competitive international politics nor (quasi-)hierarchically ordered international policy-making adequately describes the reality of politics on the global level (Mayer, Rittberger and Zürn 1993: 402). Among others, Holsti infers from a historical study of nineteenth-century European international

Table 1.3:   Ordering principles of governance

Model of governance	World state/ government	Hegemony	Horizontal policy coordination/ International governance[35]	Global governance
Ordering principle	Hierarchy	Anarchy	Anarchy	Heterarchy

politics that 'there are half-way houses between systems of governance based on principles of anarchy and those based on hierarchy. There are alternatives to pure self-help systems, on the one hand, and command systems, on the other' (Holsti 1992: 56f.).

If neither the concept of anarchy nor the concept of hierarchy can adequately describe the ordering principle of the international system today, then a third ordering principle might exist, and it is necessary to define it (Waltz 1979: 115–25). Here, we suggest that 'heterarchy' may be appropriate to conceptualize this third ordering principle (see Table 1.3).

Heterarchy

An etymological definition of 'heterarchy' can be traced back to its Greek origin, i.e. 'heteros' (the other, the alien) and 'archein' (to reign, to govern), i.e. under the governance of an other. While hierarchy can only be considered in a context of sub- or superordination; heterarchy is characterized by coordination. All definitions of heterarchy stem from this idea: a form of organization resembling a network or fishnet (Bennhold 2005: 1, 20).

The concept of heterarchy was originally developed to grasp the functioning of the human brain as a neural net whereby the brain is composed of a network-type structure with the capacity to process inputs on several levels at once. The concept of heterarchy has since been incorporated into organization theory and especially been embraced in the subfield of organization of corporations.[36] As part of systems theory, sociology and law also embraced the concept in recent years (cf. Neyer 2002: 15).

Applied to social systems, the argument is as follows: Modern societies increasingly consist of functionally differentiated subsystems and this functional differentiation causes complexity. Due to its high complexity a social system cannot be understood as hierarchically structured. Rather complexity requires heterarchy or a network form of steering (Willke 1996: 64).

Heterarchy as an ordering principle has the characteristic that neither decision-making authority nor channels of communication are uniformly standardized. In an ideal heterarchical system, rules of order are flexible to allow for innovative approaches to dealing with problems of varying nature.

Thus, problem solving is approached, designed and activated according to situational need.

Heterarchy builds on the initiative of different actors and draws on the knowledge and expertise of its members whose creativity is stimulated through benevolent competition. Patterns of cooperation can then be built spontaneously and problem oriented. Heterarchy can therefore be envisaged as a system of 'potential leadership.' Leadership is exercised by the part of the system which is – under the given circumstances – best suited to deal with a certain problem. No actor or social subsystem is a priori given preferential authority (Willke 1996: 65).

Autonomous actors are only loosely connected, are problem-oriented in their approach to each other and are generally cooperative (even when conflicts of interest occur). Despite the high autonomy of the different sub-systems each actor in the system is obliged to use its capabilities to the benefit of the system as a whole (Willke 1996).

While systems theory uses heterarchy as an ideal type of structure, our understanding is that heterarchy can also be conceptualized as an empirical-analytical concept (for a very useful elaboration on heterarchy as an empirical concept see Neyer 2002).

Heterarchy as an ordering principle in global governance

The heterarchical order in global governance can be observed in the form of a dense network of institutions for global governance. These institutions might take different forms such as (1) intergovernmental, (2) global inclusive institutions such as those examined in this chapter, or even (3) purely private institutions for the collective management of transsovereign problems. These institutions neither exist independently of one another nor is there a hierarchical order between them. They are (more or less) loosely connected, might overlap in their competence and/or tasks, are activated according to a specific situation, and cooperate if necessary.[37]

Heterarchy as an ordering principle does not mean that states and their institutions definitely lose importance, rather they are part of a network of institutions for global governance.

Notes

1. The authors would like to thank the following people for valuable comments on earlier versions of this chapter: Doris Fuchs and other the participants of the Conference 'Changing Patterns of Authority in the Global Political Economy', University of Tübingen, October 2004, the participants of the AGFF (Tüebingen Working Group on Peace and Conflict Research) and participants of the IR Convention of the DVPW (German Political Science Association), Mannheim, October 2005. The authors also thank Malte Firlus for research assistance.

2. Inside the World Trade Organization civil society organizations have only limited access. One notable exception is that *Amicus Curiae* Briefs may be submitted during WTO dispute settlement procedures.
3. On executive multilateralism see Zürn 2004: 264.
4. See for example Hasenclever, Mayer and Rittberger 1997; Rittberger and Zangl 2006.
5. It is crucial to separate the understanding of 'governance' from the notion of 'government'. The term 'government' refers to formal institutions that are part of hierarchical norm- and rule-setting, monitoring of compliance with rules, and rule enforcement; governments allocate values authoritatively. 'Governance', in contrast, is more encompassing (Rosenau 1992: 4). Governance refers to identifying promising and sustainable approaches to solve societal problems, translating these solutions into rules for conduct, ensuring adherence to these rules and, where necessary, adjusting them to changing conditions (Rittberger 2004b: 247–9). It therefore refers to a purposive system of rules or normative orders apart from the regularities (natural orders) emerging from unrestricted interactions of self-interested actors in a state of anarchy. It also implies that the actors recognize the existence of certain obligations and feel compelled, for whatever reason, to fulfil them (Mayer, Rittberger and Zürn 1993: 393).
6. The most prominent example is the consultative status arrangement for NGOs with the UN Economic and Social Council according to Art. 71 UN Charter.
7. These institutions provide good examples of informal engagement with non-state actors.
8. UN ECOSOC Res. 1996/31, 25th July 1996.
9. 'These networks are loose alliances of government agencies, international organizations, corporations, and elements of civil society such as nongovernmental organizations, professional associations, or religious groups that join together to achieve what none can accomplish on its own' (Reinicke 1999/2000: 44).
10. A partnership is a voluntary and collaborative agreement between state and non-state actors, in which all participants agree to work together to achieve a common purpose or undertake a specific task and to share risks, responsibilities, resources, competencies and benefits (Nelson and United Nations 2002: 46).
11. In our understanding, inclusiveness and openness constitute two different concepts. The concept of openness still departs from state-centrism and implies that state actors or IGOs themselves are able to either 'open up' or 'close' international institutions to private sector actors. This implies that openness is a behavioural pattern of institutions (Staisch 2003). In contrast, the concept of inclusiveness refers to the structure of an institution.

    For a different definition of 'inclusiveness' only relating to membership of states in international institutions see Koenig-Archibugi 2006. Zürn and Koenig-Archibugi also discuss the role of public and private sector actors in global governance and conclude that 'there has been a proliferation of hybrid arrangements in a number of policy domains' which has 'deep implications for the nature of governance' (2006: 251) without elaborating on these implications, however.
12. As of 28 April 2006.
13. The third major organ is the ILO's secretariat, the International Labour Office.
14. The ILO Constitution's Preamble states that 'the failure of any nation to adopt humane conditions of labour is an obstacle in the way of other nations which desire to improve the conditions in their own countries'.
15. As of 8 May 2006, www.ilo.org/ilolex/english/info/index.htm.

16. Ten out of the 28 government representatives (countries 'of chief industrial importance' and often the largest contributors to the ILO) have quasi-permanent seats in the Governing Body (executive council of the ILO). They are appointed for an indefinite period; appointments can be reviewed if necessary (Art. 7 ILO Constitution).
17. Even today, one of the main criticisms is that in certain states workers' and employers' representatives are not independent from their governments. Moreover, member states are required 'to nominate non-Government delegates and advisers chosen in agreement with the industrial organizations, if such organizations exist, which are most representative of employers or workpeople, as the case may be, in their respective countries' (Art. 7 ILO Constitution).
18. United Nations Global Compact Office Press Release 20 April 2006. Accessed 1 June 2006: www.unglobalcompact.org/NewsAndEvents/news_archives/2006_04_20.html.
19. The 10th principle addresses the issue of corruption.
20. Website of the The Global Fund to Fight AIDS, Tuberculosis and Malaria. Accessed 1 June 2006: www.theglobalfund.org/en/faq.
21. One developing country CSO, one developed country CSO, one CSO representative of the communities living with the diseases, one representative of the business sector, and one representative of a private foundation.
22. The ILO, as noted above, is an outlier case, and does not fit into the above scheme.
23. The Onchocerciasis (Riverblindness) Control Programme in West Africa was sponsored by the World Bank, WHO, UNDP, and FAO. The African Program for Onchocerciasis Control has since superseded it (Worldbank 2004).
24. Like resource dependency or exchange theory the principal–agent approach draws from rational choice theories of domestic and international politics. It argues that instrumentally rational actors delegate powers to executive and judicial agents in order to lower the transaction costs of policy-making and implementation. The main focus of attention is usually devoted to the discretion function of agents. Power dependency approaches imply that motivation to act is asymmetrical, but the power of the interested parties is enough to coerce others to act (Edele 2006: 43).

    This can be dependent on a number of factors, such as the demand for credible commitments or policy-relevant information, or the expected and presumed preference gap between the principal and the agent (Majone 2001, Pollack 1997).
25. A discussion of the United Nations' or other international organizations' interest, as a principal, in delegating and/or pooling resources to new types of governance institutions deserves further attention and constitute an interesting field of research.
26. Some authors have analysed the prospects of transnational alliances, however mostly with a focus on the inclusion of civil society organization or the functioning of multi-level governance within the European Union (Take 2002; Brühl 2003).
27. This approach leans on the concept of Max Weber that legitimacy rests on a *belief* in legitimacy and is to be approached as an empirical phenomenon rather than a philosophical concept (Weber 1968: 213).
28. Some authors consider transparency and fairness of processes to be part of a third dimension of legitimacy, the 'throughput' dimension (Zürn 2000).
29. Output legitimacy is also referred to as substantive legitimacy, as it relies on empirical measures of success (Barnett and Finnemore 2004: 168f).

30. Other inclusive institutions take this further by giving NGOs voting rights, such as in the The Global Fund, or by providing for rules-based business and CSO involvement in formal networks, such as in the Global Compact.
31. UNAIDS procedural guidelines for NGOs clearly state that representatives are expected to attend all meetings.
32. For example, UNAIDS partners with the Global Business Coalition on HIV/AIDS.
33. As of April 2006 there were over 2900 participants in the Global Compact. Accessed 1 June 2006. www.unglobalcompact.org/ParticipantsAndStakeholders/index.html.
34. Funds donated to UNAIDS increased from just over $US57 million in 1999 to just over $US 171.5 million in 2005. Accessed 1 June 2006. data.unaids.org/Governance/PCB01/Core_1995–2005_en.pdf?preview=true.
35. See also Rittberger 2004b.
36. The following discussion is based on Reihlen 1998 (Reihlen and Rohde 1998).
37. A good example might be the UN system: the UN and its specialized agencies as well as various special programmes or funds, and public–private partnerships that emerged at the periphery of the UN system.

References

Alger, C. (2002): The Emerging Role of NGOs in the UN System. From Article 71 to a People's Millenium Assembly. *Global Governance* 8(1): 93–117.

Altman, D. (2003): Understanding HIV/AIDS as a Global Security Issue. In: Lee, K. (ed.), *Health Impacts of Globalization*. New York: Palgrave Macmillan.

Altmann, J. and M. Kulessa (1998): *Internationale Wirtschaftsorganisationen. Ein Taschenlexikon*. Stuttgart: Lucius & Lucius.

Anheier, H., M. Glasius and M. Kaldor (eds.) (2004): *Global Civil Society 2004/5*. London: Sage.

Annan, K. (2004): Addressing Business Leaders at Global Compact Summit, Secretary General says Experience Shows that Voluntary Initiatives 'Can and Do Work'. United Nations, New York, 24 June 2004 (SG/SM/9387, ECO/71).

Barnett, M. and M. Finnemore (2004): *Rules for the World: International Organizations in Global Politics*. Ithaca, NY: Cornell University Press.

Beisheim, M., S. Dreher, G. Walter, B. Zangl and M. Zürn (1999): *Im Zeitalter der Globalisierung?: Thesen und Daten zur gesellschaftlichen Denationalisierung*. Baden-Baden: Nomos.

Benner, T., W. H. Reinicke and J. M. Witte (2004): Multisectoral Networks in Global Governance: Towards a Pluralistic System of Accountability. *Government and Opposition* 39(2): 191–210.

Bennhold, K. (2005): Taking Networking to the Next Level. *International Herald Tribune* 26 January 2005: 1, 20.

Böge, V., Chr. Fitzpatrick, W. Jaspers and W.-Chr. Paes (2006): *Who's Minding the Store? The Business of Private, Public and Civil Actors in Zones of Conflict*. Bonn: Bonn International Centre for Conversion (BICC brief 32).

Boutros-Ghali, Boutros (1996): Foreward. In: Weiss, Thomas G. and Leon Gordenker (eds.), *NGOs, the UN, and Global Governance*. London: Lynne Rienner: 7–12.

Brozus, L., I. Take and K. D. Wolf (2003): *Vergesellschaftung des Regierens? Der Wandel nationaler und internationaler politischer Steuerung unter dem Leitbild der nachhaltigen Entwicklung*. Opladen: Leske + Budrich.

Brühl, T. (2003): *Nichtregierungsorganisationen als Akteure internationaler Umweltver-handlungen: Ein Erklärungsmodell auf der Basis der situationsspezifischen Ressourcennach-frage*. Frankfurt am Main u.a.: Campus.

Brühl, T. and V. Rittberger (2001): From International to Global Governance: Actors, Collective Decision-making, and the United Nations in the World of the Twenty-First Century. In: Rittberger V. (ed.), *Global Governance and the United Nations System*. Tokyo/New York: United Nations University Press: 1–47.

Charnovitz, S. (2001): International Law Weekend Proceedings: Economic and Social Actors in the World Trade Organization. *ILSA Journal of International and Comparative Law* 7: 259–74.

Clark, I. (1999): *Globalization and International Relations Theory*. Oxford: Oxford University Press.

Coicaud, J.-M. (2001a): International Democratic Culture and its Sources of Legitimacy. In: Coicaud, J.-M. and V. Heiskanen (eds.), *The Legitimacy of International Organizations*. Tokyo/New York: United Nations University Press: 256–308.

Coicaud, J.-M. (2001b): International Organizations, the Evolution of International Politics, and Legitimacy. In: Coicaud, J.-M. and V. Heiskanen (eds.), *The Legitimacy of International Organizations*. Tokyo/New York: United Nations University Press: 510–52.

Cusimano, M. K. (2000): Beyond Sovereignty: the Rise of Transsovereign Problems. In: Cusimano, M. K. (ed.), *Beyond Sovereignty: Issues for a Global Agenda*. Boston: Bedford/St. Martin's: 1–40.

Cutler, A. C., V. Haufler and T. Porter (1999): *Private Authority and International Affairs*. Albany, NY: State University of New York Press.

Czempiel, E.-O. (1981): *Internationale Politik: ein Konfliktmodell*. Paderborn: Schoeningh.

Edele, A. (2006): All Hands on Deck – The Establishment of Global Public–Private Partnerships for Devlopment from a Resource Exchange Perspective. Unpublished Masters Thesis, University of Tübingen, Institute of Political Science.

European Commission (2001): Promoting a European Framework for Corporate Social Responsibility. Brussels, Directorate General for Employment and Social Affairs. Luxemburg: Office for Official Publication of the European Communities.

Global Fund to Fight Aids, Tuberculosis and Malaria (2003): *A Force for Change: the Global Fund at 30 Months*. Geneva: The Global Fund.

Global Public Policy Institute (2004): About GPPi. Available: www.globalpublicpolicy. net/ (accessed on 10 December 2004).

Gordenker, L. and T. G. Weiss (1996): Pluralizing Global Governance: Analytical Approaches and Dimensions. In: Gordenker, L. (ed.). *NGOs, the United Nations, and Global Governance*. Boulder, CO: Lynne Rienner: 17–47.

Hamm, B. (2006): Neuere Entwicklungen des Global Compact. In: von Schorlemer, S. (ed.), *'Wir, die Völker (…)' – Strukturwandel in der Weltorganisation*. Frankfurt a.M. et al.: Peter Lang: 95–113.

Hasenclever, A., P. Mayer and V. Rittberger (1997): *Theories of International Regimes*. Cambridge: Cambridge University Press.

Held, D., A. G. McGrew, D. Goldblatt and J. Perraton (1999): *Global Transformations: Politics, Economics and Culture*. Stanford, CA: Stanford University Press.

Holsti, K. J. (1992): Governance without Government: Polyarchy in Nineteenth-Century European International Politics. In: Rosenau, J. N. and E. O. Czempiel (eds.), *Governance without Government: Order and Change in World Politics*. Cambridge: Cambridge University Press: 30–57.

Howse, R. (2001): The Legitimacy of the World Trade Organization. In: Coicaud, J.-M. and V. Heiskanen (eds.), *The Legitimacy of International Organizations*. Tokyo/New York: United Nations University Press: 355–407.

Huckel, C., R. Reusch and F. Scholtes (2005): 'Legitimität' im Globalisierungsdiskurs: Teilhabe, Kompetenzzuweisung, Wohlfahrt. In: Badura, J., L. Rieth and F. Scholtes (eds.), *Globalisierung – Problemsphären eines Schlagwortes im interdisziplinären Dialog*. Wiesbaden: VS-Verlag: 141–62.

Hurd, I. (2003): Labour Standards through International Organisations. The Global Compact in Comparative Perspective, *Journal of Corporate Citizenship* 3(11): 379–408.

International Labour Organization (2001): International Labour Organization. Information Leaflet. Available: www.ilo.org/public/english/bureau/inf/download/leaflet/pdf/leaflet2001.pdf (accessed on 11 September 2005).

International Labour Organization (2004) 'The ILO: What it is. What it does. Available: www.ilo.org/public/english/bureau/inf/download/brochure/pdf/broch_0904.pdf (accessed on 11 September 2005).

IPPPH (2004): The Initiative on Public–Private Partnerships for Health Partnerships, Database. Available: www.ippph.org/index.cfm?page=/ippph/partnerships (accessed on 10 December 2004).

Junne, G. C. A. (2001): International Organizations in a Period of Globalization: New (Problems of) Legitimacy. In: Coicaud, J.-M. and V. Heiskanen (eds.), *The Legitimacy of International Organizations*. Tokyo/New York: United Nations University Press: 189–220.

Kaldor, M. (1999): *New and Old Wars: Organized Violence in a Global Era*. Cambridge: Polity Press.

Kaul, I. (2006): Exploring the Policy Space between Markets and States. Global Public–Private Partnerships. In: Kaul, I. and P. Conceição (eds.), *The New Public Finance. Responding to Global Challenges*. New York: Oxford University Press: 219–68.

Kaul, I., I. Grunberg and M. A. Stern (eds.) (1999a): *Global Public Goods: International Cooperation in the 21st Century*. New York: Oxford University Press.

Kaul, I., I. Grunberg and M. A. Stern (1999b): 'Introduction'. In: Kaul, I., I. Grunberg and M. A. Stern (eds.), *Global Public Goods: International Cooperation in the 21st Century*. New York: Oxford University Press: 1–38.

Kaul, I. and R. U. Mendoza (2003): Advancing the Concept of Public Goods. In: Kaul, I., P. Conceição, K. Le Goulven and R. U. Mendoza (eds.), *Providing Global Public Goods: Managing Globalization*. New York: Oxford University Press: 78–111.

Keck, M. E. and K. Sikkink (1998): *Activists Beyond Borders: Advocacy Networks in International Politics*. Ithaca, NY: Cornell University Press.

Kell, G. (2003): The Global Compact: Origins, Operations, Progress, Challenges. *Journal of Corporate Citizenship* 3(11): 35–49.

Kell, G. and D. Levin (2003): The Global Compact Network: an Historic Experiment in Learning and Action. *Business and Society Review* 108(2): 151–81.

Keohane, R. O. (1984): *After Hegemony: Cooperation and Discord in the World Political Economy*. Princeton, NJ: Princeton University Press.

Keohane, R. O. and J. S. Nye (1974): Introduction: the Complex Politics of Canadian-American Interdependence. *International Organization* 28(4): 595–607.

Keohane, R. O. and J. S. Nye (2000a): 'Introduction'. In: Nye, J. S. and J. D. Donahue (eds.), *Governance in a Globalizing World*. Washington DC: Brookings Institution Press: 1–49.

Keohane, R. O. and J. S. Nye (2000b): *Power and Interdependence: World Politics in Transition*. Boston: Longman, 3rd edn.

Keohane, R. O. and J. S. Nye (2003): Redefining Accountability for Global Governance. In: Kahler, M., and D. A. Lake (eds.), *Governance in a Global Economy: Political Authority in Transition*. Princeton, NJ: Princeton University Press: 386–411.

Koenig-Archibugi, M. (2002): Mapping Global Governance. In: Held, D. and A. G. McGrew (eds.), *Governing Globalization: Power, Authority and Global Governance*. Cambridge: Polity Press: 46–69.

Lomborg, B. (ed.) (2004): *Global Crises, Global Solutions*. Cambridge: Cambridge University Press.

Majone, G. (2001): Two Logics of Delegation: Agency and Fiduciary Relations in EU Governance. *European Union Politics* 2(1): 103–21.

Martens, K. (2005): *NGOs and the United Nations. Institutionalization Professionalization and Adaptation*. Basingstoke, New York: Palgrave Macmillan.

Mayer, P., V. Rittberger and M. Zürn (1993): Regime Theory: State of the Art and Perspectives. In: Rittberger, V., and P. Mayer (eds.), *Regime Theory and International Relations*. Oxford: Clarendon Press: 391–430.

Muldoon, J. P. (2004): *The Architecture of Global Governance: an Introduction to the Study of International Organizations*. Boulder, CO: Westview Press.

Nelson, J. and United Nations (2002): *Building Partnerships: Cooperation between the United Nations System and the Private Sector*. New York, NY: United Nations Department of Public Information.

Neyer, J. (2002): Politische Herrschaft in nicht-hierarchischen Mehrebenensystemen. *Zeitschrift für Internationale Beziehungen* 9(1): 9–38.

Nölke, A. (2000): Regieren in transnationalen Politiknetzwerken? Kritik postnationaler Governance-Konzepte aus der Perspektive einer transnationalen (Inter-) Organisationssoziologie. *Zeitschrift für Internationale Beziehungen* 7(2): 331–58.

Nye, J. S. (2002): The American National Interest and Global Public Goods. *International Affairs*: 233–44.

O'Brien, R., A. M. Goetz, J. A. Scholte and M. Williams (2000): *Contesting Global Governance: Multilateral Economic Institutions and Global Social Movements*. Cambridge: Cambridge University Press.

Pfeffer, J. and G. R. Salancik (1978): *The External Control of Organizations: a Resource Dependence Perspective*. New York: Harper & Row.

Pollack, M. A. (1997): Delegation, Agency, and Agenda Setting in the European Community. *International Organization* 51(1): 99–134.

Reihlen, M. (1998): Die Heterarchie als postbürokratisches Organisationsmodell der Zukunft?. Arbeitsberichte des Seminars für Allgemeine Betriebswirtschaftslehre, Betriebswirtschaftliche Planung und Logistik der Universität zu Köln (Arbeitsbericht Nr. 96).

Reihlen, M. and A. Rohde (1998): Das heterarchische Unternehmen: Ein flexibles Organisationsmodell im Wissensbasierten Wettbewerb. Unpublished Paper.

Reinicke, W. and F. Deng (2000): *Critical Choices: the United Nations, Networks, and the Future of Global Governance*. Washington DC: Brookings Institution Press.

Reinicke, W. H. (1999/2000): The Other World Wide Web: Global Public Policy Networks. *Foreign Policy* 117: 44–57.

Rieth, L. (2004): Der VN Global Compact: Was als Experiment begann . . ., *Die Friedens-Warte* 79(1–2): 151–70.

Rieth, L. and T. Göbel (2005): Unternehmen, gesellschaftliche Verantwortung und die Rolle von NGOs. *Zeitschrift für Wirtschafts- und Unternehmensethik*, 6(2): 244–61.

Rittberger, V. (1973): *Evolution and International Organization: Toward a New Level of Sociopolitical Integration*. The Hague: M. Nijhoff.

Rittberger, V. (2003): Weltregieren: Was kann es leisten? Was muss es leisten? In: Küng, H. and D. Senghaas (eds.), *Friedenspolitik: Ethische Grundlagen Internationaler Beziehungen*. Munich/Zürich: Piper: 177–208.

Rittberger, V. (2004a): Transnationale Unternehmen in Gewaltkonflikten. *Die Friedens-Warte* 79(1–2): 15–34.

Rittberger, V. (2004b): Weltregieren zwischen Anarchie und Hierarchie. In: Rittberger, V. (ed.), *Weltpolitik Heute: Grundlagen und Perspektiven*. Baden-Baden: Nomos: 245–70.

Rittberger, V., Chr. Schrade and D. Schwarzer (1999): Introduction: Transnational Civil Society and the Quest for Security. In: Inoguchi, T. (ed.), *International Security Management and the United Nations. The United Nations System in the 21st century*. Tokyo/New York: United Nations University Press: 109–38.

Rittberger, V. and B. Zangl (2006): *International Organization: Polity, Politics and Policies*. Basingstoke, New York: Palgrave Macmillan.

Rosenau, J. N. (1992): Governance, Order, and Change in World Politics. In: Rosenau, J. N. and E. O. Czempiel (eds.), *Governance without Government: Order and Change in World Politics*. Cambridge: Cambridge University. Press: 1–29.

Rosenau, J. N. and E. O. Czempiel (eds.) (1992): *Governance without Government: Order and Change in World Politics*. Cambridge: Cambridge University Press.

Ruggie, J. G. (2002): The Theory and Practice of Learning Networks: Corporate Social Responsibility and the Global Compact. *Journal of Corporate Citizenship* 5(1): 27–36.

Sampson, G. P. (ed.) (2001a): Overview. In: Gary Sampson (ed.), *The Role of the World Trade Organization in Global Governance*. Tokyo: United Nations University Press: 1–18.

Sampson, G. P. (2001b): *The Role of the World Trade Organization in Global Governance*. Tokyo/New York: United Nations University Press.

Scharpf, F. (1998): Interdependence and Democratic Legitimation. Working Paper 98/2. Cologne: Max Planck Institute for the Study of Societies.

Scharpf, F. W. (1999): *Regieren in Europa – effektiv und demokratisch?* Frankfurt am Main: Campus.

Schechter, M. G. (2001): *United Nations-sponsored World Conferences: Focus on Impact and Follow-up*. Tokyo/New York: United Nations University Press.

Schorlemer, S. von (2006): Vorwort. In: Schorlemer, S. von (ed.), '*Wir, die Völker (...)' – Strukturwandel in der Weltorganisation*. Frankfurt a.M. et al.: Peter Lang, 7–22.

Scott, W. R. (2003): *Organizations: Rational, Natural, and Open Systems*. Englewood Cliffs, NJ: Prentice-Hall, 5th edn.

Senti, M. (2002): *Internationale Regime und nationale Politik. Die Effektivität der Internationalen Arbeitsorganisation (ILO) im Industrieländervergleich*. Bern, Stuttgart, Vienna: Haupt.

Shaffer, G. C. (2003): *Defending Interests: Public–Private Partnerships in WTO Litigation*. Washington, DC: Brookings Institution Press.

Simmons, P. J. and C. de Jonge Oudraat (2001): *Managing Global Issues: Lessons Learned*. Washington DC: Carnegie Endowment for International Peace.

Smith, M. K. (2002): False Hope of New Start. Oxfam Briefing Paper No. 24, June 2002.

Spar, D. L. and L. T. La Mure (2003): The Power of Activism: Assessing the Impact of NGOs on Global Business. *California Management Review* 45(3) (spring 2003): 78–101.

Staisch, M. (2003): Reaching Out, or Not: Accounting for the Relative Openness of International Governmental Organizations Towards NGOs. Unpublished Masters Thesis, University of Tübingen, Institute of Political Science.

Stoll, P.-T. and F. Schorkopf (2002): *WTO – Welthandelsordnung und Welthandelsrecht*. Köln et al.: Carl Heymanns.

Suchman, M. C. (1995): Managing Legitimacy: Strategic and Institutional Approaches. *Academy of Management Review* 20(3): 571–610.

Take, I. (2002): *NGOs im Wandel: Von der Graswurzel auf das diplomatische Parkett*. Wiesbaden: Westdeutscher Verlag.

Tussie, D. and M. P. Riggirozzi (2001): Pressing Ahead with New Procedures for Old Machinery: Global Governance and Civil Society. In: Rittberger, V. (ed.), *Global Governance and the United Nations System*. Tokyo/New York/Paris: United Nations University Press: 158–80.

UNAIDS (1999): Modus Operandi of the Programme Coordination Board of the Joint United Nations Programme on HIV/AIDS (UNAIDS) (Revised June 1999).

UNAIDS (2004a): 2004 Report on the Global AIDS Epidemic. Geneva: United Nations Publications.

UNAIDS (2004b): A Joint Response to HIV-AIDS. New York: United Nations Publications.

UNAIDS (2004c): UNAIDS and Nongovernmental Organizations. Geneva: United Nations Press.

UNAIDS (2005): Report of the Seventeenth Meeting of the UNAIDS Programme Coordinating Board. Geneva, 27–9 June 2005. data.unaids.org/Governance/PCB04/PCB_17_05_10_en.pdf?preview=true, accessed 20 April 2006.

UNCTAD (2002): World Investment Report. United Nations Publications.

Underdal, A. (2002): One Question, Two Answers. In: Miles, E. L., A. Underdal, A. Steiner et al. (eds.), *Environmental Regime Effectiveness. Confronting Theory with Evidence*. Cambridge, MA/London: MIT Press: 3–45.

UNDESA (2004): Partnerships for Sustainable Development – CSD Database. Available: webapps01.un.org/dsd/partnerships/public/browse.do (accessed 10 December 2004).

UNFIP (2004): Mission Statement. Available: www.un.org/unfip/2004Website/mission.htm (accessed 10 December 2004).

United Nations (1995): Joint and Co-sponsored United Nations Programme on Human Immunodeficiency Virus/ Acquired Immunodeficiency Syndrom. United Nations, ECOSOC 1995/2, 21st Plenary Meeting, 3 July 1995.

United Nations (1997): The World Conferences: Developing Priorities for the 21st Century. United Nations Briefing Paper. www.un.org/geninfo/bp/worconf.html, accessed 10 December 2004.

United Nations (2004a): Report of the Secretary General on the Implementation of the Report of the Panel of Eminent Persons on United Nations – Civil Society Relations. General Assembly, A/58/ Agenda Item 55 (unedited, advance version).

United Nations (2004b): We the Peoples: Civil Society, the United Nations, and Global Governance (known as 'Cardoso Report'). United Nations, General Assembly, A/58/817, 11 June 2004.

United Nations Global Compact Office (2005): The Global Compact's Next Phase. New York.

Waltz, K. N. (1979): *Theory of International Politics*. Reading, MA: Addison-Wesley.

Weber, M. (1968): *Economy and Society, Vols. 1 and 2*. Berkeley, CA: University of California Press.

Wendt, A. (1999): *Social Theory of International Politics*. Cambridge: Cambridge University Press.

Willke, H. (1996): *Ironie des Staates: Grundlinien einer Staatstheorie polyzentrischer Gesellschaft*. Frankfurt am Main: Suhrkamp.

Winston, M. (2002): NGO Strategies for Promoting Corporate Social Responsibility. *Ethics and International Affairs* 16(1): 71–87.

Wolf, K. D. (2000): *Die Neue Staatsräson. Zwischenstaatliche Kooperation als Demokratieproblem in der Weltgesellschaft*. Baden-Baden: Nomos.

Wolf, K. D. (2003): Normsetzung in internationalen Institutionen unter Mitwirkung privater Akteure? 'International Environmental Governance' zwischen ILO, öffentlich-privaten Netzwerken und Global Compact. In: Schorlemer, S. von (ed.), *Praxishandbuch UNO. Die Vereinten Nationen im Lichte globaler Herausforderungen*. Berlin: Springer: 225–40.

Worldbank (2004): Reform of World Bank-Administred Trust Funds: the Way Forward. Washington, DC: World Bank Publications.

World Trade Organization: Available: www.wto.org.

Young, O. R. (1999): *Governance in World Affairs*. Ithaca/London: Cornell University Press.

Zürn, M. (1998): *Regieren jenseits des Nationalstaates. Globalisierung und Denationalisierung als Chance*. Frankfurt am Main: Suhrkamp.

Zürn, M. (2000): Democratic Governance beyond the Nation-State. *European Journal of International Relations* 35(2): 183–221.

Zürn, M. (2001): Political Systems in the Postnational Constellation: Societal Denationalization and Multilevel Governance. In: Rittberger, V. (ed.), *Global Governance and the United Nations System*. Tokyo/New York: United Nations University Press: 48–87.

Zürn, M. (2004): Global Governance and Legitimacy Problems. *Government and Opposition* 39(2): 260–87.

Zürn, M. and M. Koenig-Archibugi (2006): Conclusion II: the Modes and Dynamics of Global Governance. In: Koenig-Archibugi, M. and M. Zürn (eds.), *New Modes of Governance in the Global System. Exploring Publicness, Delegation and Inclusiveness*. Basingstoke/New York: Palgrave Macmillan: 236–254.

2

The WTO Constitution, Judicial Power and Changing Patterns of Authority

Jeffrey L. Dunoff

Introduction

This chapter addresses judicial power and changing patterns of authority in the context of the World Trade Constitution. Of course, posing the topic in this way presupposes the existence of a world trade constitution. One purpose of this chapter is to explore what trade scholars mean when they refer to the World Trade Constitution. To do so, I'll discuss three leading versions of WTO constitutionalism that have been developed in the literature. I will then suggest that these otherwise divergent views of constitutionalism share an impulse to channel or minimize world trade politics. Paradoxically, however, the call for constitutionalism has sparked precisely the sort of politics that it seeks to pre-empt. Hence, another goal of this chapter is to illustrate the self-defeating nature of the turn to constitutionalism.

This analysis will raise a larger question, one that relates to this volume's focus upon changing patterns of authority in the global political economy. If there is no world trade constitution, and if the calls for such a constitution trigger the world trade politics that constitutionalism seeks to avoid, why do leading trade scholars continue to engage in the turn to constitutionalism? The answer to this question will lead us not only to the question of whether there are changing patterns of authority, but to deeper and more troubling questions about the current status of the discipline of international law.

In the current post-September 11 environment – where realist approaches to international relations are ascendent – international law is a discipline under siege. In this context, we might understand the turn to constitutional discourse among academics as a response to deep disciplinary anxieties about the current status and role of international law. The invocation of constitutional rhetoric at the WTO (and elsewhere in international law) may be an effort to invest international law with the power and authority that domestic constitutional structures and norms possess. However, in this regard, the turn to constitutionalism may be self-defeating. Critical evaluation of constitutional claims may simply highlight the *lack* of constitutional structure, legitimating foundations, or popular acceptance of the WTO or international law more generally.

This chapter will proceed in five parts. Part one reviews the three leading conceptions of constitutionalism outlined in international trade law scholarship. Part two analyses whether WTO dispute settlement reports support any of the three leading constitutional theories. Part three discusses whether there are commonalities among the three leading theories of constitutionalism at the WTO. Part four locates the debate over constitutionalism at the WTO within the context of the volume's larger preoccupation with changing patterns of authority in international economic law. Finally, Part five examines the allure of constitutional discourse, and suggests that international lawyers' focus on constitutionalism may reflect deeper anxieties over international laws current status and role.

The turn to constitutionalism: competing conceptions of constitutionalism at the WTO

Although international lawyers have long invoked constitutional imagery, constitutional discourse has become more prominent in recent years. The increased salience of this discourse reflects, in part, radical constitutional changes in the former Eastern Bloc states following the fall of the Berlin Wall and dissolution of the Soviet Union; the increased use of comparative constitutional techniques by various constitutional courts and, of course, the ongoing project to draft a treaty establishing a Constitution for Europe.

In addition to debates over specific domestic and supranational constitutions, international lawyers increasingly use constitutional analogies to describe the activities of the United Nations and other international organizations. Even a cursory review of writings addressing the use of force in Iraq and Kosovo; the dissolution of the former Yugoslavia; the Lockerbie saga; and international responses to civil unrest in Africa and elsewhere reveals the hold of constitutional imagery on the international legal imagination.[1] In almost every instance, the scholarly invocation of constitutional discourse has both commented on and contributed to highly visible contemporaneous developments in the social and political world.[2]

In recent years, WTO scholarship has also experienced a turn to constitutionalism. It is tempting to locate the constitutional turn in trade scholarship within the context of the turn to constitutionalism in international law generally. But there is an immediate and dramatic contrast between the WTO context and the other contexts mentioned above: in the WTO there is no ongoing political process of creating a constitutional document, nor any likelihood of such a process in the foreseeable future. There is no constitutional convention, no constitutional drafting process, and no readily identifiable constitutional moment.

Moreover, the Uruguay Round texts do not appear to create a constitutional system. The Uruguay Round Agreements neither create a world trade legislature nor vest autonomous legislative or regulatory capacity in a WTO body. These agreements do not refer to a vertical division of powers or a formal separation of powers doctrine. Finally, most states, including major trading powers such as the US and the EU, have refused to give direct effect to the obligations created by the WTO agreements, meaning that WTO rules cannot be invoked by private parties in domestic courts.[3] Immediately, then, we are struck by a puzzle: What do WTO scholars mean when they speak of constitutionalism at the WTO?

Not surprisingly, constitutionalism is a highly contested term that is used in different ways by different authors.[4] Nevertheless, it is possible to characterize the most prominent of this scholarship as falling into one of three different categories. As described below, the most influential trade scholarship understands the WTO constitution to consist of either (1) the WTO's institutional architecture; (2) a set of normative commitments; or (3) a process of judicial mediation among conflicting values. Each of these understandings is briefly described.[5]

The WTO constitution as institutional architecture

The most significant strand of trade scholarship understands the WTO constitution primarily in institutional terms, and the most visible known advocate of this understanding is John Jackson.[6] As he notes 'my focus is on the institutional side, on what I call the "constitution" of the world trading system' (Jackson 2001: 71).

Jackson's preoccupation with the constitutional dimensions of institutional design is present in his earliest writings. The final chapter of Jackson's 1969 trade law treatise is entitled: 'The Constitutional Structure of a Possible International Trade Institution'. It concludes:

> The perpetual puzzle . . . of international economic institutions is . . . to give measured scope for legitimate national policy goals while preventing the use of these goals to promote particular interests at the expense of the greater common welfare. An additional function of the international institutions is that of any government unit to allow a society of persons or nations to organize in such a way as to enable its members to pursue common goals without being defeated by competing antisocial conduct of members of the group. . . . What is needed in an institution . . . is the structure and machinery to enable man [*sic*] as efficiently as possible . . . the pursuit of common goals. In the long run, it may well be the machinery that is most important . . . rather than the existence of any one or another specific rule of trade conduct (Jackson 1969: 788).

Despite Jackson's influence, for many years few in the trade world pursued his call to understand questions of institutional structure in constitutional terms.

Twenty years after issuing his call for an institutional machinery to govern international trade relations, and in the context of the then-ongoing Uruguay Round negotiations, Jackson published *Restructuring the GATT System* (1990). This book proposes a 'constitutional' status and structure for the international trade system. In part, Jackson urges a constitutional structure as a pragmatic means to address the GATT's famous birth defects, including the 'provisional' nature of GATT obligations; a losing party's power to veto adverse dispute settlement reports; the doctrinal and practical complications arising out of the existence of multiple GATT agreements and understandings; and the practical difficulties associated with changing GATT rules.[7]

In addition to these characteristically 'pragmatic' arguments,[8] Jackson advances a bold historical-descriptive and normative claim: 'To a large degree the history of civilization may be described as a gradual evolution from a power oriented approach, in the state of nature, towards a rule oriented approach' (Jackson 1990: 52). He emphasizes that, in the economic context, only a rule-oriented approach will provide the security and predictability necessary for decentralized international markets to function. And how is this new rule-orientation to be realized? Jackson argues that this new approach can best occur through a 'constitution' creating a new international organization, the World Trade Organization.

Jackson's ideas about the need for a new institutional architecture, presented at a London seminar attended by Uruguay Round negotiators and elsewhere, caught the attention of several trade diplomats and Arthur Dunkel, then the GATT's Director-General.[9] As a result, Jackson was hired as an advisor to the Government of Canada and drafted papers outlining the need for a new international organization and a proposed agreement. At roughly the same time, various EC officials became interested in institutional issues. Eventually, a draft Agreement Establishing the Multilateral Trade Organization was included in the Dunkel Draft Final Act, released in late 1991. After various diplomatic twists and turns, trading nations established a new World Trade Organization at the conclusion of the Uruguay Round. It is no exaggeration to state that the WTO's innovative and controversial institutional structure owes much to Jackson's writings and advocacy.[10]

Jackson's post-Uruguay Round writings continue to focus on the theme of institutional architecture as constitution. In recent years, Jackson has critiqued the WTO's institutional structure, focusing on the strengths and limitations of the WTO's innovative dispute resolution system and on the institutional obstacles to rule-making at the WTO. While Jackson's immediate concerns have, shifted over time, and he sometimes uses the terms 'constitution' and 'constitutionalism' in different ways, in general, his writings continue to focus on questions of institutional architecture in the trade regime.

The WTO constitution as normative commitment

A second strand of constitutional scholarship views constitutionalism as the privileging of a set of normative commitments. Perhaps the most prominent advocate of this position is Ernst-Ulrich Petersmann.

Like Jackson, Petersmann has long been interested in the constitutional dimensions of international legal institutions and doctrines, with a particular focus on international economic law.[11] However, for Petersmann, constitutionalism is less an institutional arrangement than a set of normative values that protect against both government overreaching and short-sighted decisions by the population: 'The self-limitation of our freedom of action by rules and the self-imposition of institutional constraints... are rational responses designed to protect us against future risks of our own passions and imperfect rationality' (Petersmann 1999c: 1–30). In this context, Petersmann invokes the familiar story of Ulysses ordering his companions to bind him to the mast when approaching the island of the sirens;[12] constitutions consist of pre-commitments to norms that 'effectively constitute and limit citizen rights and government powers'.[13]

Constitutions are thus premised upon a series of normative values, including, inter alia, the 'rule of law'; horizontal and vertical separation of powers principles or, alternatively, Madisonian 'checks and balances' designed to produce 'rule-oriented rather than power-oriented settlement of international disputes' (Petersmann 1997: 427); and rules that limit governments by subjecting government actions that 'restrain individual freedoms (including the right to import and export)' to the tests of 'necessity and proportionality'.

Finally, constitutional systems recognize and protect inalienable human rights, 'market freedoms', and other fundamental rights as non-derogable limitations on government powers. Petersmann argues that, in this respect, the WTO performs better than domestic constitutions:

> the WTO guarantees of freedom, non-discrimination and the rule of law go far beyond national constitutional guarantees in most countries which tend to limit economic freedom to domestic citizens and, for centuries, have discriminated against foreign goods, foreign services and foreign consumers (e.g., by permitting export cartels). By extending equal freedoms across frontiers and subjecting discretionary foreign policy powers to additional legal and judicial restraints... the WTO rules... serve 'constitutional functions' for rendering human rights and the corresponding obligations of governments more effective in the trade policy area (Petersmann 2002: 644).

Petersmann's most recent writings on constitutionalism have suggested that the elevation of fundamental human rights lie at the core of his constitutional vision. Thus, he has recently argued for the 'constitutional primacy of the inalienable core of human rights' that should be applied in the WTO context (Petersmann 2002).

Perhaps most controversially, Petersmann has argued that economic freedoms lie at the heart of fundamental human rights. Following Jan Tumlir, Fredrich Hayek and others, Petersmann emphasizes the fundamental importance of economic freedoms such as the freedom to produce and exchange goods...and argues that market freedoms are indispensable for human autonomy and self-determination (Petersmann 1999c: 1–30). Repeatedly, Petersmann praises European integration law for fully recognizing that transnational 'market freedoms' for movements of goods, services, persons, capital and related payments are judicially enforceable transnational citizen rights (Petersmann 2003: 407, 457), and urges the WTO and other international organizations to follow Europe's lead in this regard.

Thus, Petersmann's understanding of constitutionalism can sharply distinguished from Jackson's. While Petersmann does not ignore institutional issues, his understanding of constitutionalism is centred upon the elevation and protection of certain normative values. Human rights are central to these values, which in Petersmann's understanding should encompass economic rights including the freedom to trade.

The WTO constitution as a judicial mediating device

Perhaps the most common conception of constitutionalism highlights the mediating and norm generating elements of WTO dispute settlement as the engine of constitutionalism. A leading exponent of this view is Deborah Cass, who argues that the WTO's Appellate Body (AB) 'is the dynamic force behind constitution-building by virtue of its capacity to generate constitutional norms and structures during dispute resolution' (Cass 2001: 39, 42).

Cass argues that the AB generates these constitutional norms through four distinct processes. First, the AB engages in 'constitutional doctrine amalgamation'; by which Cass means that the AB borrows constitutional rules, principles and doctrines from other systems and amalgamates them into the AB's own caselaw (Cass 2001: 51). Second, the AB's decisions are 'constitutive of a new system of law'. That is, through decisions that generate rules on burdens of proof, fact finding and participation by non-state actors, the AB is inaugurating a specific type of legal system. Third, the AB is incorporating into its jurisdiction issues traditionally viewed as belonging within national constitutional processes, such as public health. Finally, Cass argues that the AB 'associates itself with deeper constitutional values' in the ways that it carefully crafts and justifies its decisions. It does so by addressing such background constitutional questions as 'how to design a fair system of law...and how policy responsibility will be divided'. In addressing these sorts of issues, Cass argues, the AB associates its jurisprudence with that of other constitutional systems.

Cass argues further that these various techniques are often employed to help mediate among conflicting values that are present in the trade system, and that WTO members seem unable to resolve in WTO negotiating fora. For example, Cass discusses how the AB has carefully articulated that its standard of review of national measures is that of objective assessment. This not only steers a middle course, as a doctrinal matter, 'between full review on the merits, and the far less intrusive standard of procedural or reasonableness review' (Cass 2001: 57), but also does so in a way that 'provides a lens through which to see the constitutional issue at the foundation of the question, namely, which body national government or international tribunal has the authority to decide matters crucial to trade policy' (Cass 2001: 58). Cass argues that the AB's articulation and application of the objective assessment standard of review 'finesses a conflict between national and international institutional authority' (Cass 2001: 58).

Cass also points to the AB's choice of fact-finding method as illustrating how the AB drives the constitutionalization process. The argument here rests upon the premise that different modes of fact-finding such as inquisitorial or adversarial have deep implications for the legal system as a whole; thus, for Cass, 'fact-finding rules can code for one form of system characterization' (Cass 2001: 60). Cass argues that, in a line of cases, the AB has generated a 'procedurally relatively informal system whereby information can be elicited from a variety of sources, and the tribunal is not hemmed in by any strict rules of evidence and procedure' (Cass 2001: 60). In this regard, Cass places special emphasis on the *Shrimp-Turtle* AB report that held that panels have authority to accept information from non-parties to the WTO. She notes that this decision 'lend[s] credence to the constitutionalization claim and has significance from a democratic and constitutional design perspective' (Cass 2001: 61). It does so, in part, by potentially expanding the participants in the trade system beyond states to corporations, NGOs and civil society. This increased participation, in turn, may increase the perceived levels of the legitimacy and fairness of the trade system.

Cass argues that, taken in the aggregate, the four features she identifies are the mechanisms through which 'the emerging jurisprudence of the WTO is beginning to develop a set of rules and principles which share some of the characteristics of constitutional law; and that this in turn is what contributes to the constitutionalization of international trade law' (Cass 2001: 52). Behind the doctrine, Cass argues, is a preoccupation with the sorts of issues that preoccupy constitutional courts: 'questions about the division of powers; ... [of] state sovereignty ... [questions] about how a legal system is constituted, its overall validity, its democratic contours, its very legitimacy' (Cass 2001: 72). In short, for Cass, the AB is 'building a constitutional system by judicial interpretations emanating from the judicial dispute resolution institution' (Cass 2001: 52).

The writings of Jackson, Petersmann and Cass represent three of the most prominent understandings of constitutionalism at the WTO. But, as even the brief descriptions above suggest, there are profound and perhaps intractable differences among these various uses of the term.[14] Is there any way to determine which, if any, of these understandings best captures WTO law and practice? In the next section of the chapter, I turn from scholarship to WTO practice. In particular, I examine the practices of WTO dispute resolution panels and the AB to see if their reports are consistent with any of the constitutional understandings developed in trade scholarship.

WTO dispute settlement: what constitution?

The Uruguay Round Agreements do not explicitly announce themselves to be a world trade constitution; they do not explicitly set out a system of separation of powers or checks and balances; they do not explicitly enshrine a 'freedom to trade'; and they do not explicitly empower the AB to establish a constitutional system through judicial interpretation. So if a WTO constitution exists, its nature and contours are not to be found – directly at least – in the Uruguay Round texts.

The next most obvious place to look for evidence of constitutionalism is in WTO dispute settlement reports. If there was a constitution, and if it centred upon either the WTO's institutional architecture, a fundamental freedom to trade, or the AB's norm-generating capacities, then it is likely that this constitutional structure would find expression in panel or AB reports.

Moreover, it is logical to examine dispute resolution reports because WTO dispute settlement lies near the heart of many discussions of constitutionalism at the WTO. As is well-known, the WTO dispute settlement system is far more legalized than the predecessor GATT system. While some suggest that the changes in dispute settlement alone can be characterized as constitutional (Steinberg 2004: 248), more frequently the claim is that the changes have permitted a form of judicial lawmaking. And there can be little doubt that the dispute settlement system is extraordinarily active, or that much of the effective work of trade diplomats and WTO secretariat is now focused on the dispute settlement process.

Of course, it is far more common to find robust judicial systems at the domestic level than at the international level. Domestic systems often include several different forms of judicial power, the most controversial of which is 'judicial review'. In the United States, for example, the Constitution expressly states that federal law is supreme over state law.[15] This provision is commonly understood to authorize federal courts to evaluate whether state acts conform to federal law. This exercise of judicial power is a form of vertical judicial review, in that the courts of a hierarchically superior government are reviewing the laws of a hierarchically inferior government for conformity with the laws of the superior entity (Vasquez 2004: 587, 595). In the United States, this form of 'vertical' judicial review today is relatively uncontroversial. In contrast, the concept of vertical judicial review in the European Union remains rather controversial (Berman 2004: 557).

In addition, from time to time US federal courts review the acts of executive branch officials for conformity with federal law or the Constitution. Federal courts also review the constitutionality of federal legislation. These forms of judicial review can be considered horizontal, because federal courts are reviewing the acts of coordinate branches of the same government to determine their conformity with the laws of that government. To the extent that judicial review remains controversial in the United States, debate centres around horizontal versions of judicial review. Horizontal judicial review has proven to be less problematic in Europe.[16]

For present purposes, these observations suggest a few avenues of inquiry. First, in analysing judicial power at the WTO, it is necessary to specify what type or types of judicial power are at stake. Perhaps more importantly, the above discussion suggests that different constitutional systems might utilize different types of judicial power: 'As is true in other institutions, both national and international, a tribunal-like institution must be understood in the context of its place in a broader governmental and institutional constitution' (Jackson 2000).

For example, a theory that adopted a process-oriented view of the constitution would likely see a primary purpose of judicial power as allocating different types of decisions to the institutions with the greatest capacity for generating results appropriate to the issues presented. In contrast, a theory that understood the constitution primarily as a vehicle for enshrining a particular set of substantive values would likely understand judicial settings in which to defend and enforce those values.

Do panels or the AB exercise a form of judicial power consistent with any of the three models of constitutionalism set out above? If the Jacksonian concept of constitutionalism at the WTO were descriptively accurate, we might expect to see a number of dispute settlement reports that explore the relationships among the various constituent elements of the WTO's institutional architecture. However, only a handful of cases address these institutional issues.

The most prominent dispute in this regard is *India Quantitative Restrictions on Imports of Agricultural, Textile and Industrial Products (India-QRs)*.[17] The dispute involved a challenge to certain trade measures imposed, India claimed, for balance of payments purposes. India argued that the panel had only limited competence to examine this issue as 'jurisdiction over this matter has been explicitly assigned to the BOP (Balance of Payments) Committee and the General Council'. More broadly, India argued that a principle of institutional balance mandated that the panel adopt a limited and deferential role lest it upset the 'distribution of powers between the judicial and the political organs of the WTO'.

In advancing these arguments, India was clearly seeking to have the AB adopt an understanding of the WTO architecture akin to a 'separation of powers' understanding of domestic governmental systems. Indeed India explicitly invoked domestic separation of powers systems and argued that 'the drafters of the WTO Agreement created a complex institutional structure under which various bodies are empowered to take binding decisions on related matters. These bodies must cooperate to achieve the objectives of the WTO, and can only do so if each exercises its competence with due regard to the competence of all other bodies. In order to preserve a proper institutional balance between the judicial and the political organs of the WTO with regard to matters relating to balance-of-payments restrictions, review of the justification of such measures must be left to the relevant political organs'.

Notably, the AB flatly rejected this theory. After reviewing the relevant WTO texts and prior panel reports, the AB concluded that 'India failed to advance any convincing arguments in support of a principle of institutional balance that requires panels to refrain from reviewing the justification of balance-of-payments restrictions'. Instead, the AB relied upon the text of the DSU and a footnote to the Balance of Payments Understanding that explicitly provided for dispute settlement mechanisms to be available 'with respect to any matters arising from the application of restrictive import measures taken for balance of payments purposes'.

In one sense, of course, the *India-QR* report addresses issues at the heart of a Jacksonian constitutional vision: the relationship between different parts of the WTO's institutional architecture. However, what is more significant is the AB's explicit and unequivocal rejection of the invitation to adopt a theory of separation of powers or to articulate a theory explaining the relationships between the WTO's 'political and judicial organs'. The AB does not understand – or at least declare – itself to be articulating a constitutional vision of the relationships among coordinate branches of an overarching institution or to be policing the jurisdictional lines that separate these coordinate branches.

To the contrary, the *India-QRs* report is written in an extremely narrow manner that studiously avoids constitutional rhetoric or reasoning. And whether or not the AB's reasoning is persuasive,[18] there can be little doubt that the AB's larger, if implicit, message – that it will not adopt or articulate a 'constitutional' understanding of the WTO's institutional architecture – was widely understood. In no subsequent panel or AB report did the tribunal mention or did a WTO member even deign to raise an argument invoking 'institutional balance', 'separation of powers', 'checks and balances' or similar arguments.

In short, there have been few opportunities for the AB to articulate a vision of constitutionalism as institutional architecture.[19] Moreover, on the one occasion where the AB did have the opportunity to adopt and articulate a constitutional vision of the relationships among the political and judicial branches, it explicitly rejected this understanding of the WTO system, and instead decided the case on narrow textual grounds. While there is surely no 'magic number' of reports which would confirm that the AB is exercising a form of judicial power consistent with an understanding of the WTO constitution as institutional architecture, it does seem fair to say that, to date, the reports that do so are few and far between.

To be sure, there are many potential explanations for the lack of such cases. Perhaps it is because claims can only be brought by member states against other member states. That is, unlike in the EU, WTO organs cannot initiate (or be named as respondents in) WTO dispute settlement proceedings. Another is that the WTO's political organs have little legislative or executive power, and hence challenges to their powers are likely to be infrequent (Vasquez 2004). Or maybe few cases discuss these issues because once the AB speaks, as in *India-QRs*, there is no need to relitigate the issue.

But even if separation of powers arguments are not addressed, one might expect a discussion of other facets of the WTO's institutional architecture. In short, the fact that very few reports discuss these issues and that none of the reports explore the WTO's institutional architecture suggest that they are doing so in the service of a vision of a WTO 'constitution' tends to confound theories that rest upon a vision of the WTO constitution as institutional architecture.

Similarly, neither the AB nor any panel has embraced the freedom to trade that Petersmann advocates.[20] The panel report in the *Section 301* case, arguably, provides the most relevant discussion:

> Neither the GATT nor the WTO has so far been interpreted by GATT/WTO institutions as a legal order producing direct effect [i.e., as creating legally enforceable rights and obligations for individuals]. Following this approach, the GATT/WTO did *not* create a new legal order the subjects of which comprise both ... Members and their nationals.[21]

The panel goes on to say that 'it would be entirely wrong to consider that the position of individuals is of no relevance to the GATT/WTO legal matrix', for a primary purpose of the GATT/WTO is 'to produce market conditions that permit individual activity to flourish'.[22] The panel therefore opines that it may be convenient 'in the GATT/WTO legal order to speak not of the principle of direct effect but of the principle of indirect effect'.[23] While this passage is surely an important acknowledgment of the role of individuals in the international trade system, it is hardly a ringing endorsement of a legally binding freedom to trade of constitutional dimension. No other WTO panel or AB report has discussed the direct effect (or indirect effect) of WTO law on individuals or a freedom to trade.

Finally, relatively few reports use the various mediating methods that Cass identifies and, when they do, their reports often fail to resolve the underlying value conflicts. Consider one of the examples that Cass relies upon to illustrate 'the way the [AB's] decisions herald a constitutionalization process', namely the AB's decision to permit submissions from a range of sources, including non-state actors. Close examination of what panels and the AB *do*, rather than what they *say*, with these submissions tends to undermine, rather than support, Cass's thesis about the constitutional dimensions of judicial norm-generation.

For several years, non-state actors, including NGOs, trade associations and individuals, have attempted to participate in WTO dispute resolution through submission of amicus briefs. In *Shrimp-Turtle*, the panel held that such amicus briefs were inadmissible as a matter of WTO law.[24] However, the panel then invited the parties to append relevant provisions of NGO briefs to their own; one party, the United States, did so.

On appeal, the AB explicitly rejected the panel's legal conclusion that NGO briefs were inadmissible, and held that panels had discretionary authority to accept amicus briefs.[25] But the AB expressly approved the panel's decision to permit parties to append NGO briefs to their own. It even adopted a similar procedure itself. Again, the United States appended NGO briefs to its own. In oral proceedings, the AB specifically asked the US to state whether it 'agree[d] with or adopted' the NGO arguments. The United States replied that '[it] agrees with the arguments in the NGO submissions to the extent those arguments concur with the [arguments in the main US brief]'. The Appellate Body proceeded to focus solely on the NGO arguments that were already in the US submission. Nevertheless, the AB's decision to admit amicus submissions prompted criticism from many WTO members.[26]

Thereafter, from time to time, a disputing party would incorporate an NGO brief into its own. However, the issue remained controversial, and came to a head in the *Asbestos* dispute. This case involved a Canadian challenge to a French ban on the sale of asbestos. Before the panel, the EC attached two amici briefs to its submission; the arguments in these briefs were considered by the panel.[27] But three other NGO submissions, that were not incorporated into any party's brief, were not 'taken into consideration' by the panel.[28]

After an appeal was filed in the Asbestos dispute, it became clear that many NGOs wished to submit briefs. Sua sponte, the Appellate Body issued a 'communication' with a procedure for interested parties to request leave to file amicus briefs.[29] Several developing states requested a special meeting of WTO members to discuss this communication and the larger issue of amicus briefs. An overwhelming majority of states who spoke at this meeting severely criticized the Appellate Body for issuing this communication. The Chair of the meeting announced he would forward a note to the Appellate Body urging it to exercise 'extreme caution' on this issue. The Appellate Body denied each of the seventeen applications for leave to file an amicus brief that were submitted in the *Asbestos* appeal.[30] Since then, in almost every dispute involving amicus briefs, panels and the AB have not addressed the arguments presented in NGO briefs that were not appended to a party's submission.[31]

The *Shrimp-Turtle* AB report represents an apparently significant doctrinal advance with respect to civil society participation in WTO dispute resolution. However, in practice, briefs submitted by non-state actors are only considered when adopted by a party to the dispute. This practice undermines the claim that the AB is playing a constitutional, norm-generating role here. In fact, after a large number of WTO members strongly objected to the norm that the AB tried to generate, supposedly constitutional, the AB backed away from the new norm. As one recent panel report stated – 'in light of the absence of consensus among WTO Members on how to treat amicus submissions', that it would not accept amicus briefs.[32]

In short, the AB's decisions lend little support any of the leading theories of constitutionalism. Few dispute settlement reports address the issues of institutional architecture that Jackson's scholarship would suggest is central to the WTO's 'constitution'. Few address the individual freedom to trade that Petersmann would have at the heart of the WTO's constitution; the one report to even address individual rights finds that they do not exist under WTO law. And few resolve the sorts of disputes that Cass says are central to the constitutionalization process, such as whether non-state actors will have access to WTO dispute resolution. Thus, we are left with a puzzle. Sophisticated and experienced trade scholars are developing increasingly elaborate theories of constitutionalism at the WTO; but the most prominent example of WTO practice, WTO dispute settlement reports, provides little evidence to support any of the specific theories of constitutionalism, let alone a move to constitutionalism in general. What explains this apparent discrepancy between WTO scholarship and practice?

Constitutionalism as antidote to trade politics

The discussion above illustrates just some of the diverse ways that trade scholars have used the term 'constitutionalism'. For now, I am less interested in determining which of the three constitutional visions is accurate than in exploring whether the various uses of the term suggest that constitutionalism is too protean and indeterminate to carry any analytic weight. In other words, is there a conceptual – or even ideological – link between these competing conceptions of constitutionalism at the WTO? What purchase is obtained through the invocation of constitutional discourse?

For current purposes, each of the three visions of constitutionalism at the WTO can be understood as standing in opposition to a broad and inclusive vision of world trade politics. That is, in each vision, we can understand constitutionalism as a mechanism for withdrawing an issue from the battleground of power politics and as a vehicle for resolving otherwise politically destabilizing political disputes through reference to a meta-agreement. This constitutional agreement – whether embodied in institutions, in foundational text, or in judicial doctrine and traditions that gloss the text – can then be used to resolve and pre-empt debate over what would otherwise be controversial issues that threaten the realm of ordinary politics. In short, the constitutionalist move is designed to 'bring international power politics under the strong arm of the "rule of law" ' (Broude 2004).

Consider again, for example, Jackson's constitutional vision, which as noted, is fixed on institutional architecture. This attention is eminently understandable; structural design is the basic hardware for constitutional practice, and the most familiar, visible and tangible index of constitutional continuity and change (Walker 2004: 23). However, recall the purpose of this institutional architecture: to introduce a 'rule based' system to replace the pre-exisiting 'power based' trade system. Jackson is explicit that, at bottom, the new rules based system is designed as an antidote to the corrupting influence that the exercise of power – that is politics – has heretofore exerted on international trade politics.

Petersmann similarly understands constitutionalism as a necessary corrective to the pathologies of politics: 'constitutionalism emerged in response to negative experiences with abuses of political power in order to limit such abuses through rules and institutions' (Petersmann 1999: 733, 758). Or, as Petersmann memorably suggests, constitutionalism's foundational insight is that the central political question is not who shall govern, but rather 'how must laws and political institutions be designed . . . so that even incompetent rulers and politicians cannot cause too much harm' (Petersmann 1997).

Cass, as well, presents a vision of constitutionalism that can be understood in opposition to politics. Her focus, as we have seen, is on the generation of constitutional norms by the WTO's judicialized dispute resolution process. But to use a highly judicialized process for generating and applying norms is effectively to turn legislative and interpretative powers to a small cadre of Appellate Body members. And while this may be a highly deliberative process, WTO dispute resolution is hardly a site for participatory or democratic politics.

Thus, a common link between these three different understandings of the WTO's constitution is that, for each of the scholars surveyed, the turn to constitutionalism is part of a larger turn away from politics. That is, for each of the scholars surveyed, the rise of the WTO as a constitutional entity can be understood as a corrective of, or replacement for, unruly and potentially destructive trade politics.

In this sense, however, the turn to constitutionalism can be understood as more a step backwards than a step forwards.[33] As Robert Keohane and Joseph Nye have argued, the original GATT was premised upon a 'Club Model' of international cooperation (Keohane and Nye 2003: 264). That is, during GATT's early years a relatively small number of economists and diplomats from like-minded states worked quietly to make trade policy without much public input or oversight: 'The GATT successfully managed a relative insulation from the outside world of international relations and established among its practitioners a closely knit environment revolving around a certain set of shared normative values (of free trade) and shared institutional (and personal) ambitions situated in a matrix of long-term first-name contacts and friendly personal relationships. GATT operatives became a classical network' (Weiler 1999: 334).

This Club Model persisted for many years because it was successful, in the sense that it oversaw dramatic decreases in tariffs and other trade barriers, and a corresponding increase in global trade and prosperity.

Paradoxically, however, the advantages of the Club Model of trade policy-making contained the seeds of their own destruction. First, increasing trade liberalization caused citizens to be more sensitive to further liberalization. This sensitivity complicated future efforts at liberalization (Dunoff 1999: 733). In addition, the Club Model was not sustainable in a context where developing states and civil society began to demand a greater role in trade negotiations and policy-making.

Today, the WTO is no longer an obscure body dealing with tariffs, but is understood as a central element of an emerging regime of global governance. Ministerial meetings in Seattle and Cancun 'teach that business as usual at the WTO is no longer acceptable. The days of major agreements being hammered out in Geneva hotels by trade experts operating under the radar of public view are gone forever. In short, the Club Model no longer represents a politically viable management structure for the international economic system' (Esty 1998: 123). The pressures on the WTO strongly suggest that whatever replaces the old Club Model must be more transparent and participatory. In this sense, the turn to constitutionalism – a turn away from politics – is precisely *not* what the WTO needs.

The deeper paradox, of course, is that constitutionalism – at least the kind advocated by Jackson, Petersmann and Cass – cannot possibly deliver the escape from politics that it promises. Jackson would house trade politics within the WTO's institutional apparatus. Of course, only states can be members of the WTO. But this means that WTO institutions reinscribe the very state-centric political order that many of the most controversial trade disputes put at issue (Dunoff 2001: 979). The most dramatic examples of world trade politics, including the Seattle Ministerial and controversies over access to essential medicines, highlight the ways in which trade politics can no longer be understood simply as inter-state politics and – more importantly – that in their current configurations the WTO's institutions do not and cannot contain world trade politics. That is, the structural limitations of this architecture almost guarantees an inadequate foundation of the democratic participation and accountability necessary for the social legitimacy that any effort to constitutionalize the trade system needs to succeed.

Similarly, Petersmann would enshrine and elevate economic freedoms, including a 'right to trade'. Petersmann argues that, in proper constitutional orders, government restrictions on economic rights, including the right to trade, should be subject to a strict 'necessity' test (Petersmann 1997: 431). As Howse and Alston have persuasively argued, this necessity test reveals how significantly Petersmann's vision of constitutionalism privileges economic rights as opposed to important social interests.[34] In practice such an elevation of economic rights would necessarily limit governments' ability to pursue many non-economic goals, such as environmental protection and other social policies.

More specifically, Petersmann's arguments about the need to integrate market freedoms into human rights law reflect one very particular – and contested – vision of human rights. There is a much larger debate, or political struggle here, both within and among nations, over the appropriate balance between economic and non-economic policy goals. To constitutionalize one controversial view of that balance is, in effect, to pre-empt that debate and that struggle.

Trade scholars invoke constitutional discourse because of the undoubted power that this discourse has in legal circles. However, the ideological and symbolic power associated with constitutional discourse has prompted powerful responses from those who would counterclaim or deny constitutional authority. Paradoxically, while the turn to constitutionalism can be seen as a method of closing down debate and removing issues from the domain of political contestation, in practice the advocates of constitutionalism have inadvertently triggered a robust and productive normative debate. Jackson's vision of constitutionalism has sparked a growing literature on whether the WTO's institutional structure is or should be considered 'constitutional'.[35] Similarly, Petersmann's efforts to constitutionalize a human right to trade within WTO law prompted a vigorous response.[36] And Cass's vision of the AB's constitutional powers joins a large literature debating the norm-generating and constitutional dimensions of WTO dispute resolution. In short, the advocates of constitutionalism have – perhaps inadvertently – helped to fuel a vociferous debate over the empirical validity and normative desirability of conceptualizing the WTO as a constitutional policy.

Changing patterns of authority

The present volume explores changing patterns of authority in the global political economy. The juxtaposition of the phrases 'world trade constitution' and 'judicial power' with changing patterns of authority would seem to imply a greater centralization of authority over international economic issues at the WTO. Indeed, two features of the Uruguay Round agreements are generally understood to support this centralization hypothesis.

First, the agreements are marked by a significant expansion in the reach of WTO disciplines into new areas, including intellectual property, services and some areas of foreign direct investment. Indeed, the expanding reach of the WTO has given rise to a significant debate among trade diplomats and scholars over whether the WTO should expand even further. Some, such as Andrew Guzman, suggest that since the WTO 'cannot avoid environmental, labor or other issues it ought to incorporate more regulatory issues within its mandate'.[37] The list of potential issues is enormous, including labour standards, competition policy, human rights issues, investment rules, environment and more. The advocates of expansion do not minimize the difficulties associated with developing rules in new areas, but argue that 'the alternative of reduced international economic cooperation is inconsistent with the needs of an increasingly global economy'.[38]

The other dramatic change is in the dispute resolution area. As is well-known, panel and AB reports are now automatically adopted, unless there is a consensus against such action. In addition, losing parties are obliged to reform their GATT inconsistent practices within a reasonable time period, or offer satisfactory alternative trade concessions. If the party fails to do so, then the aggrieved party may request authorization from the Dispute Settlement Body to suspend concessions 'equivalent to the level of the nullification or impairment' of its benefits under the relevant WTO agreement. Again, such authorization will be automatically granted absence of a consensus to the contrary. In the aggregate, these changes mark a significant 'legalization' of the dispute resolution process. They are also commonly understood to represent a shift in power to the dispute settlement system.

The centralization hypothesis contains much truth, but is often overstated. While it may be true that many more substantive areas – such as intellectual property – are now within the WTO, it does not follow that authority in international economic relations is flowing in only one direction – into the WTO. Rather, it appears that authority is flowing in at least two other directions.

First, the WTO's authority is flowing out toward other international legal regimes. The invocation of WTO norms in negotiations and treaty text in a variety of fora – including the Kimberly Process, the WHO Framework Convention on Tobacco Control, the Cartagena Protocol on Biosafety, and the ILO's June 2000 recommendation regarding Burma demonstrate how the WTO's shadow is falling on other regimes. Sometimes these other regimes adopt texts that seem to suggest that WTO norms are superior to those of the other regime;[39] sometimes the other regimes generate texts that suggest that their norms are superior to WTO norms;[40] and sometimes the texts suggest both positions at once.[41]

Second, many of the issues within the WTO's ambit are also being addressed in other international bodies. Consider, for example, international intellectual property (IP) issues. For many years, these issues were primarily addressed in the World Intellectual Property Organization (WIPO). During the 1990s, the United States and the EC, at the urging of their respective IP industries, pushed to move IP issues from WIPO to the trade regime. The motivation for this shift arose, in part, out of a dissatisfaction with the handling of IP issues within WIPO. Moreover, the United States and the EC perceived the GATT/WTO system to have several features that made it a superior venue, including significant bargaining leverage and a much stronger dispute resolution system than that found in WIPO. As a result of US and EC pressure, IP issues came into the WTO through the Uruguay Round Agreement on Trade-Related Aspects of Intellectual Property Rights (TRIPs).[42]

The move of IP issues from WIPO to the WTO was soon perceived to be disadvantageous for many developing states and their citizens. Not surprisingly, the TRIPs Agreement sparked a backlash. Developing states, NGOs and others launched a strategy that Laurence Helfer has usefully termed 'regime shifting' (Helfer 2004). This term refers to the deliberate effort to move law-making initiatives from one international venue to another. IP issues are now on the agenda at a variety of international bodies, including multilateral organizations, such as the World Health Organization, and the Food and Agriculture Organization; international negotiating fora such as the Biodiversity Treaty's Conference of Parties; and numerous expert or political bodies, such as the United Nations Commission on Human Rights. Helfer argues that developing state and NGO actions in these, and other bodies, are part of a concerted effort to create IP norms that recalibrate, revise or supplement TRIPs norms.

The result is that, at least with respect to international IP rights, we inhabit a polycentric world marked by multiple norms from a proliferating number of international regimes, including the trade, biodiversity, plant genetic resources, public health and human rights regimes.[43] Significantly, the norms, principles and rules generated outside of TRIPs are often in tension with TRIPs norms (Helfer 2004: 9). This is not to deny that the WTO in fact now exercises authority in policy domains where it previously did not do so; rather it is to suggest that authority is fragmenting and flowing in more than one direction, and that the flows in any particular issue area are highly contingent, and often conflicting and contradictory.

Simultaneous moves towards both centralization and dispersion of authority are evident along other dimensions as well. Compare, for example, the halting progress in the on-again, off-again Doha Development Agenda, with the proliferation of regional and bilateral trade agreements. For example, in the Western hemisphere in 2003 alone, the United States signed Free Trade Agreements with Chile and Singapore; concluded negotiations on the Central American Free Trade Agreement with El Salvador, Guatemala, Honduras and Nicaragua (and later finalized negotiations with Costa Rica and the Dominican Republic); launched negotiations with Morocco, Australia, the five member states of the South African Customs Union, and announced its intent to begin negotiations with Panama, Bolivia, Colombia, Ecuador and Peru, Bahrain and Thailand. During the same year, Canada concluded an FTA with Costa Rica, and negotiated FTAs with four Central American states, EFTA and Singapore, and announced intentions to negotiate with the Andean Community, CARICOM and the Dominican Republic. In addition, Mexico was in negotiations with Argentina, Uruguay, and Japan; Bolivia with Chile; the Andean Community with Mercosur, and CARICOM concluded negotiations with Costa Rica. There have also been intense activities on the bilateral and regional fronts in Europe and in Asia/Pacific.

To be sure, these agreements may reflect, in part, frustration with the slow pace of multilateral negotiations. They may also be understood, in part, as strategic moves designed to influence Doha Development Agenda negotiations. And in the long run regional liberalization may serve to prompt multilateral liberalization. But there should be little doubt that this level of activity on the regional and bilateral front cannot help but deflect energy and attention from multilateral efforts. They also increase the risks of multiple agreements with conflicting terms, and the creation of vested interests will resist dilution of preferential treatment at the multilateral level. The substantial activity directed towards regional and bilateral agreement suggests that, at least in certain respects, authority is flowing away from the WTO.

Finally, with respect to international trade disputes, authority is flowing both towards and away from formal WTO dispute resolution. On the one hand, states are submitting to WTO dispute resolution an unprecedented number of trade disputes.[44] However, substantial empirical evidence suggests that a majority of disputes are terminated prior to a panel ruling and, of these disputes, most are settled without even a request for a panel (Busch and Reinhard 2000: 158). To be sure, these disputes may be settled in the 'shadow of the law', and in this sense the panels and AB might be understood to be exercising power even outside of formal proceedings. On the other hand, absent empirical evidence, '[we] should not readily assume that the shadow of adjudication under which some parties settle their disputes makes such settlements less political or more faithful to the law' (Alvarez 2003: 405, 412).

More importantly, the overwhelming majority of trade disputes never enter the WTO's dispute resolution system. Consider one particularly controversial area – the role of panels in the areas of sanitary and phytosanitary (SPS) measures. The work of panels and the AB in this area, including the *Beef-Hormones* reports, have garnered significant attention. However, the overwhelming majority of the WTO's SPS-related work occurs in the SPS Committee, and this work receives virtually no attention from legal scholars. Since the SPS Agreement came into force in 1995, over 180 specific trade concerns have been raised in the SPS Committee, ranging from complaints about restrictions on imports of hard cheeses made from non-pasteurized milk to labelling requirements on shelled eggs and the shelf life requirements for canned food products.

Several points bear attention. First, of course, is the sheer volume of disputes that are raised in the Committee, as opposed to the relatively small number of SPS disputes that are considered within WTO's formalized dispute resolution procedures. The number of SPS concerns raised in the SPS Committee outnumbers the number of SPS disputes considered by panels by a ratio of approximately 45:1.

More importantly, SPS Committee proceedings have been a relatively useful forum for the resolution of conflicts and potential conflicts between member states. Members' submissions to the committee,[45] as well as a series of WTO reports,[46] detail a significant number of food safety concerns that were satisfactorily resolved before the Committee. Moreover, these official documents may understate the number of successful resolutions; the number of safety concerns are not limited to those formally discussed in the SPS Committee, and 'many concerns regarding food safety measures are solved bilaterally before they come to the WTO, or around the edges of the SPS Committee meetings without actually having been raised at the meeting itself'.[47] In stark contrast, the panels and the AB have not enjoyed a similar degree of success in resolving the SPS disputes that have come before them.

In other words, while legal analysis tends to focus upon treaty text and panel and AB reports to determine the impact of the SPS Agreement (as well as other Uruguay Round agreements), these materials constitute only a small part of states' SPS-related activities. As Robert Hudec observed:

> dispute settlement is only the tip of the GATT legal system. GATT law applies to a very wide range of day-to-day government behavior, very little of which ever comes before a GATT legal proceeding. An analysis of the relative success of formal legal proceedings is manifestly not a description of this larger whole. (Hudec et al. 1993: 1, 3)

In short, WTO dispute resolution is neither the most common nor the most important institutional mechanism available for resolving international trade disputes.[48] Accordingly, while substantial authority has flowed into WTO dispute settlement, it is a mistake to overlook the powerful countervailing flows of authority outside of WTO dispute settlement.

In sum, the centralization thesis suggests that the WTO is the architectonic trade body that, through its expanded reach and strengthened dispute resolution system, is exercising greater control and authority over international economic policy. Reality, in contrast, is significantly more complex and nuanced. First, many of the issues addressed by the trade regime are simultaneously being addressed in competing international institutions. If the WTO's expanding reach into new issue areas is the conventional story here, the less-noticed counter-story is that authority is simultaneously flowing away from the WTO as issue areas within the WTO's ambit are increasingly being addressed by multiple international bodies. In addition, many of the largest and most important WTO members are increasingly turning to regional and bilateral trade agreements that contain rules that are not always consistent with WTO norms.

Hence, rather than centralization, we see polycentricity. Instead of authority being consolidated in one place, authority over international economic issues is flowing in various directions simultaneously. To some extent, power and authority are flowing into the multilateral trade system; at the same time, these flows move outward from the trade regime as trade-related issues are considered in multiple fora simultaneously. The changing patterns of authority are kaleidoscopic, rather than unidirectional. In the near-future, the meta-task facing the international economic system will be to develop mechanisms to acknowledge and coordinate multiple sources of authority.

The allure of constitutionalism

Heretofore, the argument has been primarily negative; in effect, that there is no constitutionalism at the WTO, there is no exercise of judicial power at the WTO consistent with leading theories of constitutionalism, and there is no centralization of international economic policy making at the WTO. But if this analysis is accurate, we confront an even bigger puzzle than the ones explored above: why are so many scholarly resources and energy being devoted to debating constitutionalism at the WTO?

The maturation of international law

The arguments set forth above are in deep tension with most of the major trends in contemporary trade scholarship. Conventional wisdom understands the WTO system as 'a supreme achievement of international legal enterprise... bringing international power politics under the strong arm of the rule of law'. For constitutionalism's advocates, constitutional discourse hence provides a useful vocabulary with which to understand the WTO's robust and legalistic approach to dispute resolution, innovative enforcement mechanisms, and the superiority of WTO norms over conflicting domestic statutes. Indeed, some WTO scholars have advocated extending (or replicating) the WTO's 'constitutional' model to other areas of international relations (Bronkers 2001: 41).

More broadly, the conventional wisdom understands the general turn to constitutionalism in international law to reflect a broadening and deepening of international legal norms and a welcome maturation of the field. From this perspective, the turn to constitutionalism reflects a welcome and, indeed, overdue development in international law.

Others see the WTO as one element in a rich constitutional landscape at the international plane (Trachtmann 2006: 646).

The constructivist gambit

A second potential explanation for the scholars' turn to constitutional discourse focuses on the self-referential nature of constitutional discourse. That is, constitutional traditions find expression in self-conscious constitutional discourse and there can be no constitutional tradition without this form of discourse. This observation is not, of course, a suggestion that the mere existence of constitutional discourse can, as if by magic, generate a constitutional entity. But it does suggest that constitutionalism's advocates may hope that their claims can spark a tradition of discourse that itself can help transform the WTO into an entity understood in constitutional terms.

The turn to constitutionalism can be understood as an effort to find legitimating foundations for a system that, since the popular protests in Seattle and Cancun, can no longer present itself in technocratic terms in no need of popular acceptance (Howse 2002: 94). On this view, the increasingly rapid explanations of the WTO's constitution – as institutional architecture, as normative commitments, as judicial lawmaking – can be understood as an implicit acknowledgment of both the WTO's power and the lack of a broad popular basis for exercising that power.

On the other hand, the various theories about constitutionalism at the WTO – and the responses they engender – may generate a rich and ongoing debate over the constitutional status of the WTO and these debates may engage and mobilize a population that is convinced that the WTO is a constitutional entity. Efforts to generate a tradition of discussing the WTO in constitutional terms may appear to be a form of boot strapping or wish fulfillment; but such a strategy is consistent, I believe, with various strands of constructivist thought that emphasize the extent to which legal concepts such as constitutionalism rest upon intersubjective beliefs that arise out of ongoing and repeated interactions. Perhaps constitutionalism's advocates are engaged in what we might call a constructivist gambit (Cederman 2001: 139).

A discipline in crisis

Yet a third possibility presents itself. Perhaps the turn to constitutionalism is less a sign of international law's flourishing than of its crisis. A constellation of events in the 1980s and 1990s – the end of the cold war, the fall of the Berlin Wall, the apparent revitalization of the United Nations – gave rise to heady claims about the reality and the promise of international law. The creation of the WTO was just one of many developments that led prominent scholars to declare that international law had finally entered a 'post-ontological' age (Franck 1995) and proclaim that 'international legal rules, procedures and organizations are more visible and arguably more effective than at any time since 1945' (Slaughter Burley 1993: 205). In this context, international lawyers occupied themselves with arguments regarding how to manage the welcome but potentially problematic proliferation of international norms, institutions and tribunals,[49] and the central jurisprudential task was to determine which of the various theoretical explanations of why nations comply with international law was the most persuasive.[50]

But international law's triumphal moment quickly faded, and today the discipline faces severe challenges, both from within and without. From within, empirical studies raise serious questions about international law's effectiveness.[51] From without, political leaders and scholars question international law's relevance and endorse realist approaches to international relations.

Moreover, international lawyers today are more likely to fear the implications of a hegemonic era than to celebrate the arrival of a post-cold war era. These anxieties are even more pronounced when the hegemon seems to denigrate international law and institutions, as illustrated by the refusal to ratify the Kyoto Protocol, the 'unsigning' of the Rome Treaty creating the International Criminal Court, the rejection of the Land Mines and Comprehensive Test Ban Treaties, the repudiation of the ABM treaty, and, perhaps most ominously, the assertion of a doctrine of preventive war that is in considerable tension with conventional understandings of the norms governing the use of force. In such a world, traditional international law can (d)evolve into hegemonic international law.[52]

Against this backdrop, might we understand the turn to constitutionalism to reflect not international law's strength or vigour, but precisely the opposite? The fact that international law and international relations scholars are seemingly obsessed with issues of constitutionalism may well signal a discipline in crisis. Formerly the existence of an international body or institution provided its own justification; today something more is required. Is it possible that international lawyers invoke rhetorical tropes, like constitutionalism, out of a felt need to invest international legal bodies with the power and authority that parallel legal mechanisms on the domestic level possess?

The disciplinary anxiety that international lawyers have would also explain the excessive attention given to WTO dispute resolution. WTO dispute resolution has the magic bullet that international law is always criticized for lacking: effective enforcement mechanisms. WTO dispute resolution thus possesses the allure of an international legal regime with teeth, and hence a simple and compelling answer to sckeptics who doubt that international law is really law (Dunoff 2004b: 196).

In this context, it is not surprising that the turn to constitutionalism should occur in trade scholarship. There can be little doubt that '[w]hatever its flaws, the [WTO] is the envy of international lawyers who are more familiar with less efficient and more compliance-resistant legal regimes, including those within the International Labour Organization (ILO), United Nations (UN) human rights bodies, and other adjudicative arrangements such as the World Court or the ad hoc war crimes tribunals' (Alvarez 2001b: 1). Perhaps the eagerness to 'constitutionalize' this system reflects a deeper insecurity or defensiveness about our field, a defensiveness that, perhaps, may find reflection in our larger theme of changing patterns of authority in the international economic domain.

The irony, of course, is that constitutionalism cannot deliver on its promise to remove disputed issues from the domain of politics. Just as courts in the US cannot quiet debate over same-sex marriage or affirmative action with their 'constitutional' decisions, even less can WTO institutional architecture, or panels and AB reports end debate over controversial topics in the trade world. Attempts to do so simply highlight constitutionalism's conceits.

Conclusion

Trade scholars are preoccupied with the debate over constitutionalism at the WTO. While this phrase is used in many different ways, I've tried to demonstrate that constitutionalism is almost invariably seen as a mechanism to defuse or resolve potentially destabilizing political conflicts. However, constitutionalism – whether on the international or domestic plane – cannot pre-empt or displace political debate on controversial issues. Paradoxically, constitutionalism creates precisely the sort of politics that it seeks to pre-empt. Hence, one goal of this chapter has been to demonstrate the self-defeating nature of the turn to constitutionalism.

But if the turn to constitutionalism triggers the very world trade politics that constitutionalism seeks to avoid, why do leading trade scholars engage in this debate? Another goal of the chapter has been to inquire into the conditions that have given rise to the debate over constitutionalism at the WTO. I've suggested that the timing and prominence of this debate may shed light on the current status of the discipline of international law. In short, the turn to constitutionalism may reflect a deep disciplinary anxiety that has been heightened by international events since September 11, 2001. Constitutional discourse may be a defensive reaction of international lawyers who perceive that international law is under severe stress.

These arguments suggest that at this point in the development of the WTO system, we can best understand the term 'constitutionalism' as a metaphor. Here, I understand metaphor in a conceptual, rather than a literary, sense; a metaphor's significance lies not only in its images, but in its implications. That is, if we accept the metaphor that life is a journey, then the implication is that we should expect obstacles and seek movement toward a destination. If the WTO is a constitutional system, then the implication is that we should expect WTO norms and institutions to have a strength and importance that 'ordinary' rules of international law may lack. More importantly, we should expect this 'constitution' to remove contested issues from the domain of ordinary politics and resolve them by reference to some meta-agreement.

Finally, the arguments above should not be understood as a categorical rejection of the turn to constitutionalism at the WTO. As the discussion above suggests, constitutionalism can come in many different forms. The forms most prominent in the legal scholarship to date seem designed to pre-empt political debate and contestation. But other forms of constitutionalism may be designed to invite political debate and contestation, or to empower democratic and deliberative decision-making. Institutional architecture can be used to support or to undermine broader political participation and contestation. Many scholars have suggested ways for the WTO to be more open and inclusive. Similarly, to the extent the emerging trade constitution is under-stood as privileging certain values over others, or as the result of judicial decision-making, those values and decisions can be directed toward openness and participation. In short, as a general theoretical matter, there is no simple answer to normative questions about the desirability of constitutionalism at the WTO.

Notes

1. See, e.g., J. E. Alvarez (2001); P.-M. Dupuy (1997); C. Tomuschat (1997); J. Crawford (1997); B. Fassbender (1998); W. M. Reisman (1993). Parts of the analysis that follows can be found in J. L. Dunoff (2006a).
2. The European context provides a particularly rich example. For a sample, see G. de Burca and J. Scott (eds.) (2001); Weiler, J. H. H. (1999).
3. See Case C-149/96, Portugal v. Council, [1999] ECR I-8395; Uruguay Round Agreements Act (Pub. L. No. 102–465, 108 Stat. 4809), sec. 102(a)(1) ('No provision of any of the Uruguay Round Agreements, nor the application of any such provision to any person or circumstance, that is inconsistent with any law of the United States shall have any effect'). For more on the use of WTO law by US courts, see J. L. Dunoff, Death, Dumping and Domestic Courts (unpublished paper).
4. In addition to the authors discussed, important discussions of constitutionalism at the WTO can be found in J. P. Trachtman (2006); T. Broude (2004); R. H. Steinberg (2004); R. L. Howse and K. Nicolaides (2003); N. Walker (2001); R. Howse and K. Nicolaidis (2001); M. Krajewski (2001); J. O. McGinnis and M. L. Movsesian (2000); H. L. Schloemann and S. Ohlhoff (1999); W. Benedek (1999).
5. For another effort to describe this scholarship, see J. L. Dunoff (2005). For a different version of some of the arguments developed below, see J. L. Dunoff (2006a).
6. 'Constitutional' arguments run through much of Jackson's international trade scholarship. For a sampling, see, e.g., J. H. Jackson 1998, 1990, 1969, 2001, 1997, 1996, 1980. Because Jackson's 'constitutional' vision has been ably discussed elsewhere, I will offer here only a brief summary of his arguments. See, e.g. J. H. Jackson (1999).
7. Jackson has discussed these 'birth defects' in numerous writings. See, e.g., J. H. Jackson (1969, 1997, 1980).
8. For an analysis of Jackson's pragmatic style, see R. L. Howse (1999).
9. This account is drawn from D. P. Steger (1999).
10. Id. ('Indeed, he [Jackson] can be credited with having sown the seeds of the idea to establish a World Trade Organization.')
11. An incomplete listing of Petersmann's writings linking constitutionalism with international economic law includes E.-Ulrich Petersmann 1991, 1993, 1996, 1997, 1998, 2000a, 2000b, 2002.
12. E.-U. Petersmann (1997–98); Petersmann (1996). In invoking this image, Petersmann follows Jon Elster's pathbreaking work. See, e.g., J. Elster (1979).
13. Petersmann (1998). As neither international law nor the UN Charter effectively provide restraints on public and private abuses of power, neither are properly considered constitutional. Id.

14. This is not to deny that it may be possible to harmonize these understandings. For example, it might be that a focus on institutional structure can be predicated upon substantive political and moral values, and can use adjudicatory fora as the central mechanism for vindication of these values.
15. US Const. art VI.
16. Id. at 561. Unlike the US Constitution, the EC Treaty articles expressly vest the ECJ with authority to review the legality of acts of EU institutions.
17. WT/DS90/AB/R (23 Aug., 1999).
18. For a critique of the AB's rationale, see L. Bartels (2004).
19. In Turkey–Textiles, the panel addressed whether dispute settlement panels have the competence to assess the GATT consistency of a measure taken under a regional trade agreement, particularly given the existence of the WTO Committee on Regional Trade Agreements which evaluates the overall WTO compatibility of regional trade agreements. Turkey Restrictions on Imports of Textile and Clothing Products, WT/DS34/R (31 May, 1999), paras 9.52–9.54. While this specific issue was not raised on appeal, the AB went out of its way to 'note in this respect' its ruling in India-QRs. Turkey – Restrictions on Imports of Textile and Clothing Products, WT/DS34/AB/R (22 Oct., 1999), at para. 60.

    Many cases have explored the relationship between different Uruguay Round texts, such as the relationship between the GATT and GATS. While these cases involve examination of the scope and relationship of the WTO's substantive obligations, they generally do not call for an examination of different parts of the WTO's institutional architecture.
20. This may mean that we should understand Petersmann's writings as largely normative rather than descriptive.
21. United States–Sections 301–310 of the Trade Act of 1974, WT/DS152/R, para. 7.72, (27 Jan., 2000).
22. Id. at para. 7.73.
23. Id. at para. 7.78.
24. United States Import Prohibitions of Certain Shrimp and Shrimp Products, WT/DS58/R (98-1710) (15 May, 1998).
25. United States Import Prohibitions of Certain Shrimp and Shrimp Products, WT/DS58/AB/R (98–000) (12 Oct., 1998).
26. G. P. Sampson (2000). The amicus controversy has also sparked substantial scholarly literature. See, e.g. J. L. Dunoff (1998); S. Charnovitz (2000).
27. European Communities – Measures Affecting Asbestos and Asbestos-Containing Products, WT/DS135/R (18 Sept., 2000).
28. Id.
29. European Communities – Measures Affecting Asbestos and Asbestos-Containing Products, Communication from the Appellate Body, WT/DS135/9 (20 Nov., 2000).
30. European Communities – Measures Affecting Asbestos and Asbestos-Containing Products, WT/DS135/AB/R (3 Dec., 2001) at para. 55.30–56.32.
31. For example, in United States Investigation of the International Trade Commission in Softwood Lumber from Canada, WT/DS277/R (22 March, 2004), the AB 'did not find it necessary' to take two amicus briefs that were not incorporated into parties briefs into account in rendering its decision. In United States Countervailing Measures Concerning Certain Products from the European Communities, WT/DS212/AB/R (9 Dec., 2002), an industry association submitted a brief. After confirming that the brief was not part of either party's submission, the AB stated that '[t]he brief has not been taken into account by us as we do not find it to

be of assistance in this appeal'. Id. at para. 76. In United States: Import Prohibition of Certain Shrimp and Shrimp Products: Recourse to Article 21.5 of the DSU by Malaysia, WT/DS58/RW (15 June, 2001), two different NGO briefs were submitted to the panel. One was attached to the United States's submission; this brief was considered part of the record. The other brief was not attached to any party's submission, and the panel 'decided not to include it in the record in this case'. Id. at paras. 5.15–5.16. On appeal, two amicus briefs were again submitted. One was attached to the United States's brief, and was considered 'prima facie an integral part of that participant's submission'. The other brief was not attached to any party's submission, and the AB did not take it into account. United States: Import Prohibition of Certain Shrimp and Shrimp Products: Recourse to Article 21.5 of the DSU by Malaysia, WT/DS58/AB/RW at paras. 76, 78 (22 Oct., 2001).

   There are a few exceptions to this general practice. In Australia: Measures Affecting Importation of Salmon: Recourse to Article 21.5 by Canada, WT/DS18/RW (18 Feb., 2000), the panel accepted a letter from the 'Concerned Fisherman and Processors in South Australia'. Id. at paras. 7.8–7.9. In United States: Preliminary Determinations with Respect to Certain Softwood Lumber from Canada, WT/DS236/R (27 Sept., 2002), the panel 'accept[ed] for consideration' an unsolicited amicus brief from a Canadian NGO. However, the panel rejected three other amicus briefs. Id. at para. 7.2.

32. United States Investigation of the International Trade Commission in Softwood Lumber from Canada, WT/DS277/R at 88, n. 75 (22 March, 2004).
33. For an insightful account, see R. Howse (2002a).
34. See, e.g., P. Alston (2002); R. Howse (2002b).
35. See, e.g., Howse and Nicolaidis (2003): 227; P. M. Gerhart (2003).
36. See, e.g., G. Marceau (2002); Alston (2002); Howse (2002a).
37. See, e.g., A. Guzman (2004).
38. Id. Not unexpectedly, calls for an expanded WTO have sparked counterarguments against such an expansion of the WTO's ambit. See, e.g., J. O. McGinnis and M. L. Movsesian (2004). For more on this debate, see J. L. Dunoff (2001).
39. Thus, a June 2002 draft of the WHO Framework Convention on Tobacco Control provides that 'nothing in this Convention and its related protocols shall be interpreted as implying in any way a change in rights and obligations of a party under any existing international treaty' and that tobacco control measures 'shall be ... implemented in accordance with ... existing international obligations, and shall not constitute a means or arbitrary or unjustifiable discrimination in international trade'.
40. The final draft of the WHO Tobacco treaty dropped the provisions; the WHO now claims that under general rules of international law, including the lex posterior and lex specialis principles, Tobacco treaty provisions would trump inconsistent WTO norms.
41. For example, the preamble of the Biosafety Protocol provided that 'this Protocol shall not be interpreted as implying a change in the rights and obligations of a Party under any existing international agreements', suggesting that pre-existing WTO norms would trump any inconsistent Protocol norms – but then states that this provision 'is not intended to subordinate this Protocol to other international agreements'.
42. Agreement on Trade-Related Aspects of Intellectual Property Rights, 15 Dec., 1993, Marrakesh Agreement Establishing the World Trade Organization, Annex 1C,

Legal Instruments–Results of the Uruguay Round vol. 31, 33 I.L.M. 81 (1994) [hereinafter TRIPs Agreement].
43. International law exhibits these polycentric tendencies in other issue areas as well. See, e.g., J. L. Dunoff (2007); J. L. Dunoff (2004), Book Review, *American Journal of International Law*, 98: 224–29 (reviewing Scott Barrett, Environment and Statecraft); K. Raustiala and D. G. Victor (2004).
44. As of 16 June, 2004, some 312 different complaints had been notified to the WTO. See Update of WTO Dispute Settlement Cases, WT/DS/OV/21 (30 June, 2004).
45. G/SPS/GEN/265 (10 July, 2001).
46. G/SPS/GEN/204/Rev.4 (2 March, 2004); G/SPS/GEN/204/Rev.3 (26 March, 2003); G/SPS/GEN/204/Rev.2 (15 February, 2002); G/SPS/GEN/204/Rev.1 (5 March, 2001).
47. WTO Annual Report 65–66 (2004). See also S. Jaffe and S. Henson (2004) (complaints to the SPS Committee 'probably represent the "tip of the iceberg" as most concerns and disputes are raised bilaterally and the majority of negotiations are handled by technical organizations rather than country trade representatives').
48. For a fuller discussion of this point, both in the context of SPS disputes and more generally, see J. L. Dunoff (2006b).
49. On the proliferation of international courts and tribunals, see, e.g., Y. Shany (2003); T. Buergenthal (2001): 267; J. Charney (1998): 101.
50. See, e.g., A. Chayes and A. Handler Chayes (1995) (managerial theory of compliance); T. M. Franck (1995), compliance as function of law's legitimacy; H. Hongju Koh (1997): Why Do Nations Obey International Law? *Yale Law Journal*, 106: 2599 (transnational legal process explanation for compliance).
51. See, e.g., O. A. Hathaway (2002): Do Human Rights Treaties Make a Difference? *Yale Law Journal*, 111: 1935.
52. A large literature addresses the challenges that US hegemony poses to international law. See, e.g., Byers, M. and G. Nolte (eds.) (2003): *United States Hegemony and the Foundations of International Law*; J. E. Alvarez (2003); D. F. Vagts (2001): Hegemonic International Law, *American Journal of International Law*, 95: 843.

References

Alston, P. (2002): Resisting the Merger and Acquisition of Human Rights by Trade Law: a Reply to Petersmann, *European Journal of International Law* 13: 815.
Alvarez, J. E. (2001a): Constitutional Interpretation in International Organization. In: Coicaud, J.-M. and V. Heiskanen (eds.), *The Legitimacy of International Organizations*. Tokyo: United Nations University Press.
Alvarez, Jose E. (2001b): How Not to Link: Institutional Conundrums of an Expanded Trade Regime. Widener Law Symposium, 7, J. 1.
Alvarez, J. E. (2003): Hegemonic International Law. *American Journal of International Law* 97: 873.
Bartels, L. (2004): Separation of Powers in the WTO: How to Avoid Judicial Activism. *International Law and Comparative Law Quarterly*, 53: 861.
Benedek, W. (1999): Developing the Constitutional Order of the WTO – The Role of NGOs. In: Benedek W. et al. (eds.), *Development and Developing International and European Law*. The Hague 1999: 228, 232.
Braithwaite, J. and P. Drahos (2000): *Global Business Regulation*. Cambridge University Press: 566.
Bronkers, M. (2001): More Power to the WTO? *Journal of International Economic Law* 4: 41.

Broude, T. (2004): *International Governance in the WTO: Judicial Boundaries and Political Capitulation*. London: Cameron May.

Buergenthal, T. (2001): The Proliferation of International Courts and Tribunals: Is It Good or Bad? *Leiden Journal of International Law* 14: 267.

Busch, M. L. and E. Reinhardt (2000): Bargaining in the Shadow of the Law: Early Settlement in GATT/WTO Disputes. *Fordham International Law Journal* 2: 158.

Byers, M. and G. Nolte (eds.) (2003): *United States Hegemony and the Foundations of International Law*. Cambridge: Cambridge University Press.

Cass, D. Z. (2001): The Constitutionalization of International Trade Law: Judicial Norm-Generation as the Engine of Constitutional Development in International Trade. *European Journal of International Law* 12: 39, 42.

Charney, J. (1998): Is International Law Threatened by Multiple International Tribunals? *Recueil des Cours* 217: 101.

Charnovitz, S. (2000): Opening the WTO to Nongovernmental Interests. *Ford International Law Journal* 24: 173.

Chayes, A. and A. H. Chayes (1995): *The New Sovereignty: Compliance with International Regulatory Agreements*. Cambridge, MA: Harvard University Press.

Cottier, T. (1998): The WTO Dispute Settlement System: New Horizons. *American Society of International Law: Proceedings* 92: 86.

Crawford, J. (1997): The Charter of the United Nations as a Constitution. In: Fox, H. (ed.), *The Changing Constitution of the United Nations*. London: British Institute of International and Comparative Law, 3.

de Burca, G. and J. Scott (2001): *The EU and the WTO: Legal and Constitutional Issues*. Oxford: Hart.

Dunoff, J. L.: Death, Dumping and Domestic Courts (unpublished manuscript).

Dunoff, J. L. (1998): The Misguided Debate over NGO Participation at the WTO. *Journal of International Economic Law* 1.

Dunoff, J. L. (1999): The Death of the Trade Regime. *European Journal of International Law* 10: 733.

Dunoff, J. L. (2001): The WTO in Transition: of Constituents, Competence and Coherence? *George Washington International Law Review* 33: 979.

Dunoff, J. L. (2002): The WTO's Legitimacy Crisis: Reflections on the Law and Politics of WTO Dispute Resolution. *American Review of International Arbitration* 13: 197.

Dunoff, J. L. (2004a): Book Review. *American Journal of International Law* 98: 224, 224–9.

Dunoff, J. L. (2004b): Compliance at the WTO: Seduced by the Dispute Settlement System? *Proceedings of the Canadian Council on International Law* 196.

Dunoff, J. L. (2005): Why Constitutionalism Now? Text, Context and the Historical Contingency of Ideas. *Journal of International Law and International Relations* 1: 191.

Dunoff, J. L. (2006a): Constitutional Conceits: the WTO's 'Constitution' and the Discipline of International Law. *European Journal of International Law* 17: 647.

Dunoff, J. L. (2006b): Lotus Eaters: the Varietals Dispute, the SPS Agreement, and WTO Dispute Resolution. In: Bermann, G. and P. Mavroidis (eds.), *Trade and Human Health and Safety*. Cambridge University Press.

Dunoff, J. L. (2007): Multilevel Environmental Governance. In: Bodansky et al. (eds.), *The Oxford Handbook of International Environmental Law*. Oxford University Press.

Dupuy, P.-M. (1997): The Constitutional Dimension of the Charter of the United Nations Revisited. *Max Planck Yearbook of United Nations Law* 1.

Elster, J. (1979): *Studies in Rationality and Irrationality*. New York: Cambridge University Press.

Esty, D. C. (1998): Non-Governmental Organizations at the World Trade Organization: Cooperation, Competition, or Exclusion. *Journal of International Economic Law* 1: 123.

Fassbender, B. (1998): The United Nations Charter as Constitution of the International Community. *Columbia Journal of Transnational Law* 36: 529.

Franck, T. M. (1995): *Fairness in International Law and Institutions*. New York: Oxford University Press.

Gerhart, P. M. (2003): Two Constitutional Visions of the World Trade Organization. *Journal of International Economic Law* 24: 1.

Guzman, A. (2004): Global Governance and the WTO. *Harvard International Law Journal* 45: 303.

Helfer, L. R. (2004): Regime Shifting: the TRIPS Agreement and New Dynamics of International Intellectual Property Lawmaking. *Yale Journal of International Law* 29: 1.

Hilf, M. and E.-U. Petersmann (eds.) (1993): *National Constitutions and International Economic Law*. Deventer, The Netherlands: Kluwer Law International.

Howse, R. L. (1999): The House that Jackson Built: Restructuring the GATT System. *Michigan Journal of International Law* 20: 107.

Howse, Robert L. (2002a): From Politics to Technocracy and Back Again: the Fate of the Multilateral Trading Regime. *American Journal of International Law* 96: 94.

Howse, R. L. (2002b): Human Rights in the WTO: Whose Rights, What Humanity? *European Journal of International Law* 13: 651.

Howse, R. and K. Nicolaidis (2001): Legitimacy and Global Governance: Why Constitutionalizing the WTO Is a Step Too Far. In: Porter, R. B., P. Sauvé, A. Subramanian and A. B. Zampetti (eds.), *Efficiency, Equity, and Legitimacy: the Multilateral Trading System at the Millennium*. Washington, DC: Brookings Institution Press, 227–52.

Howse, R. L. and K. Nicolaides (2003): Enhancing WTO Legitimacy: Constitutionalization or Global Subsidiarity. *Governance* 16: 73.

Hudec, R. E., D. L. M. Kennedy and M. Sgarbossa (1993): A Statistical Overview of GATT Dispute Settlement Cases: 1948–1989. *Minnesota Journal of Global Trade* 2: 1.

Jackson, and John H. (1969): *World Trade and the Law of GATT*. Indianapolis: Bobbs-Merrill.

Jackson, J. H. (1980): The Birth of the GATT-MTN System: a Constitutional Appraisal. *Law and Policy in International Business* 12: 21.

Jackson, J. H. (1990): *Restructuring the GATT System*. London: Royal Institute of Strategic Affairs.

Jackson, J. H. (1996): Reflections on Constitutional Changes to the Global Trading System. *Chicago Kent Law Review*: 511.

Jackson, J. H. (1997): The Great 1994 Sovereignty Debate: United States Acceptance and Implementation of the Uruguay Round Results. *Columbia Journal of Transnational Law* 36: 157.

Jackson, J. H. (1998): *The World Trade Organization: Constitution and Jurisprudence*. London: Royal Institute of International Affairs.

Jackson, J. H. (2001): The WTO 'Constitution' and Proposed Reform: Seven 'Mantras' Revisited. *Journal of International Economic Law* 4(1): 67–78.

Jaffe, S. and S. Henson (2004): Standards and Agro-Foods Exports from Developing Countries: Rebalancing the Debate. *World Bank Policy Research Working Paper* 3348: 25.

Keohane, R. O. and J. S. Nye (2003): The Club Model of Multilateral Cooperation and the World Trade Organization: Problems of Democratic Legitimacy. In: Porter, R. B., P. Sauvé, A. Subramanian and A. B. Zampetti (eds.), *Efficiency, Equity, and Legitimacy: the Multilateral Trading System at the Millennium.* Washington, DC: Brookings Institution Press, 264, 294.

Koh, H. H. (1997): Why Do Nations Obey International Law? *Yale Law Journal* 106: 2599.

Krajewski, M. (2001): Democratic Legitimacy and Constitutional Perspectives of WTO Law. *Journal of World Trade* 35: 167.

Marceau, G. (2002): WTO Dispute Settlement and Human Rights. *European Journal of International Law* 13: 753.

McGinnis, J. O. and M. L. Movsesian (2000): The World Trade Constitution. *Harvard Law Review* 114: 511.

Petersmann, E.-U. (1991): *Constitutional Functions and Constitutional Problems of International Economic Law.* Fribourg: Fribourg University Press.

Petersmann, E.-U. (1993): Theories of Justice, Human Rights, and the Constitution of International Markets. *Loyola of Los Angeles Law Review* 37: 407.

Petersmann, E.-U. (1996): Constitutionalism and International Organizations. *Northwestern Journal of International Law and Business* 17: 398.

Petersmann, E.-U. (1997): How to Reform the UN System? Constitutionalism, International Law, and International Organizations. *Leiden Journal of International Law*: 421.

Petersmann, E.-U. (1997–98): How to Reform the United Nations: Lessons for the International Economic Law Revolution. *UCLA Journal of International Law and Foreign Affairs*, 2: 185.

Petersmann, E.-U. (1998): How to Constitutionalize the United Nations? Lessons from the International Economic Law Revolution. In: Volkmar Gotz, Peter Selmer and Rudiger Wolfram (eds.), *Liber Amicorum Gunther Jaenicke*, Berlin: Springer, 313–52.

Petersmann, E.-U. (1999a): Legal, Economic and Political Objectives of National and International Competition Policies: Constitutional Functions of WTO Linking Principles for Trade and Competition. *New England Law Review* 34: 145.

Petersmann, E.-U. (1999b): Constitutionalism and International Adjudication: How to Constitutionalize the UN Dispute Settlement System? *New York University Journal of International Law and Politics* 32: 733.

Petersmann, E.-U. (1999c): How to Constitutionalize International Law and Foreign Policy for the Benefit of Civil Society? *Michigan Journal of International Law* 20: 1.

Petersmann, E.-U. (2000a): The WTO Constitution and the Millennium Round. In: Bronkers, M. and R. Quick (eds.), *New Directions in International Economic Law.* Deventer, The Netherlands: Klawer Law International.

Petersmann, E.-U. (2000b): The WTO Constitution and Human Rights. *Journal of International Economic Law* 3: 19.

Petersmann, E.-U. (2002): Time for a United Nations 'Global Compact' for Integrating Human Rights into the Law of Worldwide Organizations: Lessons from European Integration. *European Journal of International Law* 13: 621.

Petersmann, E.-U. (2003): Theories of Justice, Human Rights, and the Constitution of International Markets. *Loyola of Los Angeles Law Review* 37: 407.

Reisman, W. M. (1993): The Constitutional Crisis in the United Nations. *American Journal of International Law* 87: 83.

Schloemann, H. L. and S. Ohlhoff (1999): Constitutionalization and Dispute Settlement in the WTO: National Security as an Issue of Competence. *American Journal of International Law* 93: 424.

Shany, Y. (2003): *The Competing Jurisdictions of International Courts and Tribunals.* Oxford: Oxford University Press.

Slaughter Burley, Anne-Marie (1993): International Law and International Relations Theory: A Dual Agenda. *American Journal of International Law* 87: 205–39.

Steger, D. P. (1999): A Tribute to John Jackson. *Michigan Journal of International Law* 20: 165.

Steinberg, R. H. (2004): Judicial Lawmaking at the WTO: Discursive, Constitutional and Political Constraints. *American Journal of International Law* 98: 247.

Tomuschat, C. (1997): International Law as the Constitution of Mankind. In: *International Law on the Eve of the Twenty-First Century: Views from the International Law Commission*: 37–50.

Trachtman, J. P. (2006): The Constitutions of the WTO. *European Journal of International Law* 17: 646.

Walker, N. (2001): The EU and the WTO: Constitutionalism in a New Key. In: de Burca, G. and J. Scott (eds.), *The EU and the WTO: Legal and Constitutional Issues*.

Walker, N. (2004): After the Constitutional Moment. In: Pernice, I. and M. P. Maduro (eds.), *A Constitution for the European Union: First Comments on the 2003 Draft of the European Convention*. Baden-Baden: Nomos, 23–43.

Weiler, J. H. H. (1999): *The Constitution of Europe: Do the New Clothes Have an Emperor? And Other Essays on European Integration*. World Trade Organization, Annual Report 2004: 68–9.

Part 2
Providing and Managing Global Public Goods

3
Providing (Contested) Global Public Goods

Inge Kaul

Introduction

Many perceive globalization as a chequered process that has, in part, highly appreciated aspects, and in part, highly controversial and therefore contested dimensions. Many, for example, enjoy the enhanced connectivity that has been brought about by the expanding international communication and transportation networks or the ease with which commerce can be conducted today, due to integrating banking systems and financial markets.

At the same time, views on various aspects of the multilateral trade regime or the international financial architecture often differ widely, for example assessments of where best to focus international health efforts or how to approach building and maintaining international peace and security.

The welcomed dimensions of globalization are frequently being taken for granted, while the more controversial ones tend to attract considerable political attention, contributing to making globalization's threats and short-comings stand out more than the new, added opportunities that greater openness of national borders affords. Controversy stalls international cooper-ation, trapping the world in a 'bad' equilibrium of sub-optimal global public good provision, continuing, and perhaps even, exacerbating global crises?

But what contributes to some aspects of globalization being contested while others are welcomed? And what are desirable and feasible policy options for reducing the risk of controversy?

These are the questions at the centre of this chapter. The aim is to suggest, based on existing literature and data, first answers in the form of predictions to be tested in future research and studies.*

The predictions emerging from the discussion are:

- I – Contestation occurs where low publicness in utility coincides with high publicness in either consumption, provision or both. This means, the net-benefits of the global public good in question are distributed unevenly across countries/population groups, generating significant gains for a few,

"

yet only limited benefits, or even, costs for many others. However, all are potentially affected by the good and compelled to contribute to its provision.

- II – Prominent among the contested global public goods are global norms that seek to redraw conventional lines between 'private' and 'public' – to the detriment of influential incumbent actors.
- III – Competitive – that is, participatory – global governance reduces the risk of controversy, notably at the negotiation stage of global public goods provision, as it facilitates a swifter alignment of divergent interests.
- IV – Greater reliance on private goods as building blocks of global public goods is another possible way of reducing controversy, notably at the stage of follow-up to international agreements and other global norms and expectations, as it offers individual actors stronger incentives and more flexibility to contribute to a common goal.

These points will be developed as follows. Part one introduces the concepts of public goods and global public goods. Part two presents empirical evidence on some of the key characteristics of non-contested and contested global public goods, leading to predictions I and II. Part three discusses possible policy options for avoiding contestation, distilled as predictions III and IV. The concluding section summarizes the main arguments set forth in this chapter.

Differences in preferences are normal, and in many respects, 'here to stay'. Public goods, especially global public goods are more prone than private goods to be subject to varying views and valuations, precisely because they are in the public domain, affecting all. So the goal cannot be to avoid discussion about these differences but to bring them out into the open. In a globalizing and increasingly interdependent world, problems need to be resolved lest they continue to roam the globe. To resolve them, effective international cooperation is often required. And this means that win–win bargains are required – agreements that provide strong positive incentives for all to cooperate, in their own self-interest as well as to their mutual benefit.

Introducing public goods and global public goods

The goods (and services) that people consume or use in other ways fall into two main categories: private goods and public goods.[1] Private goods are those that can be made exclusive: Property rights to them can be clearly established; they can be owned – and traded, for example, against payment of a price in markets.

Publicness in consumption

In contrast to their private counterparts, public goods are non-exclusive: available for all to consume. And often, people may have to consume a public good, that is, live with its effects whether they enjoy doing so or not. For example, they may benefit from medical and pharmaceutical research and development efforts that have been undertaken by previous generations to develop a cure against diseases such as polio or tuberculosis. Or, they may suffer from the more violent weather patterns that are predicted to be associated with global warming, although they themselves may have contributed to the current levels of greenhouse gas emissions in the atmosphere only in a marginal way.

Public goods are the goods that people encounter in the public domain.[2] There are two aspects that are particularly important to know about these goods in the context of the present chapter.

First, publicness or privateness is in most instances not an innate property of the good. Rather, it often reflects a choice made by society or various societal groups. To illustrate, given today's state of knowledge and technological development, it would be feasible to reduce various environmental pollutants, provided the requisite political will and willingness to pay existed. Hence, continuing pollution often reflects a political choice (e.g. unwillingness on the part of policymakers to take corrective action so as not to lose the support of important constituencies).

Second, the benefits or costs of public goods can be of a different geographic and/or temporal span: local, national, regional or global.[3] They may even span across one or several generations. Accordingly, global public goods are public goods with costs and/or benefits that reach across national borders and geographic regions, and sometimes, also across generations.[4]

In other words, globalness constitutes a special dimension of publicness, and in most instances, also results from a political choice – e.g. the removal of at-the-border barriers like international trade taxes or capital controls, allowing markets to integrate and the public domains of countries to become interlocked. Only some global public goods are by nature global and public. The moonlight or the warming rays of the sun are examples. Many other global issues constitute globalized (formerly essentially national) public goods.[5]

Publicness in production

The main attribute of a public good is its publicness in consumption, being available for all. However, public goods are also increasingly marked by publicness in provision – requiring inputs or contributions in cash or in kind from a multitude of actors, public and private, and in the case of global public goods, national and international.

The production-side definition of public goods still offered by standard public finance/economics theory is that these goods are state-provided. However, this definition echoes how things were at an earlier time, around the mid to late 1950s, when public goods were first defined in a rigorous way (see especially Samuelson 1954). But today, after several decades of rebalancing the roles of markets and states, leading to greater partnering between the private and the public sector, public goods are generally *multi-actor products*,

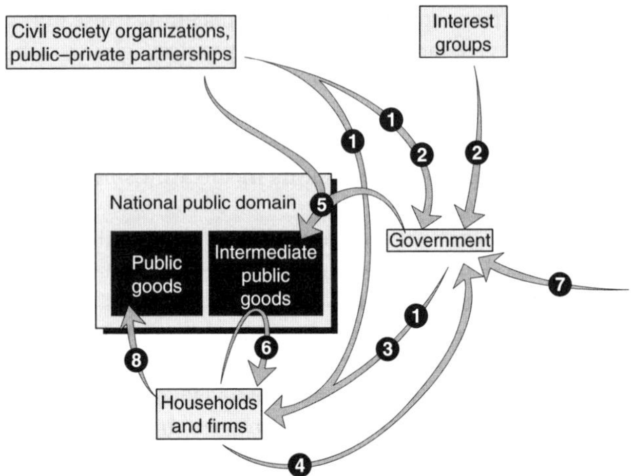

❶ Incentives
Encouraging actors to deliver direct and indirect inputs or to change behaviour to account for social concerns

❷ Political pressure
Lobbying governments to fund or deliver goods and services

❸ Coercion
Compelling individuals and firms to change their behaviour to account for social concerns

❹ Domestic preferences
Reflecting the choices on desired state action by national constituents

❺ Opportunity
Offering households and firms the possibility of consuming goods and services that generate externalities that enhance the provision of the public good

❻ Consumption
Consuming goods and services made available to enhance the provision of the public good

❼ External preferences
Reflecting the choices on desired state action by international constituents

❽ Externality
Emerging as a result of individual action

Figure 3.1: Production path of national public goods
Note: The figure is based on the assumption that the good follows a 'summation' aggregation technology. Intermediate public goods (like norms and standards) serve as inputs to a final public good.
Source: Kaul and Conceição (2006b: 12).

emerging from public (state) as well as private contributions (see also Figure 3.1).[6] The role of the state is often focused on providing incentives to private actors, encouraging them to take not only private interests but also social concerns into account (e.g. for a private actor to consider not only the ill-effects of smoking on one's own health but also the ill-effects of smoking on by-standers).

Many global public goods are multi-actor products not only in the sense that both public and private actors contribute to their production,

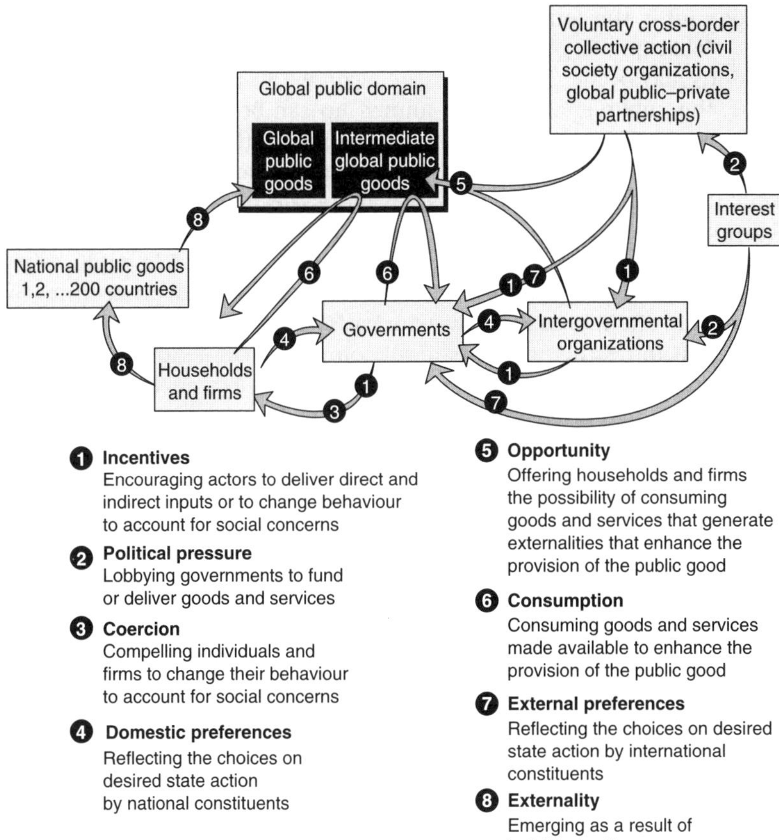

1 Incentives
Encouraging actors to deliver direct and indirect inputs or to change behaviour to account for social concerns

2 Political pressure
Lobbying governments to fund or deliver goods and services

3 Coercion
Compelling individuals and firms to change their behaviour to account for social concerns

4 Domestic preferences
Reflecting the choices on desired state action by national constituents

5 Opportunity
Offering households and firms the possibility of consuming goods and services that generate externalities that enhance the provision of the public good

6 Consumption
Consuming goods and services made available to enhance the provision of the public good

7 External preferences
Reflecting the choices on desired state action by international constituents

8 Externality
Emerging as a result of individual action

Figure 3.2:   Production path of global public goods
Note: The figure is based on the assumption that the good follows a 'summation' aggregation technology. Intermediate public goods (like norms and standards) serve as inputs to a final public good.
Source: Kaul and Conceição (2006b: 14).

including their financing. But they also require both national-level as well as international-level action (see also Figure 3.2).

National and global public goods are often closely linked (arrow 7 of Figure 3.1). National public goods are the main building blocks of summation-type global public goods (Figure 3.2). International cooperation of various types (arrows 1, 2, 4 and 5) may alter the behaviour of individual states or private actors (arrows 3 and 6), generating the required national contributions (arrow 8) to the global public good.

Important in the context of the present chapter is to underline that while many global public goods follow such a summation process, significant variations may occur.[7] Two aspects are again worth noting.

First, the public effects to be summed up can be either perfectly substitutable or non-substitutable. Substitutable public effects lend themselves to trading arrangements. Reductions in carbon dioxide emissions are a case in point. If actor B can reduce emissions more cheaply than actor A, actor A might pay actor B to provide A's contribution.

By contrast, if the challenge is to correct non-substitutable public effects, corrective action is location-specific: it has to be undertaken on a country-by-country, and often, even actor-by-actor basis. For example, only to the extent that certain infrastructure exists in all countries, will a globally integrated civil aviation system emerge. Or, public health services, including monitoring arrangements have to be improved everywhere to achieve an effective control of such communicable diseases as SARS or tuberculosis.

In summation cases like disease (e.g. polio) eradication, which involve non-substitutable effects, the smallest contribution will determine the overall provision level of the good. The same holds for terrorism control through improvements in aviation security. If such 'weak link' situations arise because an underproviding country lacks adequate resources, it might be in the enlightened self-interest of resource-richer countries to financially support the poorer country. For example, as Sandler (2006) argues, richer countries gain little from continuing to upgrade their airport screening facilities if other countries are not doing the same.

Second, cross-border collective action differs from that at the national level in that the latter can rely on the coercive powers of government but the former depends on sovereign states making their own policy choice. This does not imply that states don't face political pressures or other compulsions (like the more and more real threat of global climate change). Rather, it means that they will weigh all likely – economic and non-economic – costs and benefits associated with investing or not investing in the provision of a particular global public good and then perhaps choose the most preferred course of action from their perspective, even if this is only the least-cost one.

The 'voluntary' nature of cross-border collective action thus brings into focus the incentive challenges that a global public good presents, notably the distribution of its costs and benefits across actor groups. It raises questions like: Who is motivated, and how strongly, to enhance the provision of a good? If preferences do not overlap, how could a better match of incentives be achieved? By offering a 'carrot' such as compensatory finance? Or by adding 'teeth' to an agreement, stipulating for example, that non-compliance will lead to trade sanctions?

In sum, then, global public goods are public in consumption – potentially affecting all; and many of these goods are also public in provision – no individual actor could – or, would be strongly enough motivated to – provide them unilaterally.[8]

Why some global public goods are of a contested nature and others are not

Although most global public goods share the two basic characteristics of publicness in consumption and provision, they meet with quite different policy responses. Some are generally welcomed by *the public* – people at large; and others become embroiled in controversy and conflict. Just think of the protests that have accompanied discussions about issues of international trade and finance at meetings of the World Trade Organization (WTO), the International Monetary Fund (IMF) and World Bank, or the Group of Seven/Eight major industrialized countries (G-7/8).

Yet among the contested global public goods are not only issues like the trade regime and the international financial architecture but also cultural and political norms like those pertaining to gender equality and reproductive rights, banning corruption, practices to observe when constructing large dams, or the international community's right to intervene into domestic affairs of sovereign nations.

Among the generally appreciated – non-contested – global public goods are: the international postal system; the international transportation system, including for example, civil aviation; the technical norms and standards like those formulated by the International Organization for Standardization (ISO); or even, the harmonized form of national passports that facilitates emigration and immigration worldwide.

So, why are some global public goods welcome while others stir up controversy?

Factors contributing to contestation

A thorough investigation of this question calls for issue-specific empirical research as well as comparative analyses across issues and studies. As this lies beyond the scope of this chapter, the aim here will be to formulate, based on available studies and the data they contain, tentative answers to be tested in future research.

The tentative answer to 'Why do some global public goods encounter controversy?' is:

> *Prediction I:*
> Contestation occurs where a global public good is marked by low publicness in utility but high publicness in either consumption, provision, or both.

Low publicness in utility: a necessary but not sufficient condition of controversy

International relations theories and other social science literature examining issues of international cooperation argue that critical to effective international cooperation is that the cooperating parties perceive collective action as yielding significant and fair net-benefits for all (Axelrod 1984).

By implication, one could assume that contested global public goods will be marked by a highly uneven distribution of net-benefits, generating relatively large gains for a few and modest benefits, or even, costs for others. In other words, contestation is likely to arise where the good is marked by low publicness in utility.

A frequently cited example is the use of trade distorting agricultural subsidies and tariffs by industrialized countries.[9] Farmers in these countries demonstrate against their removal, while developing countries as well as some foreign aid agencies and non-governmental organizations like OXFAM and Third World Network, which are concerned about global development, support their abolishment so as to enhance income opportunities for many farmers in poor nations. Removing agricultural trade distorting measures in rich countries could increase economic welfare in developing countries by about \$42 billion according to one estimate (Anderson, Martin and Valenzuela 2006: 6). Yet, to understand contestation around trade, the distinction between industrialized and developing countries may need to be refined further. For example, fully abolishing current restrictions to trade could make some developing countries, notably those in sub-Saharan Africa, relatively worse-off than in the current system, given that their exports presently benefit from preferential treatment by some importing industrialized countries, and the fact that liberalization would make other large developing countries very competitive (see also Figure 3.3).

This illustrates that the question of who benefits or incurs losses from which design aspect – and/or which provision level – of a global public good is often a highly complex issue to determine. Furthermore, the data on the multilateral trade regime presented in the Appendix shows that to reap the benefits from international trade, spending on trade facilitation, e.g. on constructing and maintaining new ports, roads and other infrastructure, notably to get domestic products to international markets, would be required. For many countries, the costs involved in these types of investment may be unaffordable, rendering the promises of these additional benefits for trade elusive.

Or, take the case of climate stability – also presented in the Appendix. According to the figures shown, the 'big' gainers seem, at first sight, to be the developing countries. However, the figures do not take into account that industrialized countries have contributed most to the over-burdening of the atmosphere with greenhouse gases, and hence, to the emergence of the risk of climate change. Considering this fact, many developing countries feel that industrialized countries should shoulder the primary responsibility for

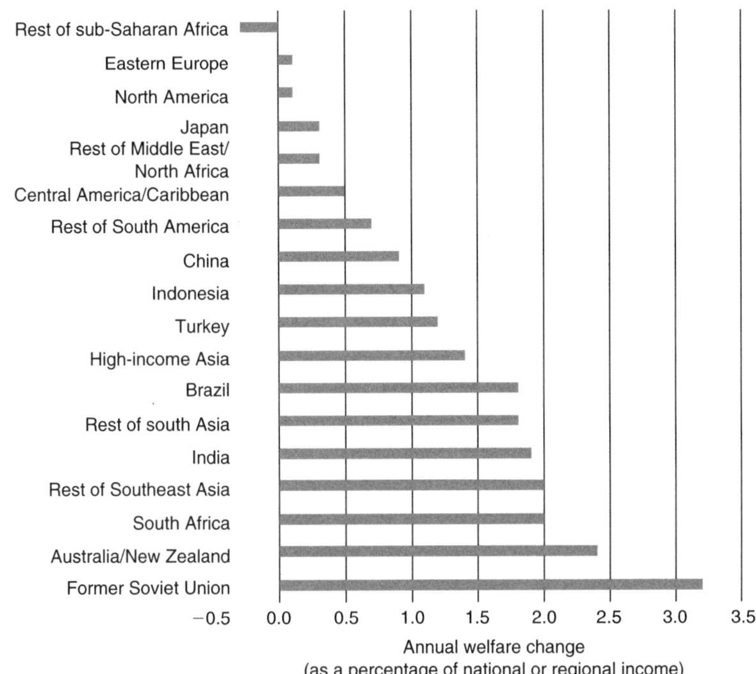

Figure 3.3: Differentiated impact of trade policy reform
Source: Conceição and Mendoza (2006: 342).

corrective action. The net-benefit potentially accruing to developing countries thus indicates not a real gain, but rather the damage, that will be inflicted on these countries if industrialized countries do not take decisive corrective action in good time.[10]

The estimates of benefits and costs underlying the first part of the Appendix only take account of the direct financial implications of the current underprovision of the global public good in question and of the suggested corrective action. They do not reflect actors' valuations of these goods, i.e. the relative priority or preference they may assign to the good. Yet actors' preferences are usually shaped by more than just these direct financial considerations. Variations in preferences also stem from factors like differences in levels of development and income, geographic and climatic conditions, or socio-cultural and political traditions. In fact, such differences are often wider globally, i.e. between people worldwide (without considering the national borders between them) as well as between countries than within countries.[11] Yet, to express them in monetary terms and to include them in cost/benefit assessments presents many methodological problems, as the literature on contingent valuation has shown (Carson, Flores and Meade 2001).

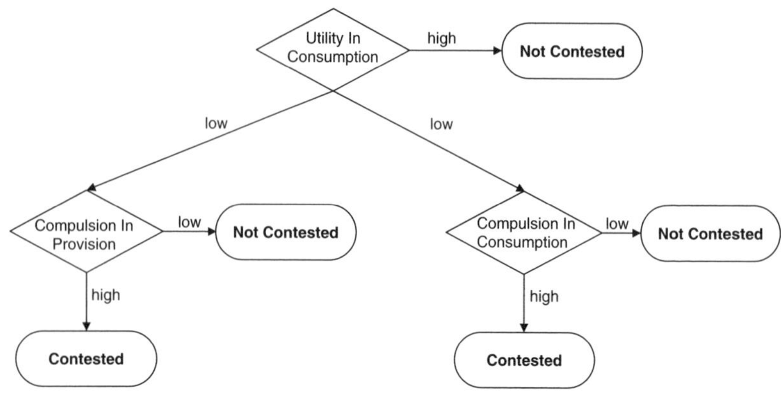

Figure 3.4:   Political-economy tree of global public good provision

Nevertheless, even based on the limited data available, it seems that an uneven distribution of net-benefits or low publicness in utility tends to be associated with contested global public goods. But does this condition alone explain contestation?

It seems not. Some global public goods also generate such unevenness but they are not subject of controversy. For example, many elements of scientific knowledge are potentially available for all to consume, in a nonrival way. Yet, at least in the short and medium term, some (e.g. richer and older population groups) may benefit much more than others (e.g. younger and poorer people). And yet, there seem to be few, if any protests against the provision of such research.

High publicness in consumption and/or provision

Evidently, low publicness in utility is not a sufficient condition for open dispute about a global public good. While perhaps a necessary condition, it appears that low publicness in utility has to coincide with other, additional factors in order to generate controversy. These factors might include: 1) high publicness in consumption; and/or 2) high publicness in provision (see also Figure 3.4).[12]

Consider for example, the policy wave towards privatization and economic liberalization that has, especially since the early 1980s, swept across countries worldwide. They contributed among other things, to the production of the global public good 'economic openness' or 'integrated markets'. Yet, at least in the short and medium term, they often entailed high costs for many population groups and many countries, notably developing countries. Yet, they were often handed down by international donors to developing countries in the form of loan conditionality: they had to be implemented and complied with – provided and consumed.

The result often was protracted and severe protest against these reforms, nationally and internationally. The realization that 'institutions matter' and reforms – in order to be less costly – need to be designed and implemented in a country-specific way came in large measure, through the pressure exerted through these protest movements (Teunissen and Akkerman 2004).

Or, take some of the initial proposals for the agreement on Trade-Related Aspects of Intellectual Property Rights (TRIPS) that many perceived as generating outright disutility – a threat to people's health and survival. It was feared that TRIPS would increase the costs of pharmaceutical products – pricing them out of the reach of poorer people. Yet, at the same time, TRIPS like other trade rules, are subject to close monitoring and enforcement of compliance – production and consumption. The reason is that in order to be effective, these rules need to be institutionalized and adhered to as widely as possible. In other words, trade rules like many other global norms are marked by high publicness in provision and consumption. Not surprisingly, thus, TRIPS, too, became the subject of considerable controversy.[13]

Prediction II: recognizing potentially controversial global public goods

Determining publicness in consumption, provision and utility is not an easy task, as it often requires extensive data collection and research. So, is it possible to recognize – in advance, before controversy erupts – the global public goods that are likely to stir up controversy? What distinguishes them from non-contested global public goods?

Again, a tentative answer to this question might be:

> *Prediction II:*
> Prominent among contested global public goods are global norms that seek to redraw conventional lines between 'public' and 'private' – to the detriment of influential incumbent groups.

To illustrate, one of the implications of TRIPs is to reinforce the protection of intellectual property rights, or in other words, to limit more stringently public access to knowledge, at least for a certain number of years. Or, take the Kyoto Protocol on climate change. By proposing to cap countries' emission levels, it restricts public access to the atmosphere through the introduction of a new private good, viz. emission allowances. Similarly, the often hotly debated issues of removal of national trade barriers or capital controls imply a shift from national 'closedness' (which can be viewed, as discussed before, as a special case of privateness) to national openness or globalization (which can be seen as a special case of publicness).

In the same vein, efforts aimed at the universalization of basic human rights, including rights of women and children, often run counter to conventional norms of who can and cannot participate in public life, including the work sphere, and what can and cannot be done within the private sphere of one's home (like violence against women or child abuse).

By contrast, a key feature of the non-contested global public goods like the universal postal system or the international civil aviation regime is that they are relatively distribution-neutral: Most people would perceive them as offering new, added opportunities. Some may benefit more than others; but few, if any, may feel that these costs are placing a direct net-cost on them.

Interestingly, these goods are also often of a network-type: While their benefits increase with the number of network members, they function for those that are part of the network, even if not all potential members are in the loop – not everybody has to have a phone for telephones to be useful, even though the usefulness of having a phone increases the more there are. Therefore, pressures on individual actors to consume and contribute also tend to be lower in the case of these goods. And much the same holds for technical norms and standards. For example, most people not only consume, but also enjoy, the fact that credit, debit or cash card sizes and machines (notably the slots for inserting the cards) are standardized. Not surprisingly, therefore, an organization like ISO is embroiled in much less controversy than the international financial institutions or WTO.

But again, redrawing the lines between 'public' and 'private' is not the whole story. Important is the second part of prediction II: 'to the detriment of influential groups'. The reason is that influential groups find it easier to make their interests known and insert them into international negotiations. And they also have better ways and means of supporting the 'roll-out' of norms that they prefer, or to stall the implementation of agreements that they perceive as being disadvantageous to their interests.

Consider once again, the case of 'climate change'. When powerful actors like the United States perceive disutility, they may choose to opt out of international cooperation. Or, they may delay implementation, as is the case with respect to agricultural subsidies. No doubt all governments have to undertake complex balancing acts to accommodate the often quite diverse interests of different constituencies. But industrialized countries and other influential actors – being the policymakers in many global public good situations – are likely to try harder and to be better able to assert their preferences than other, less influential actors, the policy-takers, including the least-developed countries and poor or disease-stricken people.[14]

Enhancing the provision of contested global public goods: possible policy options

The perception of incurring net costs or receiving an unfair share of the total net benefits generated by an international cooperation effort may hamper the participation of countries in international negotiations and complicate reaching an agreement (Albin 2003: 263–79; Chasek and Rajamani 2003: 245–62). As a result, global welfare may suffer, potentially making all worse off. To avert the risk of the world getting caught in such a 'bad' equilibrium, it would be important to clarify, what could be done to reduce controversy and encourage a more mutually beneficial – and hence acceptable for all – outcome of international negotiations.

The scope for such a mutually beneficial outcome seems to exist in many instances. The data in the Appendix suggest that the global gains to be derived from enhancing the provision of the global public goods discussed in this box could, in all cases, be quite significant. So, a 'simple' way forward could be for the 'winners' to compensate the 'losers' so that cross-border cooperation would make sense for all. In fact, this is what happened in the case of the Montreal Protocol aimed at restoring the ozone layer by phasing out chlorofluorocarbons (CFCs).

Yet, the Montreal Protocol is one of the few examples of successful international cooperation that was stimulated by compensatory financing.[15] Even where such financing occurs, it is often couched in other terms, notably in terms of foreign aid or development assistance as in the case of the Global Environment Facility (GEF). The GEF compensates developing countries for the incremental costs they incur when providing global environmental services like biodiversity preservation or reduction of greenhouse gases – an offer that developing countries do not always find attractive, because it does not reflect the true scarcity value of the service they render.[16]

Relying on intergovernmental agreements to make available compensatory financing may not be the best, most reliable entry point into facilitating consensus building on (potentially) controversial issues. Moreover, controversy may arise at both stages of international cooperation, viz. at the negotiation stage, when forging international agreements and at the implementation stage, when translating agreements into policy action, notably at the country level.

Promoting competitive global governance

Turning first to the stage of negotiations, in international venues states usually appear and act as individual, quasi-private actors. Their primary goal in these venues is to pursue national – particularistic – interests of their country or of one or the other domestic constituency. Therefore, international negotiation venues resemble in many respects a market: a bargaining and exchange forum.

In fact, international negotiations often suffer from failures quite similar to those failures that occur in markets, e.g.: limited competition (due to some parties being more powerful than others); information asymmetries (due to differences in national research and policy analysis and design capacity); and of course, free-riding in the presence of global public goods and cross-border spillovers. Like in economic markets limited competition in 'political markets' leads to inefficient outcomes. These may be ill-fitting policy recipes that a few actors formulate for application by many others, and which, because they are ill-fitting, risk being circumvented or causing more global harm than good.

It could thus be argued that just like their economic (including financial) counterparts, more competitive international political markets (speak, negotiation processes) will produce more mutually acceptable, and hence, more efficient outcomes. Thus, a further prediction that emerges is:

Prediction III:

More competitive – participatory – global governance reduces the risk of controversy, as it facilitates swifter as well as more durable policy consensus.

The most feasible way move towards more competitive, less distortion-inducing global governance may be: *firstly* to promote an adequate voice for all concerned; and *secondly* to enable all to have access to relevant information.[17] These two measures would go a long way in bringing international negotiations closer to being perfectly competitive. Also, they could be introduced through one-time decisions, e.g. a decision on changing voting rights and other decision-making patterns in a particular international organization. Yet they would fundamentally alter the dynamic of the organization: Rather than ignoring or suppressing differences in preferences and interests, they would facilitate bargaining between different parties, realizing that under conditions of openness and globalization private/national interests are often best served by expanding public/global gains.

A voice for all concerned

In many respects, global realities seem to be already moving in this direction. In particular, following the series of extensive public protests in the late 1990s/early 2000s that accompanied some of the major international gatherings and heeded policy signals sent by the more advanced developing countries like Brazil, China, India and South Africa, the recognition is now growing that controversy could be reduced, possibly even avoided, if all concerned had an adequate voice in the process. This may mean placing greater emphasis on consulting stakeholders and/or creating room at the decision-making tables for all relevant actors. The airing of differences in preferences appears gradually to become a more integral, built-in and orderly part of international negotiations.

For example, in the International Monetary Fund (IMF) there is an ongoing discussion on how to rebalance the distribution of voting power amongst member countries – which in large measure still reflects the original formulation in the 1940 – and how to make it more reflective of the changes in members' relative positions in the global economy since then (Bryant 2004, Buira 2005, World Bank and IMF 2005).

A similar reform process can also be observed for the G-7/8 group of major industrialized countries. The G-7/8 has now established a 'tradition' of inviting select developing countries to its summits. For example, at the Group's 2005 summit in Gleneagles, Scotland, a number of developing countries were also in attendance, including Algeria, Brazil, China, Ethiopia, Ghana, India, Mexico, Nigeria, Senegal, South Africa and Tanzania.[18] Furthermore, proposals also exist for the creation of new entities to avoid the frequently observed trade-off between being representative, and being an effective decision-making body.[19]

However, global policy formulation and norm and standard setting today are no longer (or perhaps more correctly, decreasingly) a matter of intergovernmental decision-making. Non-state actors, including civil society and business, have an increasingly decisive say. As Ruggie (2004: 519) points out, the international policy domain is:

> constituted by interactions among non-state actors as well as states. It permits the direct expression and pursuit of a variety of human interests, not merely those mediated (filtered, interpreted, promoted) by states. It 'exists' in transnational non-territorial spatial formations, and is anchored in norms and expectations as well as institutional networks and circuits within, across and beyond states.... The effect...is not to replace states, but to embed systems of governance in broader global frameworks....

This implies that ways also need to be found to foster multi-actor dialogue, especially dialogue between state and non-state actors. Again, under the pressures of reality, international negotiations appear to be reforming themselves along these lines. Virtually all intergovernmental bodies today pride themselves on having established procedures for consulting non-state actors. And venues like the World Economic Forum, the World Social Forum or the Clinton Global Initiative seek to promote multi-actor dialogue and follow-up action.[20]

In all cases the goal seems to be to bring all different actors and stakeholders *into* the negotiations: make the bargaining process more participatory, and thus, competitive so as to reduce the risk of protracted and costly controversy later.

Reducing information asymmetries

But effective voice depends on more than a fair distribution of voting rights, a seat at the table or money to support advocacy initiatives. It also depends on all parties having access to adequate information to assess their room for policy manoeuver. Yet many governments and other actors in poor countries often lack precisely this: analyses to guide their decision-making and to allow them to identify policy priorities, high-return investments and the scope for policy manoeuver they have in international negotiations. Therefore, reducing the number of contested global public goods – and the degree of controversy surrounding these goods – would also require more systematic assessments of how different public goods affect a particular country, or even, population groups within the country.[21]

The goal of such policy analyses would be to create greater transparency of global net gains that would result from an international cooperation effort for summation type global public goods, and the room that different actors have to compensate potential losers – be it through transfer payments, or also through cross-bargaining.

An improved distribution of voice, coupled with access of all to relevant information, would certainly enhance the competitiveness of international negotiations, and possibly, generate more efficient, better fitting, more effective, and ultimately perhaps also, fairer agreements. It would replace today's – often noisy and messy – disputes and protests against various global public goods – by competitive global governance, providing arrangements for the orderly workout of differences in preferences.

Promoting the availability of private good contributions to global public goods

International norm and rule setting is often indispensable for countries and other actors to have a sense of the direction in which the world is moving. However, the implementation of international agreements has in most instances to follow a country-specific path. As noted, much controversy has erupted in the past, because this point was ignored.

The fourth prediction of this chapter indicates a way to overcome controversy that may result from over-harmonized ('one size fits all') policy approaches:

Prediction IV:
Where private goods are available, allowing individual actors to contribute to global public goods while meeting their own private/national purposes, the implementation of international agreements on global public goods is less controversial than where it relies on intergovernmental cooperation.

Intriguingly, private sector actors have for some time understood much better than their intergovernmental counterparts that cooperation works if the intended bargain promises a fair distribution of net-gains to the parties involved. The result has been that, in a number of issue areas, intergovernmental cooperation schemes were replaced by market-based arrangements.

Just think of the international commodity agreements that existed in the past, e.g. those for cocoa, coffee, sugar or tin. Most are now defunct; and in their stead commodity futures and options markets have emerged.

Or, consider the debt crises from which notably the developing countries have suffered and the arduous negotiations to resolve them, often led by the IMF and other 'donor' country agencies. By now, a number of new market-based instruments have emerged to help prevent crises, or should a crisis occur, to resolve it in a more orderly fashion.

Take for example, the case of growth-indexed sovereign bonds, also known as gross domestic product (GDP)-indexed bonds. The public actors (issuing governments) benefit from this instrument, because the debt service is tied to the economic performance of the economy. In a period of lower growth, the payments to bond holders are lowered proportionally to the decrease in the growth rate. But investors in the bonds – which include many private actors in international capital markets – gain, too. With low growth, a country's debt position can rapidly become unsustainable and the country could default. International investors would be better off receiving lower debt repayments in a predictable and organized way, rather than face uncertain recovery values through a chaotic default process.[22]

The insertion of collective action clauses into sovereign bonds generates a similar win–win situation. These clauses are included in bond contracts issued by sovereign governments and bind bondholders to agreeing to a common debt restructuring process, if default occurs. This discourages opportunistic and costly behaviour by one or two investors, who may seek to gain better terms than other investors. It also makes the debt restructuring process more orderly and less onerous for the issuing government and helps reduce the likelihood of global financial crises.[23]

Mention could also be made of carbon markets, catastrophe bonds, and weather or terrorism insurance. The interesting feature of all these and other instruments is that governments and investors cooperate to their mutual advantage – without any underlying multilateral agreement of complex international negotiations, generating private/national as well as public/global gains. The cooperative and mutually beneficial outcome is imbedded in the use of the financial tools, which both parties voluntarily agree to use because it is clearly in their best interest.

The lesson to be drawn from this experience perhaps is that an enhanced availability of private goods, which generate such a combination of significant private/national as well as public/global gains, could, where feasible, be a desirable, effective and efficient way towards promoting a fuller provision of global public goods. Such private goods would give individual actors, including individual governments, a better chance to fine-tune their contributions to global public goods to their particular circumstances, easing the necessity to contribute a fixed amount in a pre-determined way that often accompanies intergovernmental cooperation schemes. This flexibility as well as the possibility to capture at least a significant part of the benefits generated for their own purposes (i.e. to enhance their utility) is likely to strengthen their incentive to cooperate – and help unlock the promise of the considerable welfare gains that an enhanced provision of global public goods could generate.

Thus, private goods that serve global-public-good ends lower compulsion to contribute, consume or both and enhance utility for all. They correct the conditions that according to prediction I set forth in this chapter are likely to give global public goods a contested nature. However, many of these goods are still new and innovative. Considering the promise they hold and the lengthening list of global crises, the time may be ripe for more decisive action to move some of the existing private-good instruments towards more broad-based adoption and initiate research and development (R&D) on further such goods that might allow individual actors to break free from stalled intergovernmental collective action.

Conclusion

This chapter has addressed the issue of why some global public goods are contested and how to reduce the risk of controversy, stalled negotiations, and hence, underprovision of global public goods, resulting in important global welfare losses. The purpose has been to provide tentative answers, in the form of four predictions that would need to be tested in future research and study.

The main message emerging from the discussion is that many global public goods are non-contested, or put differently, generally appreciated by the global public – people at large. According to prediction I, contestation occurs where publicness in utility is low (only a few derive significant net-gains from international cooperation) and publicness in both, consumption and provision is high (all are affected by the good and compelled to contribute to its provision). Global public goods that are marked by such a mismatch between publicness in utility, on the one hand, and publicness in consumption and provision, on the other hand, are, as prediction II suggests, those that seek to redraw the conventional lines between 'public' and 'private' – to the detriment of often relatively few but influential actors.

Yet, power politics are unlikely to change. So, is it possible to reduce the risk of continuing underprovision of global public goods and the lengthening list of global crises?

Prediction III suggests possible reform steps towards more competitive global governance, or in other words, an orderly working out of differences in preferences. Prediction IV proposes greater reliance on private-good inputs to global public goods as a more efficient way of providing these goods, since they offer individual actors stronger incentives to contribute, coupled with greater flexibility to tailor the way in which they contribute to their particular circumstances.

Appendix

Publicness in consumption does not necessarily imply publicness (even distribution) of utility

The main defining property of public goods, including global public goods, is that they are available for all, that is, there for all to consume, sometimes whether an actor enjoys doing so or not. Public goods are in the public domain; and global public goods span across borders and often also generations.

While global public goods tend to affect all, the distribution of their costs and benefits, and hence, the net-gain they generate for different actors or stakeholders can vary widely. It appears that the goods that are known to have generated considerable international debate and controversy are also often those that are characterized by an uneven distribution of net-benefits.

Contested global public goods: uneven distribution of net-benefits

Consider for example, the following global public goods.

Global Climate Stability. By some estimates, the damages that could result from a doubling of carbon dioxide in the atmosphere would imply global costs of $270 billion (in 1988 dollars). Industrialized countries would bear $180 billion, or about 1.3 per cent of their gross national product (GNP) in 1988, and developing countries (non-OECD countries) would bear $89 billion, or about 1.6 per cent of their combined GNP (Fankhauser 1995: 55, table 3.15). So both groups of countries have a similar interest in avoiding these costs.

However, if one were to assume that only industrialized countries would reduce emission levels to 5 per cent below their 1990 levels, as foreseen in the Kyoto Protocol, and assuming further that emission allowances can be globally traded, the industrialized countries would be net losers by $39 trillion under this scenario; and developing countries would enjoy net benefits of $111 trillion (Cline 2004: 31).

It is, of course, important to note that, historically, industrialized countries have tended to be the primary polluters. Yet, the greenhouse gas emissions of some developing countries are rising so fast that emission reductions by industrialized countries alone, may be a fair first step to reduce these countries' environmental 'debt'. But in the longer run such an approach would accomplish little in terms of fostering climate stability.

Thus, it is not surprising that many developing countries are keen to see industrialized countries take a first step towards corrective action; and that industrialized countries are keen to see a commitment to reducing emission levels on the part of developing countries. It is around these sorts of issues that the current international debates on climate stability revolve, and often, also stall.

Global Financial Architecture. The efficient functioning of international markets, including that of international financial markets, depends on a series of institutions, including policy principles and codes and standards as well as various organizational mechanisms, which must be in place, nationally and internationally – in other words, on an effective global financial architecture. Such an architecture is also essential for countries, especially developing countries, to avoid over-indebtedness that may result from external shocks to their economy.

Some analysts (e.g. United Nations 2005) argue that the current global architecture lacks several components that could help developing countries avoid financial crises; and it may even contain elements that lead to – rather than prevent – financial crises in emerging markets.

The period between 1975 and 1998 was an era of rapid financial liberalization and removal of capital controls. And it was also during this era that 158 currency crises, 54 banking crises, and 32 twin (currency and banking) crises occurred – the majority of which occurred in emerging market countries (116 currency, 42 banking, and 26 twin crises). Recent major crises in addition to those include the Russian Federation's 1998 debt crisis, Brazil's 1999 currency crisis, Turkey's 2001 currency crisis, and Argentina's 2001–2002 debt crisis. The costs of a selection of banking crises between the late 1970s and 2000 illustrate the costs involved: lost output totalled $1 trillion – or about $50 billion per annum – for the developing and transition countries (Caprio and Klingebiel 2002: 17; Honohan and Klingebiel 2003: 1541).

Even today many dimensions that could help prevent such crises in an efficient way are still missing in the global financial architecture. Yet, while governments find it difficult to agree on various policy options like a resumption of the issuance of Special Drawing Rights, private investors are seeking solutions, because they have realized that increased financial stability is also rewarding for them: it reduces 'investor haircuts' (calculated as the percentage difference between the present values of old and new debt instruments, discounted at the yield prevailing immediately after the exchange). The costs to investors from recent debt restructuring episodes (e.g. Russia, Ukraine, Pakistan, Ecuador, Argentina and Uruguay) range from 13 per cent to as high as 74 per cent of the value of investments (Sturzenegger and Zettelmeyer 2005: 4). A similar motivation propels, as noted, the discussion on sovereign bond indexation.

Multilateral Trade Regime. Taking the multilateral trade regime from the agreement level (that is, the level of declared intentions) to the level of a new, changed policy reality of market integration, requires effecting changes in national trade policy and making improvements in infrastructure for trade facilitation. According to one study (Hertel 2004: 24), making these changes could bring global net benefits of well over $5 trillion (in net present value terms in 2001 dollars). The benefits are fairly evenly distributed, with $2.9

trillion in welfare gains for industrialized countries and $2.5 trillion for developing countries.

However, the costs of corrective action would fall primarily on developing countries, which are expected to pay a one-time cost of about $23 billion and annual costs of $20 billion (e.g. for investments in, and the maintenance of, infrastructure), while industrialized countries incur only a one-time cost of about $6 billion (ibid.). Thus, even though developing countries could benefit, they may not be able to pay for the costs of corrective action. The large potential benefits that could accrue to them – and to the world – from enhancing the provision status of the multilateral trade regime are therefore not being realized.

Looking at the distribution of the net-benefits of free trade within countries rather than just across groups of countries, the de facto cost of being part of the multilateral trade regime also entails being open to increased competition from abroad, notably for particular sectors within a country. While such competition could be efficiency enhancing, its benefits will materialize only if the countries or sectors concerned are ready, so that they thrive rather than whither with the influx of foreign trade and investment. Certain sectors even in highly industrialized countries will not be spared from facing intense competition, notably from developing countries that have to some degree ascended the competitiveness ladder, like China and India. Outsourcing, for example, is hitting some sectors in the United States hard – software and service companies have been losing about 100,000 jobs per year – even as that country, on the whole, gains immensely from international trade (Bhagwati, Panagariya and Srinivasan 2004: 99). Finally it seems that structural adjustment (e.g. to increased openness to trade) may be no less controversial among domestic constituencies in industrialized countries than it was in developing countries was in the 1980s and early 1990s (see, Cornia, Jolly and Stewart 1987).

Polio Eradication. Polio eradication is an underprovided global public good. It is about 99.7 per cent provided (expressed as the reduction in the number of cases since the eradication programme started), with 1,263 new cases of polio virus in the 'wild' in 2004 (there were 350,000 in 1988, when the eradication effort was officially launched through a World Health Assembly resolution; www.polioeradication.org/progress.asp).

One study estimates the global cost of corrective action at $67 billion in present value terms (Khan and Ehreth 2003: 704, table 3). Of this, $24 billion accrues to developing countries and $43 billion to industrialized countries. If one considers only the benefits from savings in medical costs (derived through historical analysis of costs back to 1970 and projected into 2040) – costs that would be avoided through immunization and eradication assessed against the baseline scenario of no immunization – and the cessation of vaccination after 2010, this suggests global present benefits of $128 billion (in 2000 dollars discounted at 5 per cent) (Khan and Ehreth 2003: 704, table 3).

Most of the benefits ($115 billion) flow to the largely industrialized and middle-income countries of Europe and the Americas (World Health Organization regions), with the remaining benefits ($13 billion) flowing mostly to developing countries (Khan and Ehreth 2003: 704, table 3).

Thus, based on the preceding information, enhanced provision of polio eradication could bring global net benefits of more than $60 billion (in net present value terms in 2000 dollars). However, the benefits would likely be unevenly distributed: industrialized countries experience a net benefit of $72 billion, and developing countries experience a net cost of about $11 billion. This does not include the additional benefits from mitigating the risk of polio as a weapon of bioterrorism – and these benefits will likely stack in favour of the major industrialized countries facing the highest terrorist threat. This uneven distribution does not mean that polio eradication would not be in the self-interest of developing countries, but only that within the assumptions of the study used to derive the estimates, it would be costly to developing countries, while industrialized countries would achieve net savings. Polio eradication would still be a good global investment.

Consensual global public goods: even distribution of net-benefits (or, at least, no net-cost to any party)

Contrast the foregoing accounts then with that of smallpox eradication, which is mentioned here as an example of a consensual global public good with a rather even distribution of net-benefits across countries.

Smallpox Eradication. The World Health Assembly declared smallpox eradicated in 1980 (Barrett 2004: 3). This means that this global public good is currently fully provided. The global net present value benefits of this achievement stand around $47 billion (in 1967 dollars discounted at 3 per cent), with some $35 billion flowing to developing countries and about $12 billion to industrialized countries. Developing countries gain more because the disease had already been eliminated in industrialized countries when the international eradication effort began in 1966 (Fenner et al. 1988). Industrialized country gains are limited to the savings from not having to vaccinate once the disease is eradicated. Yet, clearly, both industrialized and developing countries achieved substantial net gains – a win-win result – from the full provision of this global public good.

Notes

* The views expressed are those of the author and do not necessarily reflect the views of the organization with which she is affiliated. The author thanks Pedro Conceição, Ronald Mendoza and Nena Terrell for useful comments.

1. For reasons of brevity, the term 'good' will be employed here to refer to both goods and services. Also, the term 'good' denotes things like tangible objects (e.g. bread, cloth or a road) as well as conditions (e.g. peace and security, law and order, climate

stability or disease control). Thus, the term 'good' is used here without indication of the utility a thing/condition may have for a particular (group of) actors.

2. The more conventional definition is that, in their pure form, public goods are nonexcludable and nonrival in consumption – their consumption by one actor does not diminish their availability for others, which, more simply stated, means they are available for all. If a good exhibits both characteristics, viz. nonexcludability and nonrivalry in consumption, it is said to be a pure public good. If it is marked only by one of these properties, it is categorized as an impure public good. See for the standard treatment of the concept of public goods, for example, Cornes and Sandler (1996).

3. It is important to note that the word 'global' here means cross-cutting or stretching across various types of natural or human-made boundaries. 'Global' should not be confused with 'international', i.e. a space that exists between nations, or extraterritorial.

4. For further discussion of public goods and global public goods interested readers may also wish to consult Barrett (2006); Cornes and Sandler (1996); Ferroni and Mody (2002); Kanbur, Sandler, and Morrison (1999); Kaul, Grunberg, and Stern (1999); Kaul et. al. (2003); and Sandler (1997, 1998, 2004, 2006).

5. Economic globalization is largely an intended, deliberate process, which comes about based on public policy decisions to remove national borders and harmonize the design and provision level of national public goods so as to facilitate the integration across borders of markets and infrastructure. However, as these intended globalization efforts progress and cross-border economic activity increases, unintended globalization also increases, resulting from the externalities that may accompany this activity – including spillovers/spillins like pollution, communicable diseases, international terrorism or technology, knowledge and information transfer. However, spillovers may occur whether borders are open or not. For example, greenhouse gas emissions have always risen, whether the world found itself in an era of more open or more closed borders, more extensive or more limited travel across countries and regions.

6. Figure 3.1 clearly illustrates how public goods are multi-actor products to which all groups might potentially contribute. For example, civil society and lobbyists might nudge the government into taking action (arrows 1 and 2) while also seeking to influence the general public through their advocacy activities (arrow 1). As a result, public demand for a certain public good, say smoke-free public spaces, might increase (arrow 4). In response, the government might provide an intermediate public good such as an information campaign on the ill effects of smoking in public places (arrow 3), hoping to alter the behaviour of individual actors (arrow 6). Coercive measures might also be needed, such as a ban on smoking in public places (arrow 3). Together, the positive externalities resulting from the changed behaviour of individuals (voluntary and coerced) would then produce the desired public good, smoke-free public spaces (arrow 8). The government might also be influenced by external preferences (arrow 7), for example, by foreign visitors who demand smoke-free airports and hotel rooms or by international conventions such as the World Health Organization Framework Convention on Tobacco Control (www.who.int/tobacco/framework/en).

7. The concept of aggregation technology was introduced by Hirshleifer (1983) and by Cornes and Sandler (1984) and elaborated on by Cornes (1993).

8. Unilateral provision is a technical possibility especially where the good abides by a best-shot aggregation technology. A case in point is an innovation like a new

pharmaceutical product. For example, a particular vaccine must only be invented once to exist; and it can be invented by one researcher or one laboratory. However, some pharmaceutical companies could, of course, succeed on their own to develop, say, a malaria vaccine. Yet, since such a vaccine would primarily benefit poor people in poor countries, they may not see a realistic possibility of ever recouping related research and development (R&D) costs, and hence, lack the incentive to undertake related investments.

9. Trade distorting measures include domestic support, export subsidies, and tariffs. While domestic support measures distort the producer side, market price support distorts the consumer side of the market.

10. Industrial countries having the primary responsibility for taking corrective action on the risk of climate change does not imply that they should not trade emission allowances or reduction credits with developing countries. They can do so and still meet what some see as their international obligation, if the trade is in the mutual interest of both trading partners.

11. See, on this point, the empirical evidence provided among others, in the *Human Development Reports* (UNDP various years). To mention a few statistics here, the world's wealthiest 500 individuals have a combined income greater than that of the poorest 416 million people. The 2.5 billion people living on less than $2 a day (some 40 per cent of the world's population) account for only 5 per cent of the world's income. The richest 10 per cent, on the other hand, almost all of whom live in high-income countries, account for 54 per cent (UNDP 2005, 4).

12. Many of the points made here about the contested nature of global public goods might also apply to regional and national public goods. However, in the case of national public goods, it is often easier to design policy packages, including compensatory financing for potential losers, than it is in the case of regional and global public goods. The latter tend to be negotiated on a good-by-good or international agency-by-agency basis, which renders the structuring of policy packages difficult.

13. See for a more detailed discussion on the global public good dimensions of TRIPS and other aspects of the multilateral trade regime, also Mendoza (2003).

14. A rich and growing literature exists on these and related points. Yet again, the information it presents is mostly of a qualitative nature. Quantitative analyses are rare. See, among others, Addison and Roe (2004); Keohane and Milner (1996); Mkandawire and Soludo (1999); Rajan and Zingales (2003); and Weiss (2003).

15. For more detail on this point, see www.unep.org/ozone/Montreal-Protocol/Montreal-Protocol2000.shtml.

16. The purpose of the GEF is to support projects with global environmental spillover effects in developing countries and to compensate countries for any efforts that they undertake over and above what they would have done had they been motivated by national interests only. See www.gefweb.org/What_ is_the_GEF/what_is_the_gef.html.

17. Other elements that introduce governance imperfections like, for example, large differences in economic and military power that sometimes introduce 'monopoly competition' into negotiations, are evidently more difficult to change so that the measures suggested here appear to be the more feasible.

18. See www.g8.gov.uk for the Gleneagles Summit and also www.whitehouse.gov/g8/2004/ for the Sea Island Summit, g8.fr/evian/english/ for the Evian Summit, and www.g8.gc.ca/sumdocs2002-en.asp for the Kananaskis Summit.

19. These proposals include, among others, suggesting the creation of an L-20, a group of 20 political leaders to advise the world on global issues (see, Kaul and Conceição

2006a and Bradford and Linn 2004) and the establishment, for a similar purpose, of a G-29, composed of member states of the United Nations, some of whom would have a permanent seat on the Security Council and others a rotating one (see Kaul et al. 2003).
20. See, for further information www.forumsocialmundial.org.br/: and www.clintonglobalinitiative.org
21. A possible methodology for such assessments has been outlined by Conceição and Mendoza (2006). The authors differentiate between the distribution of net-benefits between the groups of industrialized countries and developing countries. However, the suggested methodology could also be applied to undertaking country-level assessments.
22. For further a discussion of GDP-indexed bonds, see for example, Borensztein and Mauro (2004), and UN and UNDP (2005, 2006).
23. For further a discussion of collective action clauses, see for example, Eichengreen (2006).

References

Addison, A. and A. Roe (eds.) (2004): *Fiscal Policy for Development: Poverty, Reconstruction and Growth*. Basingstoke: Palgrave Macmillan.

Albin, C. (2003): Getting to Fairness: Negotiations over Global Public Goods. In: Kaul I., P. Conceição, K. Le Goulven and R. U. Mendoza (eds.), *Providing Global Public Goods: Managing Globalization*. New York: Oxford University Press.

Anderson, K., W. Martin and E. Valenzuela. (2006): Why Market Access is the Most Important of Agriculture's 'Three Pillars' in the Doha Negotiations. World Bank, Trade Note 26. Washington DC: World Bank. [siteresources.worldbank.org/INTRANETTRADE/Resources/2390541126812419270/TradeNote26_Revised.pdf].

Axelrod, R. (1984): *The Evolution of Cooperation*. New York: Basic Books.

Barrett, S. (2004): The Provision Status of Disease Eradication. UNDP/ODS Background Paper. United Nations Development Program, Office of Development Studies, New York: [www.thenewpublicfinance.org/background/barrett_eradication.pdf].

Barrett, S. (2006): Making International Cooperation Pay: Financing as a Strategic Incentive. In: Kaul, I. and P. Conceição (eds.), *The New Public Finance: Responding to Global Challenges*. New York: Oxford University Press.

Bhagwati, J., A. Panagariya and T. N. Srinivasan. (2004): The Muddles over Outsourcing. *Journal of Economic Perspectives*, 18(4): 93–114.

Borensztein, E. and P. Maur (2004): The Case for GDP-indexed Bonds. *Economic Policy*, 19(38): 166–216.

Bradford, C. and J. F. Linn. (2004): Global Economic Governance at a Crossroads: Replacing the G-7 with the G-20. *Brookings Policy Brief* 131. Washington, DC: The Brookings Institution.

Bryant, R. C. (2004): *Crisis Prevention and Prosperity Management for the World Economy*. Washington DC: The Brookings Institution.

Buira, A. (2005): The IMF at Sixty: an Unfulfilled Potential?. In: Buira, A. (ed.), *The IMF and the World Bank at Sixty*. London: Anthem Press.

Caprio, G. and D. Klingebiel (2002): Episodes of Systemic and Borderline Financial Crises. In: Klingebiel, D. and L. Laeven (eds.), *Managing the Real and Fiscal Effects of Banking Crises*. World Bank Discussion Paper 428. Washington DC: The World Bank.

Carson, R. T., N. E. Flores and N. F. Meade (2001): Contingent Valuation: Controversies and Evidence. *Environmental and Resource Economics*. 19(2): 173–210.

Chasek, P. and L. Rajamani. (2003): Steps Towards Enhanced Parity: Negotiating Capacity and Strategies of Developing Countries. In: Kaul, I., P. Conceição, K. Le Goulven and R. U. Mendoza (eds.), *Providing Global Public Goods: Managing Globalization*. New York: Oxford University Press.

Cline, W. R. (2004): Climate Change. In: Lomborg, B. (ed.), *Global Crises, Global Solutions*. Cambridge: Cambridge University Press.

Conceição, P. and R. U. Mendoza (2006): Identifying High-Return Investments: a Methodology for Assessing when International Cooperation Pays – and for Whom. In: Kaul, I. and P. Conceição (eds.), *The New Public Finance: Responding to Global Challenges*. New York: Oxford University Press.

Cornes, R. (1993): Dyke Maintenance and Other Stories: Some Neglected Types of Public Goods. *Quarterly Journal of Economics* 108(1): 259–71.

Cornes, R. and T. Sandler (1984): Easy Riders, Joint Production, and Public Goods. *Economic Journal* 94(3): 580–98.

Cornes, R. and T. Sandler (1996): *The Theory of Externalities, Public Goods, and Club Goods*. Cambridge: Cambridge University Press.

Cornia, A., R. J. and F. Stewart (eds.) (1987): *Adjustment with a Human Face*. 2 vols. Oxford: Clarendon Press.

Eichengreen, B. (2006): Assessing Contractual and Statutory Approaches: Policy Proposals for Restructuring Unsustainable Sovereign Debt. In: Kaul, I. and P. Conceição (eds.), *The New Public Finance: Responding to Global Challenges*. New York: Oxford University Press.

Fankhauser, S. (1995): *Valuing Climate Change*. London: Earthscan.

Fenner, F., D. A. Henderson, I. Arita, Z. Jezek, and I. D. Ladnyi (1988): *Smallpox and its Eradication*. Geneva: World Health Organization.

Ferroni, M. and A. Mody (eds.) (2002): *International Public Goods: Incentives, Measurement and Financing*. Washington, DC: Kluwer Academic Publishers and World Bank.

Hertel, T. (2004): Assessing the Provision of International Trade as a Global Public Good. UNDP/ODS Background Paper. United Nations Development Programme, Office of Development Studies, New York: [www.thenewpublicfinance.org/ background/hertel.pdf].

Hirshleifer, J. (1983): From Weakest-Link to Best-Shot: the Voluntary Provision of Public Goods. *Public Choice* 41(3): 371–86.

Honohan, P. and D. Klingebiel (2003): The Fiscal Cost Implications of an Accomodating Approach to Banking Crises. *Journal of Banking and Finance* 27(8): 1539–60.

Kanbur, R., T. Sandler and Kevin Morrison. (1999): The Future of Development Assistance: Common Pools and International Public Goods. Policy Essay 25. Overseas Development Council, Washington, DC.

Kaul, I., I. Grunberg and M. A. Stern (eds.) (1999): *Global Public Goods: International Cooperation in the 21st Century*. New York: Oxford University Press.

Kaul, I., P. Conceição, K. Le Goulven and R. U. Mendoza (2003) (eds.): *Providing Global Public Goods: Managing Globalization*. New York: Oxford University Press.

Kaul, I. and P. Conceição (2006a): The L-20: an Important Beginning of a New Era of International Cooperation. Presented at the L-20 Conference on Financing Global Public Goods. Princeton, NJ, February 26–27. [www.l20.org/publications/Phase%20III/Publicgoods/L20%20Princeton%20Background_Kaul%20&%20Conceicao.pdf].

Kaul, I. and P. Conceição (2006b) (eds.): *The New Public Finance: Responding to Global Challenges*. New York: Oxford University Press.

Keohane, R. O. and H. V. Milner (1996) (eds.): *Internationalization and Domestic Politics*. Cambridge: Cambridge University Press.

Khan, M. M. and J. Ehreth (2003): Costs and Benefits of Polio Eradication: a Long-Run Global Perspective. *Vaccine* 21(7–8): 702–5.

Mendoza, R. U. (2003): The Multilateral Trade Regime: a Global Public Good for all? In: Kaul, I., P. Conceição, K. Le Goulven and R. U. Mendoza (eds.), *Providing Global Public Goods: Managing Globalization*. New York: Oxford University Press.

Mkandawire, T. and C. C. Soludo (1999) (eds.): *Our Continent, Our Future: African Perspectives on Structural Adjustment*. Trenton, NJ and Asmara: Africa World Press.

Rajan, R. G. and L. Zingales (2003): *Saving Capitalism from the Capitalists: Unleashing the Power of Financial Markets to Create Wealth and Spread Opportunity*. New York: Crown Business.

Ruggie, J. G. (2004): Reconstituting the Global Public Domain – Issues, Actors and Practices. *European Journal of International Relations* 10(4): 499–531.

Samuelson, P. A. (1954): The Pure Theory of Public Expenditure. *Review of Economics and Statistics* 36(4): 387–9.

Sandler, T. (1997): *Global Challenges: an Approach to Environmental, Political and Economic Problems*. Cambridge: Cambridge University Press.

Sandler, T. (1998): Global and Regional Public Goods: a Prognosis for Collective Action. *Fiscal Studies* 19(3): 221–47.

Sandler, T. (2004): *Global Collective Action*. Cambridge: Cambridge University Press.

Sandler, T. (2006): Recognizing the Limits to Cooperation Behind National Borders: Financing the Control of Transnational Terrorism. In: Kaul, I. and P. Conceição (eds.), *The New Public Finance: Responding to Global Challenges*. New York: Oxford University Press.

Sturzenegger, F. and J. Zettelmeyer (2005): Haircuts: Estimating Investor Losses in Sovereign Debt Restructurings, 1998–2005. IMF Working Paper 05/137. International Monetary Fund, Washington, DC [www.imf.org/external/pubs/ft/wp/2005/wp05137.pdf].

Teunissen, J. J. and A. Akkerman (eds.) (2004): *Diversity in Development: Reconsidering the Washington Consensus*. The Hague: FONDAD.

UN (United Nations) (2005): *World Economic and Social Survey*. New York.

UN (United Nations) and UNDP (United Nations Development Programme) (2005): Report on the Meeting on GDP-indexed Bonds: Make it Happen. New York, 25 October 2005 [www.un.org/esa/ffd/GDP-indexed%20Bonds].

UN (United Nations) and UNDP (United Nations Development Programme) (2006): Report on the Meeting on GDP-indexed Bonds: an Idea Whose Time Has Come. Washington DC, 21 April 2006 [www.un.org/esa/ffd/GDP-indexedbonds-DC-report.doc].

UNDP (United Nations Development Programme) (2005): *Human Development Report 2005, International Cooperation at a Crossroads: Aid, Trade and Security in an Unequal World*. New York: Oxford University Press.

UNDP (United Nations Development Programme) (various years): *Human Development Report*. New York: Oxford University Press.

Weiss, L. (2003) (ed.): *States in the Global Economy: Bringing Domestic Institutions Back*. Cambridge: Cambridge University Press.

World Bank and IMF (2005): Development Committee Comunique. 25 September 2005, Washington, DC [www.imf.org/external/np/cm/2005/092505.htm].

4
Global Public Goods:
the Governance Dimension

Peter-Tobias Stoll

Introduction

The global public goods approach is based on and strongly appeals to economic thought (Kaul et al. 1999; Kaul et al. 2001). Its foundations and merits in this regard are dealt with elsewhere.[1] Importantly, it addresses institutional, political and legal aspects by highlighting that the poor supply of public goods at the international level results from a lack of adequate structures for their production and governance (Kaul et al. 2003a).

The global public goods approach has been well received in academia. Research in a number of areas of international relations has made use of this concept (Kaul et al. 1999; Kaul et al. 2003). Furthermore, some governments and international institutions have also heavily supported the elaboration and further development of this approach.[2] As this may indicate, the notion of global public goods appears to address relevant questions both from an academic perspective as well as from the point of view of international policy-making. It seems to appropriately reflect a deficit that so far has been described as a demand for the production and/or provision of public goods at the global level which is not properly reflected by the existing political structures.

From a traditional internationalist and international law perspective, the notion of global public goods sounds quite familiar.[3] Many issues discussed under this new approach have formed part of the international agenda for years, not to say decades. Furthermore, diplomacy and academia have created a rich variety of concepts and formulas, which appear to be quite close to the public goods approach. The concept of the common heritage of mankind as discussed in relation to deep-seabed minerals, technology, the geo-stationary orbit and a number of other issues can be used to illustrate this point (Wolfrum 1984: 331ff.), as can the 'common concern', which has been voiced in regard to many international environmental issues (Brunnée 1989: 800ff.). From the point of view of international law, the issue of *ius cogens*, *erga omnes* and the concept of public interest norms may also be mentioned, which rely on the idea of communality in order to justify binding effects on states, irrespective of whether they are bound by explicit consent.

The global public goods approach, however, goes further than these concepts, taking on board economic implications and the political economy in the issue areas addressed. Thus, it highlights, that in addressing today's international challenges, the economic dimension is key, including the regulatory system of the world economy and the underlying political structures.

In order to explore the governance dimension of such findings, the causes for the rising demand for such global public goods merits a closer look as well as the modes of their supply. As will be shown in section one, the demand for global public goods does not merely result from the real world effects of increasing transborder interactions but is also due to policy interactions, which restrict access to those goods, which so far have been openly accessible. Likewise, the possible modes of supply are more complex at the global level than within a domestic framework as will be addressed in section two. Because of these circumstances, the task of governing the provision of global public goods is a challenging one. This is even more so the case, as such provision requires properly addressing the many cross-cutting issues involved. Often, such cross–cutting issues have implications for different international regimes and their work. Due to what may be considered a 'sectoral divide', the existing international regimes have difficulty adequately responding to such challenge (section three).

The demand for global public goods

As is often stated, the demand for the provision and production of public goods at the global level results from the decline in the role that states play in this regard. Traditionally, states provided public goods. However, the intensification of transboundary economic activity, trade, communication, travel and migration increasingly renders it difficult to define and effectively provide public goods within the confines of national boundaries.

For example, established national structures for the production and distribution of public goods, such as rules on access and the structure of finance may be put into question by globalization and the resulting problem of free-riding. Also, established national regulatory policies in the area of health and consumer protection now face the need to comply with international developments and the requirement of international compatibility. In view of international trade and transboundary economic activities, such compatibility of national policies is an imperative. Accordingly, maintaining such compatibility is a high priority in policy-making.

In addition to these effects, globalization may also confront states with new demands concerning public goods; clearly, the facilitation and intensification of communication, travel, trade and social interaction may cause a spread of diseases and encourage criminal activities and international terrorism.

The privatization of knowledge, technology and intellectual works

However, the recent demand for global public goods is not only due to the decreasing role that states play. Much to the contrary, the availability of such goods has been put into question by a number of policy measures, both at the national and international levels, which have significantly affected the access to and production of such goods. Such measures include the assignment and strengthening of intellectual property rights, the claiming of sovereign rights over certain resources and the privatization of the production and distribution of certain public goods or services.

This is especially true for knowledge, technology and other intellectual property goods. Under the Agreement on Trade-related Aspects of Intellectual Property Rights of the World Trade Organization (TRIPs), the protection of intellectual property rights has become comprehensive and very effective over the last few years. The free use of patented technology and copyrighted materials, which so far has been a reality in many countries on the basis of legal exemptions or poor enforcement, will be much more severely restricted in the coming years. Furthermore, new developments in patent law and copyrights will reduce the so-called *domaine public* which is considered an important global public good. For instance, the patentability of computer software may restrict the use of software elements by third-party programmers and limit the activities of the open source community.[4] An extensive patent protection for genes and gene sequences may hamper third party technology developments (Wolfrum et al. 2002: 42ff.). In the issue-area of biotechnology, a further restriction applies, as countries of origin claim sovereign resource rights on genetic material situated within their jurisdiction.[5]

An example: plant genetic resources and the decline of the public domain

The impact of intensified protection of intellectual property and the creation of additional entitlements can be exemplified by the case of plant genetic resources, i.e. the genetic material required to grow plants for food and agriculture and to further develop such plants by means of breeding.

For a long time, such plant genetic resources have been freely available in most cases, allowing for an exchange of seeds between farmers at the community level as well as between breeders and agricultural research centres around the world. However, over the last 25 years, such availability has been dramatically reduced by the establishment of property rights and similar entitlements driven by different actors and their particular interests.

Advances in plant breeding in recent decades have considerably changed patterns of agriculture and land use. New and promising plant varieties have been developed by commercial breeding companies and distributed around the world with considerable support from development assistance programmes. In many areas, such varieties replaced the cultivation of regional and local breeds and were even grown in places, which, so far, have not been cultivated at all. The resulting decline in diversity in many regions, including those, which can be considered 'centres of origin' or 'centres of crop diversity' has given rise to some concerns such as the loss of species as an input for future agricultural research and breeding as well as general environmental considerations (Perrings and Gadgil 2003). Apart from these considerations, the spread of new and commercially developed crops also had an impact on traditional forms of agriculture.

What followed was a series of impacts, negotiations and agreements that exemplify conflicting claims and interests. Legal claims put into question an exchange of seeds in the local community and the use of some portion of the harvest as propagating material.[6] Those concerns led to discussions in the FAO, which resulted in the adoption of a legally non-binding Undertaking on PGRFA in 1983.[7] Most significantly, that undertaking proclaimed that PGRFA are the 'common heritage' of mankind.[8] The common heritage principle, developed through UN negotiations concerning the uses of the deep seabed and its resources contains little more than an idea of free access and an air of distributional justice (Schrijver 1988: 87ff.). Today, it looks quite strange, that the undertaking proclaimed such a principle to be applicable to any germplasm with relevance for food and agriculture, including wild species, landraces as well as highly developed commercial varieties.[9] Indeed, the undertaking was soon modified. In 1989 the FAO Conference made it clear, that plant breeder's rights under the UPOV Convention should not be affected by the undertaking.[10] Also, it was stated, that 'the term "free access" does not mean "free of charge"'.[11] In turn, developing countries successfully asked for a recognition of the rights of farmers.[12] Two years later, the FAO conference again modified the system of the undertaking. At the FAO conference it was decided, that 'breeders' lines and farmers' breeding material should only be available at the discretion of their developers during the period of development'[13] and thereby acknowledged the proprietary character of such lines. However, in turn, the Conference decided, that 'nations have sovereign rights over their plant genetic resources'. Thus within just a few years, the former 'common heritage' has been divided up into various proprietary claims (Correa 1994; Stoll 2004). It cannot be overlooked, that the different claims made in this case clearly represent the conflicting interests involved. The recognition of plant breeder's rights and the proprietary character of breeding lines were of comfort to the breeding industry – which in those days was mainly situated in the North. The so called 'farmers' rights' and the concept of a sovereign right on genetic resources can be roughly considered a counterclaim of the South. In sum, the example amply shows, that plant genetic resources, which can be considered a public good have become the subject of claims of different stakeholders. This is likely to cause conflicts in demand, intensive negotiation and result in inefficiencies. Meanwhile, a Treaty on Plant Genetic Resources for Food and

Agriculture has been concluded to enable facilitated access to resources while accommodating the various different entitlements.

The privatization of public services

A similar development has taken place in view of public services, an area which includes communications, energy, water supply and waste disposal. Whereas the provision of such services has traditionally been taken care of by public authorities, (which had to take into account a number of public policy objectives), there is now a strong tendency to transfer such service provision to the private sector. National developments in this regard are often seconded or even initiated by international efforts to liberalize the trade in services. For example, under the WTO Agreement on Trade in Services, negotiations have been initiated on a number of services, including, for energy, water supply and even secondary education.

Summary

As has been seen, the demand for the provision of public goods at the global level is not merely caused by globalization but also results from the assignment of exclusionary rights and the privatization of public services. It has to be highlighted, that not only the latter developments but also the process of globalization are subject to policy choices and thus cannot be considered inevitable in an inescapable process of globalization. It also has to be emphasized, that choices concerning globalization, liberalization and privatization often have a sound basis. The liberalization and subsequent intensification of trade may importantly contribute to world economic growth. The assignment and strengthening of intellectual property rights may foster research and development and technological advancements around the world. Lastly, the privatization of public services may be an imperative of limited budgets and may result in a better quality and a lower price. Despite these advantages, it cannot be overlooked that such policy decisions apparently have been made without fully taking into account the resulting impact on the need for, and availability of, public goods.

The supply of global public goods

In order to provide a public good, a number of activities may be required, depending on the nature of the good at hand. Goods may need to be produced – as is the case with telecommunications, health services or food; or need to be preserved – as is the case with the environment. In many cases, the supply of a good may require some system of distribution at different levels in order to be supplied to potential beneficiaries at the local level. Of course, the supply of a public good also often requires considerable resources, both in terms of funding, technical, and organizational capacities and contributions by different actors.

States, which so far have been the major supplier of public goods, have developed different and often highly sophisticated structures to achieve successful supply. They can rely on existing administrative institutions and a system of public finance. Furthermore goods are produced, distributed and used within a well established system of economic, social, health and environmental policies and related preferences. If such goods are to be made available to beneficiaries around the world and/or require action taken in different countries, supply is considerably more complex.

Changing rather than decreasing: a new role for states

The increasing necessity to produce and/or provide public goods at the global level will most likely considerably *change* rather than reduce the role of states. While, according to the reasons outlined above, the provision of public goods within a national framework will become less relevant, there will be an increasing demand for states to commit themselves to contribute to and participate in the global production of public goods.

Such demand may quickly arise and even touch upon the status of states in the international system, as the case of international terrorism, laid out below amply, shows.

For a long time, international security issues have been dominated by the two hegemonial powers. After the fall of the Berlin Wall, the US, for obvious reasons, was not willing and probably not capable, to take on the burden of acting as a sole power providing international security on its own. Without much success, a participation and contribution of other states was discussed. The attacks of September 11, 2001 made it clear, that international terrorist organizations had come into a position to carry out strikes, which in terms of impact come close to state military actions. Also, obviously such terrorist organizations had benefited from the inability or unwillingness of states to exercise control and to effectively prevent terrorist activities.

All of a sudden it became clear that international security is a public good, which has to be provided for globally (Mendez 1999: 383ff.). Within a short period of time spanning from the international operations in Afghanistan to the Report of the Secretary General on 21 March 2005[14] and including the war in Iraq and related discussions, the role of both international institutions and the states changed considerably, both in practice as well as in terms of general concepts about statehood.

In practice, the Security Council assumed a central role in the fight against international terrorism. It not only set up an impressive institutional machinery for the coordination and cooperation of action against international terrorism[15] but also acted as a quasi-legislator by mandating all states to abide by the provisions of the international terrorism conventions, which hitherto had been ratified only by a limited number of states (Talmon 2005: 177ff.).

In terms of general concepts, the notion of sovereignty became the subject of considerable change. The International Commission on Intervention and State Sovereignty, which has been set up by the Canadian government in response to an initiative by the Secretary–General of the United Nations, voiced the idea of a 'responsibility to protect'. It based the concept on a 'recharacterization', where sovereignty is no longer exclusively a device of control, but is to be understood as 'sovereignty as responsibility'.[16] In view of the particular importance of international security and the clear-cut and far-reaching authority of the UN Security Council, such developments cannot be generalized. However, it can hardly be overlooked, that the idea of a responsibility as inherent in the concept of sovereignty has also gained relevance in view of other global public goods (Kaul et al. 2003a: 12).

Common but differentiated responsibilities

A stronger commitment of states in view of the provision of public goods at the international level requires taking into account differences in terms of resources, skills and the level development. This need is reflected by the principle of common but differentiated responsibilities of states, which has become well established in international policy-making on sustainable development and also forms part of a number of international environmental instruments (Stone 2004; Kellersmann 2000: 35ff.). Under this principle, measures have been developed to grant developing countries additional funding for measures fulfilling national environmental objectives while at the same time contributing to global environmental objectives. The international environmental funding institutions, and primarily the global environmental facility, may fund the incremental costs, which reflect the contribution of the national measure at hand to global environmental objectives. As this example may show, means and mechanisms can, and have been, developed to accommodate the different responsibilities and the potential of states in order to enable and to persuade them to participate in the provisions of public goods at the global level.

Limited relevance of traditional intergovernmental cooperation and organizations and the emerging role of private actors

Of course, the issue of providing public goods at the international level is not entirely new. International cooperation is well established in a number of sectors and can rely on long-standing institutions, in particular international organizations. Multilateral and bilateral development assistance often relates to the provision of public goods, e.g. health services or the maintenance of food security. Also, a number of international institutions are engaged in the production of normative public goods, such as technical standards, health regulations and liberalization of international trade.

However, it is highly questionable whether intergovernmental structures can meet the increasing demand for the supply of public goods at the global level. Such structures have become quite specific and efficient, but generally still have limited means, tools and financial resources.

This may be demonstrated by the case of protecting human health against threats like HIV/AIDS and other infectious diseases (Arhin-Tenkorang and Conceição 2003). The activities of existing international institutions, such as the World Health Organization (WHO) cannot be underestimated as a resource in terms of provision of the global public good human health. It has for example invaluable scientific expertise as a resource and is well equipped to design and execute programmes and campaigns. However, the enormous demand for efficient medicines clearly exceeds its resources and mandate. To provide more financial resources, the 'Global Fund to Fight AIDS, Tuberculosis and Malaria' has been established outside the WHO to finance the provision of such medicines.[17]

Furthermore, means were sought to produce such medicines at terms more favourable than the patent holders were offering. Patent law, both at the national and international level envisages such production under a non-voluntary licence. However, it turned out to be difficult to make effective use of the relevant provisions of the WTO agreement on trade-related aspects of intellectual property rights (Shaffer 2004: 463ff.). Thus, it became necessary to discuss and eventually resolve the issue through relevant WTO bodies (Abbott 2002: 470ff.). As trade is often relevant for the provision of global public goods, the WTO will very likely have to be involved in many of those issues. As these examples show, the provision of public goods at the international level often requires a combination of resources, skills, authority, regulatory policies and institutional machinery, which exceeds the limits of most international organizations.

These and many other instances of attempts at new solutions for global problems have shown that states and international organizations can hardly cope with the demand for global public goods by means of traditional forms of intergovernmental cooperation. In view of the supply of public goods at the global level, it is essential to explore and develop the potential of contributions by individuals, civic groups, society and business.

Within the issue area of environmental protection, this idea was developed long ago and embodied in the principle of sustainable development. The 1992 United Nations Conference on Environment and Development endorsed this principle, an insight of which is that the protection of the environment cannot be sufficiently achieved by governmental intervention, but needs to become an integral part of economic and social structures that govern the decision-making of private actors, particularly including consumers and businesses.

From a similar but much more limited and instrumental perspective, new concepts such as the public–private partnership highlight the potential to link public objectives with business activity. Public–private partnerships are fairly common in the field of infrastructure and the provision of public services, including energy supply, waste disposal and telecommunications. They are also fairly well established in international development cooperation and finance. The projects all have different underlying concepts regarding access and funding. However, in most cases, they envisage that the beneficiaries of a certain public good or services have to contribute to its funding. One thus has to be reminded that this form of the supply of public goods has important distributional consequences, as most of them imply that the good or service at stake is not entirely financed by public sources and made available free of charge.

Linking public goods to private benefit – biodiversity resources

A number of new approaches for the supply of public goods have been developed in view of environmental goods, especially biodiversity (Perrings and Gadgil 2003). According to the Convention on Biological Diversity, the conservation of such diversity is a common concern of mankind. There is no doubt that biodiversity has important eco-system functions and can also serve as an input for the development of agriculture and biotechnology and thus qualifies as a global public good. A number of approaches have been developed within the context of the convention in order to link the conservation of biodiversity to potential private benefits. The most important issue in this regard relates to the fact that biodiversity represents a wealth of genetic information which may be used for the development of new materials, medicines and crops. In order to provide incentives for the conservation of biodiversity, the convention endorses a sovereign right of states to determine access to genetic material and its uses, and links this right to entitlement to receiving a share of potential benefits from such uses. Thus, potential private users of such genetic or biological material, mainly including chemical and pharmaceutical companies, would have to share some of the benefits they receive with the respective country of origin.

Another mechanism envisaged by the Convention on Biological Diversity relates to traditional forms of living and agriculture which may be considered to be supportive to the conservation of biological diversity. The convention calls for the development of mechanisms to ensure that local indigenous communities practising traditional lifestyles and agriculture may profit from offering their innovations and knowledge to third parties for commercial use. Furthermore, a number of initiatives aim at exploring the potential that sustainable tourism may have in view of the conservation of biodiversity. In each of these cases, certain actors are entitled to collect benefits from the commercial uses of such public goods in order to persuade them to protect biodiversity and invest in its conservation.

Private actors also play an important role in the conservation and use of plant genetic resources for food and agriculture. As outlined above, the interests of business, public institutions and of states have made it difficult in the past to organize the conservation and availability of those resources, which represent a global public good which is highly relevant for food and agriculture at the international level. In order to bring the different actors and interests together, the International Treaty on Plant Genetic Resources for Food and Agriculture envisages a so-called 'multilateral system', which facilitates access and exchanges of such resources between international and national public institutions, mainly seed banks, and private agencies: private seed banks and private plant breeders.[18] A mechanism is envisaged to allow for a sharing of benefits, including those resulting from commercialization.

Privatization in the communications sector – satellite communication and the internet

In some areas, the supply of public goods at the global level has been fairly well-developed. International satellite communication, including INTELSAT and the INMARSAT system, which is specifically designed to meet the need for maritime communication, were developed by adding an international governmental structure to existing US initiatives and organizations. It has to be highlighted, that from the very beginning, this structure included a private element because the leading US agency was organized as a private company. Because of the fact that telecommunication providers in many countries around the world were privatized in recent years, the structure of both systems has been undergoing important changes. Today, both systems mainly rely on a cooperation between providers based on private forms.[19]

There are striking similarities to this in the development of the internet. The internet has been developed with the support of US governmental institutions which have transferred their responsibilities step by step to commercial entities. In addition, an international governance structure has been established (Brady 2003; von Bernsdorff 2003).

In sum, these examples from the telecommunications sector show that public goods may be provided for by private actors at the global level. The subsequent withdrawal of governmental resources and control obviously results from technological advances and developments around the world, which renders those services stable and affordable and reduces the need for intervention.

Public goods and social responsibility – multinational enterprises and non-governmental organizations

As the preceding considerations have amply shown, the provision of public goods at the international level importantly relies on non-governmental actors and particularly the private sector. In this regard, it has sometimes been discussed, whether the public sector may assume a more general governance role beyond engaging in the supply of particular public goods.

In this vein, a social responsibility of multinational enterprises is worth mentioning, which recently has been the subject of much discussion. There is a long history of initiatives aimed at requiring multinational enterprises to take into account social, environmental and political objectives in their overseas business operations and especially when doing business in developing countries. Currently, the OECD, the International Chamber of Commerce and a number of UN bodies have discussed and adopted standards and codes of conduct in this respect.[20] Furthermore, some attempts have been made to link the provision of certain social services to investment projects. In some cases, partnerships have been set up to provide certain public services like energy and water supply, schools and hospitals along with investment projects.

Another aspect concerning the role of the private sector in the provision of global public goods concerns rule-making and standard-setting. As is well known, such rules and standards figure as public goods – and in the case of their international character – as global public goods. It has been emphasized in this regard, that private actors may engage in rule-making and standard set-ting and thus can contribute to the further development of the international body of regulation, which is needed to cope with the effects of globalization. International merchant law and commercial arbitration often are discussed in this regard (Teubner 1997a, 1997b).

Indeed, international commercial rules and structures and procedures pro-vide for important public good and services, mainly regulation and dispute settlement. It may be added, that private entities also play an important role in the definition of commercial and industrial standards. In many states, the elaboration of technical, industrial and commercial standards has been the task of private institutions. Regional and international standard setting bodies that build on such private structures are also to be considered private entities.

A closer look at the body of law of many states may show that such law often refers to commercial practices and customs. This involvement and contribution of private actors to rulemaking and standard setting in the field of commerce, industry and technology has been, to some extent, underestimated in the past.

Regarding its future potential, however, caution is to be applied. Private standard setting and rule making, as well as dispute settlement, hitherto has been confined to issues and areas where the potential actors should be able to act on an equal footing regarding their interests and strengths. However, such private standard-setting can hardly be considered appropriate in instances where the interest of individuals and groups, who cannot fully participate in such rule making exercises appropriately, are concerned. In view of the new enthusiasm for private rulemaking within some parts of academia, it should be noted that proper stakeholder involvement is an essential precondition for private activity in this regard.

However, non-state and non-governmental action for the supply of global public goods is by no means an exclusive domain of the private sector. To the contrary, non-governmental organizations can also play an important role in this regard. Today, the role of NGOs is no longer confined to giving pub-lic information and lobbying national and international institutions. NGOs widely engage in international development cooperation by providing education; running public awareness campaigns, providing technical expertise, education and medical services. In some areas, their know-how and capacities are indispensable for fulfilling functions which are important for the provision of public goods.

Summing up: multiplicity of forms

The increasing need to produce and/or distribute public goods at the global level is likely to change the role of states and international organizations and will require the establishment of new forms of organization including non-state and non-governmental actors e.g. the private sector and NGOs. A number of rather different structures have been established for the supply of public goods at the global level. They all reflect the particular nature of the good at hand and the related interests of actors concerned.

Global governance for global public goods

The urgent demand for and the various and complex patterns of supply of public goods at the global level require adequate structures of governance.

Providing public goods is quite demanding in terms of governance. It requires complex political decisions, which include the determination of the goods to be made available to the public in terms of quality, quantity and conditions and necessitates allocating means and resources for its production and availability. Furthermore, the implementation of such decisions may be complex and involve regulatory action, institution-building, and the establishment of an adequate administrative structure for the production and distribution and funding.

Most importantly, however, decision-making on the provision of public goods requires make difficult choices. In a world of scarce resources, we cannot expect public goods to be available free and without limitations. Moreover, public goods may be conflicting by their very nature, as is the case, for instance, with intellectual property protection and public health (Shaffer 2004: 461). Ways and means have to be in place, to reconcile such conflicting priorities or to offer compensation.

Decision-making on public goods requires taking into account the positions, interests and views of various stakeholders, including potential beneficiaries as well as potential private providers. At the national level, formal political institutions and many informal network structures exist, which are competent and experienced in this regard.

The provision of public goods beyond the national framework cannot rely on similar structures (Peterson 2000: 356ff.; Kindleberger 1986: 8ff.). Also, doubts arise as to whether the existing international regimes can be considered fit to provide for such governance. Very likely, additional means and new ways have to be explored for that purpose.

Governing public goods at the European level – different conditions at the global level

In the European context, a regional structure of governance emerged, which can, by and large, be considered to provide the kind of governance required to effectively control the supply of public goods. Parallel to the progress made during the course of economic integration, the mandate and authority of the European Union was broadened in order to cover issues such as consumer protection, health, the environment, infrastructure, science and technology. Nowadays, the provision of those public goods is widely governed by European institutions. They have the authority to implement their decisions by means of legislation and administration. Furthermore, the European Parliament (although still in a limited way), represents the Union citizens as potential beneficiaries or providers of public goods. Individuals enjoy a set of rights, which they may enforce in the courts, including the European Court. With all necessary cautions, therefore, the EU system can be considered as properly addressing the need for governance beyond the national framework.

The international system certainly lacks the homogeneity which is required to develop such structures of governance. Certainly, such structures require a sound basis of common values and institutions. In terms of membership, mandate and coverage, the United Nations system might appear to come close to the idea of an international governance structure. However, with a few important exceptions, most notably in the field of collective security, the system lacks the authority to implement its decisions effectively. The United Nations thus may play an important role as a political forum but is poorly equipped to exercise all of the functions which are required to govern the provision of public goods at the global level.

Indeed, the international system to date is mainly built on states who have retained their right to exclusively create obligations through issue-specific, separate agreements and to design separate institutional structures for particular issues as they deem fit to respond to their particular interest.

The system of international regimes: a problem of a sectoral divide

Thus, in the international system, a whole number of regimes exist, which deal with particular issues. This includes regimes as powerful as the WTO or as specific as the International Plant Protection Convention. Their interrelationship is based on equality. The existence of these different regimes is due to the peculiarities of the processes of development of the international system.

Their creation and structure each reflects a particular consensus on a certain issue, agreed upon by a coalition of states within a specific setting and through specific procedures. Most regimes mirror exactly the circumstances of their creation in terms of a specific combination of subject matter, objectives, rules, decision-making procedures, mechanisms and measures. A good example here is the WTO, which is built on a quite peculiar set of issues, and reflects the different interests of states involved.

However, this sectoral structure of the international order does not easily match with the challenging task to govern the provision of public goods at the international level. Global public goods as discussed here, by their very nature, their means of production and availability and the potential choices to be made between conflicting other public goods and policy objectives often concern more than one international regime. For instance, many of the numerous environmental regimes address subjects which are closely interrelated. The conflict between the protection of biodiversity and climate-change policies may serve as an example in this respect (Matz 2005: 149ff.).

Examples concerning the WTO

Regarding a sectoral divide, the numerous difficult debates surrounding the WTO are a particularly good example which deserves elaboration. Most of the issues debated in the WTO concern some public good, e.g. human rights, human health, food security or the environment. In almost all of these debates, reference is made to other international regimes, which are established to provide for those public goods.

The environmental cases brought to WTO dispute settlement highlight this point. In the *Shrimp-Turtle* case, the Convention on International Trade in Endangered Species was at stake, because sea turtles are among those species listed in Annex 1 to the Convention as being under threat of extinction.[21] The *Swordfish* case (which was eventually settled otherwise), should have referred to the United Nations Convention on the Law of the Sea and its implementing provisions for highly migratory species and straddling stocks (Stoll and Vöneky 2002). In both of these cases, there were obviously strong links to other international regimes. However, they could not be fully explored and taken into account within the confines of the WTO dispute settlement system. Rather than explicitly referring to rules and activities of the other regimes, the dispute settlement institutions of the WTO had to stick to the laws of the WTO as a basis for their considerations. Thus, rather than referring to rules and decisions of other international bodies, the Panels and the Appellate Body had to base their decisions on Article XX of the GATT 1994. This article is a national exception type of provision, which was originally meant to allow for sovereign policy measures in certain policy areas. Thus, the international context of the measures taken hardly could be appropriately reflected.

The divide between international regimes which becomes clear at this point may be particularly significant in dispute settlement procedures. However, it is also present in other fields of activity of the organization. The previously mentioned medicines controversy can be considered a good example in this regard. The problem of providing a cure against HIV/AIDS and other infectious diseases has been discussed in a number of international regimes.

In particular, the Committee of the Covenant on Social, Economic and Cultural Rights adopted a General Comment on Article 12 of the Covenant, which deals with the right to health.[22] In this comment, the threat of infectious diseases in general and of HIV/AIDS in particular was highlighted and it was maintained that the availability and supply of effective medicines had a high priority. The comment also indicated that this high priority had to be taken into account when applying rules of patent law and non-voluntary licences in particular. This issue was later adopted by the Human Rights Commission of the United Nations[23] and discussed in greater detail in a special session of the General Assembly devoted to the problem of HIV/AIDS and other infectious diseases.[24] These two institutions also made the more precise point that the TRIPS Agreement, which envisaged granting licences for the local production of medicines for local markets, was ineffective because many developing countries have no domestic industrial capacities available which might allow for the local production of highly sophisticated pharmaceuticals. Instead these institutions propagated a solution which allows for the production of pharmaceuticals under a non-voluntary licence in one country, from where they are later imported by states where supply is needed. The problem was later addressed in a 2001 Doha WTO Ministerial Declaration[25] and an implementing decision by The General Council prior to the Cancun Ministerial Conference in 2003.[26] However, the discussion in the WTO on the one hand and in the UN institutions on the other took place separately, and the final WTO decision refers neither to the discussions and decisions in those UN bodies nor to Article 12 of the Covenant. As this may indicate, this kind of a sectoral divide between international regimes is a divide both of institutions and processes as well the underlying substantial legal considerations. It shows that international regimes largely stick to their own mandate and take limited account of discussions, decisions or rules of other quarters of the international system.

The need for coherence

This divide between regimes renders it difficult to effectively govern the provision of public goods in the very likely case that an issue at hand is related to more than one regime. This is especially the case in view of the need to set priorities and to arrange for some sort of compensation in order to accommodate conflicting interests.

A closer look at the structures and basic documents of the WTO reveals that a link to other international organizations or their activities is only envisaged in a small number of cases. These include, for instance, a link to the activities of the International Monetary System and to other international bodies with a mandate to adopt standards *inter alia* in the field of health protection, agriculture and consumer protection.

However, even in these examples the magnitude of the problem of regime divide becomes clear, as those other institutions decide and act independently. When elaborating and adoption standards, decision-making bodies are bound by the mandate of the respective international regime and therefore cannot openly discuss nor consider external effects such as potentially enormous trade implications. Nor can they devise any kind of political compensation in order to accommodate potential trade interests of members.

At this point, coming back to the development of the European Union is highly instructive. The international trade system heavily relies on external and other independent international regimes for guidance relating to the increasing number of public policy issues which result from the progressive liberalization of trade. In contrast, the mandate, the institutional structure and the resources of the European institutions were broadened to enable it to cope with the growing demand for coherent policy-making.

In some cases, attempts to achieve such coherence within the WTO can be seen: For instance, the global environmental facility which serves as the funding mechanism of several more recent environmental agreements exercises some overall coordination. However, it needs to be stressed that a number of tendencies are likely to result in a deepening of the structural divide rather than bridging the gap. The proposal for establishing a world environmental organization (Peterson 2000: 360ff.), for instance, while certainly possessing the potential to coordinate and harmonize existing environmental regimes, is clearly understood as an institution to counter the activities of the WTO rather than facilitate coordination. As mentioned above, governance for global public goods probably likely requires the adoption of a cross-sectoral approach, which implies that different aspects be taken into account which have so far been taken care of by different international regimes.

Thus, international organizations may contribute to the governance of global public goods by contribution each in the confines of a mandate. However, such institutions seem hardly fit for serving as a comprehensive forum to explore, discuss and decide on such issues.

Conclusion

Within the confines of a sectoral divide, the ability of international organizations to cope with new developments and the need for cross-cutting approaches is declining. States are likely to play a more important role, as they have the power to direct international bodies to liaise and establish linkages as they deem fit and to allocate funds according to their proper priorities. This important role also entails a responsibility to devise a structure of the international system, which is coherent and effective.

However, it seems all but clear that states are aware of this responsibility. At the national level, as has been shown, states have an important role to play in the provision of public goods and perform related functions of governance. Notwithstanding the many biases and intricacies of the proper reflection and representation of interests in a political system, national political institutions fulfil the task of determining the common national interest and act accordingly. However, at the international level, the conduct of states is likely to be much more oriented towards their national interests. While their activities at the national level are driven by some idea of a common national interest, in international discussions, negotiations and decision-making, they are likely to end up as stakeholders. This aspect is likely to be of critical importance for the governance of global public goods because, as explained above, there is a general tendency to shift the supply for public goods from the national to the global level.

As has been shown, public goods are supposed to serve individual beneficiaries. The proper supply of such goods requires that the specific situations and the preferences of such individual beneficiaries are taken into account. Furthermore, such supply has to rely on private contributions – be it by individuals or private business actors. They can provide important input to the governance related to the supply of such public goods. While a number of formal and informal political and administrative structures exist at the national level in order to take care of this need, the provision of public goods at the global level cannot rely on such favourable structures. Traditionally, states and their governments were entrusted with the task to properly reflect the preferences, needs and the potential of individuals at the international level. However, they can hardly be deemed fit to adequately exercise this function in view of the growing complexities of international politics and the challenging demand to govern the provision of global public goods.

Obviously, a more comprehensive and inclusive structure of international policy-making is required, which enables potential beneficiaries and providers of public goods to be more adequately involved.[27] This need becomes even more apparent when considering that recent developments highlight the relevance of the individual and his/her rights. The right to food, the right to water, the farmers' rights and the right to health may serve as examples in this regard. This coincides with a renaissance of the more classical social human rights, witnessed by the recent activities of the Committee on the Convention on Economic, Social and Cultural Rights.

However, in view of the fact that a public good may be relevant for a potentially vast number of beneficiaries all over the world, any direct involvement of those individuals in decision-making seems to be impossible. More likely, there will be a need to develop some political structures which represent the preferences, needs and the potential of the various possible stakeholders. Importantly, it has to be taken into account that the supply of a public good relies on local, national and regional activities and structures even if that public good is to be considered a global one.

The challenge of building up a structure of governance for global public goods is therefore one of establishing the necessary linkage between very different types of actors all acting upon their own proper roles. As shown, the different international organizations to be involved can hardly communicate and coordinate on their own. The preparedness and ability of states to act as actors in the common interest is fairly limited. Furthermore, the provision of global public goods has to take into account the needs, preferences and the potential of individuals around the world. Non-governmental organizations already play an important role in order to foster awareness and to exercise political influence to bring the view, the potential and the preferences of those different actors together. They are very likely to need to play an even bigger role in the future. To this end, however, it would be necessary that their role be more adequately defined.[28]

Notes

1. See Kaul in this volume.
2. In 2003, France and Sweden did set up jointly an International Task Force for Global Public Goods, see: www.gpgtaskforce.org/. An International Policy Workshop on Global Public Goods, Concepts, Experience, Financing has been held by the German Development Policy Forum in 2001, www.dse.de\ef\gpg\index.htm.
3. The same holds true, of course, for the national level. See, for a German perspective: Engel (1997) passim.
4. See the ongoing discussion on the Proposal for a European Directive on the patentability of computer-implemented inventions, EU Doc. COM (2002) 92 final of 20.02.2002.
5. See section on 'Linking public goods to private benefit', below.
6. See the Final Report of the Commission on Intellectual Property Rights, London 2002, www.iprcommission.org/papers/pdfs/final_report/CIPRfullfinal. pdf [last visited 05.05.2005] at 57 et seq.; Correa (1999).
7. ftp://ext-ftp.fao.org/ag/cgrfa/iu/iutextE.pdf [visited 05/05/2005]. See Himmighofen (2000).
8. Art. 1 of the Undertaking reads: 'The objective of this Undertaking is to ensure that plant genetic resources of economic and/or social interest, particularly for agriculture, will be explored, preserved, evaluated and made available for plant breeding and scientific purposes. This Undertaking is based on the universally accepted principle that plant genetic resources are a heritage of mankind and consequently should be available without restriction.'
9. Art 2.1 of the Undertaking reads: 'In this Undertaking: (a) "plant genetic resources" means the reproductive or vegetative propagating material of the following categories of plants: (i) cultivated varieties (cultivars) in current use and newly developed varieties; (ii) obsolete cultivars; (iii) primitive cultivars (land races); (iv) wild and weed species, near relatives of cultivated varieties; (v) special genetic stocks (including elite and current breeders' lines and mutants);…'
10. Resolution 4/89 of the 25th Session of the FAO Conference, adopted on 29 November 1989, ftp://ext-ftp.fao.org/waicent/pub/cgrfa8/Res/C4-89E.pdf.
11. FAO Res. 4/89 Art. 5 (a).
12. Resolution 5/89 of the FAO Conference, ftp://ext-ftp.fao.org/waicent/pub/cgrfa8/Res/C5-89E.pdf.
13. Resolution 3/91, of the 26th Session of the FAO Conference, adopted on 25 November 1991, ftp://ext-ftp.fao.org/waicent/pub/cgrfa8/Res/C3-91E.pdf.

14. In larger freedom: towards development, security and human rights for all, Report of the Secretary-General, A/59/2005.
15. Under Resolution 1373 a Counter-Terrorism Committee has been established under the UN Security Council.
16. The Responsibility to Protect, Report of the International Commission on Intervention and State Sovereignty, Ottawa 2001. Para 2.14 reads in part: '... there is a necessary re-characterization involved: from sovereignty as control to sovereignty as responsibility in both internal functions and external duties'.
17. For details see Matthews (2004) at 103 et seq.
18. See ftp://ext-ftp.fao.org/ag/cgrfa/it/ITPGRe.pdf and generally: www.fao.org/ag/cgrfa/itpgr.htm, Mekouar (2001); Cooper (2002); Stoll (2004).
19. Thus the operation of the international satellite organizations has been privatized. Thereby, the participating states became shareholders of the newly established, private enterprise. Polley (2002); Einhorn (1998).
20. See in this volume: Cutler, Haufler, and Utting.
21. See United States – Import Prohibition of Certain Shrimp and Shrimp Products, WT/DS58/AB/R at para. 25.
22. Committee on Economic, Social and Cultural Rights (CESCR), General Comment No. 14 (2000) , The right to the highest attainable standard of health, E/C.12/2000/4, 11 August 2000.
23. Access to medication in the context of pandemics such as HIV/Aids, Resolution 2001/33 of 23 April 2001.
24. S-26, A/RES/S-26/2, 27 June 2001.
25. Declaration on the TRIPS Agreement and Public Health, WT/MIN(01)/DEC/W/2, 14 November 2001.
26. Implementation of paragraph 6 of the Doha Declaration on the TRIPS Agreement and public health, Decision of the General Council of 30 August 2003, WT/L/540.
27. See Rittberger / Huckel / Rieth / Zimmer, in this volume.
28. See Anheier and Themudo, and Benedek in this volume.

References

Abbott, F. M. (2002): The Doha Declaration on the TRIPS Agreement and Public Health: Lighting a Dark Corner at the WTO. *Journal of International Economic Law*: 469–505.

Arhin-Tenkorang, D. and P. Conceição (2003): Beyond Communicable Disease Control: Health in the Age of Globalization. In: Kaul I. et al. (eds.), *Providing Global Public Goods*. New York et al.: Oxford University Press: 484–515.

Bernstorff, J. von (2003): Democratic Global Internet Regulation? Governance Networks, International Law and the Shadow of Hegemony. *European Law Journal* 9(4): 511–26.

Brady, G. L. (2003): International Governance of the Internet: an Economic Analysis. *New Economy Handbook* 1025–41.

Brunnée, J. (1989): 'Common Interests' – Echoes from an Empty Shell – Some Thoughts on Common Interests and International Environmental Law". *Zeitschrift für ausländisches öffentliches Recht und Völkerrecht* 49: 791–808.

Cooper, H. D. (2002): The International Treaty on Plant Genetic Resources for Food and Agriculture. *Review of European Community & International Environmental Law* 11(1): 1–16.

Correa, C. M. (1994): Sovereign and Property Rights Over Plant Genetic Resources. Background Study Paper No. 2, Commission on Plant Genetic Resources, FAO, Rome, ftp://ext-ftp.fao.org/ag/cgrfa/BSP/bsp2E.pdf.

Correa, C. M. (1999): Access to Plant Genetic Resources and Intellectual Property Rights. Background Study Paper No. 8, Commission on Plant Genetic Resources, FAO, Rome, ftp://ext-ftp.fao.org/ag/cgrfa/BSP/bsp8E.pdf.

Einhorn, M. A (1998): Restructuring and Competition in International Telecommunications: the Case of INTELSAT. *Information Economics and Policy* 10(2): 197–218.

Engel, C. (1997): Das Recht der Gemeinschaftsgüter. *Die Verwaltung* 30: 429–79.

Himmighofen, W. (2000): Work Going on in the FAO. In: Wolfrum, R. and P. T. Stoll (eds.), *European Workshop on Genetic Resources Issues and Related Aspects*. Berlin: Berichte des Umweltbundesamtes, 5/2000: 173 ff.

Kaul, I., I. Grunberg and M. A. Stern (1999) (eds.): *Global Public Goods – International Cooperation in the 21st Century*. New York et. al.: Oxford University Press.

Kaul, I., I. Grunberg and M.A. Stern (2001): *Global Public Goods: International Cooperation in the 21st Century*. New York: Oxford University Press.

Kaul, I., P. Conceição, K. Le Goulven and R. U. Mendoza (eds.) (2003): Providing Global Public Goods. Managing Globalization. New York et al.: Oxford University Press.

Kaul, I., P. Conceição, K. Le Goulven and R. U. Mendoza (2003a): Why Do Global Public Goods Matter Today? In: Kaul, I. et al. (eds.), *Providing Global Public Goods*. New York et al.: Oxford University Press: 2–20.

Kellersmann, B. (2000): *Die gemeinsame, aber differenzierte Verantwortlichkeit von Industriestaaten und Entwicklungsländern für den Schutz der globalen Umwelt*. Berlin et. al.: Springer.

Kindleberger, C. P. (1986): International Public Goods without International Government. *American Economic Review* 76(1): 1–13.

Matthews, D. (2004): WTO Decision on Implementation of Paragraph 6 of the Doha Declaration on the TRIPS Agreement and Public Health: a Solution to the Access to Essential Medicines Problem? *Journal of International Economic Law*, 73–107.

Matz, N. (2005): *Wege zur Koordinierung völkerrechtlicher Verträge: völkervertragsrechtliche und institutionelle Ansätze*. Berlin et al.: Springer.

Mekouar, M. A. (2001): Treaty Agreed on Agrobiodiversity: the International Treaty on Plant Genetic Resources for Food and Agriculture. *Environmental Policy and Law* 32(1): 20–5.

Mendez, R. P. (1999): Peace as a Global Public Good. In: Kaul I. et al. (eds.), *Global Public Goods*. New York et al.: Oxford University Press: 382–416.

Perrings, C. and M. Gadgil (2003): Conserving Biodiversity: Reconciling Local and Global Public Benefits. In: Kaul, I. et al. (eds.), *Providing Global Public Goods*. New York et al.: Oxford University Press: 532–55.

Peterson, E. and F. Wesley (2000): The Design of Supranational Organizations for the Provision of International Public Goods: Global Environmental Protection. *Review of Agricultural Economics* 22(2): 355–69.

Polley, I. (2002): *INTELSAT: Restrukturierung einer internationalen Telekommunikationsorganisation*. Berlin: Duncker & Humblot.

Schrijver, N. J. (1988): Permanent Sovereignty over Natural Resources versus the Common Heritage of Mankind: Complementary or Contradictory Principles of International Economic Law? In: de Waart et al. (eds.), *International Law and Development*. Dordrecht: Kluwer: 87.

Shaffer, G. (2004): Recognizing Public Goods in WTO Dispute Settlement: Who Participates? Who Decides? *Journal of International Economic Law* 7: 459–82.

Stoll, P. T. (2004): The FAO 'Seed Treaty' – New International Rules for the Conservation and Sustainable Use of Plant Genetic Resources for Food and Agriculture. *Journal of International Biotechnology Law* 1: 239–43.

Stoll, P. T. and S. Vöneky (2002): The Swordfish Case: Law of the Sea vs. Trade. *Zeitschrift für Ausländisches Öffentliches Recht und Völkerrecht* 62: 21–35.

Stone, C. D. (2004): Common but Differentiated Responsibilities in International Law. *American Journal of International Law* 98(2): 276–301.

Talmon, S. (2005): The Security Council as World Legislative. *American Journal of International Law* 99(1): 175–93.

Teubner, G. (1997a): 'Global Bukowina': Legal Pluralism in the World Society. In: Teubner, G. (ed.), *Global Law without a State*. Aldershot et. al.: Dartmouth.

Teubner, G. (1997b): Breaking Frames: the Global Interplay of Legal and Social Systems. *American Journal of Comparative Law* 45: 149.

Wolfrum, R. (1984): *Die Internationalisierung staatsfreier Räume: die Entwicklung einer internationalen Verwaltung für Antarktis, Weltraum, Hohe See und Meeresboden*. Berlin et. al.: Springer.

Wolfrum, R., P. T. Stoll and S. L. Franck. (2002): *Die Gewährleistung freier Forschung an und mit Genen und das Interesse an der wirtschaftlichen Nutzung ihrer Ergebnisse*. Frankfurt am Main et al.: Lang.

Part 3
Civil Society and Global Governance

5
International NGOs: Scale, Expressions and Governance

Helmut K. Anheier, Nuno S. Themudo

Introduction

The last few decades have witnessed the expansion of non-profit or non-governmental organizations (NGOs) at, and to, levels unknown in the past, accounting for about 6% of total employment in OECD countries (Salamon et al. 1999). While most remain domestic organizations, some NGOs are increasingly international in their scope and have grown into veritable global actors (Anheier et al. 2001; Clark 2003; Lewis 2001; Lindenberg and Bryant 2001). Oxfam, Save the Children, Amnesty International, Friends of the Earth, the Red Cross and Greenpeace have become the 'brand-names' among international NGOs (INGOs) with significant budgets, political influence and responsibility. Indeed, NGOs dedicated to international relief and development have combined expenditures totalling over US$13 billion, which approximately equals the official aid budget of the United States.[1]

The growth of INGOs into global actors has brought new governance and organizational challenges (Clark 2003; Lindenberg and Bryant 2001; Young 1992). Some are characteristic of NGOs generally, and have become amplified by increased size, professionalization and other changes associated with *growth*. Others, however, seem generic to the *transnational* character of INGOs and appear closely linked to the complexity of the diverse political, economic and cultural environments in which they operate. Specifically:

- At the organizational governance level, critical challenges develop from the need to remain accountable to a diverse and dispersed membership base, which poses crucial questions of membership, internal democracy, accountability, effectiveness and legitimacy.
- At the managerial level, INGOs are not only facing problems associated with increased organizational size, they are also operating in a more competitive funding environment (Lindenberg 1999), and facing increasing needs in the developing world.

- At the policy level, challenges emerge from the variety of expressions of INGOs and the different policy contexts in which they operate.
- At the global governance level, challenges centre around the question of how INGOs fit into the system of international relations.

The purpose of this chapter is to explore these issues and suggest some of their implications for global civil society. To do so, we will first present an overview of INGOs' changing scale and scope, and look at key policy settings and civil society expressions, before turning to governance and management issues.

The contours of INGOs

Global civil society includes a vast array of NGOs, voluntary associations, non-profit groups, charities and interest associations, in addition to more informal forms of organizing such as international social movements and campaigns, Diaspora networks, 'dot-causes', and social forums. It is useful to think of INGOs as the organizational infrastructure of global civil society, connecting its different parts and giving shape to it.

Quantitative information on the scale of INGO operations is still patchy and limited to very basic indictors such as numbers of organizations and field of activity. The limitations of such counts becomes clear when we compare the number of the some 48,000 INGOs that were included in the Union of International Associations (UIA) database in 2001 (UIA 2003: 3) with the UNCTAD (2001) estimates of slightly over 60,000 transnational corporations (TNCs) for the same year. Although these respective numbers may not seem not far apart, measures of economic scale, such as organizational income or employment, would obviously dwarf the INGO totals. At the same time, as many have argued, INGO presence, operations and impact are not primarily economic. Non-economic aspects such as membership base, volunteers, clients served, people mobilized, or indicators of achievements in terms of social and political change would be more in line with the organizational characteristics and *raison d'être* of civil society organizations like INGOs (Clark 2003). To obtain a fuller picture of the contours of INGOs and their role within global civil society, we examine below their scale, dispersal, organizational links and composition.

Scale

Unfortunately, comprehensive financial and employment data on INGOs are not available to us at the transnational level and we are therefore limited to examining different facets of the phenomenon. Based on data collected by the UIA, INGO numbers grew exponentially from 13,000 in 1981 to over 47,000 by 2001 (Anheier and Themudo 2002). Another set of data provided by the Johns Hopkins Comparative Non-profit Project (Anheier and Salamon

2003, Salamon and Anheier 1996) aims to measure basic economic indicators on the size of international non-profit organizations in a broad cross-section of countries. These data allow us to fathom at least some aspects of the scale of INGO activities, albeit from a country-based perspective. For the 28 countries for which such data are available, INGOs amount to 1–2% of total non-profit sector employment, or 134,000 full-time equivalent jobs. They also attracted a large number of volunteers, who represent another 154,000 jobs on a full-time basis.

For some countries, it is possible to examine INGO growth. Between 1990 and 1995, employment in INGOs in France grew by 8% (Archambault et al. 1999: 89), over 10% in Germany (Priller et al. 1999: 115), and by over 30% in the UK (Kendall and Almond 1999: 188). Even though the data is limited, the resulting pattern is in line with some of the other evidence we present below: the activities of international non-profit organizations have expanded significantly, and, while they continue to represent a small portion of national non-profit economies, their share has nonetheless increased.

In terms of revenue structure, INGOs, as measured by the Johns Hopkins team, receive 29% of their income through fees and charges, including membership dues, 35% from both national and international governmental organizations in the form of contracts, grants and reimbursements, and 36% through individual, foundation or corporate donations. With volunteer input factored in as a monetary equivalent, the donation component increases to 58% of total 'revenue', which makes the international non-profit field the most 'voluntaristic and donative' parts of the non-profit sector after religious non-profit (73%), national civic and advocacy (56%), and national environmental groups (56%). Significantly, it is far more 'voluntaristic and donative' than domestic service-providing non-profit organizations.

This suggests that INGOs benefit more from volunteer commitment and general mobilization of the population behind particular international causes (e.g., human rights; humanitarian assistance; international development; peace and international understanding) than more conventional non-profit organizations in social services, culture and the arts or housing, which are increasingly financed by the public sector and commercial revenue sources.

The pronounced donative and volunteer element also applies to INGOs of significant size and with complex organizational structures that span many countries and continents (Anheier and Themudo 2002; Anheier and Katz 2003). Examples include Amnesty International with more than 1.8 million members, subscribers and regular donors in over 150 countries. The Friends of the Earth Federation combines about 5,000 local groups and one million members. The International Union for the Conservation of Nature brings together 735 NGOs, 35 affiliates, 78 states, 112 government agencies, and some 10,000 scientists and experts from 181 countries in a unique worldwide partnership. Much of the work undertaken by these INGOs is done on a volunteer basis.

INGOs' share of foreign aid flows has increased significantly since the 1970s. At that time INGO aid, including both private and official aid channelled through INGOs, was 11% of all aid flows from OECD countries to developing countries. In the late 1990s, INGO aid totalled over US$13 billion (Fowler 2000) equivalent to around 23% of total aid flows (see UNDP 2003, chapter 8, for official aid flows). Most of the growth took place in the 1990s, a period which coincides the significant expansion of INGO operations more generally. In the 1990s, INGO contributions increased in both relative and absolute terms as official aid flows decreased.

The change in the economic weight and political importance of INGOs is highlighted even further when we look at the composition of INGO aid flows, using estimates compiled by Clark (2003: 130). Whereas in the 1980s, INGOs increasingly became an additional avenue for official development and humanitarian assistance flows, the 1990s saw a reversal of this trend: official aid flows declined overall, as did their channelling via INGOs. Official grants to INGOs fell from US$2.4 billion in 1988 to US$1.7 billion in 1999 (measured in 1990 US dollars). By contrast, private donations, including individual, foundation and corporate contributions, more than doubled from $4.5 to $10.7 billion. These figures underscore the significant expansion of INGOs in the changing development field of the 1990s, and the private mobilization effort they represent.

Dispersal

The growth of INGOs and their organizational presence is, of course, not equally spread across the world. Not surprisingly, Europe and North America show the greatest numbers of INGOs and higher membership densities than other regions of the world (Anheier and Katz 2003). Nevertheless, as we will show below, although cities in Europe and the United States still serve as INGO capitals of the world, a long-term dispersion process has decreased the concentration of INGOs to the effect that they are now more evenly distributed around the world.

INGO memberships increased in all regions, but more in some than in others. The highest expansion rates are in Central and Eastern Europe, including Central Asia, followed by East Asia and Pacific. The growth in Central and Eastern Europe is clearly linked to the fall of state socialism and the introduction of freedom of association, whereas the growth in Asia is explained by economic expansion and democratic reform in many countries of the region. INGO membership growth in relation to economic development shows that growth rates throughout the 1990s were higher in middle-income countries (East Asia, Central and Eastern Europe, parts of Latin America) than in the high-income countries of Western Europe, Pacific and North America. What is more, the expansion rate of INGOs in low-income countries is higher than that for richer parts of the world (Anheier and Katz 2003).

To further illustrate the process of dispersion, it is useful to review some basic patterns of NGO locations over time, and to go back briefly to the beginnings of modern NGO development. In 1906, only two of the 169 INGOs (2%) had their headquarters outside Europe; by 1938, 36 of the 705 existing INGOs (5%) were located outside Europe. By 1950, with a significant increase of US-based INGOs, and with the establishment of the United Nations 124 of the 804 existing INGOs (15%) were not based in Europe. With the independence movement and the generally favourable economic climate of the 1950s and early 1960s, the number of INGOs increased to 1,768, of which 83% were located in Europe, 10% in the United States, and between 1–2% in each of the following regions; Asia, South America, Central America, Africa, Middle East and Australia (Tew 1963).

By 2001, much of this concentration had given way to a more decentralized pattern around an emerging bipolar structure of INGOs, with two centres: Western Europe and North America (Anheier and Katz 2003). Europe still accounts for the majority of INGO headquarters, followed by the United States, but other regions such as Asia and Africa have gained ground. Nonetheless, among the ten countries hosting the greatest number of intercontinental organization headquarters in 2001, we find eight European countries (United Kingdom, France, Switzerland, Belgium, Netherlands, Germany, Italy, and Austria), next to the USA and Canada (UIA 2002/3: Vol. 5: 81).

In terms of cities, by 2001 the traditional role of Paris as preferred headquarters to INGOs (729) has hardly diminished in absolute terms, with other European and American cities also being major INGO headquarter cities including London (807), Brussels (1,392), Geneva (272), and New York (390). They are however less dominant in relative terms: over ten other cities in four continents have more than 100 INGO headquarters and another 35 on five continents have over 50 (Anheier and Katz 2003).

Together, these data indicate that the growth of the organizational infrastructure of global civil society does not involve concentration but dispersion, and points to inclusion rather than exclusion. In organizational terms, global civil society today is a less Western-based phenomenon than in the past. Significant growth rates of recent years led to expansion outside North America and the European Union. Using terms coined by David Held (1999), the organizational infrastructure of global civil society (INGOs) has attained wider reach (extensity) and higher density (intensity) (Anheier and Katz 2003).

Organizational links

The infrastructure of global civil society in terms of INGOs has not only become broader in geographical coverage (scale), it also became much more interconnected. In 2001, the UIA reported over 90,000 such links among NGOs, and 38,000 between INGOs and international governmental organizations.[2] The average number of links jumped from an average of 6.7 in 1990 to 14.1 in 2000 – an increase of 110%. The infrastructure of global civil society has not only become bigger and broader, it has also achieved greater density and connectedness. These links measure a range of inter-organizational activities from consultations, joint projects and financing to publications and outreach campaigns. The data also suggest that INGOs have become more interconnected with international institutions of global governance like the United Nations or the World Bank.

Composition

Next to scale and connectedness, field of activity or purpose is another important dimension in describing the infrastructure of global civil society. When looking at the purpose or field in which INGOs operate, we find that among the INGOs listed in 2001 by the UIA, two fields dominate: economic development and economic interest associations (26.1%) and knowledge-based NGOs in the area of research and science (20.5%). At first, the pronounced presence of these activities and purposes among INGOs comes as a surprise, yet it is in the these fields that need for international cooperation, exchange of information, standard-setting and other discourses have been long felt. There are thousands of scholarly associations and learned societies that span the entire range of academic disciplines and field of human learning. Likewise, there is a rich tradition of business and professional organizations reaching across national borders, from international chambers of commerce, consumer associations, and professional groups in the field of law, accounting, trade, engineering, transport, civil service and health care.

Indeed, the earliest available tabulation of INGOs by purpose, lists 639 organizations in 1924, with nearly half being either economic interest associations (172) or learned societies and research organizations (238) (Otlet 1924). Only 55 organizations fell into the category 'political', 28 in 'sports', 25 in 'religion', and 14 in 'arts and culture'. In other words, the political, humanitarian, moral or religious value component to INGOs is a more recent phenomenon. Although some of the oldest humanitarian organizations date back to the nineteenth century, i.e., the Red Cross or the Anti-Slavery Society, their widespread and prominent presence at a transnational level is a product of the latter part of the twentieth century.

By 2002, value-based NGOs in the areas of law, policy and advocacy (12.6%), politics (5.2%), religion (5.2%), made up the second largest activity component, with a total of 23% all INGOs. This is followed by a service provisions cluster, in which social services, health, and education together account for 21% of INGO purposes. Smaller fields like culture and the arts (6.6%), the environment (2.9%), and defence and security make up the balance (Anheier and Katz 2003).

Yet next to a greater emphasis on values, the changes in the composition of purposes that took place in the 1990s, brought a long-standing yet often overlooked function of INGOs to the forefront: service delivery has become a visible and important part of INGOs. Indeed, social services as a purpose grew by 79% between 1990 and 2000, health services by 50%, and education by 24%. This function of INGOs is primarily connected to the public management expression of global civil society, which we outlined below.

Although INGOs only provide a partial picture of global civil society, looking at INGO data shows that the infrastructure of global civil society has expanded significantly since 1990, both in terms of scale and connectedness. The relative focus on these organizations, taken together, shifted more towards value-based activities and service provision. Overall, the expansion of INGOs and the value-activity shift, imply both quantitative and qualitative changes in the contours and role of global civil society organizations, which are manifested in the various expressions of global civil society.

Expressions of global civil society

One of the main characteristics of global civil society, celebrated by some, deplored by others, is its multifaceted nature. We believe it is helpful to think about global civil society not just in terms of its scale and scope, but also through the various forms in which it manifests itself.[3] Examining different expressions of global civil society helps us to better understand the organizational options of INGOs.

The first is the *new public management* expression, which is part of the modernization of welfare states currently underway in most developed market economies and via World Bank, EU and IMF policy prescriptions. It is also affecting the social welfare systems in developing countries and transition economies. At the international level, new public management is replacing conventional development assistance policies (Deacon et al. 1997; Clark 2003) and seeks to capitalize on what is viewed as the comparative efficiency advantages of non-profit organizations through public–private partnerships, competitive bidding and contracting out under the general heading of privatization.

The main actors involved in this approach, are the professionalized organizational components of global civil society, in other words, NGOs and INGOs. Prompted in part by growing doubts about the capacity of the state to cope with its own welfare, developmental and environmental problems, political analysts across the political spectrum have come to see NGOs as a strategic middle way between policies that put primacy on 'the market' and those that advocate a greater reliance on the state (Giddens 1999). Institutions like the World Bank (Fowler 2000), the United Nations (UNDP 2002) or the European Union (1997), together with bilateral donors and many developing countries, are searching for a balance between state-led and market-led approaches to development, and are allocating more responsibility to INGOs. It is therefore hardly surprising that, as described above, service-provision has been the fastest growing area of INGO activities in the 1990s.

With the rise of new public management, the emphasis on NGOs as service providers and instruments of privatization casts them essentially in a sub-contracting role. Consequently, many NGOs have become instruments of national and international welfare state reform guided by the simple equation of 'less government = less bureaucracy = more flexibility = greater efficiency' (Kettle 2000).

For some, the new public management expression is associated with co-option (Chandhoke 2002). This takes different forms. In some cases, NGOs are artificially created, as a fig leaf for states unable or unwilling to act. In other cases, NGOs are supported if not created by international donors and institutions, and then hand-picked during consultation rounds, to provide a semblance of democratic legitimacy for the institution.

Now perhaps more frequent than new public management is global civil society's *corporate* expression. This expression is caused by the 'corporatization' of NGOs as well as the expansion of business into local and global civil society. It consists of two aspects. On the one hand, corporations use extended social responsibility programmes to provide, jointly with non-profit organizations, services previously in the realm of government (health care, child care, and pensions, but also community services more widely) (Perrow 2001, 2002). On the other hand, many NGOs are increasingly 'professionalizing' (Lewis 2001). Guided by management gurus they increasingly adopt corporate strategies, and are increasingly open to partnerships with business. We suggest that the corporatization of NGOs will gather momentum, encouraged by a resource-poor international community eager to seek new forms of cooperation, particularly in development assistance and capacity building.

Given that a significant share of the world's 100 largest 'economies' are TNCs, there are growing 'points of contact' between global businesses and INGOs (Lindenberg and Bryant 2001). TNCs and INGOs often work together in addressing global problems (e.g., environmental degradation, malnutrition, low skills and education levels) as well as many local issues in failed states and areas of civic strife and conflict. Cases in point are the partnerships between the Rainforest Alliance and Chiquita and between Greenpeace and Innogy to build an offshore wind farm in the UK.

Partly as a reaction to, and partly as an implication of, neoliberal policies and 'lean states,' public opinion in developed market economies is expecting greater corporate responsibility and a higher degree of 'caring' on behalf of multinational corporations about the societies in which they operate. Increasingly, this is expected to go beyond adherence to principles of corporate governance and core principles of conduct; it implies greater emphasis on service delivery to employees and their communities (e.g., educational programmes, child care), addressing negative externalities or the 'bads' produced by business operations (e.g., pollution, resource depletion), and public goods (health, sustainability). Willingly or reluctantly, companies and NGOs team up to divide responsibilities the state is failing to meet.

A third expression of global civil society is *social capital* or self-organization. Here the emphasis is not so much on management as on building relations of trust and cohesion. It is based on the idea that norms of reciprocity are embodied in transnational networks of civic associations. What is important, according to this approach, is that self-organization across borders creates social cohesion within transnational communities. In contrast to the basically neoliberal role NGOs assume in the public management expression, in this expression they are linked to the perspective of a 'strong and vibrant civil society characterized by a social infrastructure of dense networks of face-to-face relationships that cross-cut existing social cleavages such as race, ethnicity, class, sexual orientation, and gender that will underpin strong and responsive democratic government' (Edwards, Foley and Diani 2001: 17). Norms of reciprocity, citizenship, and trust are embodied in national and transnational networks of civic associations. Put simply, the essence of this expression is: civil society creates social capital, which is good for society and good for economic development.

According to this view, NGOs are to create, as well as facilitate, a sense of trust and social inclusion that is seen as essential for the functioning of modern societies both nationally (e.g. Putnam 2000; Anheier and Kendall 2002; Dasgupta and Serageldin 2000; Offe and Fuchs 2002) as well as transnationally (Lindenberg and Bryant 2001; Edwards and Gaventa 2001). The main argument is that participation in voluntary associations, including social movements, creates greater opportunities for repeated 'trust-building' encounters among like-minded individuals, an experience that is subsequently generalized to other situations such as business or politics. Thus, what could be called the Neo-Tocquevillian case for NGOs is largely an argument based on the positive and often indirect outcomes of associationalism.

The final form is the *activist* expression.Here the main actors are social movements, transnational civic networks and social forums. INGOs play key roles as mobilizing structures within these organized efforts (Smith et al. 1994). They are as a source of dissent, challenge and innovation, a countervailing force to government and the corporate sector (Keane 2001). They serve as a social, cultural and political watchdog keeping both market and state in check, and they contribute to and reflect the diversity, pluralism and dynamism of the modern world.

The first two expressions – new public management and corporatization – are more top-down and professional. As we shall show, they dominated global civil society during the last decade, and are important for providing the infrastructure for global civil society. The second two expressions – social capital and activism – are more bottom-up and have regained importance in recent years. They tend to provide the mobilizing impetus and agenda-setting component of global civil society. Different expressions of global civil society affect the organizational options of INGOs.

Governance and management challenges

Together, INGOs' increasing scale and scope and the various expressions of global civil society present important and unresolved challenges for the governance and management of these organizations. We will examine these challenges from the perspective of organizational theory, which points to the question of what kind of organizational models or structures are needed for INGO governance and management in complex task environments. We suggest that managing the tensions between multiple accountabilities and divergent efficiency expectations becomes the critical challenge of NGO governance (Anheier 2000; Anheier and Themudo 2002; Edwards 1999). Ultimately, both accountability and efficiency are needed for legitimacy and member commitment, and therefore, for organizational sustainability and survival.

This part of the chapter is exploratory in nature and uses a qualitative design to examine the governance and management issues INGOs face. We focus on some of the major 'brand-names' in the field: Amnesty International (Amnesty), Friends of the Earth (FoE), Greenpeace, and the International Federation of Red Cross and Red Crescent Societies (IFRC). They have in common that they work in multiple constituencies, have to balance divergent expectations from different stakeholders, work on politically as well as culturally sensitive topics, and face significant geographical imbalances in terms of needs and resources. We also draw on information collected on the World Wildlife Fund, Oxfam International, Human Rights Watch, the International Union for the Conservation of Nature, and the Coalition to Stop the Use of Child Soldiers. In selecting the case studies we also sought diversity: membership (e.g., Amnesty) vs. board owned (Oxfam); advocacy (FoE) vs. service delivery (IFRC), and the use of member volunteers in core activities (FoE and Amnesty) vs. supporting activities (Greenpeace and IFRC).[4]

Organizational theory

Organizational theory can be divided into strategic approaches and environmental approaches to examining organizational behaviour (Young et al. 1999). This division echoes the contrast between agency and structure approaches to the study of social phenomena found in the wider social sciences. Strategic approaches emphasize the role of organizational strategies in determining organizational behaviour, such as strategy choice, economies of scale and scope or transaction costs economizing. Environmental approaches on the other hand emphasize the role of the organizational environment or context in determining organizational behaviour, such as population ecology, resource dependence theory or neo-institutionalism.

Most INGOs tend to adopt a multilevel structure that involves local, national and international components to adapt to a complex task environment (Young et al. 1999). Because of the rights and obligations associated with membership and the presumption of internal democracy and participation in decision-making, the governance and management of INGO forms involves distinct challenges. Strategic approaches suggest the following key management challenges of INGOs: governance and internal accountability, organizational culture and organizational structure. By contrast, environmental approaches suggest legitimacy, external accountability and independence, and dealing with the South–North divide as the key management challenges.

Governance

Strategic approaches to organizational theory suggest that the type of organizational ownership and governance is critical in determining organizational goals (Perrow 1986), which are the ultimate *raison d'être* of the organization. In the case of INGOs this points to understanding different forms of organizational ownership, in particular the distinction between member control and board control. In the examples looked at here, the nature of ownership varied not only across different organizations but also surprisingly within the same organization. A clear difference was found between 'member-owned' INGOs, where members determine the governance of the organizations from the 'bottom-up', and 'board-owned' INGOs, in which the board of governance is self-appointed and retains control over critical decisions such as whether the organization will cease its operations. 'Board-owned' organizations can still refer to their individual or organizational supporters as 'members', which are seen primarily as a resource. In some INGOs like Amnesty and FoE, members have voting power and the entire organizational structure is built on membership. Members are seen as the 'owners' of the organization. By contrast, 'members' in organizations like Greenpeace and Human Rights Watch have no voting rights and little influence on organizational governance and decision-making. This usage of the term 'members' is actually meant in a vein similar to the term 'supporters' used by most other INGOs. This distinction in meaning is emblematic of deep organizational differences concerning the appropriate role for members in governance and internal accountability: members as organizational citizens versus members as clients, and membership as the organizational demos versus membership as organizational resource.

The terms 'member' and 'membership' become further complicated, almost ambiguous, through the introduction of various types of membership within the same organization. For example, Amnesty has different membership categories (individual, student and youth, family, senior citizen, affiliate organization). At one level, these distinctions make sense, in distinguishing levels of financial support, and allow Amnesty to cater to different membership 'markets' and 'niches' to maximize membership numbers and income. However, for member-owned organizations, such distinctions may create ambiguity and, from an internal democracy perspective, could lead to governance problems. What is the basis for representation claims – support for the cause or monetary support? For example, how to account for family membership as a voting category? Should a family vote as one (as is the case in Amnesty UK and Amnesty Thailand) or should each family individual have a vote despite the payment of lower fees?

For member-owned INGOs, the introduction of different forms of membership poses a challenge to internal democracy. Indeed, there appears to be a conflict between the income maximization logic and the democracy logic in the definition of different types of membership – a conflict that does not exist as such for member-supported organizations. For the latter, the problem of accountability remains at a more fundamental level: with no 'demos', and typically with a self-appointed board, the organization must address 'stakeholders' of various kinds to seek and maintain legitimacy for its activities.

Moreover there are variations in the rights of individual members within different national branches of the same organization. Such variations exist because of historical and legal conditions that influence the type of governance structure that is chosen in each national chapter of the INGO. In most national branches, Greenpeace members do not have voting power. For example, the board of Greenpeace US is self-appointed and members have no voting rights. In Spain, however, members have voting rights and elect Greenpeace Spain's board democratically (Greenpeace Spain URL). In contrast to Greenpeace, most FoE national branches are strongly committed to internal democracy, and members have voting power. In Canada, however, FoE members do not vote, and the national branch has a self-appointed board.

Membership can also be based on organizations rather than individuals. In this case it signals a degree of autonomy between organization-members and the association of organizations. Membership in the IFRC is an association of the 175 national societies, and individual membership exists at the national level only. The various national societies themselves, however, vary greatly in organizational structure and culture. Similarly the International Union for the Conservation of Nature is made up of a large number of member NGOs and other types of organizations, including even some member states.

While members provide resources and legitimacy, they also generate costs due to the increased complexity of setting organizational priorities (Rees 1998). The INGOs studied were generally very active in managing 'membership' to maximize financial benefits. Most INGOs have professional staff dedicated to collecting membership dues, dealing with requests for information, undertaking membership surveys, organizing major annual or bi-annual member meetings and producing membership newsletters. There seems to be a general tendency for member-owned INGOs to have higher management costs than member-supported INGOs (Young et al. 1999).

Thus, member-owned INGOs have higher costs associated with their members. They do not, however, generally have a clear idea of the actual costs involved and how they are countered by benefits derived from their members. We tried to obtain information of how much INGOs spent on their members, either as a whole or at the margins, i.e., the cost associated with adding one more member. Surprisingly, most of the INGOs examined did not collect such cost information. While some calculated how much was spent on individual actions such as fundraising, producing a newsletter or organizing specific events, they generally did not combine member-related expenditures in a systematic way. Amnesty was the only exception. It estimates that for fiscal year 2000–01, it spent 13% of its budget of £19.5 million[5] on 'membership support' (www.amnesty.org). There is however no estimate as to how much is spent at national and local levels. For Greenpeace USA, one interviewee estimated that membership-related costs are less than 10% of budget.

Similarly, none of the INGOs explicitly attempts to measure or identify the benefits of membership. While financial receipts are easy to calculate, the value of resources such as increased legitimacy, volunteer input or better access to information are less readily quantifiable, and the organizations that we observed did not attempt to do so. Membership benefit was seen either in simply financial terms or simply in terms of fundamental values expressed in the mission statement. Most of Amnesty's income for its budget of £19.5 million derives from membership dues and donations. So when compared with the costs of 'membership support', i.e. 13% of £19.5 million, the net economic yield of membership is very efficient.

For member-owned INGOs, having members is not however the result of a simple cost–benefit analysis and this in part helps to explain the absence of clear cost–benefit calculations. In some INGOs, like Amnesty and FoE, having a voting membership is a trait that defines their identity. Having membership-based governance was seen as more democratic, more accountable and more egalitarian reflecting qualities that they advocate in society. Both INGOs define themselves as a movement trying to emphasize a non-hierarchical structure and organizational culture rooted in 'grassroots' ideals. As Edwards et al. (1999: 133) put it: 'If NGOs are to become social actors in a global world, pushing for justice, equity, democracy and accountability, then clearly these characteristics need to be reflected in their own systems and structures.' The membership base and definition, however, must remain clear and unambiguous for internal democracy to function. At the same time, it is these structures that may generate tensions when INGOs attempt to maximize the economic benefits associated with membership.

While all organizations face governance challenges, INGOs' rapid expansion places renewed stress upon their governance systems. Expansion into new countries often calls for the adoption of different governance choices for different national chapters. This strategy allows INGOs to capitalize on different local conditions, but it may also create inconsistencies and power imbalances within the international organization, which may ultimately compromise its organizational legitimacy.

Organizational culture and legitimacy

A critical governance and management question INGOs have to face is the potential conflict between democracy and efficiency. Specifically, it is the conflict between the democratic values of inclusion and participation in decision-making on the one hand, and organizational needs for efficiency on the other. Public choice economics and the sociology of collective action (Michels 1962) have long suggested that democratic decision-making and participation may take too much time and scarce resources and it may, in the end, lead to untenable compromises. By contrast, centralized decision-making may not be sensitive to local conditions or may miss out on important information that can be essential for both legitimacy and efficiency. Edwards et al. (1999: 134) suggest that most NGOs 'try to defend the values-based approach of a global social movement inside an operational framework that drives the organization further into the marketplace. The result is unsurprising muddle and a great deal of internal tension.'

Not giving members the right to vote does not automatically mean the organization is fully 'undemocratic', since internal democratic processes may take place at different levels (local, national and international) and involve different voting actors (individuals or organizations). Greenpeace for example still elects its international board through an assembly of representatives from its national affiliates. But not all of its national affiliates have democratic procedures themselves. Amnesty and FoE, in contrast, have individual voting rights at local and national levels. In terms of international governance, the most common pattern was that national organizations (internally democratic or not) elect an international council to elect an international board that, in turn, chooses and oversees the international executive organs. None had direct individual membership voting at the global level.

Clearly, large INGOs need some form of staggered, gradual representation for their highest levels of decision-making, as meetings for over 1,000,000 members at the global level would be extremely costly to organize and would very likely exaggerate inequities and thereby threaten internal democracy. But the creation of such representation systems can create ambiguity about the rights of members in different countries. One such ambiguity exists in relation to the question of whether members have a primary membership at the national or global level. The difference is significant in terms of the equality between members across all national branches. A truly global membership implies that all members have equal rights in determining the governance of the INGO in the form of 'one person – one vote', regardless of whether a member is in Britain, Uganda or Brazil. National membership on the other hand allows members to vote only to elect national representatives who in turn can determine the governance of the INGO according to 'one organizational entity – one vote'.

Such a formula, however, leads to inequities as members in countries with lower membership numbers end up having relatively more power than those have from countries with higher numbers of members. One way to address this tension is to develop corrective measures. In this respect, Amnesty uses a very complex formula for the representation of individual members at the international level. According to the Statutes of Amnesty International as amended in 2003 (www.amnesty.org):

> [Article] 15. All sections shall have the right to appoint one representative to the International Council and in addition may appoint representatives as follows:
> 10–49 groups: 1 representative
> 50–99 groups: 2 representatives
> 100–199 groups: 3 representatives
> 200–399 groups: 4 representatives
> 400 groups and over: 5 representatives
> Sections consisting primarily of individual members rather than groups may as an alternative appoint additional representatives as follows:
> 500–2,499 members: 1 representative
> 2,500 members and over: 2 representatives.

Another critical issue in democratic governance of INGOs is the dominance of the organization by a few dedicated members. Because some members are more committed than others, all democratic membership organizations have to address the dilemma between the free-riding of uncommitted members and tendency toward elite control by core activists (Romo and Anheier 1999; Olson 1965; Michels 1962).

For example, only 0.2% of all members normally attend the general assembly of FoE-US despite efforts to increase participation rates. Low participation rates are not exclusive to INGOs. Lansley (1997) observed a similar low participation rate in the case of Britain's National Trust. This probably becomes aggravated at the international level because some national chapters may have more influence than others. The result is that a small number of core activists can dominate decision-making within national chapters and, similarly, some core national chapters can dominate decision-making at the international level. As a result, the whole organization may end up being dominated by a very small number of activists.[6]

The lack of individual participation at voting events seemed common to all the INGOs looked at here. Most members participate by paying dues only but leave aspects of governance, management and organization to other, either professional staff, trustees and board members or dedicated activists. The latter stand in danger of developing into an elite group that dominates the organization, thereby undermining democratic ideals. At the same time, many membership-based NGOs could not continue to function without core activists, who are willing to dedicate time and effort to the organization and whose unpaid commitment adds legitimacy and motivation to the organization.

This problem can be compounded by a systematic lack of participation by groups that are generally underrepresented in decision-making such as women, youths and minorities. Even NGOs interested in involving minorities tend to do so by means of canvassing new members and supporters from special minorities rather than ensuring their participation in governance. It was not possible to get a breakdown of NGO membership by major social categories (gender, ethnicity, age, etc.) for any of the organizations in focus here, so we could not ascertain how representative their membership is of the wider society in which they operate. This is however an important issue that impacts directly on the broader legitimacy that INGOs can command in democratic societies. Of the cases included here, IRFC makes the strongest systematic effort to enlist minorities and youths as part of its 'Strategy 2010' to develop well-functioning national societies (IFRC 1999).

Two main solutions emerged in response to the participation and accountability problems facing INGOs. One was to increase active, rather than total, membership, which could, however, have a detrimental effect on the organizations' revenue base and even imply economic downsizing but also loss of political influence. The second solution was transparency, particularly in the sense that the decisions of the organizational core were to be made open, easily accessible and understandable to members, including passive members and potential free-riders.[7]

A final issue concerns the relation between democracy and legitimacy. Judging by their recent successes and visibility, all of the case studies are INGOs with high levels of legitimacy. Nonetheless, how much of that legitimacy stems from their membership base is unclear. As we have seen, some INGOs like Human Rights Watch, World Wild Fund or Greenpeace define themselves as membership-based organizations and yet their members have no voting power. That does not mean members are not important to the organization.

For Greenpeace,

> Greenpeace does not accept donations from government or corporations. Our 250,000 members in the United States and 2.5 million members worldwide form the backbone of our organization. (www.Greenpeace.org)

Similarly, for WWF:

> The 1.2 million people who are members of World Wildlife Fund constitute the cornerstone of support for our ambitious conservation agenda. (WWF USA 2000 Annual Report at www.wwf.org)

'Member' for Greenpeace and WWF means (mainly financial) 'supporter'. But despite not giving its 'members' a vote, Greenpeace enjoys a very high level of legitimacy as a global actor. In a way, Greenpeace's use of the concept membership is based on identity politics and connotes 'belonging' and 'sharing a cause'. From this perspective legitimacy does not depend on whether members can vote but whether they identify with the values the INGO supports.

Thus, the legitimacy of members without vote depends on our understanding of the basis for organizational legitimacy. While Amnesty and FoE claim legitimacy through 'democratic representativeness', Greenpeace and Human Rights Watch claim legitimacy through 'extent of public support' (measured both in supporter numbers and financially). Generally, member-owned INGOs believe they are 'true' membership organizations in the spirit of 'associations' of citizens, whereas member-supported INGOs reject this interpretation. Instead, they argue, their members 'belong to the cause' and continued support for their organization demonstrates this fact.

We should recall that only a small proportion of members participate in NGO governance through exercising voting rights. With the great majority abstaining, the distinction between member-owned and member-supported INGOs may be less pronounced in reality. In board-owned INGOs, economic incentives push managers to conduct surveys of actual and potential members to gauge their preferences and opinions. Since these INGOs depend on individual contributions to organizational income they must ensure 'public support' by keeping its actions in alignment with supporter preferences. By avoiding complex governance structures extra resources are freed up and can be dedicated to the organizational mission. The cases of Greenpeace and Human Rights Watch question the view of Edwards et al. (1999: 133) that 'few NGOs have democratic systems of governance and accountability. As service providers they do not need them; as social actors they certainly do.' It seems that there are other ways of gaining legitimacy (see also Hudson 2000).

Nonetheless, the ability to vote does provide members with a voice option which non-voting members do not have. Moreover despite low participation rates members arguably will exercise their voting option when it matters most, i.e. in extreme circumstances, and in situations when important questions about the mission and the future of the organization are at stake. A case in point was the extensive discussion generated within Amnesty when, in 1999–2000, it considered expanding its advocacy focus from civic and political rights to also include social and economic rights. In either case, member voting and democratic governance may not lead to the most efficient way and means of decision-making; if democracy is held as a value and goal, then inefficiencies related to this ideal have to be taken into account.

Organizational structure: coordination vs. local responsiveness

INGOs work in different cultural, political and economic settings, often facing very different problems and organizational tasks. Efficiency requires that decisions should be made at levels where expertise and knowledge are greatest – which may not necessarily be at the central level at all (Daft 1997; Dawson 1996; Perrow 1986). Environmental variations across local chapters and national societies are high, which suggests that a decentralized mode is best suited for achieving results locally (Young 1992).

For NGOs, being locally sensitive and responsive to local realities is not only a question of efficiency. It can sometimes be a question of life or death. By dealing with repressive states that can physically endanger its members, Amnesty faces great pressures to be locally responsive:

> The Togolese authorities, whose security forces have committed human rights violations for three decades, did nothing to bring those responsible to justice and continued to enjoy impunity. Instead, after Amnesty published a report in May detailing extrajudicial executions, 'disappearances' and torture, the authorities took reprisals against human rights defenders suspected of passing information to Amnesty.... Two members of Amnesty were arrested, beaten and threatened with death while in detention.... A Nigerian member of Amnesty was detained and tortured. (Amnesty Annual Report 2000, www.amnesty.org)

This case dramatically illustrates the need for Amnesty's international secretariat to be in close communication contact with its members in Togo. It must ensure the information published is as accurate as possible and also inform its members in Togo when a sensitive report or campaign is to be launched so that they may, in turn, seek to avoid repression by the Togolese authorities. INGOs need to be sensitive to the dangers that may befall their members and workers. The best way to do so is to keep communication channels open and to enable local sections to participate in decision-making that involves them directly.

At the same time, resources are unevenly distributed across sections and tasks do not reflect levels of support available locally. In this case, centralization rather than decentralization would allow for more efficient and equitable redistribution of resources across sections and chapters. Centralization also promotes coordination and savings through economies of scale and scope. The degree of centralization is determined by the need to ensure equity in task and resource allocation, and the need to capitalize on scale and scope economies.

Other aspects affecting the degree of centralization are preferences for self-determination, protection of the global brand, pressures for global accountability, scale of impact, and technology (Lindenberg and Dobel 1999; Lindenberg and Bryant 2001). Unitary or corporate models facilitate coordination and help maintain a single clear brand identity. On the other hand weakly coordinated networks maximize organizational autonomy. The choice between more or less centralized structures is not dictated by political preferences alone. Of central importance are two factors: communication costs among units as well as between units and the core; and coordination costs for joint action. Together, these transaction costs of having a particular structure have to be balanced against the opportunity costs of acting alone or in (typically shifting) international alliances.

INGOs must find a balance between centralization and decentralization, standardization and flexibility. According to Foreman (1999: 179), however, this is a delicate balance to maintain 'as an international NGO converts national staff and board members to its mission, core values, and management style, it gradually eliminates the benefits of diversity and representation of legitimate national interests' (Foreman 1999: 194), which in turn makes the organization less sensitive to local conditions.[8]

All INGOs studied defined their own organizational structure as a federation. The management structures followed the federation model where much autonomy is retained at national level. Generally, the international core tends to be responsible for the execution of global actions, coordination of national affiliates' efforts within global actions, and provide support services such as information technology, web page maintenance, and administration. Sometimes, the core also has redistributive functions between well off and less well off national affiliates.

Federations help avoid the pitfalls of organizational partnerships and unitary associations, and they arguably provide the best structure to deal with the organizational challenges faced by INGOs (Foreman 1999). However, a variety of federation models exist, and as INGOs become global entities they tend to move away from simple federation structures toward more complex, even hybrid models (Lindenberg and Dobel 1999: 14).[9]

There is significant variation within federation structures. Foreman (1999) divided federations into donor-member dominated federations and bumblebee federations. In donor-member dominated federations the strongest power is held by members organizations or national affiliates that are also donors to the federation. This structure attempts to reflect donor-member stakes in the organization as both donors that want their funds to be adequately used and as members that want to influence organizational mission and operation. The argument is that donor-members have higher stakes in the federation than other members do, so they should also have greater power in deciding its work – which helps avoid the free-rider problem. In its past, World Vision International adopted the donor-member led federation structure (Foreman 1999).

The 'bumblebee' type federation has its particular name after the complex and evolving interactions between core and affiliates. In this structure affiliates are given increased power as they prove their reliability and ability to operate autonomously. As an affiliate unit joins the federation it will be under close supervision by the international core. As it demonstrates its commitment to the organizational mission, its probity and its reliability it acquires more autonomy and a greater voice in the federation (Lindenberg 1999). Amnesty has a structure that partly resembles a 'bumblebee' federation. As discussed above Amnesty's national sections gain increasing voice in the federation as they establish themselves and increase their number of local groups and members. National sections and local groups are given increasing autonomy as they demonstrate their ability to work for the organization's goals.[10]

World Vision International and Habitat for Humanity International are also examples of bumblebee federations (Foreman 1999).

Generally, we found that the INGOs examined here differed in the extent to which affiliates or country chapters are a) autonomous and b) democratic. Some INGOs have a strong central core (Greenpeace), others like FoE have politically weak centres by design. The latter are organized according to the subsidiarity principle, i.e., a bottom up allocation of responsibilities, which leaves a small international coordinating body only with those functions that lower-level units cannot address by or amongst themselves (Handy 1989). The IFRC for example is located between these extremes. INGOs are in a continued process of negotiating the right level between more or less centralized federations (Lindenberg and Bryant 2001).

Accountability and independence

Environmental or contextual approaches to organizational theory suggest that the relationships organizations establish in search of resources and legitimacy are critical in determining organizational goals and activities. In the case of INGOs this points to understanding the differences in the relationships with various stakeholders.

With increased importance and visibility of INGOs come greater demands for their accountability (Edwards et al. 1999; Lewis 2001). Democratic or not, INGOs must be accountable to their members or supporters and their boards. Accountability of INGOs is, however, complex because of the many different stakeholders (Anheier 2000), and it becomes even more so when members and other stakeholders are distributed across different countries and cultures.

Voting is a powerful voice mechanism for accountability, of course. Moreover, members always threaten to exercise their 'exit' option in pushing forward demands for greater accountability. Yet aside from democratic representation, what other 'voice' options do members have to ensure accountability?

In member-owned INGOs members exercise 'voice' in different ways. Formally, individual members can influence decision-making mainly through their respective local group. The group coordinator can in turn present any arising issue to the national section. If necessary the national section will present the issue to the international secretariat. Members can also raise issues in person at national events such as congresses. By voting at these events members can bind the executive to members' demands. Of course members can always write directly to staff workers at national offices but this is done informally.[11]

In member-supported INGOs this approach to obtain redress or influence decision-making, i.e., writing to or otherwise contacting the staff at either national or international levels, becomes the main voice vehicle for members. Indeed, our interviews revealed that this was a commonly used procedure. There was not, however, a binding mechanism for executive accountability. There were no formal judiciary structures for grievance procedures in the sampled organizations; nor did these organizations have dedicated ombudsmen to provide additional voice to members.

There are also top-down ways for the leaders to find out about member preferences and support for alternative strategies. INGO staff often seeks membership input into decision-making by undertaking surveys of membership preferences and opinions (e.g., Greenpeace-US, WWF). This method however is unsolicited by members and aggrieved members may not be able to express their views or to get access to important organizational information within such a system.[12]

Many traditional forms of accountability for non-profit organizations collapse at the international level. Under US non-profit law members of the board are personally liable for the conduct of the organization. However, if malpractice takes place outside the US the cost of public prosecution is prohibitively high. Because INGOs have much more information about their activities across the globe than regulators do it is very difficult to exercise effective regulation. The result of this 'regulation deficit' is an increased role for the media and members to uncover malpractice. The threat of members' 'exit' in the case of a scandal is arguably the most important mechanisms of accountability for INGOs given the general inability of both national regulators and individual members or supporters to monitor international activity. To function in a transparent way INGOs need critical internal mechanisms of accountability enabling the global core to be accountable to local branches as well as the other way round.

Underlying the issue of international accountability is the allocation of responsibilities and the corresponding authority at the international level, that is, the degree of international centralization. How should power be distributed between the core and the periphery? Who should make the decisions and who should be accountable to whom? All of the organizations examined pay much attention to issues of financial dependence on their relationships with donors and Southern partners. Resource dependency can lead to external influence and even external control in relations between NGOs and their donors (Hudock 1995).

This concern is clearly manifested in the many statements made by NGO representatives and organizational websites that they do not receive any governmental funding. Such NGOs include Amnesty, Greenpeace, and FoE. These NGOs are mostly dedicated to advocacy work. Generally, however, it was not easy to find out what proportion of NGOs' funding came from external actors and what proportion derived from internal members and supporters. MSF has recently begun to reduce its financial income from the government to protect its independence as it steps up its advocacy work (Lindenberg 2001).

But when NGOs receive any funding from governmental sources it is very difficult to evaluate their organizational independence. Take Oxfam as an example. In 2002, Oxfam Great Britain received 24.4%[13] of its funding from governmental sources while Oxfam America refuses any funding from the government. On the other hand, in the same year, Oxfam International received USD 451,000, that is 23.7% from 'restricted funding' sources and the rest from 'unrestricted funding' sources (Annual Report 2002). So how financially and organizationally independent is Oxfam overall? Similarly, in 2002 the IFRC received just under 50% of its budget from 'statutory sources' (IFRC website). Each national Red Cross however receives different proportions of funding from governmental sources. How independent is the Red Cross as a group? And is the Red Cross less independent than Oxfam if they receive more funding from governmental sources? These questions have important accountability implications. High dependence on government funding may reduce NGOs' ability to be responsive to its members' interests, risking further alienation of its membership and, in turn, greater dependence on government funding. To avoid this, membership INGOs must balance the opportunities from increased resources from government sources with greater accountability to its membership.

South–North divide

A presence in both the South and the North presents one final set of issues for INGOs governance and management. This presence is an opportunity to INGOs but also a potential source of tension within the organization. The North–South divide refers to a set of issues that cut across all of the previous issues: governance, organizational culture, organizational structure, accountability and relationship with donors. This divide can lead to confusion and conflict between the international core of an INGO, normally located in the North, and affiliates located in the South. These tensions were unequivocal in the Jubilee 2000 campaign. Southern national affiliates engaged in direct confrontation with some of their Northern counterparts because the Northern affiliates were not radical enough in their demands for greater equality between North and South (Anheier and Themudo 2002; Grenier 2003). Another good example of the South–North divide is the importance of development issues for environmental NGOs. Development issues are much more important for environmental NGOs in the South than for environmental NGOs in the North (Princen and Finger 1994).

Northern INGOs run the danger of misrepresenting Southern views when attempting to speak on behalf of the South and advocating for Southern positions and concerns without Southern membership. Particularly in the fields of humanitarian assistance and development, but also increasingly in environment, human rights and gender, analysts like Edwards (1999: 262) suggest that 'more powerful Northern NGOs have sometimes claimed a false legitimacy in speaking on behalf of constituencies in the South they do not represent, and have taken up policy positions which have not been rooted in proper consultation with Southern partners'.[14]

All international secretariats of the INGOs we looked at are located in the North: Greenpeace and FoE in Amsterdam, Amnesty in London, and IFRC in Geneva. The professional staff of the core and affiliates is very influential because they advise their boards on policy questions and decisions based on their management decisions and reports. Because of their preferential information position international secretariats should reflect diversity of membership in terms of their staffing and staffing policies. Otherwise there are strong dangers of biases. We could not however get enough information on this issue because it was very difficult to obtain gender, age or country of origin breakdowns for either the staff or the membership base. Some INGOs assured us that they were making considerable efforts in this respect.

Some of the INGOs that we looked at have developed policies to address the internal South–North tension. For example 1999 FoE's International Executive Committee (the Board) was made up of a chairperson from El Salvador, a Vice-Chair from Ghana, a Treasurer from Switzerland, and members from Australia, Bangladesh, Ecuador, Spain and the US. Amnesty has tried to hold major member meetings in the South, most recently in Dakar, Senegal. Because the ability to participate of members and representatives of Southern countries is conditioned by the ability to attend the meetings FoE started having General Assembly meetings in countries in the South as well as in the North. All organizations, except the IFRC, attempted to have a board composition that included both members from the North and the South.

These measures do not fully resolve the tensions around the sharing of resources between Northern and Southern parts of the organization. The federation may still be financially dependent on some Northern affiliates (such as from the US or Germany), but they at least they offer opportunities for more equal intra-organizational partnerships to develop. The measures may also engender the building of trust between Northern and Southern sections of the INGO – a very important element for successful partnerships (Lewis and Sobhan 1999). The ability to enable trusting and accountable relations between North and South is perhaps one of the key competitive advantages of INGOs.

Assessment

The governance and management challenges described above are intensified by INGOs' recent organizational growth; their mandate to operate internationally, sometimes even globally; and the demands accompanying the different expressions of global civil society. Simply put, New Public Management and corporatization place a premium on organizational efficiency while social capital and activist expressions place a premium on internal democracy and member participation, as well as forging lateral relationships, e.g., networks and alliances. Some have suggested that these tensions are impossible to reconcile and INGOs need to choose between activist expressions and their 'contractor' role within New Public Management. Our limited data, however, suggests that INGOs may be able to reconcile some of these conflicting sets of demands by choosing appropriate governance and management structures. While trade offs and tensions may be unavoidable, INGOs can experiment with different governance and management solutions so as to maximize their role within global civil society.

As we have seen, given the complex task and social environment in which they operate, it is not surprising to find that INGOs choose the federation structure. The combination of centralization and decentralization is better at accommodating cultural differences and allows for more effective resource mobilization and coordination. The value-added of international coordination is increased economies of scale and scope. In this context the role of the international secretariat is critical, and they seem to meet their coordination function best if they reflect the diversity of membership in terms of their staffing and staffing policies. It is important that coordination and governance are separate functions and must be understood as such by members. In other words, a clear distinction between legislature and executive is needed.

The definition and meaning of membership is critical for INGOs, with voting rights as the key issue. Having governance based on voting members profoundly affects the organization. The choice of democratic governance and transparency may not lead to the most efficient way and means of decision-making. Yet if democracy is held as a value and a goal, as is the case for most of the organizations studied, then inefficiencies related to this ideal are likely to be accepted as a worthwhile cost.

However, a number of democratic problems persist, in particular a lack of participation, and limited voice options for members. To compensate for these shortcomings, a more conscious introduction of democratic governance models may be appropriate for member-owned INGOs. In other words, the challenge is to become more like private governments rather than corporations. This would involve a clearly separated legislature (democratically elected by members), executive branch (both appointed and elected) and judiciary (elected by members). But how would the organization reconcile national with international demands? We suggest that the bumblebee structure is best suited to this task.

A strong link between accountability and legitimacy provides an important safeguard against loss of member support. Transparency emerges as the best insurance policy in this respect. The internet is a very useful tool in increasing transparency by decreasing costs and facilitating access to information. The

INGOs in our sample have extensive websites and information about their mandate, organization and activities. Particularly where members cannot vote, a visible and accessible judiciary is needed for grievance procedures, at the least an internal ombudsman to provide additional voice to members. None of the INGOs studied however have so far adopted such a strategy.

Organizational structure cannot be seen only as a design effort that maximizes benefits. Historical evolution of the INGO is a major determining factor on the role for the international secretariat and the choice of organizational structure. In choosing an adequate structure there is another obstacle: donor preferences. For Salm (1999: 102): 'the pressure to reduce administrative costs and demonstrate impact...makes it difficult...to cut costs and at the same time build internal capacity and a coherent international organizational culture. Internal capacity building requires investments of time and money, and progress on measures like leadership, inter-member coordination, and cooperation can be difficult to capture in terms of donor fund impact.' Developing adequate governance and management structures to deal with organizational challenges is itself a challenge due to theoretical and practical problems.

Nevertheless, developing adequate governance and management structures to deal with evolving organizational challenges is a critical endeavour. As mentioned above, INGOs inhabit an environment of expanding resources (human, financial and technological). However it appears that INGOs' resource base is not growing at the same pace as the number of INGOs, which has raised exponentially over the last two decades (Anheier and Themudo 2002). It is very likely therefore that competition for scarce resources will intensify among INGOs. In an environment of intensifying competition, the way in which INGOs respond to the organizational challenges facing them (e.g. by choosing an appropriate organizational structure) may be a critical source of competitive advantage and survival.

Conclusion

In his examination of international advocacy associations a decade ago, Young (1992: 27) expected the study of INGOs to become a major topic for contemporary international and voluntary sector scholars. However, since then, limited academic attention has been devoted to INGOs. This is a serious and surprising gap in our knowledge given their rise in profile mentioned above and the current revival of interest on neo-Tocquevillian ideas of associations and 'the need to bring greater democracy to global civil society' (Keane 2001: 43).

Based on our data, we have shown that the development of INGOs and global civil society over the last three decades has shown a remarkably consistent trajectory. Specifically, we suggest that:

- The growth and expansion of INGOs as a phenomenon seems closely associated with a major shift in cultural and social values that took hold in most developed market economies in the 1970s. This shift saw a change in emphasis from material security to concerns about democracy, participation, and meaning, and involved, among others, a formation towards cosmopolitan values such as tolerance and respect for human rights (Inglehart 1990).

- These values facilitated the cross-national spread of social movements around common issues that escaped conventional party politics, particularly in Europe and Latin America; and led to a broad-based mobilization in social movements, with the women's, peace, democracy and environmental movements as the best examples of an increasingly international 'movement industry' (Diani and McAdam 2003; McAdam, Tarrow and Tilly 2001).

- The 1990s brought a political opening and a broad-based mobilization of unknown proportion and scale (i.e., the *Idea of 1989*, as mentioned in Kaldor 2003), which coincided with the reappraisal of the role of the state in most developed countries, and growing disillusionment with state-led multilateralism in the Third World among counter-elites (Edwards 1999).

- In addition to this broadened political space, favourable economic conditions throughout the 1990s and the vastly reduced costs of communication and greater ease of organizing facilitated the institutional expansion of global civil society in organizational terms (Anheier and Themudo 2002; Clark 2003).

- By 2002, the changed geopolitical environment and the economic downturn challenged both the (by now) relatively large infrastructure of global civil society organizations, and the broad value base of cosmopolitanism in many countries across the world, in particular among the middle classes and elites.

- As a result, new organizational forms and ways of organizing and communications have gained in importance, with social forums and internet-based mobilization as prominent examples, as have frictions between 'Northern' and 'Southern' visions of the world's future.

We also argue that INGOs are likely to enter a new phase of restructuring in coming to terms with a changed and uncertain geopolitical situation. This process will involve both different outcomes for major policy positions and actors, and innovations like social forums, new kinds of alliances and coalitions, and increased use of internet-based forms for communicating and organizing. Indeed, the contrast between the 1990s and the 2000s is striking. The 1990s represented a period of consolidation, the construction of what appears to be a sturdy infrastructure of civil society, represented by the rapid growth of INGOs, and a growing emphasis on what we have described as the public management and corporatization approaches to global civil society. At the beginning of the twenty-first century, by contrast, we are witnessing a renewed mobilization of people and social movements and a renewed emphasis on self-organization and activism. What happens in the future depends both on the positions and values of global civil society and on the evolution of new organizational forms.

Perhaps the most positive conclusion of our chapter is that by any number of measures, INGOs as the infrastructure of global civil society has been strengthened over the last decade. At the same time, INGOs face significant governance and management problems that will become even more taxing as this form of organization gains greater policy prominence in a weakened system of international governance.

Notes

1. Fowler (2000) estimates that development NGOs spend over US$13 billion annually and USAID's annual budget is approximately US$14 billion (USAID 2003).
2. Links include different forms of cooperation and information exchange, exchange of staff, joint contracts, common campaigns, etc.
3. Global civil society manifests itself in different 'expressions' meaning the ways in which actors within civil society pursue their aims and relate to other social actors.
4. The empirical information for this chapter was collected between 2001 and 2003, using relevant documents (annual reports, organizational charts, constitutions and by-laws, special reports and studies, etc.) and expert interviews with management executives and other staff members responsible for membership issues. For three organizations (Greenpeace, FoE and Amnesty) the data was collected at different levels of the organization: local (for UK only), national (US, Canada, Sweden, UK, Spain, and Mexico), and from the relevant international secretariats.
5. Spending on membership support was £2,486,700.00. Given that Amnesty has around 1,000,000 members we estimate that around £2.50 was spend per member in the year 2000–01.
6. That tendency would probably hold even if there were global assemblies for all members, as very few members can afford the logistical expenses involved in participation. This is an additional reason why membership voting at global level tends to be done through national representatives.
7. A related solution is to develop and use internet-based mechanisms of voting and membership participation.
8. Within a multilevel INGO, it is also important to design adequate systems of horizontal coordination. Horizontal relations are more complicated than the core–national affiliates relations, but essential to allow for learning in a system of mutual control rather than central control (Foreman 1999). Mutual control rather than central control appears to be easier in membership-owned organizations than in board-owned INGOs.
9. Alongside national affiliates INGOs can also have national sections, local groups and regional sections (e.g., European Union sections in Brussels). In some countries INGOs had international individual members, that is, members who are not affiliated with any national section because there isn't one in their country (e.g., Amnesty). Some sections have paid staff while others are made up of essentially one committed volunteer.

10. Amnesty's Statutes read 'A section of Amnesty International may be established in any country, state, territory or region with the consent of the International Executive Committee. In order to be recognized as such, a section shall: (a) prior to its recognition have demonstrated its ability to organize and maintain basic Amnesty International activities, (b) consist of not less than two groups and 20 members' (Amnesty Statutes in www.amnesty.org).
11. Interview with FoE (UK) and Amnesty (UK).
12. In terms of the top-down provision of information to members, transparency efforts tended to be very sporadic and inconsistent. Information available on the INGOs web page is still very limited but it is increasing rapidly. Some INGOs have started publishing their annual reports on the web for easy inspection. Most INGOs mentioned also that they would send a paper copy of their annual report on request by members.
13. In its 2001/2002 Annual Report Oxfam Great Britain reported earnings of £46.265 million ('resources from government and other public authorities', Oxfam GB 2002: 28) of a total income of £189.398 million for the year.
14. The North–South tension is not exclusive to INGOs but present in many forms of North–South cooperation. Funding is central to North–South relations. Can a real partnership be possible if Northern NGOs continue to play the role of donors? Generally the Southern NGO is dependent on the Northern NGO (Lewis 1998). It is impossible to offer here a full description of all the issues involved but we would like to stress that INGOs offer opportunities to address this tension, which are not present in a relation between separate Northern and Southern NGOs.

References

Amnesty URL. www.amnesty.org

Anheier, H. K. (2000): Managing Nonprofit Organisations: Towards a New Approach. *Civil Society Working Paper, 1*. London: Centre for Civil Society. London School of Economics.

Anheier, H. K., M. Glasius and M. Kaldor. (2001): Introducing Global Civil Society. In: Anheier, H., M. Glasius and M. Kaldor (eds.), *Global Civil Society 2001*. Oxford: Oxford University Press: 3–23.

Anheier, H. K. and J. Kendall (2002): Trust and the Voluntary Sector. *British Journal of Sociology* 53(3): 343–62.

Anheier, H. K. and N. Themudo (2002): Organisational Forms of Global Civil Society: Implications of Going Global. In: Glasius, M., M. Kaldor and H. K. Anheier (eds.), *Global Civil Society 2002*. Oxford: Oxford University Press: 191–216.

Anheier, H. K. and H. Katz (2003): Mapping Global Civil Society. In: Kaldor, M., H. K. Anheier and M. Glasius (eds.), *Global Civil Society 2003*. Oxford: Oxford University Press: 241–58.

Anheier, H. K. and L. M. Salamon (2003): The Nonprofit Sector in Comparative Perspective. In: Powell, W. W. and R. Steinberg (eds.), *The Nonprofit Sector: a Research Handbook*. New Haven: Yale University Press: 191–216.

Archambault, E., et al. (1999): From Jacobin Tradition to Decentralization. In: Salamon, L., et al. (eds.), *Global Civil Society Dimensions of the Nonprofit Sector*. Baltimore: Johns Hopkins Center for Civil Society Studies: 81–97.

Chandhoke, N. (2002): The Limits of Global Civil Society. In: Glasius, M. et al. (eds.), *Global Civil Society 2002*. Oxford: Oxford University Press: 35–54.

Clark, J. (2003): *Worlds Apart: Civil Society and the Battle for Ethical Globalization*. London: Earthscan/Kumerian.

Daft, R. (1997): *Management*. Fort Worth: Harcourt Brace College Publishers.

Dasgupta, P. and I. Serageldin (2000): *Social Capital: a Multifaceted Perspective*. Washington DC: World Bank.

Dawson, S. (1996): *Analysing Organisations*. London: Macmillan.

Deacon, B., M. Hulse and P. Stubbs (1997): *Global Social Policy: International Organisations and the Future of Welfare*. London: Sage.

Diani, M. and D. McAdam (eds.) (2003): *Social Movements and Networks*. Oxford: Oxford University Press.

Edwards, M. (1999): *Future Positive: International Co-operation in the 21st Century*. London: Earthscan.

Edwards, B., E. Foley and M. Diani (2001) (eds.): *Beyond Tocqueville: Civil Society and the Social Capital Debate in Comparative Perspective*. University of New England Press.

Edwards, M. and D. Hulme (eds.) (1995): *Beyond the Magic Bullet: NGO Performance and Accountability in the Post-cold War World*. London: Macmillan.

Edwards, M., D. Hulme and T. Wallace (1999): NGOs in a Global Future: Marrying Local Delivery to Worldwide Leverage. *Public Administration and Development* 19: 117–136.

Edwards, M. and J. Gaventa (eds.) (2001): *Global Citizen Action*. Boulder, CO.: Lynne Rienner.

FoE URL. www.foei.org.

Foreman, K. (1999): Evolving Global Structures and the Challenges Facing International Relief and Development Organizations. *Nonprofit and Voluntary Sector Quarterly* 28(4) Supplement: 178–97.

Fowler, A. (2000). *The Virtuous Spiral*. London: Earthscan.

Giddens, A. (1999): *The Third Way and its Critics*. London: Polity.

Greenpeace Spain URL. www.greenpeace.es.

Greenpeace URL. www.greenpeace.org.

Greenpeace USA URL. www.greenpeaceusa.org.

Grenier, P. (2003): Jubilee 2000: Laying the Foundations for a Social Movement. In: Clark, J. (ed.), *Globalizing Civic Engagement: Civil Society and Transnational Action*. London: Earthscan: 86–108.

Handy, C. (1989): *The Age of Paradox*. Boston: Harvard Business School Press.

Held, D., A. McGrew, D. Goldblatt, and J. Perraton (1999): *Global Transformations: Politics, Economics and Culture*. London: Polity.

Hudock, A. (1995): Sustaining Southern NGOs in a Resource-dependent Environment. *Journal of International Development* 7(4): 653–67.

Hudson, A. (2000): Making the Connection: Legitimacy Claims, Legitimacy Chains and Northern NGOs' International Advocacy. In: Lewis, D. J. and T. Wallace (eds.), *New Roles and Relevance: Development NGOs and the Challenge of Change*. Hartford: Kumarian.

Inglehart, R. (1990): *Culture Shift in Advanced Industrial Society*. Princeton: Princeton University Press.

International Federation of Red Cross and Red Crescent Societies (IFRC) (1999): *Strategy 2010: Learning from the Nineties and Other Supporting Documents*. Geneva: IFRC.

Kaldor, M. (2003): *Global Civil Society*. Cambridge: Polity.

Keane J. (2001): Global Civil Society? In: Anheier, H. K. M. Glasius and M. Kaldor (eds.), *Global Civil Society 2001*. Oxford: Oxford University Press.

Kendall, J. and S. Almond (1999): United Kingdom. In Salamon et al. (eds.), *Global Civil Society Dimensions of the Nonprofit Sector*. Baltimore: The Johns Hopkins Center for Civil Society Studies.

Kettle, D. (2000): *The Global Public Management Revolution: a Report on the Transformation of Governance*. Washington: Brookings Institution Press.

Klingemann, H. D. and D. Fuchs (eds.) (1995): *Citizens and the State*. New York: Oxford University Press.

Lewis, D. J. (1998): Development NGOs and the Challenge of Partnership: Changing Relations between North and South. *Social Policy and Administration* 32(5): 501–12.

Lewis, D. J. (2001): *The Management of Non-governmental Development Organisations: an Introduction*. London: Routledge.

Lewis, D. J. and B. Sobhan (1999): Routes of Funding Roots of Trust? Northern NGOs, Southern NGOs, Donors, and the Rise of Direct Funding. *Development in Practice* 9(1–2): 117–29.

Lindenberg, M. (1999): Declining State Capacity, Voluntarism, and the Globalization of the not-for-profit Sector. *Nonprofit and Voluntary Sector Quarterly* 28(4) Supplement: 147–67.

Lindenberg, M. and C. Bryant (2001): *Going Global: Transforming Relief and Development NGOs*. Bloomfield, CT: Kumerian Press.

Lindenberg, M. and J. P. Dobel (1999): The Challenges of Globalization for Northern International Relief and Development NGOs. *Nonprofit and Voluntary Sector Quarterly*, 28(4) Supplement: 2–24.

McAdam, D., S. Tarrow and C. Tilly (2001): *Dynamics of Contention*. Cambridge: Cambridge University Press.

Michels, R. (1962): *Political Parties*. New York: Collier.

Offe, C. and S. Fuchs (2002): A Decline of Social Capital? In: Putnam, R. (ed.), *Democracies in Flux*. Oxford: Oxford University Press.

Otlet, P. (1924): Tableau de l'Organisation Internationale. Rapport General à la Conference des Associations Internationales, Geneva (UIA publication number 114).

Perrow, C. (2001): The Rise of Nonprofits and the Decline of Civil Society. In: Anheier, H. K. (ed.), *Organizational Theory and the Nonprofit Form*. Report No. 2. Centre for Civil Society, London School of Economics: 33–44.

Perrow, C. (1986): *Complex Organisations*. New York: Basic Books.

Perrow, C. (2002): Organizing America: Wealth, Power, and the Origins of Corporate Capitalism. In: *The Nonprofit Form and Organizational Theory*. London: Centre for Civil Society, London School of Economics.

Priller, E. et al. (1999): Germany. In: Salamon, L. et al. (eds.), *Global Civil Society Dimensions of the Nonprofit Sector*. Baltimore: The Johns Hopkins Center for Civil Society Studies.

Princen, T. and M. Finger (1994): *Environmental NGOs in World Politics: Linking the Global and the Local*. London/New York: Routledge.

Putnam, R. D. (2000): *Bowling Alone: the Collapse and Survival of American Community*. New York: Simon & Schuster.

Rees, S. (1998): *Effective Nonprofit Advocacy*. Working Paper Series. Aspen, Aspen Institute.

Romo, F. P. and H. K. Anheier (1999): Organizational Success and Failure: a Network Approach. *American Behavioral Scientist* 39(8): 1057–79.

Salamon, L. et al. (1999): *Global Civil Society: Dimensions of the Nonprofit Sector*. Baltimore, MD: Johns Hopkins University Institute for Policy Studies.

Salamon, L. M. and H. K. Anheier (1996): *The Emerging Nonprofit Sector.* Manchester: Manchester University Press.

Salm, J. (1999): Coping with Globalization: a Profile of the Northern NGO Sector. *Nonprofit and Voluntary Sector Quarterly* 28(4) Supplement: 87–103.

Smith, J., R. Pagnucco, and W. Romeril (1994): Transnational Social Movement Organisations in the Global Political Arena. *Voluntas* 5(2): 121–54.

Tew, E. S. (1963): Location of International Organizations. *International Organizations* 8: 492–3.

UNCTAD (United Nations Conference on Trade and Development) (2001): World Investment Report. www.unctad.org/wir/pdfs/wir_tnc_top100.en.pdf.

UNDP (2002): *Human Development Report 2002.* Oxford: Oxford University Press.

UNDP (2003) *Human Development Report 2003.* Oxford: Oxford University Press.

Union of International Associations, UIA (2002/3): *Yearbook of International Associations. Guide to Global Civil Society Networks.* Vol. 5. Munich: Saur.

USAID: USAID Budget. Frontlines, Nov/01/2003.

WWF USA URL: www.worldwildlife.org/.

Young, D. (1992): Organizing Principles for International Advocacy Associations. *Voluntas* 3(1): 1–28.

Young, D., B. Koenig, A. Najam, and J. Fisher (1999): Strategy and Structure in Managing Global Associations. *Voluntas* 10(4): 323–43.

List of organizations studied

Amnesty International (Amnesty)
Friends of the Earth (FoE)
Greenpeace
Human Rights Watch (HRW)
International Federation of Red Cross and Red Crescent Societies (IFRC)
International Union for the Conservation of Nature
Oxfam
World Council of Churches
World Wildlife Fund (WWF)

6

The Emerging Global Civil Society: Achievements and Prospects

Wolfgang Benedek

The phenomenon of civil society organizations

Global CSOs have emerged as a response to the deficiencies of global governance, of a 'gap' left by states and international organizations in representing public concerns and interests of citizens (Scholte 2000: 281 ff.). Governments often show a lack of adequate attention to 'global concerns', like environmental degradation, the depletion of natural resources needed also by future generations, epidemic illnesses, preservation of ecosystems and biodiversity, global warming, human security including food security and water security. Increasingly, citizens do not feel adequately represented at the global level, where no parliamentary institutions exist. Critique addressed to the United Nations exemplifies this trend. There appear to be certain imbalances in the international agenda, namely neglect of developmental and environmental concerns and of the social dimension of international economic relations (Weinz 2000: 94ff.). The main deficit of global governance, however, derives from the preoccupation of governments with short-term national, mainly executive interests, leading to the neglect of long-term global concerns. International public goods tend to be neglected also by private economic interests. One reaction was the organization of public interests through CSOs as non-state actors (Thürer 1999: 37 ff.) representing an emerging global civil society.

Definition

This raises the issue of the definition of civil society. It should also be clarified, whether civil society organizations as non-governmental organizations can pursue any kind of legitimate private interests including the pursuit of profit as do business corporations or whether this categorization should strictly be limited to organizations pursuing public interests. For the purposes of this contribution, civil society organizations are understood as non-profit organizations, based on the right to associate, that pursue primarily public policy interests by private means. In this way they are distinguished from corporate or business organizations, which are for-profit and pursue primarily private interests, and from inter-state organizations like international organization, which pursue public interests by public means. In practice the distinction is often blurred as CSOs may also pursue economic or private interests and business associations or corporations may also promote public interests as shown by the corporations committing themselves to respect the ten principles of the Global Compact.

Forms and functions

Civil society is covering a public space which is different from the state or the market. It is focused on the human person, its development, security and rights. The state can set framework rules, but is supposed to respect the autonomy of NGOs, which is a precondition of their proper functioning. A possible way of distinction can be found in the functional approach, which allows delimiting the space of civil society versus business and the state. Typical CSOs are human rights NGOs, environmental NGOs, peace and conflict resolution NGOs, consumer organizations, etc. In this chapter, the terms CSOs and NGOs are used interchangeably as it is common practice, but the focus is on NGOs acting as CSOs in the public interest, which also corresponds to the terminology used by the United Nations (UN).

There is a large plurality of CSOs, which mainly results from the diversity of their purposes and the heterogeneity of their approaches. The variety of NGOs can be seen from the many functions they pursue, which is reflected also in the acronyms in use for certain groups of NGOs like PINGOs, i.e. Public Interest NGOs, TANGOs, i.e. Transnational Advocacy NGOs, etc. Some governments have tried to bring NGOs under their control or to establish NGOs which pursue governmental interests. This has created a problem of independence reflected in organizations called GONGOs, i.e. Government-sponsored NGOs, or QUANGOs, i.e. Quasi-NGOs. Finally, NGOs are not only used by civil society, but also by 'uncivilized society' as a convenient form to cover networks of organized crime. Such NGOs are called CRINGOs, i.e. Criminal NGOs. These various types and practices call for quality control, which can be achieved through various types of regulation as will be discussed later in the chapter.

The participation of CSOs as actors in new forms of global governance (Benedek 2005b: 257ff.) has resulted in more inclusive and participatory approaches. Global CSOs contribute successfully to international 'agenda-setting', to advocacy of public concerns, and to challenging the lack of accountability observed in international organizations. International NGOs are increasingly taking part directly or indirectly in negotiations of agreements like the Cartagena Protocol on Biosafety (UNDP 2002: 122). They can perform an *amicus curiae* role by writing briefs for the attention of WTO panels and the Appellate Body. They may enjoy consultative status with ECOSOC and be invited to meetings of informal groups and networks like the

'Human Security Network' of 14 states, which usually invites international organizations and non-governmental organizations to its meetings.

In terms of their function, international CSOs aim at gaining better access to information and at ensuring procedures of participation that lead to more inclusiveness in international decision-making processes and organizations. For example, international economic organizations have come under attack for a lack of democratic accountability since the early 1990s and the World Bank, the GATT and the WTO have faced severe criticism on this point from many international CSOs. The major strength of CSOs in this respect lies in their power of prevention (Benedek 2001: 239ff.), as was demonstrated in the case of the Ministerial Conference in Seattle, which failed, at least partly, because of CSO public protests and CSOs lobbying for a better standing in international organizations for themselves, but also for developing countries. Under the traditional world trade regime, the governments of only few countries used to negotiate compromises among themselves, which the other states were then expected to accept. The problem of democratic participation raised by this process is obvious.

This lack of democratic participation, or 'democracy gap', that CSOs criticize on the international level is related to the fact that the division of power, which characterizes democratic nation-states does not exist on the international plane. If international parliamentary bodies exist, they have only very limited powers. In addition, their members are often delegates of, in certain cases, non-democratic governments. Therefore, CSOs are filling a gap of representation of public interests on the global level. This calls for a new division of powers to be developed in which the interests of the people versus the state can be more democratically represented. Since the mid-1990s the rise of global civil society and its potential to create such a 'power shift' has become topical (Mathews 1997: 50ff.).

Potential and pitfalls

The strengths of global CSOs can be seen in their capacity to represent civil society, influence international public opinion, provide expertise and organize international networks. Some global NGOs have a large expert staff and an international network of affiliate organizations and are therefore able to provide expertise and mobilize funds, which often even go beyond the possibilities of smaller, in particular developing states. However, CSOs also have weaknesses. The weaknesses can be seen in the existence of 'single purpose NGOs', who sometimes pursue only very limited interests and are neither able nor willing to take other legitimate interests into account. In advocating their concerns, they are acting like lobbyists for their 'just cause' leaving the task of balancing interests to others. In this regard they are not acting differently from lobbyists that act, for example, on behalf of certain corporate interests. Therefore there is reason for caution regarding the limits and possibilities for NGOs to harmonize their efforts.

This leads to a heterogeneity of approaches, which might make it difficult to decide which concern needs to be addressed first by the international community. Furthermore, there are very different degrees of sophistication in the approaches of NGOs. Sometimes, like in the 'Stop GATS campaign' they push their cause by using extreme examples in their arguments and ignore justified counter-arguments. As the dynamics of the media usually provides most attention to those who have the most extreme arguments or behaviour, this may lead to a certain escalation of the debates as global CSOs often seek maximal visibility for their concerns. Generally, this is an example of the problem of quality control of NGOs. Accountability needs to be 'a two-way street' (United Nations Development Programme (UNDP) 2002: 112).

Legal status and funding

With regard to their international legal status, CSOs may have partial, i.e. functional, international legal personality in certain circumstances, i.e. if they are assigned certain tasks by international organizations or bodies or granted consultative status (Hobe 1999: 152ff.; Kamminga 2005). However, their formal *de iure* status is not decisive. In practice, it is their *de facto* status that is more important, because this is what is necessary for international NGOs to use the 'soft power' of shaping agendas and discussions through the media. They therefore neither depend on the formal role attributed to them nor on the participation in formal procedures. Accordingly, the *de facto* status of NGOs is based on their 'authority', which is a result of their competence in the field, together with the size of their membership and their capacity to mobilize public opinion.

The legal status of CSOs is closely linked to their funding, which has developed into new challenges to the role of CSOs. For example, the public interest function of CSOs is challenged by the increasing role of national and international consultancies, i.e. companies, which specialize in implementing projects which are put on tender. The implementation of projects has been a major function of civil society organizations, which compete for public funding through projects available from states, and the European Union in particular. Direct state funding for NGOs creates dependency relationships and some NGOs, e.g. Amnesty International do not accept such funding as a matter of principle. However, in general, implementing projects allows NGOs a larger degree of autonomy even if in certain cases a level of dependency on the state or other funding organization may arise. In any case, CSOs depend, to a significant extent, on the implementation of projects to maintain their organizational capabilities, which allows them at the same time to pursue their public policy objectives. The increasing competition from consultancy groups, which mainly pursue economic interests and specialize in tenders from the European Union or individual states, may undermine the capability of CSOs to maintain their public interest activities. Therefore, the general tender policies of the European Union and states may have the effect of weakening civil society even though the European Union and a number of democratic states have committed themselves to strengthening civil society.[1] One solution to this problem could be to establish criteria for the implementing organizations in the tenders, expressly favouring non-profit associations above for-profit corporations.

Accountability and challenges to CSOs

Another challenge facing CSOs is the need to show accountability – both to their members and supporters and to the public at large – to the same extent as the international organizations CSOs criticize. This requires transparency, regular reporting and public relation activities to explain their policies and achievements. Usually regular reports are published on the website of the respective NGO, that sum up the activities undertaken to meet the objectives and clarify the sources and the use of funding received. Accountability is one of the principles of good governance, an aim worth pursuing for CSOs.

One way to show more inclusiveness by international CSOs, which are mainly located in the North, would be to give a larger role to Southern CSOs in their networks and top positions. This, however, creates further problems as CSOs from the South sometimes become dependent on funding through NGOs from the North, which are then often criticized for patronizing their partners, and acting as intermediaries for quality assurance for Northern governments and the EU. Further criticism focuses on the salaries paid to the staff in Southern NGOs as it distorts the local standards of remuneration and may lead to a loss of capacity in the state sector. In addition, it might attract people seeking work in well-paid jobs for their personal interest only. Therefore, the relationship between Northern and Southern NGOs can be a delicate matter, requiring sensitivity and a balancing of interests. In a similar way, Western support of CSOs in Eastern Europe may have distorting effects, due also to the absence of a civil society tradition there (Howard 2003; Narozhna 2004: 243ff.).

Developing countries, in the South and Eastern Europe in particular, are generally critical of CSOs as they fear for their sovereignty and are afraid of the political impact of CSOs domestically. Developing country governments often perceive CSOs as extra-parliamentary opposition. Especially if NGOs receive outside funding, they may be suspected of pursuing foreign interests and acting as Trojan horses. Weak states, which are struggling for stability and sovereignty, and do not want to be criticized at the international level, argue that CSOs should present their arguments at the national level, but hardly offer adequate possibilities of participation to do this. Therefore, NGOs, in cooperation with others, may find more attention for their concerns on the international level than with the national governments often suspicious of their work. However, it should also be noted that certain successes like the case of South Africa against a number of pharmaceutical companies, where international NGOs have had a significant role in support of the South African Government, have led to a more welcoming attitude of some developing countries towards NGOs (Abbott 2002).

In order to achieve, on the national level, an environment conducive to CSO participation, CSOs need to ensure that they are seen as defenders of common public concerns. They should therefore avoid mixing private with public interests. For example, in order to strengthen public confidence of their operations, Austrian NGOs collecting funds from private citizens have established a common 'quality seal' (Gütesiegel) in 2001, which includes the obligation to submit their books to a supervisory mechanism.[2]

Accountability is key to the legitimacy of CSOs, which must be assured on both the national and international levels (Kovach, Neligan and Burell 2003: 21ff.). On the national level, there are the national laws of association and sometimes specific laws regulating the establishment, benefits and obligations of NGOs. In order to be recognized and registered, NGOs, in most democratic states, need to meet various requirements, which can be more or less burdensome, and accept some measure of state control. Accordingly, their statutes need to clearly identify their purposes and objectives, and define responsibilities, financial accountability, representativeness, structures of internal decision-making, dispute settlement procedures etc.

With the absence of any possibility to establish NGOs on the international level, national registration is also obligatory for those NGOs that act globally. In practice, international or global NGOs tend to be registered in those countries that provide the best conditions, like the Netherlands, or where the headquarters of the NGO is situated. However, although the principle of national supervision remains, this does not prevent NGOs from creating international federations.

Accountability is also a main condition for recognition by international institutions and bodies, such as ECOSOC, which will be addressed in the section below. Finally, specific accountability is requested by donors, which set very elaborate accounting and reporting requirements. Funding institutions may require NGOs to provide a variety of data and information, i.e. the statute, annual reports and a track record of previous projects.

In conclusion, the global civil society manifests itself in a variety of CSOs/NGOs, which seek larger participation in order to pursue their public interest goals. They derive their authority from their competence and membership, but also have to live up to the very standards they propagate for other actors, in particular with regard to accountability.

Problems and regulation of CSOs

Critique of CSOs targets their inner democracy, their lack of a wider responsibility and capacity to balance interests, their limited accountability and their dependency on donors. These are all elements on which CSOs may be judged for their legitimacy, which is also increasingly coming under scrutiny

(Atack 1999: 855ff.). To be considered legitimate, NGOs are therefore required to show transparency and accountability, e.g. by disclosing their funding sources, decision making structures and procedures. Accordingly, this section explores various critiques of CSOs, which can undermine their legitimacy and the ways how the activities of CSOs are being regulated.

Points of critique

First and foremost, there is the question of the democratic nature of CSOs, both internally and in terms of representing public interests on the global level. This is related to whether CSOs are broadly based and thus show a certain degree of representativity, which gives them more authority in pursuing public interests. Internal democratic accountability relates to the constituency of CSOs, whereas external democratic accountability relates to the public at large.

The increasing professionalization of CSOs raises questions of distinguishing them from profit-oriented and state organizations. On the one hand, there is a need for a professionalization of CSOs as they take on more responsibilities and become important stakeholders. On the other hand, there is a danger of blurring distinctions between CSOs, the for-profit sector and the state, which sometimes 'co-opt' with NGOs to pursue various state functions. This may raise certain dangers for CSOs and their legitimacy, if the state is trying to contract out to NGOs functions which go together with state responsibilities. This can even be found unconstitutional as was the case in respect of certain aspects of the out-sourcing of the administration of the obligatory community service replacing the military service in Austria to the Austrian Red Cross.[3] It can also make NGOs dependent on the state. This may result in losing support from their constituencies and transforming CSOs into for-profit associations or de facto-corporations.

There are also forms of cooperation between Transnational Corporations (TNCs) and global CSOs (despite the fact that CSOs also follow a logic that makes them the main critics of TNCs) that can be problematic for CSO reputation and legitimacy. Local and global CSOs may be sponsored by TNCs, for example in the framework of Global Compact activities, as TNCs today have significant budgets for public relations and social and goodwill activities. This has partly evolved out of NGO critique and discussions on the social responsibility of TNCs, and basically constitutes a positive development, for example in the case of public–private partnerships. However, being directly supported by corporate funds may create a credibility problem for CSOs as their constituency often is critical of both globalization and TNCs. CSOs need to insist on full transparency and independence in relation to the funding offered. This applies also when funding is chanelled through independent foundations such as the Ford Foundation.

Quality control can be exerted by NGOs themselves, e.g. through self-control or by extending recognition only to such organizations which meet criteria commonly agreed upon. This might be necessary in certain circumstances in order to prevent business NGOs, CRINGOs or GONGOs from misusing the reputation of CSOs for their own interests. For example, during and after the war in Bosnia-Hercegovina, the International Coalition for Voluntary Agencies (ICVA) kept a register of recognized humanitarian NGOs, which alone could benefit from certain privileges like tax exemptions or special license plates on cars.

CSO recognition in and contribution to international organizations

The positive role of CSOs/NGOs in global governance has been recognized by the UN which have provided for the possibility of consultations with NGOs in Article 71 of the UN Charter. This possibility has been foreseen in the statutes of most specialized organizations, the financial and monetary organizations being the main exception. Accordingly, several forms of regulation of CSOs exist on the international level as in particular the consultative status administered by ECOSOC. Its relationship to NGOs is based primarily on ECOSOC Resolution 1996/31 of 25 July 1996, which, pursuant to Article 71 of the Charter, introduced a clear set of rules guiding the consultative relationship between the UN and NGOs.

Certain specialized organizations like WIPO or ILO have their own regulations. These different forms of regulation offer differing degrees of privilege and restriction for CSOs and their work depending of the requirements CSOs fulfil. Thereby they provide not only avenues for CSOs to confirm formal recognition of the legitimacy of their organization but also address the issue of quality control on the international level by way of stated preconditions for being granted consultative status. Such quality assurance mechanisms can have different elements, starting from the definition of criteria for obtaining consultative status allowing for participation, monitoring of the work of the NGO by evaluation based on reporting and observation, and decisions on the continuation or suspension of their status.

ECOSOC for example, in its Resolution 1996/31, distinguishes between three different categories of accreditation. NGOs have to demonstrate their mandate, governance and financial regime in order to obtain a general, specific or Roster status with ECOSOC, which then determines which specific rights and obligations the CSO receives, like proposing items for the agendas of UN bodies, speaking at meetings, circulating documents, etc. (Otto 1996: 107ff.). Among the requirements is also the obligatory presentation of a report every four years, on the basis of which the status may be extended. This quadrennial report is subject to review by the ECOSOC Committee on NGOs, which consists exclusively of states. A CSO's status can also be suspended or withdrawn or special reports can be requested from the NGO on its activities at any time.

The World Trade Organization (WTO) is an example for global economic governance (Benedek 2004: 225ff.). Article V:2 of the Agreement on the

Establishment of the WTO foresees the possibility for 'appropriate arrangements for consultation and cooperation with non-governmental organizations concerned with matters related to those of the WTO'.[4] However, in contrast to the ECOSOC consultative system, the WTO and its various bodies so far have not established a registration procedure allowing NGOs to participate in their work. Instead, NGOs can register only for the Ministerial Conferences, where they can assist in the public meetings and are given briefings on the progress of the work. For example, the 5th WTO Ministerial Conference in Cancún has been attended by about 800 NGOs with about 1,600 representatives.[5] In addition, there is an annual seminar on matters of particular interest to the WTO to which a number of NGOs is admitted. The WTO has changed its policies on information and transparency and now allows NGOs to present position papers, which can then be downloaded from the WTO website. However, there is no regular registration procedure allowing NGOs to obtain a consultative-like status as it is the case with ECOSOC (Benedek 1999: 228ff.). This has been much criticized by NGOs, which would like to assist in meetings of WTO bodies and are not satisfied with the briefings organized by the WTO Secretariat on an ad hoc basis. With regard to dispute settlement procedures under the WTO, the Appellate Body has clarified that NGOs may submit *amicus curiae* briefs, for which guidelines have been formulated. However, in no single case so far has an *amicus curiae* brief of an NGO been formally taken into account, and WTO member states, in particular from the South, have vehemently criticized this possibility of NGO participation (Benedek 2005a: 123f.).

The example of ECOSOC shows that international organizations are free to select for cooperation those NGOs they want according to criteria they can define themselves and that there is also a possibility for constant quality control. This raises the issue why international economic organizations like the WTO and the World Bank as well as the International Monetary Fund have not yet made use of this possibility to develop a better institutional cooperation.

Advantages and disadvantages of CSO cooperation with international organizations

By not giving NGOs any form of consultative status, international economic organizations such as the WTO should not be surprised that they come under increasing criticism for not being open or inclusive. In the case of the WTO this has been reinforced by whole campaigns against some of the key agreements of the WTO like the GATS and the TRIPS. An example in case is the 'Stop-GATS campaign', which has reunited a number of CSOs like ATTAC[6], Oxfam, 3D -> Trade-Human Rights-Equitable Economy[7], etc. in exerting pressure on states and the European Union not to make concessions demanded in GATS, in particular in the field of public services like education, health and water supply. As a result the European Commission has not made any offers in these sectors in the ongoing negotiations of the Doha Development Round. This shows the power of prevention of CSOs to threaten the achievements, purposes and objectives of international economic organizations like the WTO. Instead of winning cooperative partners with the potential to provide important expertise, the WTO is confronted with widespread criticism. Instead of a constructive relationship with NGOs, it is confronted with obstructive attitudes undermining its work. Logically, it would be in the interest of international economic organizations to be more inclusive and develop forms of cooperation, as has been done by other organizations like the World Intellectual Property Organization (WIPO) (Abbott 2000).

Another example of international organizations taking advantage of consultative arrangements is the African Commission on Human and Peoples' Rights based in Banjul, Gambia, which originally also had limited the participation of NGOs to the opening and closing ceremonies of their meetings, but then discovered the advantage of working closely with NGOs. For this purpose a consultative status was established, which could be obtained practically by every NGO. Soon the African Commission counted more than 150 NGOs with consultative status. The NGOs supported the Commission with advice and sometimes even funds to realize its manifold tasks and at the same time provided a kind of critical conscience of its performance. After some time it turned out that numerous NGOs which had sought the status with the African Commission where not able to regularly participate in its activities and were not even able to send the required regular report. As a result, the African Commission hardened the necessary criteria for consultative status and a number of NGOs lost their status with the Commission (Evans and Murray 2002). The cooperation between the African Commission and the CSOs from all over Africa and beyond is beneficial both to the Commission and to the CSOs and can be seen as a positive example of the constructive role NGOs can play for international bodies.

In conclusion, there are several requirements for the legitimacy of NGOs and problems like quality control need to be addressed by CSOs themselves or through regulation by international organizations in which NGOs seek participation. The most common form is to offer NGOs consultative status, which is a form of institutionalization of NGO participation, from which international organizations can benefit.

The role of CSOs in global governance: opportunities and threats

> Better governance means greater participation, coupled with accountability. Therefore, the international public domain – including the United Nations – must be opened up further to the participation of the many actors whose contributions are essential … this may include civil society organizations … .[8]

What can be the role of CSOs in global governance? What issues for regulation can be defined as being of global concern for both, state and non-state actors? Global CSOs are mainly known for contesting global governance (O'Brien, Goetz, Scholte and Williams 2000). But can they also contribute constructively to the task of global governance? This contribution argues for the institutionalization of CSO participation as the most promising way to use the potential of CSOs for global governance.

Potentials of CSOs in global governance

Global CSOs provide the missing voice of civil society in global governance (Commission on Global Governance 1995: 254). They emphasize neglected issues, like sustainable development and the social dimension of the international economy. Through their participation they contribute to closing the legitimacy gap of international organizations, but also provide valuable expertise and contribute towards a more democratic governance. International CSOs are representative of active citizens organized internationally to pursue certain legitimate objectives.

Hand in hand with the growing authority of CSOs, their responsibilities grow. CSOs have to follow principles of accountability similar to international organizations and demonstrate social responsibility similar to TNCs. This is particularly true for the larger CSOs who are very sensitive to international public opinion. This growing responsibility leads to improvements of the quality of their work on the national and international level and also allows them to make a distinction between CSOs for public purposes and other NGOs, which do not pursue public interests. To the extent that CSOs are better integrated into international structures, their self-understanding changes. Quite naturally, they are moving from the role as opponent of established structures towards a more constructive, cooperative and even supportive role.

International organizations have developed different relationships to CSOs, which has resulted in different attitudes of CSOs towards specific organizations, which can be both constructive and obstructive. It depends on the attitude of the international organization, which again depends on its membership, whether CSOs are offered more or less inclusive forms of participation. It is also up to the respective organization to define the duties CSOs are subjected to in order to gain or maintain their status. This will usually consist in transparency and reporting requirements. As has been shown above, global CSOs cannot just be registered on the international level. They always have to demonstrate that they have a valid national registration too, which implies that they are always subject to national and international monitoring.

Forms of CSO participation in global governance

After a period of advocacy and agenda-setting by CSOs, resulting in standard-setting in different fields like human rights, the environment, sustainable development, economic and social relations and also security, the debate now focuses on the question of whether the contribution of CSOs should be better institutionalized in order to assure continuity and allow CSOs to pursue a broader range of interests in a more accountable way. Accordingly, the institutionalization of the role of CSOs by means of consultative status, or in other ways, can also make an important contribution to the improvement of the quality of global governance. Apart form granting consultative status, this can also be achieved by including CSOs in specific consultative bodies in order to channel their input in a more formalized way. For example, for the WTO the establishment of a consultative council as well as of an 'advisory parliamentary body' has been proposed (Benedek 2001: 236f. and Petersmann 2001: 35f.), which can deliberate over matters on the agenda of the WTO and voice its views. However, the members of WTO have, so far, not reacted positively to such proposals made and the WTO Secretariat, which has preferred to actively promote its contacts with parliamentarians in particular through the Inter-Parliamentary Union (IPU) in order to increase the democratic legitimacy of the WTO, has not pursued this approach. Even when a number of deputies, particularly from the European Parliament, started to build a kind of 'Parliamentary Assembly' of the WTO, the WTO Secretariat showed no reaction. Obstacles to this idea are also due to differences of interest between the US Congress and the European Parliament (Shaffer 2004: 629ff.; Petersmann 2004).

Instead, the director-general of WTO established a 'consultative board' of eight eminent persons, coming from governmental, academic, business, trade and economic policy-making backgrounds to draw up a report on the institutional challenges faced by the WTO in the future (Sutherland 2004: 41ff., 80). The report contains a special section on 'dialogue with civil society' emphasizing responsibilities on both sides. While identifying a primary responsibility of WTO member states to engage with civil society in trade policy matters, the report suggests setting up clear objectives for relations between the WTO, civil society and the public at large by further developing the guidelines on relations with NGOs from 1996. In this respect 'no single set of organizations should be constituted to the permanent exclusion of others' (Sutherland 2004: 80, para. 12). Local civil society organizations from least-developed countries, especially Africa should be provided with assistance. Pointing to the extensive relations developed by World Bank and other intergovernmental organizations with civil society, the report also emphasizes that improved WTO relations with civil society require more resources. Regarding the attempts to move towards a 'Parliamentary Assembly' of the WTO, the report notes the opposition of developing and some developed countries. In view of the lack of adequate support it recommends more involvement of parliamentary institutions on the national level (Sutherland 2004: 80 and 46). This shows the difficulties and reluctance faced in making WTO structures more inclusive.

Towards 'cosmopolitan legality' through CSO participation

The involvement and institutional participation of CSOs can contribute to strengthening the democratic legitimacy of international organizations. Some even speak of a 'cosmopolitan legality' (Buchanan 2003: 673ff.) of global governance which includes global civil society organizations. This points to a major democratic deficit of international economic relations, where oligarchic groupings like the 'G7(8)' play a key role. These groups, however, are neither representative of the international community of states nor do they provide for any form of participation of global civil society organizations.

There are also potential disadvantages that can stem from the institutionalization of CSO activities. For example, there is the danger of dividing the CSO movement by offering privileged access to some and not to others, who have the same ambition. Also, a sort of co-optation of less critical CSOs may weaken the general critical aims of the movement as a whole. In day to day cooperation, CSOs may become more pragmatic and risk losing their attractiveness amongst supporters as critical voices. International organizations, which allow for the participation of CSOs will have to accept different views from within, which may make consensus-building even more difficult.

However, positive effects prevail as positions reached in more inclusive consultations will have more authority and a better chance of being widely accepted. Regular participation of specific recognized NGOs allows for a better understanding for each others' concerns and constraints. The possibility to place requirements on CSOs for consultative status provides an opportunity to establish criteria like expertise, representativity or capacity which make pursuing a broader range of interests more likely. The practice of temporary status with regular reviews strengthens the accountability of admitted CSOs, which may lead to a 'responsibilization' of NGOs. There is also a tendency within CSOs to form coalitions and networks, which may increase the elements of representativity and coverage.

In conclusion, the inclusion of CSOs is in the interest of the quality and efficiency of global governance. There are several ways of increasing participation of NGOs, including making full use of existing forms of consultative status with international organizations. Finally, the institutionalization of the participation of CSOs provides more democratic legitimacy for international organizations and global governance. It can also contribute to building a global citizenship, which will form the democratic basis of the emerging global civil society and its organizations.

Notes

1. See The Commission and Non-Governmental Organizations: Building a Stronger Partnership, COM (2000) 11 final. See also para. 3.2.2. of the Thematic Programme

for the promotion of democracy and human rights worldwide under the future Financial Perspectives (2007–2013) on strengthening the role of civil society in promoting human rights and democratic reform, in supporting conflict prevention and in developing political participation and representation, Communication from the Commission to the Council and the European Parliament, COM (2006) 23 final.
2. See Zwei Jahre Spendengütesiegel [Two years quality seal for donations], Press Release, 14 November 2003 (www.osgs.at), accessed 28 February 2005.
3. Decision of the Austrian Constitutional Court of 16 January 2004, B1248/03 on the Constitutionality of the Organization of the Austrian Civil Service.
4. See also Guidelines for Arrangements on Relations with NGOs of 18 July 1996, WTO Doc. WT/L/162 of 23 July 1996. See also Krajewski 2001: 183f. and Esty 1998: 123 ff.
5. World Trade Organization – News of 6 October 2003, webmaster@wto.org.
6. The acronym for this organization founded in 1998 stems from its original French name 'Association pour une Taxation des Transactions financières à l'Aide aux Citoyens'; see Kübelböck 2001: 201ff.
7. See for Oxfam International, www.oxfam.org, and, for 3D, www.3dthree.org.
8. United Nations, Report of the Secretary-General, We the Peoples: the role of the United Nations in the Twenty-first Century (Millenium report), GA Doc. A/54/2000 of 27 March 2000, para. 46.

References

Abbott, F. M. (2000): Distributed Governance at the WTO-WIPO: an Evolving Model for Open-Architecture Integrated Governance. *Journal of International Economic Law* 2000: 63–81.
Abbott, Frederick M. (2002): The Doha Declaration on the TRIPS Agreement and Public Health: Lighting a Dark Corner at the WTO. *Journal of International Economic Law* 2002: 469–505.
Anheier, H. K., M. Glasius. and M. Kaldor (eds.) (2001): *Global Civil Society 2001*. Oxford: Oxford University Press.
Atack, I. (1999): Four Criteria of Development NGO Legitimacy. *World Development* 27(5): 855–64.
Benedek, W. (1999): Developing the Constitutional Order of the WTO – the Role of NGOs. In: Benedek W. et al. (eds.), *Development and Developing International and European Law, Essays in Honour of Konrad Ginther*. Frankfurt am Main: Lang Verlag: 228–50.
Benedek, W. (2001): Internationale Gemeinschaft und Zivilgesellschaft. In: Nautz J. et al. *(eds.)*, Das Rechtssystem zwischen Staat und Zivilgesellschaft. Vienna: Passagen Verlag: 239–46.
Benedek, W. (2004): Demokratisierung internationaler Wirtschaftsorganisationen am Beispiel der WTO. In: Kopetz, H., J. Marko and K. Poier (eds.), *Soziokultureller Wandel im Verfassungsstaat, Phänomene politischer Transformation, Festschrift für Wolfgang Mantl*. Vienna: Böhlau Verlag: 225–38.
Benedek, W. (2005a): *Die Europäische Union im Streitbeilegungsverfahren der WTO*. Vienna Graz: Neuer Wissenschaftlicher Verlag.
Benedek, W. (2005b): Globale Governance der Weltwirtschaft. In: Koller, P. (ed.), *Die globale Frage. Empirische Befunde und ethische Herausforderungen*. Vienna: Passagen Verlag: 257–74.

Buchanan, R. (2003): Perpetual Peace or Perpetual Process: Global Civil Society and Cosmopolitan Legality at the World Trade Organization. *Leiden Journal of International Law*, 16: 673–99.

Colás, A. (2002): *International Civil Society: Social Movements in World Politics.* Cambridge: Polity Press.

Commission on Global Governance. (1995): *Our Global Neighbourhood.* Oxford: Oxford University Press.

Esty, D. C. (1998): Non-governmental Organizations at the World Trade Organization: Cooperation, Competition or Exclusion. *Journal of International Economic Law* 1: 123–47.

Evans, M. D. and R. Murray (eds.) (2004): *The African Charter on Human and Peoples' Rights: the System in Practice, 1986–2000.* Cambridge: Cambridge University Press.

Guidelines for Arrangements on Relations with NGOs of 18 July, 1996. WTO Doc. WT/L/162 of 23 July 1996.

Hobe, S. (1999): Der Rechtsstatus der Nichtregierungsorganisationen nach gegenwärtigem Völkerrecht. *Archiv des Völkerrechts* 37(2): 152–76.

Howard, M. M. (2003): *The Weakness of Civil Society in Post-Communist Europe.* Cambridge: Cambridge University Press.

Kamminga, M. (2005): The Evolving Status of NGOs under International Law: a Threat to the Inter-State System. In: Alston, P. (ed.), *Non-State Actors and Human Rights.* Series: Collected Courses of the Academy of European Law. Oxford: Oxford University Press: 93–111.

Kovach, H., C. Neligan and S. Burell. (eds.) (2003): *The Global Accountability Report 1/2003: Power without Accountability?* The One World Trust.

Krajewski, M. (2001): Democratic Legitimacy and Constitutional Perspectives of WTO Law. *Journal of World Trade* 35(1): 167–86.

Kübelböck, K. (2001): ATTAC – Potential für gesellschaftliche Veränderung oder Domestizierung von Konflikten? *Journal für Entwicklungspolitik* XVII (2): 201–9.

Mathews, J. T. (1997): Power Shift. *Foreign Affairs* 76(1): 50–66.

Narozhna, T. (2004): Foreign Aid for a Post-euphoric Eastern Europe: the Limitations of Western Assistance in Developing Civil Society. *Journal of International Relations and Development* 7: 243–66.

O'Brien, R., A. M. Goetze, J. A. Scholte and M. Williams. (2000): *Contesting Global Governance. Multilateral Economic Institutions and Global Social Movements.* Cambridge: Cambridge University Press.

Otto, D. (1996): Non-governmental Organizations in the United Nations System: the Emerging Role of the International Civil Society. *Human Rights Quarerly* 18(1): 107–14.

Petersmann, E.-U. (2001): Human Rights and International Economic Law in the 21st Century. *Journal of International Economic Law* 4: 3–39.

Petersmann, E. U. (ed.) (2004): *Preparing the Doha Development Round: Challenges to the Legitimacy and Efficiency of the World Trade Organization.* Robert Schumann, Florence, Centre for Advanced Studies, European University Institute.

Sutherland, P. et al. (eds.) (2004): Report by the Consultative Board to the Director-General Supachai Panitchpakdi. *The Future of the WTO, Adressing Institutional Challenges in the New Millennium.* Geneva: World Trade Organization.

Shaffer, G. (2004): Parliamentary Oversight of WTO Rule-Making: the Political, Normative, and Practical Contexts. *Journal of International Economic Law* 7: 629–54.

Scholte, A. (2000): Civil Society and Democracy in Global Governance. *Global Governance* 3: 281–304.

Thürer, D. (1999): The Emergence of Non-Governmental Organizations and Transnational Enterprises in International Law and the Changing Role of the State. In: Hofmann, R. (ed.), *Non-State Actors as New Subjects of International Law: International Law – From the Traditional State Order Towards the Law of the Global Community.* Berlin: Duncker & Humblot: 37–58.

United Nations (2000): We the Peoples: the Role of the United Nations in the Twenty-first Century. *Report of the Secretary-General (Millennium Report)*, GA Doc. A/54/2000 of 27 March 2000.

United Nations Development Programme (UNDP) (2002): Deepening Democracy in a Fragmented World. *Human Development Report 2002.* Oxford: Oxford University Press.

Van Boven, T., C. Flinterman, F. Grünfeld and R. Hut (1995): *The Legitimacy of the United Nations: Towards an Enhanced Legal Status of Non-State Actors.* Maastricht/Utrecht: Studie-en Informatiecentrum Mensenrechten.

Weinz, W. (2000): Weltsozialordnung und globale Zivilgesellschaft. *Vereinte Nationen* 2000 3: 94–98.

Part 4
Business in Global Governance

7
Problematizing Corporate Social Responsibility under Conditions of Late Capitalism and Postmodernity

A. Claire Cutler

Introduction

We are said to be witnessing a transformation in political authority associated with a revolution in the global activities of corporations. The 'corporate social responsibility movement' is heralded as revolutionary in providing enhanced corporate accountability in international commerce. This movement is widely regarded by students of business, law, and politics as an innovative dimension of global governance that is contributing to greater sociality in the global political economy (Ougaard 2006; Testy 2002; Haufler 2001, 2006). Indeed, John Ruggie (2004), the former Assistant to the Secretary-General of the United Nations (UN), and a major architect of the UN Global Compact, which seeks to govern corporations through voluntary commitments to socially responsible practices, regards the movement as evidence of a new 'transnational public sphere' and a new non-state-based public space. Comprised of statements of best practices, codes of conduct, standards, and voluntary arrangements concerning corporate labour, human rights, environmental, and governance practices, the corporate responsibility movement is seen as governing corporate behaviour at home and abroad, whilst also opening up space for broader participation and the articulation of a variety of social concerns that are not routinely addressed in corporate decision-making. For Ruggie, this signals the provision of much needed public goods and the articulation of an incipient global civil society and global public sphere. However, others challenge the publicness of the goods being provided and question the sincerity and propriety of rooting global sociality in voluntary and predominantly private, self-governing corporate arrangements (Lipschutz with Rowe 2005; Cutler 2006).

This chapter problematizes the conceptualization of the corporate social responsibility movement as the normative foundation for an emerging global public sphere by challenging its nature as a regime of 'global governance'. Rather, this chapter argues that this movement is regarded more critically as

"

constituting the material and ideological foundations for legitimating corporate regimes of private appropriation and accumulation. The movement is presented, not as a dimension of *public governance*, but as an element of *privatized governance* that is integral to transformations in international law and state–society relations that are associated more generally with the contemporary historical bloc. The contemporary historical bloc is characterized by a complex of material, institutional, and ideological influences that are reframing local and global political economies according to the related logics of late capitalism and post-modernity (Cutler 2003: 100–4). Conditions of late capitalism are reflected in the growth of transnational corporate laws that facilitate the mobility and expansion of capital and related patterns of flexible accumulation through privatized legal norms and institutions. Postmodernity is reflected in legal pluralism as corporate governance structures and processes are increasingly multiple, cross-secting, porous, and soft (Cutler 2003, 2004). These conditions give rise to dialectical tensions between local and global political economies, hard and soft legal regulation, and delocalizing and relocalizing tendencies. While corporations have engaged in self-regulation before (Hummels 2004), this chapter argues that the contemporary corporate social responsibility (CSR) movement, as a voluntary, soft, and self-regulatory movement, is specifically associated with the contemporary historical bloc.

The chapter begins by problematizing the conceptions of a global public sphere. It then considers the ontology of the corporation through a review of the history and political economy of the modern corporate form. This review illustrates the changing ontology of the corporation from that of a public-regarding to a private-regarding entity and raises the problem of attempting to infuse private entities with public purposes. It also raises conceptual and theoretical problems with viewing the CSR movement as a dimension of global governance involved in the supply of public goods. The next section argues that public international law and international institutions have failed to regulate corporations effectively. These failures resulted in the establishment of bilateral investment treaties as the central legal form engaged in the regulation of corporate conduct and the emergence of privatized regulatory social responsibility regimes. The final section places the CSR movement in the context of the contemporary historical bloc. This historical bloc is argued to be characterized by the proliferation of transnational regimes of private accumulation and governance, involving a mix of public and private authorities, interacting in multiple often cross-secting and contradictory ways. Despite such apparent regulatory pluralism, the transnational, global, and national orders are embedded in deeper cultural expectations and understandings about political economy, law and acceptable business practices deriving from neoliberal political ideology and economic theory and articulated by the CSR movement. They are forming a consensus concerning the type of regulatory order appropriate for the 'underbelly' of transnational capitalism, which is taking shape in an emerging business civilization defined by a culture of 'efficiency'. The paper concludes with the problematic nature of grounding the nascent 'public sphere' in private corporate governance and considers the possibilities for public contestation of privatized regulation.

Analysing the global public sphere

The conception of the public sphere has a rich lineage in liberal thinking and is linked to certain understandings of legitimate authority and governance. Liberal theorists identify the element of 'publicness' as an inherent characteristic of authority (Cutler 1999), which may or may not take the form of governmental institutions and processes, but nonetheless constitutes a form of authority (Hall and Biersteker 2002). Moreover, liberal theory judges the quality of the public sphere according to criteria of democratic legitimacy and the functional capacity of authorities to provide the conditions conducive to the health of the public weal. Democratic legitimacy is assessed variously by the inclusivity of a polity and generalized participation in deliberative and discursive processes of collective decision-making (Benhabib 1996; Rawls 1997; Habermas 1996, 1999). It may also be judged by the efficacy of the rule of law and constitutionalism (Held 1995, 2000), by the transparency of rules and laws, and the accountability and responsiveness of authorities.

The health of the public sphere is also assessed by the ability of authorities to provide order and to supply public goods, both of which liberal political economists argue go under-provided in the absence of a government willing to assume the costs of supplying them. According to Inge Kaul et al. (2003: 21) public goods are 'usually defined as goods with non-excludable benefits and non-rival consumption. Non-excludability means that it is technically, politically, or economically infeasible to exclude someone from consuming the good. Nonrivalry means that one person's consumption of the good does not detract from its availability to others.' Indeed, the provision of public goods is regarded as a particularly acute problem in the global order. Global public goods are defined as 'goods where benefits extend to all countries, people and generations' (Kaul and Mendoza 2003: 95). The absence of a global state to provide global public goods and the weakness of global civil society and global democratic processes to articulate and legitimate notions of the 'global public good' are regarded as providing profound obstacles to a robust global public sphere. The obstacles are both material and analytical/theoretical. They are material in the sense that there are only rudimentary institutions of global governance to create and distribute global public goods. The obstacles are also analytical/theoretical in that liberal analysis posits the absence of the appropriate incentive structure for private entities to provide public good voluntarily and thus theorizes the requirement for public intervention to ensure their provision. To further compound these problems, the very notions of public and private are deeply contested and different historical periods have constructed the private and public spheres with variable content (Desai 2003).

Notwithstanding these obstacles, the provision of global public goods has been taken up by a multiplicity of actors, including international governmental and non-governmental organizations (IGOs and NGOs), transnational corporations (TNCs), and private business associations (Kaul et al. 2003; Cutler, Haufler, and Porter 1999). Indeed, the CSR movement is regarded by many as instrumental in the constitution of a global public domain by building a framework for deliberative and discursive decision-making and in providing under-provided global public goods. Ruggie (2004) asserts that the 'states system is becoming embedded in a broader, albeit still thin and partial, institutionalized arena concerned with the production of global goods'. Ruggie draws upon the idea of a 'world civic politics' and 'private governance' as the 'two building blocks' of a 'broadening and deepening sociality at the global level' in a 'new global public domain: an increasingly institutionalized transnational arena of discourse, contestation and action concerning the production of global public goods, involving private as well as public actors'. He notes that corporations are creating a '*new* transnational world of transaction flows that did not previously exist', which he describes as 'non-territorial spaces and management systems' that 'may also provide a historically progressive platform by creating a more inclusive institutional arena in which, and sites from which, other social actors, including CSOs (civil society organizations), international organizations, and even states, can graft their pursuit of broader social agendas onto the global reach and capacity of TNCs'. Ruggie stresses that governance refers to the conduct of public business and following Max Weber defines public authority as a 'fusion of power with legitimate social purpose'. He regards the CSR movement, which he argues is being driven by global civil society groups and not governments, as an important source for accountability and social capacity building at the global level and offers the (UN) Global Compact as an important mechanism for creating learning networks, policy dialogues, and facilitating private–public partnerships in developing countries that are creating new expectations of corporate conduct and fleshing out global social purposes.

Other proponents of similar views marshal numerous reasons to support the provision of global public goods through private, corporate rule-making. The natural and organic nature of corporate self-regulation is suggested as fully consistent with corporate legal theory that naturalizes the corporation as a private entity, analogous to a private individual, with its own legal personality and rights to autonomy and self-direction.[1] In addition, liberal political economy posits that all sorts of economic efficiencies result from private, self-regulation.[2] However, these rationales beg the question of the nature of the goods that are being supplied by the CSR movement. Indeed, they raise a more fundamental issue of the nature and ontology of the corporation as a 'private' entity ostensibly engaged in the pursuit of public purposes and the provision of 'public' goods.

The ontology of the modern corporation

This section reviews the historical development and ontology of the business corporation, whose legal identity has undergone profound transformation from that of a public-regarding to a private-regarding entity. It analyses the legal responsibility of corporations to their shareholders, as well as the political economy of corporations, illustrating the constitution of corporations as private identities. The analysis then problematizes the attempt to imbue corporations with public purposes engaged in the provision of public goods through the CSR movement.

The dawn of the corporate age

The twenty-first century has been aptly described as 'the century of the corporation', for today corporations lead and no longer follow states (Harrod 2006: 23). Nor are corporations constrained by state authority or territorial boundaries as in the past (Strange 1996). Importantly, the modern transnational corporation (TNC) is pre-eminently an American corporation, in the sense of being the product of Anglo-American business law and American styles of business management that have been globalized throughout the world (May 2006; Cutler 2003). Historically, the nature and powers of corporations were associated with the development of the European state system and with the emergence of centralized political authorities. A brief review of this history reveals changing patterns of power and authority wielded by states and by corporations. What is decisive about the dawn of the corporate age is the attribution of legal identity and autonomy to the corporation, as well as the ability to limit the liability of corporate shareholders and officers. Both attributes were crucial in facilitating the capitalization and expansion of corporations. They also worked a separation between the legal powers/capacities of corporations and their legal responsibilities, with profound implications for corporate governance and accountability.

While associations engaged in economic activity may be traced back thousands of years, the recognition of the corporation as an entity with an identity that is autonomous from its members is associated with rise of the Benedictine monastic orders (May 2006: 5). During the eleventh century in Britain and Europe, incorporation was granted to universities, religious orders, towns and cities, as well as guilds (May 2006: 5). By the end of the sixteenth century, the attribution of separate legal personality extended to the great trading corporations. Then the corporate form was conceived of as an institution with sovereign powers whose identity was bound up with the identity of the King and the great merchant empires (McLean 2003; Harris 2000). Originally regarded as a privilege granted under a charter, the corporate form was used for the achievement of what we today would regard to be public, social purposes. The great trading companies undertook to manage and facilitate colonial expansion and to advance the political interests of the great economic powers. The mandates of the first great corporations, such as the British and Dutch East India Companies and the Hudson Bay Company, were drafted very broadly and covered many rights and responsibilities that we today associate with states. In their founding charters they were granted sovereign powers over non-European peoples, including the rights to trade, to war, to make peace with indigenous peoples, and the right to create money.

While the first joint stock company was formed in England in 1553 to finance colonial expeditions, it was not until the final decade of the seventeenth century that the corporate form really began to take root. At that time colonial expansion was in full force and the total amount of investment in joint-stock companies increased significantly (Bakan 2004: 9). In fact, limiting the liability of shareholders to the value of their initial share purchase was important in ensuring adequate markets for initial stock offerings. At that time, as well, the foundations of corporate law were being worked out in the common law courts of Britain and the writings William Blackstone and Sir Edward Coke. Notable, too, is the 1702 publication of the first and anonymous book on the 'law of corporations', which articulated the principal that recognition of the independent corporate form and limited liability were 'conditional on a clear public-regarding role in promoting economic development' (May 2006: 6). Notwithstanding a few corporate stock-jobbing scandals in the eighteenth century, corporations were increasingly used by the British government for the development of infrastructure, such as the construction of the railways (May 2006: 7). In Britain, statutes governing joint stock companies and limited liability were passed in the late nineteenth century. Christopher May (2006: 7) observes that 'from the eighteenth century onward, the limitation of liability was a key mechanism underpinning the growth in size and resources of corporations, allowing them to access to disparate and unconsolidated capital to a much greater extent than did partnerships'.

Given its function as a vehicle of colonialism, the corporate form, as developed in England, was distrusted in America in its early years of independence. However, the need of the new government for funds to finance public works projects, combined with the recognition of corporations as valuable sources of such funds worked against such reservations (Pitt and Groskaufmanis 1990: 1575). As such, it did not take long for postcolonial American opposition to the corporate form to give way to the recognition of the corporation as an invaluable tool for nation-building at the dawn of the industrial age. Joel Bakan (2004: 9) notes that in 'post-revolutionary America, between 1781 and 1790, the number of corporations grew tenfold from 33 to 328'. Most of these were incorporated for the express purpose of public infrastructure development (Smith 1998: 291; Wallman 1999: 813).

In the United States, by the first half of the nineteenth century, charters of incorporation began to be distrusted as privileges granted by public authorities to private actors in exchange for political support. Given the limited granting of such charters, they were regarded as anti-competitive and as promoting corruption and monopolistic market conditions. By the middle of the nineteenth century a movement began for 'free incorporation' whereby the corporate form came to be seen less as a privilege bestowed by the state, and more as a private right. In 1889 New Jersey became the first state to enact legislation that allowed incorporation 'for any lawful business or purpose whatever'.[3] This legislative innovation proved to be so attractive to business interests that New Jersey became the forum of choice for incorporation in the United States so much so that shortly thereafter New Jersey's entire budget would come to be covered by incorporation fees (Horwitz 1987: 31). Faced with ever decreasing corporate revenues, it did not take long for other states to follow suit. With the triumph of the movement towards 'free incorporation', the corporate form eventually came to be seen not as a special privilege, but rather was naturalized as a normal mode of conducting business. As a consequence, corporations could no longer be seen as special creatures of the state. They came to be recognized as private 'persons' entitled to the same rights and privileges as all other persons.[4] Corporations thus came to be regarded as private, not public, institutions (Horwitz 1987: 20–4).

In the United States, during the latter half of the nineteenth century, the relationship of the shareholder to the corporation also began to change. This mirrored developments in Britain and also reflected the changing ontology and conceptualization of the corporate form. Prior to the recognition of limited liability, shareholders were regarded as members of the corporation, not dissimilar from partners in a partnership, who could be held personally liable for the wrongs of the corporation. Shortly after the statutory recognition of limited liability in Britain, the idea took root in the United States (Bakan 2004: 13). With the rise of the capital markets, and the concomitant dispersion of share ownership far and wide, courts began to recognize the need to limit the liability of shareholders for corporate wrongs. Accordingly, in 1891 the United States Supreme Court decided that, while liability could attach to shareholders holding original share subscriptions, such liability could not be ascribed to subsequent purchasers of corporate stock.[5] This marked the beginning of a fundamental shift in the relationship between the shareholder and the corporation. Yet, with the tremendous growth of the capital markets and the rise of investment banking in the early 1900s, this distinction would prove less and less tenable. With the ascent of mass marketing of corporate stock to institutional investors, even the purchaser of original shares could no longer be reasonably seen to have a formal private relationship with the corporation that could give rise to liability (Horwitz 1987: 45). Just as the expansion of the capital markets helped limit shareholder liability, so too did limited shareholder liability serve to facilitate the expansion of the capital markets. Unencumbered by fears of personal liability for corporate wrongs, investors were no longer as restricted from holding shares across a wide array of corporate enterprises.

This review of the history of the corporate form reveals the transformation of the corporation from a public to a private-regarding entity. This suggests conceptual obstacles to characterizing the privately constituted and operated corporation as a provider of public goods in the pursuit of public purposes. Further obstacles derive from the political economy of corporations.

The political economy of the corporation

The special treatment of corporations as natural persons subject to limited liability is justified on political economy grounds. Recognition as legal subjects is required in order to conduct the everyday business of contracting, settling disputes and so on, while limited liability is required in order to protect the interests of shareholders, who it is reasoned, will not invest in business enterprise in the absence of such limitation. Indeed, students of institutional economics trace the birth and success of capitalism to the capital accumulation made possible by the institutionalization and socialization of risk through joint stock companies and corporate law (North 1990). Historically, a key element in the institutionalization of risk was standardizing and rendering predictable the sorts of risks investors faced. In this regard, the norms of profit maximization and shareholder primacy emerged as the pillars of corporate responsibility. In the United States, for example, domestic laws imposed upon corporate managers and directors a legal duty to put the interests of shareholders first, which is typically rendered in terms of the maximization of profits. This is referred to as the 'shareholder primacy norm', which is regarded as one of the most fundamental principles of corporate law (Smith 1998: 280). The shareholder primacy norm was developed by the courts in the United States in the 1830s (Smith 1998: 296) and was well-articulated in the famous case of *Dodge* v. *Ford Motor Co.* (1919: 507):

> A business corporation is organized and carried on primarily for the profit of the shareholders. The powers of the directors are to be employed for that end. The discretion of directors is to be exercised in the choice of means to attain that end, and does not extend to a change in the end itself, to the reduction of profits, or to the non-distribution of profits among stockholders in order to devote them to other purposes.

While the managers of a corporation may take other interests into account, and even act to advance those interests, there must be a reasonable connection to the long-term interests of shareholders (Smith 1998: 283). This has been codified in over half the states in the United States into 'corporate' or 'non-shareholder constituency statutes' (ibid: 289). Typically, these statutes provide that in acting in the best interests of the corporation, the directors may take into account non-shareholder interests, such as employees, the communities in which facilities of the corporation are located, customers, and suppliers. Corporate managers, however, must take care to make judicious use of their discretion, as they can be sued by shareholders for breach of their fiduciary duty in the event that a decision cannot reasonably be seen as linked to the profit motive. Where a poor decision is based on the honest belief that it would increase profits, a manager can usually defend an action, such as a derivative lawsuit, by invoking the 'business judgement rule', which provides for a certain amount of managerial discretion in determining the best interests of the corporation. However, where the decision was not made in the *bona fide* belief that it would further the most fundamental role of the corporation, the maximization of shareholder profits, managers may be held liable for violating their fiduciary duty to the shareholders of the corporation. As such, there is only a modest amount of room for corporate philanthropy. As one scholar has put it, corporate philanthropy is 'illegal – at least when it is genuine' (Bakan 2004: 37). While the courts usually show considerable deference to any business judgement exercised by a manager (Ashford 2002: 1553), the potential for personal liability, together with the prevalent use of short-term performance indicators gives most managers little incentive to consider anything but immediate profitability.

Some regard the profit maximization motive as a problematic, if not an insurmountable obstacle to the ability of a corporation to perform public duties (Gaines and Kimber 2001: 170; Wallman 1999: 809). Gaudier (1999: 83), quoting the former CEO of Canon: 'If corporations run their business with the sole aim of gaining more market share and earning more profits, they may well lead the world into economic, environmental and social ruin.' In contrast, others link the profit motive to alleged natural efficiencies of free markets, regarding it not as an obstacle, but rather as the key to effecting socially desirable outcomes through the efficiency of the 'free market' (Friedman 1962; McCabe 1992; Rostow 1959 and Miwa 1999).

Basic to the political economy of corporations, embodied in management theory, and hence of relevance to corporate social responsibility, is the notion that in trying to optimize shareholder profits, a corporation seeks to maximize its revenues and minimize its costs. In so doing, it will seek to externalize costs onto others. For example, by trying to minimize costs, a corporation may dump the toxic by-product of its production process rather than dispose of it safely. The corporation may well incur a penalty if it breaches an environmental law, but it incorporates the cost of the penalty into its cost structure, passing the burden onto the consumer. It thereby avoids expensive waste disposal bills and instead imposes the cost onto society, which is primarily comprised of non-shareholders, consumers, and tax-payers. For the managers of a corporation, the issue is often reduced to a straightforward cost–benefit analysis, which abstracts and masks any real suffering that might result from a given decision. Indeed, it was this very cost–benefit analysis that led General

Motors to continue marketing cars that were particularly prone to explode, even though its managers knew that many people would die as a result (Bakan 2004: 62). Further examples abound. The cost of profit is all too often decreased job security, sub-optimal working conditions, a poisoned environment and so forth (Gaudier 1999: 47). The propensity for corporations to externalize costs in combination with real legal limits on corporate philanthropy in Anglo-American law, thus also suggest the rather constrained capacity for corporations to function as credible public-regarding entities.

The call for corporate social responsibility

Given the propensity of corporations to externalize costs onto society, there is real and growing concern that the costs and burdens of capital accumulation by private actors are being shifted to the public sphere. In an effort to curb corporate externalities, both state and non-state authorities are trying to encourage corporations to be more 'socially responsible'. Yet despite such effort, there is a great disparity of opinion as to just what socially responsible corporate conduct entails. At one extreme is the view that the pursuit of profits and share-holder wealth maximization are the measure of corporate social responsibility (Friedman 1962). At the other end is the view articulated by the United Nations Conference on Trade and Development (UNCTAD 1999: 15) that corporate duties, like those of a good citizen, 'rise beyond a floor of legally-mandated obligation' and involve obedience to both the 'letter and spirit of the law' (Addo 1999: 20). Underlying the notion of good citizenship is a certain voluntariness of conduct, one where a corporation is expected to take the initiative and recognize when public legal standards are inadequate or lag behind acceptable practice. This suggests a capacity for corporate reflexivity, as well as the capacity to function as a public-regarding entity, both of which do not flow easily or even reasonably from the constitution of the corporation as a private entity with legal duties to its shareholders to maximize profits.

Notwithstanding significant contestation over just what it means for a corporation to be socially responsible and over corporate capacity to operate meaningful CSR initiatives, corporations are adopting their own interpretations. In addition, governments and societies have devised a number of institutions and practices that attempt to control, or at least contain, the adverse consequences of profit maximization. Efforts to enforce corporate social responsibility range from mandatory domestic command-and-control regulation, to civil society efforts to organize boycotts, campaigns, share-holder activism, and litigation. While some of these strategies have met with considerable success, there are equally considerable obstacles to their effective deployment. For example, most require a high level of dedication and coordination among those willing to champion a cause, which in turn requires a significant amount of resources, temporal, financial, and political. Indeed, it is this very problem that prevents the effective control of corporate behaviour in many less developed countries (LDCs) (Ward 2001: 4;

Ayine 1999: 133). The desire of many LDCs to welcome foreign investment creates obstacles to monitoring corporate behaviour (Ratner 2001: 462–3; International Restructuring Education Network Europe (IRENE) 2000: 22). Ineffective monitoring may also arise from host state corruption and the prejudice of the local judiciary, particularly if the host government is involved in the business operations in question (Ward 2001: 4). Moreover, a lack of transparency and secretiveness in corporate conduct may interfere with the collection of sufficient evidence to implicate a corporation, while the fines imposed and damages awarded in many countries are insufficient incentive for corporations to modify their practices (International Council on Human Rights (ICHR) 2002: 79–80). Finally, in pursuing a legal action against a TNC, litigants often expose themselves to the risk that the TNC will launch a counteroffensive legal action (IRENE 2000: 23).

Perhaps, the greatest limitation of purely domestic responses to controlling corporate wrongs flows from the transnationalization of capital and the world economy. The abilities of corporations to shift capital and operations around the world or to shift national identity through a variety of methods, such as overseas subsidiaries, joint ventures, licensing agreements, and strategic alliances, make enforcement difficult (Roht-Arriaza 1995: 484–5; IRENE 2000:7). As the International Council on Human Rights notes, '[o]nly in exceptional cases will courts "pierce the corporate veil"' to impose liability (ICHR 2002: 81). Doctrines of limited liability and corporate personality prevent holding corporations accountable. Moreover, as a leading authority notes, 'the discrepancy between the transnational reach of MNEs' business activities and the territorial limits of national legal and administrative control over the economy constitutes the classical problem raised by MNEs' (Horn 1980: 50). The transnationalization of markets renders it quite irrelevant to define responsibility in terms of national jurisdictions alone, while the transnational corporations continue to have mobility between countries and legal jurisdictions (Addo 1999: 23). Indeed, while domestic regulation is clearly necessary, it alone is not sufficient to address corporate social responsibility in an increasingly global economy and, in fact, might be increasingly anachronistic (Williams 2002: 774; Roht-Arriaza 1995: 485).

The changing ontology and political economy of the corporation work against its recognition as a public-regarding entity and thus pose problems for corporate accountability and responsibility in the identification of public purposes and in the provision of public goods. Inadequacies of domestic regulation have led to calls for a more global approach.

Corporations, international law, and international institutions

Both public international law and international institutions have been highly ineffective in regulating the corporate social responsibility of transnational corporations (TNCs). Under the rules of public international law, TNCs are legally 'invisible', while international institutional efforts to regulate

TNCs have failed to achieve meaningful results. Transnational corporations have not exactly been unhappy with these inadequacies and failures. They are not exactly mobilizing for legal regulation and responsibilities (Cutler 2003). However, insofar as they seek to establish reasonable expectations about what is regarded as appropriate social conduct and to forestall binding legislative interventions by states, they have undertaken independent, private initiatives to establish the normative framework for their transnational operations.

Public international law is analytically and theoretically a state-based system of law. The traditional starting point is that only nation-states are recognized as having full legal rights and responsibilities, that is, international legal personality (see Cutler 2001 and 2003).[6] Other entities, such as international organizations and corporate entities may be vested with degrees of international legal personality by states, however, their legal personality or identity remains a derivative status that is contingent upon state authority. Such personality is filtered through the identity of the state, which is the main 'subject' of international law (Cutler 2001: 140).

It is difficult to impose 'command-and-control' style regulations on transnational corporations for their conduct, since they are not recognized as holding rights or duties under international law. The doctrine of state responsibility, historically the main legal mechanism for establishing responsibility under international law, addresses the responsibilities of *states* for injuries to aliens and their property (Malanczuk 1997; Ratner 2001). Again the legal focus is upon states, which as the subjects of international law, hold rights and duties thereunder. This renders efforts to control corporate conduct under international law highly problematic. It is only states that can launch and defend legal claims so that, in most circumstances, a transnational corporation can only be held indirectly responsible for their actions and must make its legal claims through the agency of a state. Typically, direct responsibility lies with the state of which the corporation is a national. This clearly poses problems for corporate accountability when corporate nationality is unclear, as in cases involving a dispersal of corporate control amongst numerous jurisdictions and the like. Moreover, it means that in order to hold a transnational corporation accountable under international law, a legal action must normally be brought against the corporation's home state, rather than against the corporation itself. Moreover, the corporate action must be imputable to the state in order for the state to be responsible.[7] As a consequence of such limitations on corporate legal responsibility, Fleur Johns (1994) has argued that transnational corporations are apparitions and 'invisible' under international law. Indeed, the statist nature of pubic international law creates a representational gap between transnational corporations and the societies within which they operate.

International institutional efforts to hold corporations accountable have also failed to produce effective regulations. After the Second World War the

International Trade Organization (ITO) was to be created as part of the Bretton Woods complex of international economic institutions that would address corporate activities. However, the ITO never materialized and was strongly opposed by the United States Congress (Cohn 2000: 27). Other international institutional efforts of note include the mobilization of the Group of 77, comprised of developing countries contesting the inadequacy of the rules of public international law to deal with their development concerns. In 1974 the United Nations Economic and Social Committee (ECOSOC) created a Commission on Transnational Corporations and gave it the mandate to develop a Code of Conduct for Multinational Corporations (MNCs). In addition, the Organization of Petroleum Exporting Countries (OPEC) and the United Nations Commission on Trade and Development (UNCTAD) undertook reviews of the impact of corporate practices on the economic concerns of the developing countries. In 1974 the United Nations established the UN Commission on Transnational Corporations (UNCTC), which engaged in drafting a Code of Conduct for MNCs that regulated matters such as tax evasion, restrictive business practices, and transfer pricing. However, opposition from the industrialized states resulted in abandonment of the Code in 1992 when the UNCTC was dissolved.[8]

Other notable intergovernmental institutional efforts to regulate corporations include the ILO Tripartite Declaration governing labour relations,[9] the Organization of Economic Cooperation and Development Guidelines for Multinational Enterprises,[10] the UN Global Compact, and the UN Norms on the Responsibility of TNCs and Other Business Enterprises with Regard to Human Rights,[11] as well as regional efforts.[12]

As a consequence of the inadequacies of international law in addressing corporate activities, bilateral investment treaties (BITs) emerged in the 1970s as the main legal instruments regulating the foreign investment activities of corporations.

Typically, BITs do not provide for CSR. They are geared towards investment protection and do not impose social performance obligations on the investor, but rather seek to limit the ability of the host state to regulate or control the investment. While BITS form only one dimension of global investment governance, they are a central or pivotal legal form that anchors and, indeed, articulates a postmodern, pluralistic system of global economic regulation. BITs have proliferated at an extraordinary rate over the past two decades.[13] In particular, developing countries have been utilizing BITs as mechanisms for attracting foreign investment. The standard rationale for BITs is the investment-enhancing function that articulating standards of protection that will be applied to investments from one country to another. BITs typically provide protection for investors and, increasingly, provide for private, delocalized processes of investor–host state dispute settlement.

Many of these treaties were negotiated under the auspices of the World Bank and directly addressed the matter of corporate legal personality by granting investing corporations with the legal right to directly sue host states for breach of their agreement. This was an important legal development that has had profound implications for corporate accountability. Bilateral investment treaties, in granting corporations the legal right to sue a host state directly, create a limited and one-sided personality for investing corporations that enables them to protect their investments, without limiting corporate conduct in any significant way. This anticipated the granting of similar corporate legal rights under the North American Free Trade Agreement (NAFTA), the Canada–US Free Trade Agreement (CUSTA), and the failed Multilateral Agreement on Investment (MAI) (Cutler 2000). Theses regimes create an interesting hybrid of public–private authority. They blur the distinction between the public and private spheres because they create protective *private* legal regimes that secure corporate investment protections, but enforce them through the *public* offices of the state signatories or international organizations, such as the World Bank's Centre for the Settlement of Investment Disputes. Under these regimes, investment transactions are delocalized as host states agree to performance standards that protect the investor and investment against local laws that might impair or interfere with the investment relationship. BITs also typically provide for private and delocalized dispute settlement under the World Bank Centre for the Settlement of Investment Disputes or other international commercial arbitration venues, which provide no or very limited access for the participation of civil society organizations.

These regimes do not provide the foundation for an emerging, participatory, global public sphere. Rather, they constitute regimes of private accumulation, which are then sanctioned and enforced by the public offices of states. These regimes socialize and communalize private commercial risks by involving public authorities in the enforcement of private agreements. This dialectical relationship between private and public spheres has been insightfully described by Robert Wai (2001–2002) as 'transnational liftoff and juridical touchdown', as the emerging regimes governing transnational corporations are freed from domestic and national regulations, but then come under their protective sphere when there is a need for binding enforcement.

Other international institutional initiatives of note are similarly limited in their one-sided regulatory focus. The agreements negotiated as part of the Uruguay Round, such as the Agreement on Trade-Related Investment Measures (TRIMS) and the Agreement on Trade-Related Intellectual Property Rights (TRIPS) function much like the NAFTA, CUSTA and MAI to protect the investor, whilst communalizing and socializing the costs and risks of private trade and investment activities. The Global Compact, the United Nations corporate social responsibility initiative, seeks a more balanced approach through the voluntary agreement of signatory corporations to abide by general principles of conduct concerning their environmental, labour, and human rights practices. However, its main defect is its voluntary nature and the general inefficacy of soft-law approaches to corporate regulation, discussed below.

For transnational corporations, the question of accountability often depends on the extent to which a parent corporation can be held liable for damage which results from activities which are directly the responsibility of a subsidiary. However, there are substantive and procedural obstacles that derive from public and private international law, as well as problems of enforcement (Cutler 2000). The consent-based nature of international law and competitive corporate capitalism create difficulties for effective enforcement of standards which protect public interests (Ayine 1999). Host countries are often unwilling or unable to impose criminal sanctions, or provide civil remedies and home countries generally do not exercise jurisdiction over the extraterritorial acts of multinational corporations (Corporate Liability 2001: 2025; Roht-Arriaz 1995: 484). Moreover, corporations are not exactly clamouring for inclusion in the state-based system of global regulation or expansion in their duties to non-shareholders (Redmond 2002: 23). This failure has led scholars to note a lack of responsiveness of international law to changes in the global political economy (Cutler 2001; Skogly 1999: 248) and has provided a regulatory gap and opening for private regulatory initiatives. The failure also accentuates the thinness of the normative and institutional foundations for global corporate governance and the so-called emergent global public domain.

As a result of the failure of international institutional regulatory efforts and in the attempt to forestall the development of binding national regulations, corporations are engaging in self-regulation and entering into voluntary arrangements with governments through private–public partnerships (OECD 2001b: 87). Indeed, as Fox et al. (2002) note, the notion of partnership is crucial to the CSR agenda. This is evident at multiple levels of governance, from domestic 'right to know' legislation that encourages dialogue between industry and the communities in which it operates, to supranational social reporting initiatives such as Social Accountability 8000 (Hess 1999).[14]

Internationally, the United Nations has invited the corporate world to partner with it in the Global Compact to define appropriate global standards of corporate conduct. As its main architect, John Ruggie (2004: 27) states that the 'Global Compact is based on principles that were universally endorsed by governments, stipulating aspirational goals of the entire international community. It engages the corporate sector, civil society, labor and governments to help bridge the gap between aspiration and reality.'

The emergence of public–private partnerships, and the concomitant emphasis on 'procedural regulation'[15] is justified on efficiency grounds. It is said to recognize that 'broad, hortatory principles have little credibility inside or outside a corporation if they do not address real operational issues and decision-making processes' (UNCTAD 1999: 34), and that '[e]ffective governance requires balancing and managing the changing relationships between states, markets and civil society' (OECD 2001b: 87). It is also premised on the notion that 'adversarial approaches to governance often do not work well and are more costly than cooperation' (OECD 2001b: 26). This is consistent with the claim by Coaseian economists that cooperation between and amongst all potential beneficiaries will achieve the most efficient provision of public goods (Dixit and Olson 2000: 312).

Similarly, voluntary corporate initiatives and self-regulating codes of conduct are justified on efficiency grounds. In fact, the limited success of intergovernmental codes of conduct, and the still nascent architecture of any reflexive international regulatory regime has given rise to perceptions of a need to find alternate ways to ensure that corporations behave responsibly. 'In this context of shifting public–private demarcations, the pressure to privatize international regulation is growing' (Williams 2001: 49). 'Self-regulation' has been defined as a 'legal regime in which the rules which govern behaviour in the market are developed, administered, and enforced by the people (or their direct representatives) whose behaviour is to be governed' (Gaines and Kimber 2001: 162). While there are many different forms of self-regulation, including both formal and informal arrangements, purely private unilateral commitments, voluntary agreement by corporations to meet public standards, and agreements negotiated between governments and private entities, the following discussion will focus primarily on private codes of conduct, which are identified by Haufler (2000: 12) as the 'most visible' measure of industry self-regulation. [16] Instead of adhering to intergovernmental instruments and rather than supporting hard, enforceable standards of corporate behaviour, industry is increasingly adopting voluntary self-regulatory governance systems. According to the OECD (2001: 17), legal complexity in the current landscape of postmodern governance 'creates a need for voluntary initiatives, since law and regulation could never spell out good practice in sufficient detail'. Moreover, its proponents argue that to do so could be prohibitively costly, unnecessary, and ultimately inefficient (Triantis 2002). Indeed, proponents argue that voluntary initiatives can serve as valuable mechanisms for filling in the governance gap between domestic and international legal regimes. According to UNCTAD (1999: 11), past failures to achieve agreement over binding, hard law precipitated the recourse to voluntary regulation: 'Faced with the apparent impossibility of generating international standards backed by legal sanctions, some governments initiated discussions aimed at developing non-binding codes of corporate conduct. These devices developed into new "soft law" alternatives, somewhat akin to a defined social contract, whereby governments would endorse and promote the agreed standards as embodying the type of conduct expected of "good corporate citizens".' Indeed, the voluntary and soft nature of CSR initiatives is characteristic of contemporary corporate regulation and reflects the fact that while corporations support a certain amount of regulation in order to provide stability, they resist too much regulation and prefer soft standards that allow them flexibility (Cutler 2003 and 2005; Rieth 2004). As they are deeply imbued with neoliberal market ideology (Black 1996), soft regulations are widely welcomed amongst the business world as an attractive new form of governance. While they have a history that may be traced to the origins of capitalism and earlier (Ratner 2001: 531; Cutler 2003), in this era of late capitalist and postmodern business regulation, they are proliferating to the point where they have 'become standard corporate fare' (Pitt and Groskaufmanis 1990: 1602).[17]

Corporate social responsibility, global governance, and the contemporary historical bloc

As noted at the beginning, it is common to characterize the corporate social responsibility movement as an instance of global governance. The idea here is that voluntary CSR initiatives give rise to a 'potential new source of global governance, that is, mechanisms to reach collective decisions about transnational problems' (Haufler 2001: 1). Significantly, the initiatives are voluntary and thus engage corporations in self-regulation. However, as noted by Morten Ougaard (2006: 232), the CSR movement involves more than self-regulation and the attainment of private, corporate values, and interests. As an instance of global governance, it implies *purposive* activity: 'defining CSR, then, is not only a question of self-regulation, but also one of identifying and delimiting the purposes that business should serve.'[18] It is an 'effort to change the understanding of what business legitimately can and ought to do' and thus must be seen as a 'field of discursive and material struggle' between profit-making and sociality; 'a range of efforts to shift the balance in current business practice toward the social ideal type of private enterprise' (Ougaard 2006: 235–6). Indeed, recognizing the constitutive and purposive dimensions of the CSR movement is a significant step in developing a critical understanding of the significance of the movement to the contemporary historical bloc.

Defining characteristics of the contemporary historical bloc are the dialectical tensions between local and global politico-legal orders, as well as between hard and soft regulation. Whether characterized as tensions between 'globalized localisms' and 'localized globalisms' (Santos 1995), between 'transnational liftoff and juridical touchdown' (Wai 2001–2002), between 'legal subjectivity and objectivity' and the 'delocalization and relocalization of law' (Cutler 2004: 205, 199), or between hard and soft law (Cutler 2003), at issue are transformations of authority and identity that are recasting the roles of states, corporations, and societies through a reconfiguration of the public and private spheres. More specifically, the complex of material, ideological, and institutional regulatory influences that form the contemporary historical bloc may be characterized as late capitalist and postmodern (Cutler 2003 and 2005). Late capitalism is evident in soft, permissive, self and market-based regulation that facilitates the transnational expansion of capital and patterns of flexible accumulation (Harvey 1989 and 2003) through deregulation, privatization, and the removal of national legal barriers to economic relations. Postmodernity reflects a plurality of legal orders operating nationally, internationally, and transnationally and increasingly in a privatized mode involving voluntary and soft regulation (Santos 1995). At the heart of this emerging normative and institutional order is the 'efficiency principle', the *grundnorm* of neoliberal market civilization (Cutler 2006). This principle elevates concerns of economic competitiveness through market-friendly regulations over competing social goals and is the defining characteristic of the contemporary historical bloc.

The CSR movement forms a vital role in constituting the ideological, material, and institutional foundations of this historical bloc. Ideologically, the CSR movement contributes to the legitimization of private transnational accumulation strategies through its articulation of the efficiency principle as the dominant criterion of value and through the naturalization of corporate self-regulation as the organic means of achieving global competitiveness and efficiency (Cutler 2006). The CSR movement establishes the parameters of appropriate corporate social conduct by shaping the expectations and discourse of business leaders, civil society organizations, governments, and international institutions. It assists in the internalization of soft and self-regulation by business elites, as well as by government and international institutional officials, as not only the most efficient, but the most commonsensical means of conducting business. In this way, the CSR movement articulates and normalizes the neoliberal normative framework and patterns of private accumulation. Moreover, in creating an environment in which social goals appear to be on the negotiating table between corporations and civil society organizations, the movement creates an appearance of inclusivity, transparency, and democratic participation and representation. However, the material and institutional dimensions of the movement suggest otherwise.

The representational gap between corporations and citizens created by statist international law and by international institutional failures to effectively regulate TNCs have resulted in the materially dominant influence of bilateral investment treaties. These treaties enable corporations to acquire contractual rights that are opposable to all, even to the publics of host states, who have no part in the negotiation or management of the treaty relationship. The rights side of corporate citizenship is thus secured through hard legal disciplines and binding dispute settlement procedures. In contrast, the duties side of corporate citizenship is addressed through voluntary CSR initiatives. Indeed, CSR initiatives constitute new fields of struggle within which corporations compete for comparative advantage. As Scott Pegg (2006: 249) observes of CSR initiatives in the resource extraction sectors, 'CSR decisions are now a form of comparative advantage and another arena in which corporations compete against one another.' This has given rise to a distinction between 'world leaders', such as Royal Dutch/Shell and British Petroleum, both of which adopted far-reaching CSR programme after scandals involving allegations of complicity in human rights atrocities, and 'bottom feeders', such as Talisman Energy, which abandoned its stake in Sudan (after controversy over its complicity in human rights abuses occurring in the context of the civil war) to an Indian corporation that does not practice CSR and is relatively immune to criticism from activists. The inability of civil society organizations to influence the activities of 'bottom feeders' suggests a very narrow range of socially inclusive participatory and democratic corporations.

Conclusion

Gunther Teubner (2002: 208) describes private corporate rule-making and self-regulation as 'breaking the frames' of territoriality, sovereignty, and modernity and as provoking one to 'look for new forms of democratic legitimacy'. He is suggesting that we must carefully consider the democratic qualifications of private governance. This involves problematizing the democratic pedigree of private-regarding corporate entities engaged in governance and, ostensibly, in the provision of 'public' goods and the pursuit of 'public' purposes. While corporate self-regulation may contribute to the provision of public goods, it may also facilitate the pursuit of private interests at public expense or enable 'private parties to influence the setting, definition, or enforcement of laws' (Barth and Dette 2001: 21), potentially rendering public opinion less audible and leaving authorities particularly vulnerable to 'regulatory capture'. Indeed, some fear that the widespread use of 'voluntary self-regulation could turn private regulation into *de facto* government regulation, with little public access to the process' (Freeman 2000: 644). The democratic legitimacy of voluntary codes of conduct turns very much upon the robustness of their provisions for participation, transparency, monitoring, and enforcement. As Robert O'Brien (1999: 264) has put it, 'the force of the argument must be matched by the argument of force'. Without appropriate enforcement, the perceived need for effective monitoring is reduced. While there are a number of ways in which firms can be monitored, including internal monitoring by the corporation or external monitoring by a foundation or independent party (Liubicic 1998: 134), few codes provide for independent oversight (Redmond 2002: 26) and lack transparency, thus making it difficult to determine to whom they are accountable or just who their beneficiaries are. Where they do, they are often worded permissively, only reserving the right to call in an external monitor (OECD 2001b: 39). This makes it difficult to verify any corporate claims that they are indeed observing their 'commitments'. Thus, many voluntary initiatives suffer from a lack of credibility (Liubicic 1998; Haufler 2001). The OECD (2003: 12) indicates that voluntary initiatives with low administration costs have a good chance of resulting in little or no change from 'business as usual', suggesting the possibility that governments may indeed be reaping cost-savings, but with little enhanced corporate social responsibility.

If voluntarism is truly the most appropriate method for creating corporate norms and for founding this newly emerging global public space, why is it that corporations insist, in contrast, upon hard, binding, enforceable rules governing their rights under trade and investment agreements with states under bilateral investment treaties and in the WTO and NAFTA regimes? It is a curious public space, indeed, when corporate *rights* are subject to hard discipline, but corporate *duties* remain soft.

The CSR movement must be conceptualized more critically as an instance of what Gramscian scholars refer to as *trasformismo*, meaning the process by which opposition and dissent are absorbed and diffused (Cutler 2005). This movement creates the appearance of active civil society participation, whilst binding trade and investment agreements effectively lock civil society out of participation in the regulation of transnational corporate conduct. The complicity of international institutions, such as the United Nations Global Compact, in the CSR movement is an attempt to give globalization a 'human face' by rendering corporate human rights, labour, and environmental practices accountable. However, the programme works a co-optation of human rights discourse without teeth. Indeed, CSR initiatives figure as part of the new management discourse and business culture that is creating a 'softer capitalism' in which the corporation is creating 'new traditions, new representations of itself and the world, and increasingly, an ethical stance towards the world' (Thrift 2000: 76). It provides the corporation with a 'legitimizing rationality', the strength of which is crucial to its longevity (Harrod 2006: 44). As Harrod notes (ibid.) the 'rationality of corporate power is the reification of the power of the market. From the beginning, the market was endowed with a mystical force – it would determine outcomes by a myriad of decisions and processes not easily discernible or predicted.' Indeed, he further argues that the legitimizing rationality of the market has become the 'major construct of the contemporary period because of the rise of the corporation as the accompanying organization'. Whereas, in the past the authority of the state and the market were linked and corporations took their instructions from the state, the rise of the corporation to dominance has shifted the relationships between states and markets and between states and corporations. Susan Strange (1996) argues that this shifting authority structure has given rise to new forms of power and of politics. The CSR movement is an increasingly significant dimension of neoliberal market discipline (Gill 2003) and the culture of late capitalism and postmodernity. It immediately raises the question of 'efficiency for whom?' and directs attention to the interests served by the privatization of corporate norms. Who benefits from and who bears the burden of voluntary corporate regulation? I have argued elsewhere (2006) that the discourse of efficiency informing the CSR movement is deeply problematic. As the *grundnorm* of this 'nascent global public sphere', the efficiency principle threatens to reduce publicness and sociality to economistic criteria of value, pushing competing social values to the margins. Even more important, and paradoxical, is its role in legitimating private regimes of accumulation as integral dimensions of the 'public sphere.' To the extent that private self-regulation is becoming the defining regulatory mode, we are witnessing the privatization of the commons. The discourse of efficiency naturalizes private, market-friendly regulation as an inherent attribute of neoliberal business civilization.

Corporations have historically, served the interests and purposes of empires and states, but under vastly different conditions and through processes controlled by states. The situation today is very different. Corporations are taking a leading role in promoting CSR initiatives and they have a vested interest in seeing that the movement remains rooted in voluntary, soft, self-regulatory norms. The triumph of the efficiency principle in environmental CSR initiatives ('eco-efficiency'), for example, reflects the building of 'a critical connection between neoliberalism and regulatory struggles over the environment in which sustainable development was retooled to become less subversive to corporate interests' (Rowe 2005). Indeed, to the extent that the CSR movement has become an integral dimension of corporate 'business "strategy" designed historically to forestall public regulation more than ensure responsible corporate behavior' (Rowe 2005; Carroll and Carson 2003; Sklair 2001), we must critically rethink the balance between public and private authority in corporate governance.

There is increasing evidence of peoples organizing and expressing their opposition to privatized global corporate law regimes, which may indicate openings for creating more participatory and collective standards and initiatives. For instance, resistance to global intellectual property law is mounting in India, Malaysia, Nepal, Indonesia, Thailand, Sri Lanka, Bangladesh, and the Philippines, as well as Nigeria where compensation and more equitable treatment are being demanded by indigenous and other peoples of leading mining, logging, pharmaceutical, and oil corporations (Cutler 2005: 13–14). Legal challenges of corporate human rights abuses increase, and increasingly human rights and environmental activists are discovering rules of private law, both domestic and international (Wai 2001, 2002) that assist in securing corporate accountability. Labour is mobilizing in Asia, Latin America, South America, and North America challenges are being made by citizen groups in Canada and the United States to corporate taxation laws that shift tax burdens to individuals, and numerous other social movements are asserting a variety of human rights and property rights against corporations.

A highly critical report has been released by Christian Aid, an agency of Churches in the UK and Ireland, which advanced 'corporate social accountability' as an alternative to 'corporate social responsibility' and advocates binding international legal standards (Christian Aid 2004). A global justice movement is taking shape and a new bloc of developing states, the G-20+, are putting the concerns of LDCs back onto the world trade agenda. In Canada, a series of Roundtables is being held to examine the human rights conduct of oil and gas corporations in zones of conflict. The goal is to explore the possibility of promoting CSR in the foreign investment activities of Canadian corporations through Canadian law and policy.

These and other similar developments reveal the corporate social responsibility movement to be a site of contested power and authority that cannot be assumed to be 'public', but that must be critically examined to determine the nature of the interests and purposes that it serves. This contestation of privatized corporate regulation also reveals fractures in neoliberal hegemony and identifies important openings for reasserting local interests and concerns as integral dimensions of the nascent global public domain.

Notes

1. This is a major rationale for regarding the rules of private international trade law and the law merchant system as an autonomous, self-referential, self-regulating, and reflexive order.
2. See in particular proponents of the law and economics movement, such as Posner 1980 and 1986.
3. NJ Laws, Ch. 269, '4: 414. Importantly, this incorporation statute was among the first to allow one corporation to own the stock of another, and thus set the stage for unprecedented concentration of corporate wealth and power.
4. In 1886, the corporation was granted status as a legal person in the United States. See Santa Clara v. Southern Pacific R.R., 118 US (1886).
5. Handley v. Stutz, 139 US 417 (1891).
6. International legal personality entails two things: being capable of possessing international rights and duties and the capacity to maintain these rights by bringing international claims (Reparations for Injuries Suffered in the Service of the United Nations, I.C.J. Rep. 1949, p. 174).
7. In addition, the lack of legal personality has meant that should a corporation wish to make a legal claim against a state, the former must make that claim through the agency of another state. However, there is no legal duty for a state to make a claim on behalf of its corporations and, as a result, corporations can be left with no recourse under international law against a state, such as a host state, that has in some way acted to impair the interests of the corporation. This motivated corporations to develop provisions in bilateral investment treaties, discussed below, that recognize direct legal claims by corporations against host states. For further discussion of the doctrine of state responsibility and for developments in the field of international human rights law that are pushing beyond the limits of this doctrine to hold corporations accountable, see Cutler 2006.
8. The ill-fated UN Code of Conduct on Transnational Corporations was one of the few intergovernmental initiatives that sought to impose binding legal obligations on transnational corporations. However, negotiations were suspended in 1992 largely because 'the need of developing states for foreign investment outweighed their desire to control [transnational corporations]' (ICHR 2002: 144).

9. Tripartite Declaration of Principles concerning Multinational Enterprises and Social Policy, adopted by the Governing Body of the ILO, at 204th Session, Geneva, November 1977.
10. Adopted 21 June 1976, 15 ILM 967; Revised in June 2000.
11. UN Doc.E/CN.4/Sub.2/2003/12/Rev.2 (2003), approved by the United Nations Sub-Commission on the Promotion and Protection of Human Rights on 13 August, 2003.
12. Now the European Union, the World Trade Organization, the Asian-Pacific Economic Cooperation Forum, the North Atlantic Free Trade Association, the Organization for Economic Cooperation and Development, and the UN Economic and Social Council have voluntary codes or standards.
13. In the 1990s alone, it is estimated that these agreements more than quadrupled, increasing from some 470 to over 2000 (Hallwood-Driemeier 2003). UNCTAD, which has been monitoring the development of BITs for the past decade, estimates that by 2003 there were over 2,265 such agreements involving 176 countries. See UNCTAD website: www.unctadxi.org/templates/Page1007.aspx accessed 12 June, 2006.
14. SA 8000 is an initiative recently promulgated by the Council on Economic Priorities Accreditation Agency. It is designed to foster independent third-party auditing of the activities of transnational corporations to ensure greater respect for fundamental labour rights.
15. Procedural regulation is a system where the focus is on designing processes and organizational structures to ensure that the association takes into account other, wider interests in its decisions (Black 1996: 30).
16. In general, self-regulatory initiatives may involve voluntary codes of conduct, environmental charters, environmental management systems, voluntary accords, voluntary agreements, co-regulation, covenants, and negotiated agreements. See Higley 2001 and Sinclair 1997: 532.
17. According to the OECD (2001b: 31), business surveys show that most major companies adopt codes of conduct. A survey conducted by the Institute of Business Ethics in the late 1990s showed that 57% of the largest UK companies had some form of code of conduct or have one in preparation, compared to 18% in 1987. Approximately 95% of Fortune 1000 companies have a code of conduct, while the World Bank (2003: 2) estimates that there may be as many as 1,000 codes in existence today, developed by individual multinational firms on a voluntary basis. Industry codes of conduct include, but are not limited to the following: the CERES Principles; Rugmark; ISO 9000 and 14000; Project XL; Responsible Care; the Apparel Industry Partnership Workplace Code of Conduct; the American Petroleum Institute's Strategies for Today's Environmental Partnership (STEPS); the American Textile Manufacturers Institute's Encouraging Environmental Excellence (E3) Programme; the British Standards Institution's BS7750; Australia's Greenhouse Challenge; the 33/50 Programme; and the Kimberley Process.
18. Implicit too, is the assumption that this purposive activity is directed at the attainment of shared or collective goals. The latter assumption has been addressed above.

References

Addo, M. (1999): Human Rights and Transnational Corporations – an Introduction. In: Ado, M. (ed.), *Human Rights Standards and the Responsibility of Transnational Corporations*. The Hague: Kluwer Law: 3–33.

Aid, C. (2004): Behind the Mask: the Real Face of Corporate Social Responsibility. Available: www.christian-aid.org.uk/indepth/0401csr/index.htm. Accessed 12 June, 2006.

Ashford, R. (2002): Binary Economics, Fiduciary Duties, and Corporate Social Responsibility: Comprehending Corporate Wealth Maximization and Distribution for Stockholders, Stakeholders, and Society. *Tulane Law Review*, 5–6: 1531–78.

Ayine, D. (1999): Improving Investor Accountability. In: Picciotto, S. and R. Mayne (eds.), *Regulating International Business: Beyond Liberalization*. New York: St. Martin's Press – now Palgrave Macmillan.'

Bakan, J. (2004): *The Corporation: the Pathological Pursuit of Profit and Power*. Toronto: Viking.

Barth, R. and B. Dette (2001): The Integration of Voluntary Agreements into Existing Legal Systems. In: Higley, C., F. Convery and F. Lévêque (eds.), *Environmental Voluntary Approaches: Research Insights for Policy-Makers*. Paris: Centre d'économie industrielle, Ecole Nationale Supérieure des Mines de Paris: 14–34.

Benhabib, S. (1996): Toward a Deliberative Model of Democracy. In: Benhabib, S. (ed.), *Democracy and Difference: Contesting the Boundaries of the Political*. Princeton: Princeton University Press: 67–94.

Black, J. (1996): Constitutionalising Self-Regulation. *Modern Law Review* 1: 24–55.

Carroll, W. and C. Carson (2003): Forging a New Hegemony? The Role of Transnational Policy Groups in the Network and Discourses of Global Corporate Governance. *Journal of World Systems Research* 18 (1): 67–102.

Cohn, T. (2000): *Political Economy: Theory and Practice*. New York: Longman.

Corporate Liability for Violations of International Human Rights Law (2001) *Harvard Law Review*: 2025–49.

Council on Economic Priorities Accreditation Agency (1998) Social Accountability 8000. See International Institute for Sustainable Development website: www.bsdglobal.com/tools/systems_sa.asp. Accessed 12 June 2006.

Cutler, A. C. (1999): Locating Authority in the Global Political Economy. *Review of International Political Economy* 43 (1): 59–81.

Cutler, A. C. (2000): Globalization, Law and Transnational Corporations: a Deepening of Market Discipline. In: Cohn, T., S. McBride and D. Wiseman (eds.), *Power in the Global Era: Grounding Globalization*. London, Macmillan Press and New York St. Martin's Press: 53–66.

Cutler, A. C. (2001): Critical Reflections on the Westphalian Assumptions of International Law and Organization: a Crisis of Legitimacy. *Review of International Studies* 27: 133–50.

Cutler, A. C. (2003): *Private Power and Global Authority: Transnational Merchant Law in the Global Political Economy*. Cambridge: Cambridge University Press.

Cutler, A. C. (2004): Critical Globalization Studies and International Law under Conditions of Postmodernity and Late Capitalism. In: Appelbaum, R. P. and W. I. Robinson (eds.), *Critical Globalization Studies*. New York: Routledge: 197–205.

Cutler, A. C. (2005): Gramsci, Law and the Culture of Global Capitalism. *Critical Review of International Social and Political Philosophy*, 8 (4): 1–16.

Cutler, A. C. (2006): Transnational Business Civilization, Corporations, and the Privatization of Global Governance. In: May, C. (ed.), *Global Corporate Power, International Political Economy Yearbook*. Boulder, CO: Lynne Rienner Publishers, 15: 199–226.

Cutler, A. C., V. Haufler and T. Porter (eds.) (1999): *Private Authority and International Affairs*. Albany, NY: State University of New York Press.

Desai, M. (2003): Public Goods: a Historical Perspective. In: Kaul I., P. Conceição, K. Le Goulven and R. Mendoza (eds.), *Providing Global Public Goods: Managing Globalization*. United Nations Development Programme, New York: Oxford University Press: 63–77.

Dixit, A. and M. Olson (2000): Does Voluntary Participation Undermine the Coase Theorem? *Journal of Public Economics* 6: 309–35.

Dodge v. Ford Motor Co. (170 N.W. 668 (1919): 507).

Fox, T., H. Ward and B. Howard (2002): Public Sector Roles in Strengthening Corporate Social Responsibility – a Baseline Study. *World Bank Corporate Social Responsibility Practice*, Retrieved 14 July 2004 from www.worldbank.org.

Freeman, J. (2000): The Private Role in Public Governance. *New York University Law Review* 3: 543–675.

Friedman, M. (1962): *Capitalism and Freedom*. Chicago: University of Chicago Press.

Gaines, S. and C. Kimber (2001): Redirecting Self-Regulation. *Journal of Environmental Law* 2: 157–84.

Gaudier, M. (1999): *Firms of the Future: Economic Efficiency and Social Performance*. Geneva: International Institute for Labour Studies.

Gill, S. (2003): *Power and Resistance in the New World Order*. Basingstoke: Palgrave Macmillan.

Habermas J. (1996): Three Normative Models of Democracy. In: Benhabib S. (ed.), *Democracy and Difference: Contesting the Boundaries of the Political*. Princeton: Princeton University Press: 21–30.

Habermas, J. (1999): *Between Facts and Norms: Contributions to a Discourse Theory of Law and Democracy*. Cambridge, MA: MIT Press.

Hall, R. and Biersteker, T. (2002): Private Authority as Global Governance. In: Hall, R. and T. Biersteker (eds.), *The Emergence of Private Authority on Global Governance*. Cambridge: Cambridge University Press: 203–22.

Hallwood-Driemeier, M. (2003): *Do Bilateral Investment Treaties Attract FDI? Only a Bit . . . and They Could Bite*. Washington DC: World Bank.

Handley v. Stutz, 139 U.S. 417 (1891).

Harris, R. (2000): *Industrializing English Law: Entrepreneurship and Business Organization*. Cambridge: Cambridge University Press: 1720–844.

Harrod, J. (2006): The Century of the Corporation. In: May, C. (ed.), *Global Corporate Power, International Political Economy Yearbook*. Boulder, CO: Lynne Rienner Publishers, 15: 23–46.

Harvey, D. (1989): *The Condition of Postmodernity*. Oxford: Blackwell.

Harvey, D. (2003): *The New Imperialism*. New York: Oxford University Press.

Haufler, V. (2000): Private Sector International Regimes. In: Higgott, R., G. Underhill and A. Bieler (eds.), *Non-State Actors and Authority in the Global System*. London/ New York: Routledge: 121–37.

Haufler, V. (2001): *A Public Role for the Private Sector: Industry Self-Regulation in a Global Economy*. Washington: Carnegie Endowment for International Peace.

Haufler, V. (2006): Global Governance and the Private Sector. In: May, C. (ed.), *Global Corporate Power, International Political Economy Yearbook*. Boulder, CO: Lynne Rienner Publishers, 15: 85–104.

Held, D. (1995): *Democracy and the Global Order: From the Modern State to Cosmopolitan Governance*. Cambridge: Polity Press.

Held, D. (2000): Regulating Globalization: the Reinvention of Politics, *International Sociology* 15: 394–408.

Hess, D. (1999): Social Reporting: a Reflexive Law Approach to Corporate Social Responsiveness. *Journal of Corporation Law* 1: 41–84.

Higley, C., F. Convery, and F. Lévêque (2001): Voluntary Approaches: an Introduction. In: Higley, C., F. Convery and F. Lévêque (eds.), *Environmental Voluntary Approaches: Research Insights for Policy-Makers*. Paris: Centre d'économie industrielle, Ecole Nationale Supérieure des Mines de Paris: 4–33.

Horn, N. (1980): Codes of Conduct for MNEs and Transnational Lex Mercatoria: an International Process of Learning and Law Making. In: Horn N. (ed.), *Legal Problems of Codes of Conduct for Multinational Enterprises*. Deventer, The Netherlands: Kluwer Law: 45–81.

Horwitz, M. (1987): Santa Clara Revisited: the Development of Corporate Theory. In: Samuels, W. and A. Miller (eds.), *Corporations and Society: Power and Responsibility*. New York: Greenwood Press: 13–63.

Hummels H. (2004): A Collective Lack of Memory. *Journal of Corporate Citizenship* 4 (14): 18–21.

ICHR International Council on Human Rights Policy (2002): Beyond Voluntarism: Human Rights and the Developing International Legal Obligations of Companies. Versoix, Switzerland: International Council on Human Rights Policy.

IRENE International Restructuring Education Network Europe (2000): Controlling Corporate Wrongs: the Liability of Multinational Corporations. Retrieved 24 July 2004 from: www.indianet.nl/irene.html.

International Labour Organization (1977): Tripartite Declaration of Principles Concerning Multinational Enterprises and Social Policy. 204th Session, Geneva.

Johns, F. (1994): The Invisibility of the Transnational Corporation: an Analysis of International Law and Legal Theory. *Melbourne University Law Review* 19: 893–923.

Kaul, I., P. Conceição, K. Le Goulven and R. Mendoza (eds.) (2003): *Providing Global Public Goods: Managing Globalization*. United Nations Development Programme, New York: Oxford University Press.

Kaul, I. and R. Mendoza (2003): Advancing the Concept of Public Goods. In: Kaul I. et al. (eds.), *Providing Global Public Goods*. United Nations Development Programme, New York: Oxford University Press: 78–112.

Lipschutz, R. with M. Rowe (2005): *Regulation for the Rest of Us? Globalization, Governmentality, and Global Politics*. London: Routledge.

Liubicic, R. (1998): Corporate Codes of Conduct and Product Labeling Schemes: the Limits and Possibilities of Promoting International Labour Rights Through Private Initiatives. *Law and Policy in International Business* 1: 111–58.

Malanczuk, P. (1997): *Akehurst's Modern Introduction to International Law*. London/New York: Routledge.

May, C. (2006): Introduction. In: May, C. (ed.), *Global Corporate Power*. International Political Economy Yearbook, Boulder, CO: Lynne Rienner Publications, 15.

McCabe, B. J. (1992): Are Corporations Socially Responsible? Is Corporate Social Responsibility Desirable? *Bond Law Review* 4: 2.

McLean, J. (2003): The Transnational Corporation in History: Lessons for Today? *Indiana Law Journal* 79: 363–77.

Miwa, Y. (1999): Corporate Social Responsibility: Dangerous and Harmful, though Maybe Not Irrelevant. *Cornell Law Review* 84: 1227–54.

North, D. (1990): *Institutions, Institutional Change and Economic Performance*. Cambridge: Cambridge University Press.

O'Brien, R. (1999): NGOs, Global Civil Society and Global Economic Regulation. In: Picciotto, S. and R. Mayne (eds.), *Regulating International Business: Beyond Liberalization*. New York: St. Martin's Press – now Palgrave Macmilln.

OECD Guidelines for Multinational Enterprises (1976): 15 ILM 967. Revised June 2000.

OECD Organization for Economic Cooperation and Development (2003): Voluntary Approaches for Environmental Policy: Effectiveness, Efficiency and Usage in Policy Mixes. Paris.

OECD Organization for Economic Cooperation and Development (2001a): Corporate Social Responsibility: Partners for Progress. Paris.

OECD Organization for Economic Cooperation and Development (2001b): Corporate Responsibility: Private Initiatives, Public Goals. Paris.

Ougaard, M. (2006): Instituting the Power to Do Good? In: May C. (ed.), *Global Corporate Power, International Political Economy Yearbook*. Boulder, CO: Lynne Rienner Publishers 15: 227–48.

Pegg, S. (2006): World Leaders and Bottom Feeders: Divergent Strategies Toward Social Responsibility and Resource Extraction. In: May C. (ed.), *Global Corporate Power, International Political Economy Yearbook*. Boulder, CO: Lynne Rienner Publishers, 15: 249–72.

Pitt, H. and K. Groskaufmanis (1990): Minimizing Corporate Civil and Criminal Liability: a Second Look at Corporate Codes of Conduct. *Georgetown Law Journal* 5: 1559–654.

Posner, R. A. (1980): The Ethical and Political Basis of the Efficiency Norm in Common Law Adjudication. *Hofstra Law Review* 8 (3): 487–507.

Posner, R. A. (1986): *Economic Analysis of Law*. Toronto: Little, Brown.

Ratner, S. (2001): Corporations and Human Rights: a Theory of Legal Responsibility. *Yale Law Journal* 3: 443–545.

Rawls, J. (1997): The Idea of Public Reason. In: Bohman J. and W. Rehg (eds.), *Deliberative Democracy: Essays on Reason and Politics*. Cambridge, MA: MIT Press: 93–131.

Redmond, P. (2002): Sanctioning Corporate Responsibility for Human Rights. *Alternative Law Journal* 1: 23–7.

Reparations for Injuries Suffered in the Service of the United Nations, I.C.J. Rep. 1949, 174.

Rieth, L. (2004): Corporate Social Responsibility in Global Economic Governance: a Comparison of the OECD Guidelines and the UN Global Compact. In: Schirm, S. (ed.), *New Rules for Global Markets: Public and Private Governance in the World Economy*. New York: Palgrave MacMillan: 177–92.

Roht-Arriaza, N. (1995): Shifting the Point of Regulation: the International Organization for Standardization and Global Lawmaking on Trade and the Environment. *Ecology Law Quarterly*: 479–539.

Rostow, E. (1959): To Whom and for What Ends is Corporate Management Responsible? In: Mason E. (ed.), *The Corporation in Modern Society*. Cambridge: Harvard University Press.

Rowe, J. (2005): Corporate Social Responsibility as Business Strategy. In: Lipschutz, R. with J. Rowe (eds.), *Regulation for the Rest of Us? Globalization, Governmentality, and Global Politics*. London: Routledge.

Ruggie, J. (2004): Reconstituting the Global Public Domain: Issues, Actors and Practices. *European Journal of International Relations* 10 (4): 499–531.

Santa Clara v. Southern Pacific R.R., 118 U.S. (1886).

Santos, B. de S. (1995): *Towards a New Common Sense – A Paradigmatic: Law, Science, and Politics in the Paradigmatic Transformation*. London: Routledge.

Sinclair, D. (1997): Self-Regulation Versus Command and Control? Beyond False Dichotomies. *Law & Policy* 4: 529–59.

Sklair, L. (2001): *The Transnational Capitalist Class*. Oxford: Blackwell.

Skogly, S. (1999): Economic and Social Human Rights, Private Actors and International Obligation. In: Addo, M. (ed.), *Human Rights Standards and the Responsibility of Transnational Corporations*. The Hague: Kluwer Law: 239–58.

Smith, D. G. (1998): The Shareholder Primacy Norm. *Journal of Corporation Law* 277–323.

Strange, S. (1996): *The Retreat of the State: the Diffusion of Power in the World Economy*. Cambridge: Cambridge University Press.

Testy, K. (2002): Linking Progressive Law with Progressive Social Movements. *Tulane Law Review* 5–6: 1227–52.

Teubner, G. (2002): Breaking Frames: Economic Globalization and the Emergence of Lex Mercatoria. *European Journal of Social Theory* 5 (2): 199–217.

Thrift, N. (2000): State Sovereignty, Globalization and the Rise of Soft Capitalism. In: Hay, C. and D. Marsh (eds.), *Demystifying Globalization*. Basingstoke: Palgrave: now Palgrave – Macmillan: 71–102.

Triantis, G. (2001): The Efficiency of Vague Contract Terms: a Response to the Schwartz–Scott Theory of U.C.C. Article. *Louisiana Law Review* 4: 1065–79.

United Nations (2003): UN Norms on the Responsibility of TNCs and Other Business Enterprises with Regard to Human Rights. Doc.E/CN.4/Sub.2/2003/12/Rev.2.

UNCTAD (1999): United Nations Conference on Trade and Development. The Social Responsibility of Transnational Corporations. New York/Geneva.

UNCTC (1986): United Nations Code of Conduct on Transnational Corporations. New York: United Nations.

Wai, R. (2001–2002): Transnational Liftoff and Juridical Touchdown: the Regulatory Function of Private International Law in an Era of Globalization. *Columbia Journal of Transnational Law* 40: 209–74.

Wallman, S. (1999): Understanding the Purpose of a Corporation: an Introduction. *Journal of Corporation Law* 24: 807–18.

Ward, H. (2001): Governing Multinationals: the Role of Foreign Direct Liability. *Royal Institute of International Affairs Briefing Paper New Series* 18: 1–6.

Williams, C. (2002): Corporate Social Responsibility in an Era of Economic Globalization. *University of California Davis Law Review* 3: 705–77.

Williams, M. (2001): In Search of Global Standards: the Political Economy of Trade and the Environment. In: Stevis, D. and V. Assetto (eds.), *The International Political Economy of the Environment: Critical Perspectives*. Boulder, CO: Lynne Rienner Publishers: 39–61.

World Bank (1998): Development and Human Rights: the Role of the World Bank. Washington, DC.

World Bank (2003): Corporate Codes of Conduct and International Standards: an Analytical Comparison. Washington, DC.

8
MNCs and the International Community: Conflict, Conflict Prevention and the Privatization of Diplomacy

Virginia Haufler

Introduction

Seemingly suddenly, in the mid-1990s the international community began to pressure multinational corporations to become more active in a positive way on issues of conflict and conflict prevention. Although some critics argue that foreign investors should withdraw from countries with unstable or illegitimate governments, an increasing number of others argue that foreign investors should instead remain invested and become more directly involved in initiatives to improve the political environment in the host country. Both groups speak out against situations in which corporations are complicit in the human rights violations of repressive governments; facilitate the international trade in commodities that finance intractable conflicts; and exacerbate societal divisions and grievances that underlie civil wars. But the second group also argues that the private sector has a responsibility to adopt new practices that would cut the link between their activities and the violence around them, by engaging in corporate conflict prevention.[1]

Does this herald the emergence of a new norm for corporate behaviour – a kind of new 'responsibility to protect' the citizens of the countries in which corporations operate?[2] Does this shift security issues out of traditional public arenas and into the hands of the private sector, at least in some weakly governed developing countries? If so, this raises the further question of why, during the last decade leading states, international organizations, and activist NGOs have chosen a strategy of pressuring the private sector to engage in conflict prevention. Concerns about the corporate role in conflict and repression are nothing new, but the idea of corporate conflict prevention is. And in any case, why would corporations accede to these demands and adopt this norm into their practices? This chapter focuses on the second of these questions: the factors that have changed the strategies of significant international actors, certain states, international organizations and activists that now seek to have corporations intervene in conflict-ridden host countries as potential agents of positive change. While the effects of corporate conflict prevention on wider issues of security, and the motivations for private sector participation, are both important questions that need to be answered, they are beyond the scope of this chapter.

These strategies are rooted in significant changes in the international environment that have altered the calculations for states and international organizations, leading them to rely more heavily on the private sector to accomplish public goals. This is combined with the entrepreneurship of activist organizations that strategically deploy new norms of corporate social responsibility as a response to political blocks to more traditional conflict prevention strategies. In order to explore this topic, this chapter examines some of the new political dynamics surrounding oil exploration and development in conflict-ridden developing countries.

The following section provides a brief survey of the literature exploring the relationship between foreign investment and political instability. This is followed by an overview of significant changes in the structure of the international political economy that have affected the strategic calculations of relevant actors, comparing an earlier era of concern over corporate misbehaviour the 1970s with the current one. I then discuss two specific initiatives that illustrate the new emphasis on corporate conflict prevention in the oil sector. The conclusion assesses the implications of these new expectations for companies, and for the conflict in values it may presage for the wider international community.

The effects of foreign direct investment on conflict

There are now around 61,000 transnational corporations firms in the world today, with over 900,000 affiliates. In the past decade, a growing amount of foreign investment has been going into the emerging markets in the developing world.[3] Many markets are now dominated by oligopolistic firms, and the largest firms have revenues that exceed those of a typical small, industrialized country. As competition in global markets has increased, corporations especially those in the extractive sectors have been moving into ever more socially and environmentally sensitive locations (Christiansen 2002). It is almost inevitable that, under these circumstances, the impact of foreign corporations on a wide array of political, economic and environmental ills would become a central focus of attention.

One of the most prominent lines of research today examines the so-called resource curse or the 'paradox of plenty'. When high-value natural resources are developed for the first time, the resulting sudden influx of wealth may distort the economy and undermine economic development, increase political conflict and ultimately retard democratization[4] (Auty 1994; Davis 1995; Sachs and Warner 1995; Karl 1997; Auty 1998; deSoysa 1999; Ross 1999;

deSoysa 2000; Ross 2000; The Fridtjof Nansen Institute 2000). There are a number of analytical arguments for why this happens. Some have analysed the role of asset-specific commodities, such as oil, on the stability and development of a country. Terry Lynn Karl analysed the role of oil in the political economy of a number of oil-exporting states in the 1990s, particularly Venezuela, and concluded that when the state owns the petroleum sector (the 'petro-state') it becomes predatory in the collection of 'mineral rents', and there are few incentives for it to develop an efficient private sector or administrative system (Karl 1997; The Fridtjof Nansen Institute 2000). Paul Collier and his colleagues at the World Bank analysed data that demonstrate that the more a country is dependent on one or a few commodities for a majority of its export revenues, the more likely it is to suffer from corruption, underdevelopment and conflict (Collier 2000; The Fridtjof Nansen Institute 2000). Others have analysed the ways in which the globalization of markets facilitates trade in 'lootable' commodities which can be used to finance war, such as diamonds, timber and cocaine. Recent research has attempted to tease out the relative importance of greed, grievance and other factors in the outbreak of civil war and the breakdown of governments (Berdal and Malone 2000; International Peace Academy 2001; Ballentine and Sherman 2003).

Scholars and others have long focused attention on the broader issue of whether or not foreign investment actually leads to, or facilitates, repression, conflict or authoritarian rule (Lopez and Stohl 1989; Frynas 1998; Global Witness 1999; Manby 1999; Pegg 1999; Nelson 2000). When foreign investors enter a region for the first time they often create conflict over access and control to particular lands and resources. This has been particularly evident where resource-rich lands are occupied by indigenous groups who do not have good access to the political system, and who may see foreign investment as a way for outsiders to exploit and plunder their lands. This has become a barrier to oil development in some regions, particularly in Latin America and also in Southeast Asia (Burke 1999). Disputes over which groups or individuals should be involved in decisions about the extent and character of natural resource development, and over the distribution of benefits, can exacerbate existing grievances. The issue of who benefits and who does not can divide local communities and groups, and increase divisions between the local and central government. Opposition to natural resource development often leads authoritarian governments to undertake repressive tactics, or can lead weak governments to fail in the face of civil war. In either case, foreign investment often supports, or has been perceived to support, authoritarian governments that repress their citizens and engage in human rights abuses, as in the recent case of oil development in Sudan.

Separate from this debate has been an extensive line of new research on the links between foreign investment, environmental degradation and security.[5] This posits that resource scarcity (instead of abundance) leads to conflict, corruption and weak governance. The development of natural resources can lead to their depletion, or to the degradation of land and water upon which peoples livelihoods depend. Thomas Homer-Dixon and his colleagues have been at the forefront in this area of research, exploring the paths through which environmental degradation and depletion cause or exacerbate differences among groups and become an important source of domestic conflict (Homer-Dixon and Blitt 1998; Homer-Dixon 1999). Homer-Dixon argues that resource scarcity drives elites to capture existing resources and marginalize others, which becomes a source of grievance. The implication, not always explicitly stated, is that corporations that exploit natural resources and pollute the environment are one source of conflict. Others, however, question the direct relationship between environmental degradation and conflict (Gleditsch 1998).

Globalization itself is posited as a new source of threat to the stability of developing countries. Economic transactions can now span the globe through networks of intermediaries, including both legitimate and illegitimate commercial actors. These networks may be instrumental in facilitating the use of revenues from resource extraction to fund the purchase of weapons, providing sustenance to rebels and repressive governments alike, as the issue of 'conflict diamonds' has demonstrated (Duffield 2000; Reno 2000; Smillie, Giberie et al. 2000). Increasingly, these global markets are implicated in transnational organized crime and even terrorism (Williams 2002).

The research on the political economy of conflict did not start from questions about the role and responsibility of corporations for violent conflict, but it provides substantive support with some caveats for activists who point to the culpability of the private sector. In recent years, the scholarly community concerned with conflict prevention and conflict management have also turned to analysing the potential positive role for the private sector; see, for instance, the recent work of Wenger and Mockli (Wenger and Möckli 2003). What exactly the private sector can and should do in order to prevent or reduce conflict is an area of great policy contestation today, with little evidence as yet about what actually works. Nevertheless, a number of leading international activist groups, and agencies of governments and international organizations, have pushed the corporate conflict prevention agenda and sought to integrate it more fully into a broad range of related policy arenas, such as development, state-building, and in recent years, post-conflict reconstruction.

Change in the international community

There are two common explanations for why so many people now want companies to engage in conflict prevention. The first is simply that corporations are everywhere and thus they are more often implicated in conflict, corruption and repression. In other words, the liberalization of economic policies worldwide and the globalization of production have facilitated the entry of corporations into places they had never gone before, including zones of conflict. The second common explanation is that it has something to do with the end of the cold war and the more permissive environment this has brought. In other words, because states are no longer concerned with the superpower struggle, they can turn their attention to other conflicts and other actors. Both of these are essentially structural arguments, pointing to the character of the global political economy and the distribution of power as factors driving towards a privatized solution to violence in peripheral nations. Neither explanation is entirely satisfactory, however, and needs to be refined and linked to more agent-centred analysis of strategic responses to the new global environment.

Both the 1970s and 1990s were two periods when multinational corporations came under especially fierce attack in international fora. In the earlier period, the United Nations, prodded by developing country governments, attempted to negotiate a global code of conduct for transnational corporations and established the Centre on Transnational Corporations. The core principles of the proposed code of conduct included a commitment by companies to uphold the law and policies of host country governments, and a reaffirmation of the sovereignty of states. After a decade of work, and agreement on about 80 per cent of the codes provisions, the entire enterprise was dropped, due to the opposition of neoliberal reformers in the Reagan and Thatcher governments, and due to a lack of interest by others (Kline 1985). Starting in the 1990s and continuing to today, there is a second surge of interest in establishing a code of conduct, but little in the way of centralized, comprehensive interstate bargaining as we saw in the past.

More corporations locate activities abroad today in large part due to the diffusion of liberalization across the international community. The decision by states to liberalize their domestic economies over the course of the last twenty-five years, whether by choice or not, has changed the entire dynamic regarding foreign direct investment. During the 1950s and 1960s, newly independent states struggled to establish authoritative control by the central government over a territory that often included many conflicting interests and ethnic groups. Governments were often authoritarian, based on patron–client politics, and called upon nationalist and anti-colonial sentiment to establish their legitimacy. Many were extremely suspicious of foreign investors, and sought to restrict their access to national resources and markets. In the early 1970s, one of the popular ways in which governing elites attempted to enhance their legitimacy and authority was by nationalizing foreign investments, especially oil production.[6] Only a few decades later, however, the world had changed dramatically. From the 1990s to today, increasing numbers of developing countries have adopted policies more favourable to foreign investment, viewing foreign investment as the key to industrialization and economic growth.[7] These efforts were supported and encouraged by the World Bank and International Monetary Fund, both of which pressed developing countries to integrate more fully into the global economy by opening their economies more fully.

While liberalization and globalization permitted wider access by corporations to a range of newly emerging economies, the end of the cold war changed the focus of security concerns. 'New' security included increased attention to non-traditional security issues such as environmental threats, but also more concern about the rise in intra-state conflicts, as opposed to the concerns about interstate war that dominated the cold war era. Many of the most conflict-ridden areas are prime locations for the development of natural resources, including oil and minerals, such as regions of Africa that have suffered from rebellions, coups, civil wars and corruption. These came to be labelled as 'failed states' or 'quasi-states' because of the limited capacity of these governments to govern effectively, with many of them experiencing prolonged civil conflict and loss of control over territory. Some observers began to point to state failure as a source of possible transnational threats[8] (Jackson 1990; Reno 2000). The countries most likely to fail are those that are neither completely democratic nor completely autocratic, but fall into a middle category in which there may be some democratic institutions or processes, but limited individual freedom and rule of law. Not all states in this category will fail – although the number of countries falling into this category increased sharply with the breakup of the Soviet Union, the number of states that have completely failed, i.e. collapsed into civil war or protracted social conflict, has declined (Marshall and Gurr 2003). These weak states are often dependent on oil wealth – the predatory or petro-states discussed above. As Dorff recently described, the study of state failure began to shift from a focus on total collapse, to an examination of state weakening, and from there to the ways in which non-state actors such as criminals and terrorists could exploit that weakness. As he points out, 'the driving force behind the new strategic environment was changing in a profound and fundamental way: From a global competition between competing ideologies to a more localized but increasingly dangerous competition between legitimate and illegitimate governance' (Dorff 2005). It is out of this environment that the concern for the complicity of corporations in conflict, corruption and criminality emerged.

In the last twenty years, the relationship between the North and South has undergone a profound shift. Two of the most important areas of change are in recent perspectives on the causes and cures for underdevelopment; and new expectations concerning the legitimacy of intervening in the affairs of weak states. After the Second World War, with the establishment of the World Bank and bilateral aid programmes in industrialized countries, a new development community of practitioners emerged with ideas about how to promote development in poorer states. In these early years, both foreign aid analysts in the North and many government representatives in the South worked from a state-centric paradigm. The donor governments and agencies financed and implemented aid projects through the host government.

The economic policies recommended and adopted in much of the developing world were protectionist import-substitution policies that encouraged government intervention in the economy, and many states nationalized or expropriated foreign investments. The model of the 'strong' developmentalist state represented by Japan was attractive to many countries, particularly in East Asia (The Fridtjof Nansen Institute 2000: 17).

Over the past fifteen years, the development paradigm has shifted, both in the donor community and in the developing countries themselves. The 'Washington consensus' emerged, in which a wide range of policymakers, particularly the US Treasury Department and the IMF and World Bank, promoted liberal policies of free trade, deregulation and privatization, and this set the stage for the policies of liberalization that opened up formerly closed markets to foreign investment. But in addition, in recent years, this liberalization has been married to an increasing concern for state capacity in the developing world (see the discussion of state failure above), under the heading of a 'good governance' agenda. The end of command-and-control economies, the crises experienced by welfare states, the state-led development of east Asian economies followed by their collapse in the east Asian financial crisis, and the increased evidence of failed states in Africa, all these changes led the development community, particularly the World Bank, to examine the role of the state in development more closely (World Bank 1997).

By focusing on 'good governance', the World Bank and others sought to limit rent-seeking by the state by promoting privatization of economic assets and reforms that would limit the discretionary power of the local government. Paradoxically, this led the international financial institutions to intervene more directly in political affairs in a way that it had not been able to do so explicitly during the cold war.[9] Non-intervention in the political affairs of a state has been a dominant norm in the international system for centuries. The principle of sovereignty was enshrined in the United Nations charter at its founding (Weiss 1996: 435). During the cold war, the United Nations was constrained not to intervene by a narrow interpretation of its Charter: it dealt only with recognized governments, and worked through those governments when it did intervene. The end of the cold war, however, resulted in an increase in humanitarian intervention in crises. As one observer noted, 'by the end of the 1990s, the idea that states should not be allowed to hide behind the shield of sovereignty when gross violations of human rights take place on their territory had firmly taken root' (JongeOudraat 2000: 4; Finnemore 2003).

The impulse to intervene has been strengthened by the emergence of an international human rights regime. International and regional laws now enshrine the principles associated with human rights. The rights of individuals, and the rights of specific groups (including women and indigenous groups), have become entrenched in world politics. The UN now has a Human Rights Commission which monitors conditions around the world, the US Department of State regularly reports the human rights status of countries, and the Canadian government has adopted 'human security' as its foreign policy theme. The norms surrounding the human rights regime are now well accepted in theory, although not always in practice. This has made it more likely that governments that violate these norms will be subject to scrutiny and sanctions (Rodman 1997). Most states still reject the *unilateral* right to intervene for humanitarian purposes, as reaffirmed by the General Assembly recently.[10] Furthermore, most would agree with the conclusions of the International Commission on Intervention and State Sovereignty, which stated that 'sovereign states have a responsibility to protect their own citizens from avoidable catastrophe ... but that when they are unwilling or unable to do so, that responsibility must be borne by the broader community of states' (International Commission on Intervention and State Sovereignty 2001: 8). In other words, it is states that are still expected to protect their own people. The problem in recent years is that many states do not have the capacity or will to do so and the international community tends to talk more about intervention than take action. Instead, those concerned about the breakdown of state authority and resulting chaos and bloodshed find themselves searching for another alternative and other actors to take responsibility; there is increasing acknowledgment of the delegation or 'privatization' of foreign policy, ranging from efforts to utilize private military forces to carry out interventions, to calls for 'responsible engagement' by corporations (Ramasastry 2002; Bomann-Larsen 2003; Avant 2005).

Failed states, a new development paradigm, and a more permissive environment for intervention all provide the larger conditions under which the turn towards the private sector to mitigate the conditions of conflict emerged. But the most dramatic difference between the earlier period of corporate criticism and the present one is the rapid increase in number and scope of non-governmental organizations (NGOs) and transnational activist networks in the current era. In the early years of postcolonial development, most activism was limited to the domestic sphere, with a few exceptions. The focus of attention by most activists tended to be their own governments and policies that directly affected their own lives. There was relatively little communication among activist groups in different countries, at least compared with today. NGOs usually did not operate in contested lands, although over time they began to mount cross-border operations which states considered to be illicit because they were without government consent (Weiss 1996: 445).

In the era of economic globalization, politics also has become increasingly globalized. Activists today organize in ways that transcend national boundaries, bringing together interested parties across the globe (Keck and Sikkink 1998; McAdam, Tarrow et al. 2001; Lichbach 2002). Keck and Sikkink argue that transnational advocacy networks emerged between 1968 and 1993; Bendell, and Broad and Cavanagh, both document a new corporate accountability movement emerging in the second half of the 1990s (Keck and Sikkink 1998; Broad and Cavanagh 1998). When local activists become frustrated with their inability to change government policy because domestic political channels are blocked, they bring in pressure from abroad in the form of transnational activist networks, in a 'boomerang effect' against the government (Keck and Sikkink 1998). Frustration at government intransigence and/or the weakness of some states has pushed local and transnational activists to look upon corporations, particularly foreign and extractive ones, to resolve issues of conflict. Firms investing in unstable regions of the world bring with them the 'spotlight' of outside media and activists, who bring worldwide attention to a conflict and to the role the company plays in it (Spar 1998).

These structural and strategic changes provide the context in which development and security agendas intersect in the area of corporate social responsibility and corporate conflict prevention. They have changed the strategic environment for companies by transforming the costs and risks of traditional strategies. In the past, in response to social and political pressures, it was often easy for firms to stonewall, or to lobby political leaders at home or in international fora for protection from societal demands. In an era of global competition and reputational risk, it has become more difficult to ignore those demands (Haufler 2003).

Corporate conflict prevention and the oil sector

The debate over corporate social responsibility is nothing new: it was over three decades ago that Milton Friedman famously defended firms against claims that they must act more responsibly, by arguing that the business of business is simply to make a profit (Friedman 1970). Others have remarked in a similar vein that it would be downright unethical for a company to do anything that might harm return to shareholders, since they are the ultimate owners of a firm (Crook 1999). And yet, a number of states, international organizations, and activists now call upon companies to adopt policies of corporate social responsibility, especially when they operate in zones of conflict.

The corporate conflict prevention agenda can be seen most clearly in the efforts to cut the link between oil resource development and violence. We can see here a number of the factors discussed above as structural factors that facilitate this new agenda. With liberalization and the end of the cold war, the competition to develop new sources of oil has heated up, with China now a driving force in oil politics. As energy companies search out new sources, they are welcomed into regions of the world they would not otherwise have explored, such as Sudan or Chad. The link between energy development, potential or existing state failure, and violence and criminality, can be seen in the domestic politics of Angola, Nigeria, Colombia and others.

The actor-centred dynamics of this agenda can be examined through the prism of government and activist efforts, particularly those based in Britain, to raise the issue of corporations and conflict prevention. These were then magnified by other activists, combined with other emerging issues of concern, and taken up by international organizations and other governments. The following is a very brief overview of some of the main instigators and enablers of this agenda during the 1990s and into the new century.

The notion of bringing business into conflict prevention efforts emerged from activist campaigns by advocacy organizations over oil in Angola, diamonds in Sierra Leone, and security forces in Nigeria and Colombia (Global Witness 1999; Freeman 2000). These campaigns brought to public attention, and to the attention of national governments and international organizations, the link between resource development and its deleterious effects on social stability. Some of the issues derived from the emerging concern over corruption and development, which was later linked to conflict. In the 1990s, activists and development specialists began to view corruption as a barrier to development and a precursor to social breakdown. A former World Bank official established the German-based NGO Transparency International (TI) dedicated to changing law and regulation regarding corruption issues, which essentially became a 'norm entrepreneur' in the area of anti-corruption initiatives.[11] TI launched a campaign to 'name and shame' countries by publishing its annual Corruption Perception Index of the most corrupt political environments, highlighting the link between perceptions of corruption and other economic variables such as foreign investment and economic growth. The campaign against corruption garnered support from its compatibility with the 'good governance' agenda of the World Bank itself, which began to incorporate anti-corruption elements into its programmes. Eventually, member states of the OECD in 1997 passed a Convention on Combating Bribery of Foreign Public Officials in International Business Transactions. The World Bank, as part of its programme of good governance initiatives, began to incorporate anti-corruption elements into its development programmes.

The anti-corruption agenda fed into and supported the emerging concerns over business and conflict. Norm entrepreneurs such as the NGO Global Witness highlighted in the global media the role of specific companies in profiting from turmoil in Africa, particularly their role in the long-drawn out civil war in Angola. Throughout the conflict, oil companies had continued to operate, doing business with both the government and the rebel forces, and essentially financing the never-ending war. With the resources at hand, there was little incentive for either side to end the conflict. Two reports by the London-based NGO Global Witness in 1998 and 1999, *Rough Trade: the Role of Companies and Governments in the Angolan Conflict*; and, more stridently, *A Crude Awakening: the Role of Oil and Banking Industries in Angolan Civil War and the Plunder of State Assets* were a wake-up call to the international community. Oil corporations, especially those based in Britain such as BP, were subject to an international spotlight for their contributions to the bloodshed in Angola. At the same time, international concern also began to focus on the Canadian company Talisman and its participation in an oil development project in Sudan, a country wrought by civil war and ruled by a repressive regime. The CEO of Talisman at first rebutted all attempts to persuade the company to withdraw from Sudan, and this became a huge issue for the Canadian public. As the stock price of Talisman shares sank under the weight of the negative publicity, eventually Talisman had to withdraw from Sudan.[12]

The broader agenda for corporate conflict prevention was set by the ground-breaking report *The Business of Peace*, produced by the Council on Economic Priorities and the Prince of Wales Business Leaders Forum (Nelson 2000). This report made the economic and moral case for why business should view conflict prevention activities as being in their own self-interest. Magnifying the impact of this report, the new UN Global Compact initiated its first Policy Dialogue on Business in Zones of Conflict at the instigation of some corporate members.[13] The Policy Dialogue brought together representatives from the UN system, the private sector, and NGOs to discuss the links between business and conflict, and potential methods of severing those links. Through this Dialogue, the participants with UN leadership were beginning to disseminate and reinforce new norms about the corporate role in conflict situations (United Nations Global Compact 2002). A policy-oriented literature emerged that attempted to tease out the economic elements of conflict, the potential role for foreign investors in conflict prevention, and the actual practical policies that this might entail (International Peace Academy 2001; Banfield, Haufler and Lilly 2003).

For the extractive industries, petroleum in particular, two issues relating to the revenues that flow from corporations to host country governments dominated the discussion at the UN, in countries that were home to oil corporations, and within the activist community: the debate over the allocation of oil revenues within society; and the transparency of those payments to the public. How a government allocates revenue is of course a responsibility of sovereign states, and typically is not considered an issue for external interest or intervention. However, a misallocation or misappropriation of these funds can deepen divisions between different groups within society, as some are advantaged and some are disadvantaged. In the case of natural resources such as oil, the revenues can be huge, dwarfing all other sources of income. The result may be that the development of natural resource wealth may stimulate competition to control revenues, fueling corruption and strengthening the position of some elite groups within society at the expense of the poor and disenfranchised. Different groups may come to fight over the revenues themselves, as greed and grievance combine in ways that lead to state failure (Collier 2000).

Many observers argued that the secrecy surrounding the payments made by large companies to host governments facilitated corruption. One mechanism to encourage a better distribution of revenues is for companies to provide the public with information about what they pay in tax revenues and fees to host country governments. Such transparency will enable local groups to hold governments and corporations accountable. In fact, the calls for increased transparency built up over the years after those initial reports and put pressure on the companies involved. British Petroleum (BP), as a major investor in Angola, found itself in the spotlight of international concern over the ongoing civil war in that country. With a new Chief Executive Officer committed to enhancing corporate social responsibility, the company published financial data regarding the signing of bonuses it paid to the Angolan government. The company made a commitment to provide more information about its operations, and to put in place systems to prevent corruption (Christiansen 2002). It put BP in a difficult position with regard to its relationship with the Angolan government and even other oil companies.

Within the next few years, the pressure on companies to adopt more transparency regarding their oil revenues became stronger. There was a realization that one single company could not adopt a policy of transparency alone, for it would later be undercut in international bidding by the less scrupulous companies that did not bother host governments with publicity in this way. George Soros, the financier who founded The Open Society Institute, helped establish the Publish What You Pay Campaign to extend the norm of transparency to oil revenue payments, in part because of their detrimental impact on conflict dynamics in host countries.

In 2002, British Prime Minister Tony Blair put forward the Extractive Industries Transparency Initiative (EITI) at the World Summit on Sustainable Development in Johannesburg. This fit perfectly with the Blair commitment to finding a 'third way' between capitalism and socialism. The UK would promote foreign investment around the world at the same time as it sought to persuade companies to adopt corporate social responsibility policies abroad that would regulate their own behaviour. The Blair administration had promised to pursue an 'ethical' foreign policy, and as part of this, established a Corporate Citizenship Unit within the Foreign Office. The EITI has, in only a few years, garnered support from other countries, including Italy, Norway, Indonesia, the Central African Republic, France and South Africa. A number of NGOs, the World Bank and the UNDP have also become involved. A British financial firm, ISIS Management, led a group of ten major investors in calling for extractive companies to be more transparent, arguing that mis-used funds can pose a significant business risk.

Another more dramatic example of the convergence of concerns about state failure, changes in norms of intervention and development, and transnational activism is the revenue-sharing agreement that is part of the Chad–Cameroon pipeline project. When major oil companies first explored the idea of developing natural gas resources and running a pipeline through Chad and Cameroon, everyone involved realized the risk that this would destabilize an already fragile society. Some in Chad were eager to obtain the wealth promised by this development, while others opposed the governing elites control and probable misappropriation of that wealth. The World Bank used its leverage in 2001 to structure a gas pipeline project in Chad and Cameroon in a new and innovative way. In return for World Bank participation, the energy companies and governments had to agree to a new kind of project conditionality. The Chadian legislature passed a law decreeing how the revenues from the project must be distributed for economic development of the country. Most of the revenue from the gas pipeline development would go directly into a separate account for improving public services and funding development projects.[14] An 'International Advisory Group' would monitor the use of pipeline profits and ensure a certain degree of transparency. While this agreement has already run into major domestic roadblocks to its implementation, it has nonetheless become a possible model for how to deal with oil development under weak and ineffectual governments (Bennett 2001; McPhail 2002). It has influenced some of the thinking about how to handle oil revenue distribution in the post-conflict reconstruction of Iraq, although so far without any real support from the US government.

The challenge to corporations

The international community appears to be inching its way, step by step, towards promoting a more significant role for corporations where states have failed to meet the standards of democracy, transparency, respect for human rights and the environment. This is not to say that corporations are free to intervene directly in the political process. There is still a strong prohibition against, for instance, corporate efforts to undermine or overthrow a government. We have reached this point through a number of converging routes. The structure of the global political economy has changed, with the adoption of policies of liberalization worldwide, the spread of globalization, and the end of East–West tension. At the same time, concerns about failed states, and the security threats posed by complex humanitarian disasters, criminalized commodity trade, and the financing of armed conflict and terrorism, have internationalized local conflicts. As Duffield has pointed out, the development and security agendas have increasingly merged.

The dominant motif of the globalization debate has been the power of corporations and the declining capacity of the state (Strange 1996). Liberal ideologues successfully have promoted a more minimal role for governments. Many critics decry the weakened authority and capacity of governments even as pro-market enthusiasts trumpet the ability of the private sector to be innovative, efficient and forward-thinking. Privatization of essential services, such as security, and the delegation of diplomacy to the private sector are elements of this change in government authority (Avant 2005). All of these ideas point us towards the business community as both the source of and solution to current problems, bestowing upon them a certain legitimacy even when they act outside of their traditional market role (Cutler, Haufler et al. 1999).

This melds with a growing corporate social responsibility movement in which firms with operations in foreign countries increasingly are pressed to behave as good 'corporate citizens' by upholding high standards for labour and the environment, and by contributing in positive ways to the local community through development and conflict management initiatives.[15]

The idea of corporate social responsibility has been taken up by an increasingly transnationalized activist community. While each separate NGO may have a different mission, the idea of promoting corporate social responsibility has become a 'focal point' in their strategies. Given the collapse of the Soviet Union and the search for 'a new world order', ideas and options are being considered today that would not have been possible previously. In a seemingly more complex political world, the idea of involving the private sector in areas previously reserved to the state may spread rapidly among policy entrepreneurs, and become a focal point for action (Schelling 1978; Finnemore and Sikkink 1998; Avant 2000). As this trend has expanded in recent years, participants could easily believe it is a logical extension to move from environmental and labour standards, where most of the action is now, to human rights, corruption, equity and conflict. Corporate social responsibility becomes a focal point for the relevant actors, a solution that, once it is viewed as reasonable, is then applied to all problems that present themselves (Goldstein and Keohane; Schelling 1978). Note that this is not about seeking to redefine or reconstitute the system itself, unlike the claims and demands of many of the anti-globalization activists (Berejikian and Dryzek 2000).[16] The participants are simply redefining behaviour at the margins by shifting the focus from corporations as the source of problems, to corporations as the potential source of solutions.

The fact that these changes are occurring cannot be denied. But do they have unintended consequences if carried through vigorously? Attempts by private sector actors to contribute to local community development, protect human rights, redistribute resources, or resolve divisions within and between societies have been beset with unintended side effects, insufficient expertise, and accusations about the lack of accountability and the illegitimacy of the firms. The tensions inherent in the move to integrate the private sector into efforts to reform societies can be summed up by two sets of competing principles: sovereignty versus global norms; and legitimacy versus capacity. Corporate conflict prevention is a form of intervention in host government affairs, posing a challenge to local sovereignty, even if it is increasingly legitimized as a global norm. However, in most cases, the private sector actually has little legitimacy in this arena. This goes against the seemingly widely held view that it is only the private sector that has the capacity to drain resources from combatants and criminals, and thus weaken the incentives for war.

Corporations can be caught between the emerging norm of corporate social responsibility, and the sovereign demands of the host state. Unlike norms about the identity and role of states in the international system, there is no comprehensive institution or regime existing today regulating multinational corporations. Thus, expectations about corporations are much more fluid and change more rapidly than expectations about other international actors. In the case of revenue-sharing issues, expectations about the actions of foreign investors are divided, pitting the host government (and in some cases the citizenry) however corrupt, repressive or illegitimate against an international community demanding reform, development, and a more equitable division of national wealth. Foreign investors become a tool of the international community when they agree to publish revenue data or participate in socially-oriented, revenue-sharing arrangements. As a result, these investors may find themselves *persona non grata* in countries that object to what they perceive is a violation of the host governments sovereign rights and prerogatives (The Fridtjof Nansen Institute 2000: 48).

As more corporations become more deeply involved in foreign aid, social policies and regulatory activities, there are some who argue that they also will undermine the capacity of national governments. When companies invest in local community development, for instance, they may make it easier for the central government to decide not to fund those functions itself. The companies also may inadvertently fund a competing political power that can challenge the central government and undermine its authority (Rondinelli 2002).

The exact boundaries of legitimate and illegitimate action are difficult to define, and change with time and circumstance. This can be seen most clearly in the debate over corporate complicity with repressive and illegitimate regimes. The debate over Second World War reparations highlights the way in which definitions of legitimacy and complicity can change. Legally, if a corporation is closely tied to a government, knows of its violations, and nevertheless continues its relationship, then it is directly complicit in its acts (Ramasastry 2002). For over fifty years, there was little attempt to revisit the issue of corporate complicity in Nazi atrocities. In the last decade, however, established companies such as IBM have found themselves hauled into court or involved in negotiations with governments and victims over reparations for past acts. Modern notions of complicity are being tested in US and European courts, as companies with foreign operations are subject to litigation over their complicity with repressive regimes. Increasingly, human rights norms developed for states are being applied in these cases to private sector behaviour (Weissbrodt 2000; Ramasastry 2002).

While foreign investors have little legitimacy for acting in the social and political realms, they do have impressive capacity. Corporations have the capital, technology, expertise and institutional capacity that many local governments lack. When the legitimate government is ineffective or incapable of supplying the public goods demanded by society, then organized interests may turn to the private sector to supply them instead. This has often been the case in the developing world, where the private sector is forced into the position of supplying the services and infrastructure that the public sector cannot provide.

Are there any wider implications that we can draw from these new expectations about the role of corporations in an emerging global society? Certainly, the idea that the private sector could contribute to human rights protection, democratization and the elimination of corruption turns our notions of world politics upside down. States are supposed to be sovereign and in charge. They are the central actor in world politics, especially on issues of war and peace. And corporations are certainly not typically viewed as the bearers of progressive values. On the one hand, corporations cannot legitimately perform the functions of governments, and should not be asked to do so. But on the other hand, there might be no other actor able to intervene as effectively.

Acknowledgements

The research for this chapter was conducted as part of a project of the Fridtjof Nansen Institute on Oil Companies in New Petroleum Provinces: Ethics, Business and Politics, funded by the Petropol Programme of the Research Council of Norway.

Notes

1. For an overview of the nexus between business and conflict, see key texts by Ballentine and Sherman 2003; Wenger and Möckli 2003; Nelson 2000.
2. The phrase 'the responsibility to protect' comes from the report of the International Commission on Intervention and State Sovereignty, which argued that, while states have the primary duty to protect and preserve their citizens, the international community has a responsibility to intervene when states fail to do so (International Commission on Intervention and State Sovereignty 2001).
3. The majority of foreign direct investment goes to the US, Europe and Japan, the so-called 'triad' countries. However, in recent years China has become a major destination for FDI. Relatively little direct investment locates in Africa, and even less in conflict-ridden and corrupt states.
4. The resource curse is often linked to the 'Dutch disease', in which the sudden vast development of one resource for export leads to an increase in the exchange rate, which makes other sectors uncompetitive, and weakens fiscal discipline. The country becomes progressively more dependent on that one resource. The Dutch suffered this problem in the early 1960s, in developing their natural gas resources.
5. See in particular the work of the Environment and Security Project of the Woodrow Wilson Institute for Scholars, and of the Minerals and Sustainable Development Project of the International Institute for Sustainable Development.
6. Earlier in the century, as an example, the Mexican Revolution led to the nationalization of all natural resources as part of the sovereignty and patrimony of the Mexican people. Even today, the decision to allow foreign investment in the oil sector is a sensitive issue in all oil producing countries.
7. The World Investment Report 2002 reports that numerous governments changed their regulations in ways favourable to foreign investors in the past few years,

marking a notable change in policy across a diverse range of states (UNCTAD 2002).

8. In fact, the US government became sufficiently concerned to fund what became known as the State Failure Task Force. Ted Robert Gurr of the University of Maryland and Barbara Harff of the US Naval Academy were commissioned by the CIA to compile information about state failures as part of an unclassified study in response to a request from senior US policy makers to design and carry out a data-driven study on the correlates of state failure since the mid-1950s. The study was carried out by a Task Force consisting of academic experts, data collection and management specialists from the Consortium for International Earth Science Information Network (CIESIN), and analytic methods professionals from Science Applications International Corporation (SAIC). See www.cidcm.umd.edu/inscr/stfail/ for more information about state failure and civil conflict.

9. The Millennium Development Goals adopted by the UN General Assembly in 2000, and endorsed by the multilateral development banks, do not directly mention any issues related to the political efficacy of regimes. It is in the implementation of programmes to achieve these goals that institutional capacity becomes a leading factor.

10. States in the developing world have spoken out against any intervention at all, even in a humanitarian crisis, since powerful states of the North are more likely to intervene in the South and not vice versa. China, India and Brazil have been particularly vocal on this point.

11. A norm entrepreneur promotes a new idea to a community, similar to the way an economic entrepreneur promotes a new product or service (Finnemore and Sikkink 1998). Ironically, until recently German law facilitated bribery by allowing German companies to write it off as a cost of doing business abroad. The US had taken the lead in this area decades earlier when it passed the Foreign Corrupt Practices Act, but it was only in the late 1990s that other states joined it in condemning corruption. This new condemnation of corruption is due in part to the active promotion of an anti-corruption norm by Transparency International, which is based in Berlin, Germany.

12. Sadly but not surprisingly, Talisman sold its participation in the Sudan project to a less scrupulous company that was not at all responsive to public pressure.

13. In this case, the interest in this topic was partly driven by the public outrage over blood diamonds that financed civil war in Sierra Leone.

14. Unfortunately, the agreement did not cover signing bonuses, and the government used this money immediately to purchase arms, displaying its lack of real commitment to share the revenue.

15. This corporate self-regulation has been criticized on a number of fronts.

16. Berjikian and Dryzek point to the possibility that all relevant actors participate in 'reflexive action' that does not necessarily shift the paradigm under which they operate (in this case, the capitalist paradigm); instead, it redefines its margins (for instance, by shifting to more sustainable industry) (Berejikian and Dryzek 2000).

References

Auty, R. (1994): Industrial Policy Reform in Six Large Newly Industrializating Countries: the Resource Curse Thesis. *World Development* 22(1): 11–27.

Auty, R. (1998): Resource-Based Industrialization and Economic Development: Improving the Performance of Resource-Rich Countries. Helsinki: World Institute for Development Research (WIDER).

Avant, D. (2000): From Mercenary to Citizen Armies: Explaining Change in the Practice of War. *International Organizations* 54(1): 41–72.

Avant, D. (2005): *The Market for Force: the Consequences of Privatizing Security.* Cambridge: Cambridge University Press.

Ballentine, K. and J. Sherman (eds.) (2003): *The Political Economy of Armed Conflict: Beyond Greed and Grievance.* Boulder and London: Lynne Rienner.

Banfield, J., D. Lilly, et al. (2003): Transnational Corporations in Conflict-Prone Zones: Public Policy Responses and a Framework for Action. London: International Alert.

Bennett, J. (2001): Public–Private Initiatives in Preventing Conflict: an Examination of Revenue Sharing Provisions in the Extractive Industry. New York: United Nations Global Compact: 1–27.

Berdal, M. and D. M. Malone (eds.) (2000): *Greed and Grievance: Economic Agendas in Civil Wars.* Boulder, CO: Lynne Rienner.

Berejikian, J. and J. S. Dryzek (2000): Reflexive Action in International Politics. *British Journal of Political Science* 193, 4.

Bomann-Larsen, L. (2003): *Corporate Actors in Zones of Conflicts: Responsible Engagement.* Oslo, Norway: Confederation of Norwegian Business and Industry (NHO) and Research Institute of Oslo (PRIO).

Broad, R. and J. Cavanagh (1998): The Corporate Accountability Movement: Lessons and Opportunities. Washington, DC: World Resources Institute: 1–36.

Burke, P. (1999): Oil Companies and Indigenous Peoples in Ecuador. In: Cutler, A. C., V. Haufler and T. Porter (eds.), *Private Authority and International Affairs.* Albany: SUNY.

Christiansen, A. C. (2002): Beyond Petroleum: Can BP Deliver?, Lysaker, Norway: The Fridtjof Nansen Institute: 1–40.

Collier, P. (2000): Economic Causes of Civil Conflict and their Implications for Policy. Washington, DC: World Bank: 1–23.

Crook, C. (1999): Why Good Corporate Citizens are a Public Menace. *National Journal* (24 April): 1087–88.

Cutler, C. et al. (eds.) (1999): *Private Authority and International Affairs.* SUNY Series in Global Politics. Albany: SUNY.

Davis, G. A. (1995): Learning to Love the Dutch Disease. *World Development* 23(10) 1765–80.

deSoysa, I. (1999): Boon or Bane? Reassessing the Effects of Foreign Direct Investment on Economic Growth. *American Sociological Review* 64(3): 766–82.

deSoysa, I. (2000): The Resource Curse: are Civil Wars Driven by Rapacity or Paucity?. In: Malone, D. M. and M. Berdal, *Greed or Grievance: Economic Agendas in Civil Wars.* Boulder, CO: Lynne Rienner: 113–36.

Duffield, M. (2000): Globalization, Transborder Trade and War Economies. In: Berdal, M. and D. M. Malone, *Greed and Grievance: Economic Agendas in Civil War.* Boulder, CO: Lynne Rienner.

Finnemore, M. (2003): *The Purpose of Intervention: Changing Beliefs about the Use of Force.* Ithaca: Cornell University Press.

Finnemore, M. and K. Sikkink (1998): International Norm Dynamics and Political Change. *International Organization* 52(4): 887–917.

Florini, A. (1998): The End of Secrecy: *Foreign Policy* 111 (Summer): 50–63.

Freeman, B. (2000): *Globalization, Human Rights and the Extractive Industries, As Prepared for Delivery: Speech by US Deputy Assistant Secretary of State*. Third Warwick Corporate Citizenship Conference, University of Warwick.

Friedman, M. (1970): The Social Responsibility of Business is to Increase its Profits. *New York Times Magazine* September 13.

Frynas, G. (1998): Political Instability and Business: Focus on Shell and Nigeria. *Third World Quarterly* 19(3): 457–87.

Gleditsch, N. P. (1998): Armed Conflict and the Environment: a Critique of the Literature. *Journal of Peace Research* 35(3): 381–400.

Global Witness (1999): *A Crude Awakening: the Role of Oil and Banking Industries in Angolan Civil War and the Plunder of State Assets*. London: Global Witness.

Goldstein, J. and R. Keohane (eds.): *Ideas and Institutions*. Princeton: Princeton University Press.

Haufler, V. (2003): Globalization and Industry Self-Regulation. In: Kahler, M. and D. Lake, *Governance in a Global Economy*. Princeton: Princeton University Press.

Homer-Dixon, T. (1999): *Environment, Scarcity, and Violence*. Princeton: Princeton University Press.

Homer-Dixon, T. and J. Blitt (eds.) (1998): *Ecoviolence: Links Among Environment, Population and Security*. Oxford: Rowman and Littlefield.

International Commission on Intervention and State Sovereignty (2001): The Responsbility to Protect. Ottawa: International Development Research Centre: 1–91.

International Peace Academy (2001): Private Sector Actors in Zones of Conflict: Research Challenges and Policy Responses. New York: Fafo Institute for Applied Social Science Programme for International Cooperation and Conflict Resolution and the International Peace Academy project on 'Economic Agendas in Civil Wars': 1–13.

Jackson, R. H. (1990): *Quasi-States: Sovereignty, International Relations, and the Third World*. New York: Cambridge University Press.

JongeOudraat, C. D. (2000): Intervention in Internal Conflicts: Legal and Political Conundrums. Washington, DC: Carnegie Endowment for International Peace Global Policy Program Working Papers 15: 1–23.

Karl, T. L. (1997): *Oil Booms and Petro-States*. Los Angeles and San Francisco: University of California Press.

Keck, M. E. and K. Sikkink (1998): *Activists Beyond Borders: Advocacy Networks in International Politics*. Ithaca, NY: Cornell University Press.

Kline, J. (1985): *International Codes and Multinational Business: Setting Guidelines for International Business Operations*. Westport and London: Quorum Books.

Lichbach, M. (2002): Global Order and Local Resistance: Structure, Culture, and Rationality in the Battle of Seattle. Unpublished paper, University of Maryland, College Park.

Lopez, G. and M. Stohl (eds.) (1989): *Dependence, Development and State Repression*. New York: Greenwood Press.

Manby, B. (1999): The Price of Oil: Corporate Responsibility and Human Rights Violations in Nigeria's Oil Producing Communities. New York: Human Rights Watch.

Marshall, M. G. and T. R. Gurr (2003): Peace and Conflict 2003. College Park, Maryland, Center for International Development and Conflict Management, University of Maryland: 1–64.

McAdam, D., S. Tarrow, et al. (eds.) (2001): *Dynamics of Contention.* Cambridge: Cambridge University Press.

McPhail, K. (2002): *The Revenue Dimension of Oil, Gas and Mining Projects: Issues and Practices.* SPE International Conference on Health, Safety and Environment in Oil and Gas Exploration and Production, Kuala Lumpur, Malaysia.

Nelson, J. (2000): *The Business of Peace: the Private Sector as a Partner in Conflict Prevention and Resolution.* London: Prince of Wales Business Leaders Forum.

Pegg, S. (1999): The Cost of Doing Business: Transnational Corporations and Violence in Nigeria. *Security Dialogue* 30(4): 473–84.

Ramasastry, A. (2002): Corporate Complicity: From Nuremberg to Rangoon; an Examination of Forced Labor Cases and Their Impact on the Liability of Multinational Corporations. *Berkeley Journal of International Law* 20(1): 91–159.

Reno, W. (2000): Shadow States and the Political Economy of Civil Wars. In: Berdal, M. and D. M. Malone, *Greed and Grievance: Economic Agendas in Civil Wars.* Boulder, CO: Lynne Rienner: 43–68.

Rodman, K. A. (1997): *'Think Globally, Punish Locally': Nonstate Actors, Multinational Corporations, and Human Rights Sanctions.* Conference paper presented at: Nonstate Actors and Authority in the Global System. University of Warwick, England, 31 Oct.–1 Nov.

Rondinelli, D. A. (2002): Transnational Corporations: International Citizens or New Sovereigns? *Business and Society Review* 107(4): 391–413.

Ross, M. L. (1999): The Political Economy of the Resource Curse. *World Politics* 51(2): 297–323.

Ross, M. L. (2000): *Does Resource Wealth Lead to Authoritarian Rule?* The Economics of Political Violence, World Bank Research Group Workshop, Princeton University.

Sachs, J. D. and A. Warner (1995): Natural Resource Abundance and Economic Growth. *Development Discussion Paper No. 571a.* Cambridge, MA: Harvard Institute for International Development, Harvard University: 1–49.

Schelling, T. (1978): *Micromotives and Macrobehavior.* New York: W. W. Norton.

Smillie, I., L. Giberie, et al. (2000): The Heart of the Matter: Sierra Leone, Diamonds, and Human Security. Ottawa: Partnership Africa Canada.

Spar, D. L. (1998): The Spotlight and the Bottom Line: How Multinationals Export Human Rights. *Foreign Affairs* 77(2): 7–12.

Strange, S. (1996): *The Retreat of the State: the Diffusion of Power in the World Economy.* New York: Cambridge University Press.

The Fridtjof Nansen Institute (2000): Petro-States–Predatory or Developmental? Final Report. Lysaker, Norway: The Fridtjof Nansen Institute: 1–52.

Transparency International (2002): Transparency International Annual Corruption Perception Index 2002. Berlin: Transparency International.

UNCTAD (2002): World Investment Report 2002. Geneva: UNCTAD.

United Nations Global Compact (2002): Dialogue on Business in Zones of Conflict: Rapporteur's Report. New York City: United Nations: 1–5.

Weiss, T. G. (1996): Nongovernmental Organizations and Internal Conflict. In: Brown, M. E., *The International Dimensions of Internal Conflict.* Cambridge, MA: MIT Press.

Weissbrodt, D. (2000): Principles Relating to the Human Rights Conduct of Companies. Working Paper. New York: Commission on Human Rights, Sub-Commission on the Promotion and Protection of Human Rights: 1–29.

Weissbrodt, D. (2000): Proposed Draft Human Rights Code of Conduct for Companies. Working Paper. New York: United Nations Commission on Human Rights, Sub-Commission on the Promotion and Protection of Human Rights: 1–35.

Wenger, A. and D. Mockli (2003): *Conflict Prevention: the Untapped Potential of the Business Sector*. Boulder and London: Lynne Rienner.

Williams, P. (2002): Transnational Organized Crime and the State. In: Hall, R. B. and T. J. Biersteker, *The Emergence of Private Authority in Global Governance*. Cambridge: Cambridge University Press: 161–82.

World Bank (1997): World Development Report: the State in a Changing World. Washington, DC: The World Bank: 1–265.

Yergin, D. and J. Stanislaw (1998): *The Commanding Heights*. New York: Free Press.

Part 5
Regulation in Global Governance

9
Rearticulating Regulatory Approaches: Private–Public Authority and Corporate Social Responsibility

Peter Utting

Introduction

The significant changes in state–market relations that have characterized the contemporary era of globalization and economic liberalization are particularly evident in the arena of corporate social responsibility (CSR).[1] Here we see 'softer', voluntary approaches to business regulation being promoted in an attempt to improve aspects of company performance that relate to social and sustainable development and human rights. Such approaches are often designed by business interests and non-governmental organizations (NGOs), and couched in a discourse that proclaims their superiority in relation to legalistic, 'harder' approaches involving state actors.

It would be wrong, however, to regard this apparent transfer of regulatory authority from state to non-state actors as simply part of a broader trend of 'deregulation' promoted by neoliberalism. What has occurred is a more complex process of 're-regulation' where the rolling back of the state in certain areas of the economy and the freeing-up of markets have gone hand in hand with the strengthening of governmental and inter-governmental rules to protect, for example, certain types of property rights, international trade and investment, and the environment (Braithwaite and Drahos 2000). Important differences in the trajectory and content of regulatory reform and approach are also apparent in different varieties or models of capitalism, North and South (Huber 2002), as well as in specific country and industry contexts. Furthermore, 'deregulation' at the national level is sometimes accompanied by new or strengthened forms of regulation at local and regional levels.

In the field of CSR, re-regulation is associated with the changing character of institutional forms that have characterized the rise of private authority in recent decades (Cutler et al. 1999; Haufler 2001). Since the late 1990s, in particular, there has been a gradual scaling-up, and ratcheting-up, of standards and implementation procedures related to CSR, with regulatory authority being assumed to a greater extent by non-governmental organizations and multistakeholder institutions or public–private partnerships, practising so-called 'civil regulation' and 'co-regulation' (Murphy and Bendell 1997; Hanks 2002; Utting 2002a). These 'collective' or more 'socialized' forms of private authority (O'Rourke 2003) are increasingly supported by governments and inter-governmental organizations. More recently still, civil society and public authorities are demanding corporate accountability through regulatory arrangements that go beyond conventional voluntary approaches by, inter alia, placing greater emphasis on corporate obligations, legalistic approaches and some form of punishment in cases of non-compliance (Bendell 2004; Broad and Cavanagh 1999; Newell 2002).

This chapter examines the theory, practice and prospects of re-regulation associated with corporate accountability and the ratcheting-up of CSR. Section one examines the shift towards non-governmental regulatory systems and multistakeholder initiatives, identifying some of their achievements and limitations. Section two describes the emerging corporate accountability agenda, highlighting its distinctive features and specific initiatives. Section three introduces the notion of 'articulated regulation', which refers to the coming together of different regulatory approaches in ways that are complementary and synergistic, and suggests that a potentially fruitful area for policy intervention lies at the interface between soft and hard, voluntary and legalistic, approaches. Articulated regulation also refers to the dual presence of forms of activism involving confrontation and collaboration, as well as greater policy coherence at both the micro level of the firm and the macro level of government and international policy. As a basis for understanding the potential and limitations of the ratcheting-up and scaling-up of CSR and corporate accountability, section four looks at the theory and dynamics of progressive institutional reform. The discussion focuses on the way in which different elements related to crisis, agency, ideas, institutions and structure intervene and interact to explain processes of institutional change; how these aspects have shaped the CSR and corporate accountability agendas; and what they tell us about the possibilities for transforming the canvas of fragmented, experimental and fledgling initiatives into a more generalized feature or variant of stakeholder capitalism.

A rapidly evolving agenda

Private regulation related to CSR has evolved considerably over the past two decades. When the contemporary CSR agenda took off, particularly in the build-up to and aftermath of the 1992 'Earth Summit' in Rio de Janeiro, it centred very much on a limited range of environmental and social initiatives; a small group of global brand name corporations, often reacting defensively to activist pressures; and a few management tools, innovations and concepts. These included, for example, selected improvements in environmental management systems, eco-efficiency, and self-prescribed and self-monitored company or industry-based codes of conduct.

Today we see more companies and industries involved, more issues on the agenda, and some transnational corporations (TNCs) and organized business interests not simply reacting to pressure but being more proactive, and attempting to apply CSR principles, policies and practices more systematically throughout corporate structures. The range of CSR interventions has broadened to include stakeholder dialogues, external monitoring and verification, 'triple-bottom line' reporting and accounting, certification and labelling, and public–private partnerships. And CSR policies and practices are reaching deeper into TNC supply chains.

The CSR agenda has also incorporated a growing number of elements associated with the international rights-based agenda, notably labour rights. Particular issues of global concern such as HIV/AIDS and violent conflict are also being addressed. More recently still, CSR is being linked explicitly to the global poverty reduction agenda, as attention focuses on how TNCs and other companies can alleviate poverty at the so-called 'bottom of the pyramid'.[2] Also evident are new institutional arrangements involving various forms of non-governmental regulatory action where civil society organizations not only attempt to exert pressures on business through confrontational activism but work collaboratively with companies, business associations, and governmental and inter-governmental organizations through various types of partnerships and service delivery activities. NGOs are participating in, and increasingly taking the lead in organizing, multistakeholder initiatives associated with standard-setting, company reporting, monitoring, certification and learning about good practice (Utting 2002a, 2004).

Such initiatives include:

- certification schemes, for example, ISO 14001 (environmental management standards); the Fair Labour Association and SA8000 (labour standards), and the Forest Stewardship Council (sustainable forest management);
- Global Framework Agreements where international trade union organizations negotiate accords with global corporations that agree to apply certain standards throughout their global structure (for example, agreements between the International Union of Food and Allied Workers (IUF) and Chiquita and Danone);
- standard-setting, reporting and monitoring schemes such as the Clean Clothes Campaign (CCC), the Worker Rights Consortium (WRC), the Global Reporting Initiative, the AA1000 Series (accountability standards), and the Extractive Industries Transparency Initiative (EITI);
- initiatives that emphasize stakeholder dialogues and learning about good practice, such as the United Nations Global Compact (promoting ten principles derived from international labour, environmental, human rights

and anti-corruption law); and the Ethical Trading Initiative (promoting social standards throughout supply chains).

Many of these initiatives have addressed some of the more obvious limitations inherent in corporate self-regulation. To some extent, certain schemes are conducive to democratic governance by engaging a broader range of actors or stakeholders in consultative and decision-making processes. They have also contributed to harmonizing standards and implementation procedures, and to imposing some order on what was becoming a confusing array of codes of conduct. And they have tried to encourage companies to internalize social and environmental standards more systematically throughout their corporate structures. As a result, CSR initiatives are penetrating deeper into TNC supply chains rather than remaining at the level of parent firms and affiliates. Multistakeholder initiatives have also played a key role in the evolution of the CSR agenda, as described above, where an increasing number of issues are being placed on the CSR table (see Haufler in this volume). The early focus on working conditions, for example, has been complemented by greater attention to labour rights such as freedom of association and collective bargaining. Procedural aspects have also been improved with companies having to accept independent monitoring as opposed to relying exclusively on internal monitoring or no monitoring at all; and they are having to measure concrete changes in performance.

To some extent, therefore, multistakeholder initiatives involve a ratcheting-up of standards and a slight hardening of the soft voluntarism that characterized the early experience of CSR that centred on corporate self-regulation. Indeed, some see company participation in such initiatives as indicative of a particular stage of an evolutionary learning and implementation curve. According to Zadek, CSR companies tend to move through various stages, described as 'defensive', in which they deny they are part of the problem; 'compliance', in which they adopt a policy which is seen as a cost; 'managerial', in which the issue is embedded in their core management processes; 'strategic', where addressing the issue is seen as good for business; and 'civil', where they encourage their peers to also address the issue. One of the ways they operationalize this latter stage is by participating in multistakeholder initiatives (Zadek 2004).

More generally, multistakeholder initiatives can be seen as important elements in new institutionalism and the drive for 'good governance' that are core features of the post-Washington Consensus, where it is increasingly recognized that there is a need for institutions that can minimize the perverse social, environmental and developmental effects of open markets, economic liberalization and corporate globalization.

In practice, some multistakeholder initiatives are more effective than others in relation to different regulatory functions. O'Rourke has placed non-governmental systems of labour regulation on a spectrum, 'from purely "privatized" regulation ... to more "collaborative" regulation, to more "socialized" regulation' (O'Rourke 2003). The 'privatized' variant, for example, is likely to facilitate easy access to the factory floor and to managers in order to obtain and disseminate information. The 'collaborative' system may be more effective at supply chain monitoring and in convincing global corporations of the need to gradually raise the bar in terms of standards and compliance. The 'socialized' system may have easier access to workers and local stakeholders, be more transparent in terms of public disclosure, and be freer to expose malpractice.

Whilst addressing some of the limitations that characterize company self-regulation, multistakeholder initiatives yield, in fact, a very mixed scorecard, reflected in the following traits. First, they involve only a small fraction of the world's 70,000 TNCs, 700,000 affiliates and millions of suppliers. For example, by December 2005, 2,323 companies had joined the world's largest CSR initiative, the United Nations Global Compact, while participation in schemes such as the Fair Labour Association and the Ethical Trading Initiative, which are associated with specific sectors, involved 15 and 39 corporations, respectively. The largest environmental certification scheme, ISO 14001, had certified some 90,000 entities (mainly companies) by December 2004.[3]

Many of the companies involved in the high profile multistakeholder initiatives are among the largest. The Global Compact, for example, has enlisted the support of approximately 100 of the Global Fortune 500 companies. But the participation of a global player in a multistakeholder initiative or its engagement with the CSR agenda should not be taken to mean that CSR practices have been internalized throughout the corporate structure, or indeed that participation will prompt any major change in corporate performance related to social, environmental and human rights aspects. In reality, CSR practices often remain limited to specific ad hoc interventions. This is apparent in to the case of the Global Reporting Initiative where by December 2005, 751 companies claimed to be using one or some of the reporting guidelines but only 120 were using them systematically. It is also apparent in relation to the reporting on CSR best practices by companies involved with the United Nations Global Compact. Indeed a 2004 evaluation of the Global Compact carried out by McKinsey & Company found that membership of the Compact stimulated only 9 per cent of the participating companies to take actions that they would not otherwise had taken had they remained outside the initiative.[4] In the vast majority of cases (91%), companies were doing things they would have done anyway (51%), albeit more efficiently or quickly, or had remained largely inactive (40%). So while some CSR commentators like to describe CSR as a stool with three legs that symbolize financial, social and environmental objectives, in reality the legs are fairly uneven, rendering the stool somewhat less effective than it may appear at first sight.

Second, the procedures adopted by certain schemes to encourage compliance with the standards they promote often remain weak. Others may be stronger on aspects to do with monitoring and verification but tend to engage very few companies. The Global Compact and the Global Reporting Initiative, for example, rely heavily on dialogue and best practice learning, and do not monitor compliance. ISO 14001 certification indicates whether or not a company has in place elements of an environmental management system, not whether it has actually improved in its impact on the environment (Krut and Gleckman 1998). Schemes, such as the Worker Rights Consortium and the Clean Clothes Campaign adopt more rigorous verification procedures but directly engage far fewer companies.

Third, some schemes tend to be exclusionary, top-down and technocratic. The voluntary approaches they promote are often packaged in a discourse that proclaims their superiority in relation to legalistic or state-based approaches, which are deemed unworkable, too slow or out-moded, and labelled pejoratively 'command and control' regulation. In contrast, voluntary approaches tend to be portrayed as innovative, pragmatic, consensual and modern. In a similar vein, various forms of protest and confrontational activism, which have played a crucial role in improving corporate social and environmental performance are deemed to be somewhat ideological or outmoded (Sustain Ability 2003).

This tendency to marginalize public policy and ignore certain aspects of the political and institutional context that drives and facilitates CSR also extends to the minimalist role often assigned to local and national institutions in developing countries in the design and implementation of CSR standards. While some multistakeholder approaches have governance structures that are genuinely participatory, others have not. Key actors or stakeholders such as workers or trade unions, and interest groups and organizations in developing countries, are sometimes poorly represented and relatively voiceless in the northern-based consultation and decision-making processes that tend to characterize multistakeholder initiatives.

Fourth, some schemes have not seriously addressed the question of what impact CSR is having on developing countries and the possible tensions and contradictions between CSR and development. It is often assumed that anything that involves improved social and environmental standards in TNC supply chains or small and medium-sized enterprises must be good for development. But this 'do-gooding' or 'win–win' approach often ignores key development issues, priorities and realities in developing countries; as well as the fact that raising social and environmental standards can imply costs that may constrain enterprise development, and that CSR supply chain management can be a way for TNCs to pass costs on to suppliers. It also tends to ignore more fundamental structural issues associated with corporate power and certain competitive and fiscal practices of TNCs that are implicated in the broader problem of underdevelopment.

Corporate accountability

The process of ratcheting-up voluntary initiatives, or the gradual hardening of softer approaches, has recently entered a new phase. This involves an approach to regulation that emphasizes not only more effective codes of conduct, monitoring, reporting and certification systems but also recourse to public policy and law. This new approach is summed up by the term 'corporate accountability'. The concept of corporate accountability is quite different to the conventional notion of CSR where the keywords are self-regulation, voluntarism and responsibility. Corporate accountability implies 'answerability' or an obligation to answer to different stakeholders, and some element of 'enforceability', where non-compliance results in some sort of penalty or costs incurred (Newell 2002; Bendell 2004). It also implies 'applicability' or 'universality', in the sense that standards apply to a far broader range of companies, rather than to those individual companies that choose to adopt voluntary initiatives.[5] Some strands of the corporate accountability movement are concerned with mechanisms that not only hold corporations to account but also curb the concentration of corporate power.[6]

In recent years there has been a wave of international agreements, proposals and campaigns associated with corporate accountability. They include the following:

- Friends of the Earth International proposed that the 2002 World Summit on Sustainable Development consider a Corporate Accountability Convention that would establish and enforce minimum environmental and social standards, encourage effective reporting and provide incentives for TNCs taking steps to avoid negative impacts.
- Several trade union and non-governmental organizations in the United States (US) have launched the International Right to Know campaign to demand legislation that would oblige US companies or foreign companies traded on the US stock exchanges to disclose information on the operations of their overseas affiliates and major contractors.
- The International Forum on Globalization has advocated the creation of a United Nations (UN) Organization for Corporate Accountability that would provide information on corporate practices as a basis for legal actions and consumer boycotts. Christian Aid has proposed the establishment of a Global Regulation Authority that would establish norms for TNC conduct, monitor compliance and deal with breaches. Others have called for the reactivation of the defunct United Nations Centre on Transnational Corporations, some of whose activities were transferred to the United Nations Conference on Trade and Development (UNCTAD) a decade ago.
- Groups, particularly in the United States, have called for the 're-chartering' of corporations, to revive a system whereby states granted corporations

a charter. This licence to operate stipulated certain responsibilities and obligations and, periodically, had to be renewed.

- A large network of trade unions and NGOs that make up the Clean Clothes Campaign (CCC) actively supported the European Union (EU) parliamentary resolution of 1999 for a code of conduct for European TNCs operating in developing countries.
- The United Nations Sub-Commission on the Promotion and Protection of Human Rights adopted, in 2003, the draft Norms on the Responsibilities of Transnational Corporations and Other Business Enterprises with Regards to Human Rights. While failing to obtain approval by the Commission on Human Rights in order to become international law the draft Norms prompted the appointment of a United Nations Special Representative on Business and Human Rights, and are being tested by a group of TNCs that form part of the Business Leaders Initiative on Human Rights.
- Various NGOs and lawyers have called not only for extending international legal obligations to TNCs in the field of human rights, but also for bringing corporations under the jurisdiction of the International Criminal Court.
- For many years trade unions and others have urged the International Labour Organization (ILO) to strengthen its follow-up activities and procedures for examining disputes related to the Tripartite Declaration of Principles concerning Multinational Enterprises and Social Policy. In 2000, the Organization for Economic Cooperation and Development (OECD) strengthened its Guidelines on Multinational Enterprises and national complaints procedures.
- In 2002, a coalition of civil society organizations and the financier, George Soros, launched the Publish What You Pay Campaign, which calls for a regulatory approach to ensure that extractive companies in the oil and mining industries disclose the net amount of payments made to national governments.
- In 2003 the Tax Justice Network was formed to address trends in global taxation that have negative development impacts, notably tax evasion and avoidance through transfer pricing and off-shore tax havens, and tax competition between states that reduces their ability to tax the major beneficiaries of globalization.

Corporate accountability implies that the rights and freedoms of companies must be balanced not just by responsibilities and voluntary initiatives but also obligations. In this sense, the concept has affinities with that of citizenship and is useful for rectifying narrow interpretations of the concept of corporate citizenship, used by many in the CSR community either as a synonym for CSR or to refer to the balancing of corporate rights and (voluntary) responsibilities, rather than the balancing of rights and (legal) obligations. While standard-setting and other regulatory action related to

CSR are often undertaken by self-appointed entities whose accountability to external agents may be very limited, the theory and practice of corporate accountability highlights issues of legitimacy and democratic governance, including the question of who decides, and who speaks for whom. It also focuses attention on complaints procedures or complaints-based systems of regulation that facilitate the task of identifying, investigating, publicizing and seeking redress for specific instances of corporate malpractice. As discussed below, this is an alternative or complementary approach to regulatory systems that involve broad but relatively superficial systems of reporting, monitoring, auditing and certification.

Corporate accountability also suggests that if CSR is to be meaningful and really work for both development and democratic governance, then it is not enough for companies to improve only selected aspects of working conditions or environmental management systems, and to engage in community projects and corporate giving. Structural and macro-policy issues also need to be addressed, including, for example, perverse patterns of labour market flexibilization and sub-contracting that can result in the deterioration of labour standards and rights; corporate taxation and transfer pricing practices that deprive developing country governments and economies of essential resources; corporate economic power and competitive advantage over small enterprises and infant industries; and the political influence of TNCs and business-interest lobbies.

Rearticulating regulatory approaches

An important contribution of some of the analysis, activism and policy proposals associated with co-regulation and corporate accountability is that they go beyond the conventional polarized debate about the virtues and limitations of voluntary versus mandatory approaches. This debate has been useful for demystifying the somewhat utopian and feel-good discourse of 'win–win' scenarios and 'partnerships' that embellishes CSR and fails to problematize the role of TNCs in global governance and development. It has also been useful in highlighting the tensions and trade-offs between different regulatory approaches, and in reminding the critics of corporate globalization of the regulatory limitations – past and present – of both state and multilateral institutions. But the polarized nature of the debate has diverted attention away from the interface of so-called soft and hard or voluntary and legalistic approaches, which is potentially a fruitful area for regulatory intervention. If 'co-regulation' refers to the coming together, through multistakeholder initiatives, participatory decision-making processes and partnerships, of different actors to facilitate the design and implementation of standards, what might be called 'articulated regulation' refers to the coming together of different regulatory approaches in ways that are complementary, mutually reinforcing and synergistic, or at least less contradictory. Some of the discussion and proposals related to corporate accountability centre on more complex or pluralistic institutional arrangements that occupy this terrain.

This section discusses four forms of articulated regulation. The first three relate to regulatory approaches that explicitly aim to promote CSR and corporate accountability. They involve complementarity between different non-governmental regulatory systems, the interface between confrontational and collaborationist forms of civil society activism, and linkages between voluntary and legalistic approaches or public policy. The fourth aspect relates to the question of policy coherence, and the need to minimize the contradictions between regulatory approaches associated with very different reform agendas.

This discussion is not meant to suggest that other regulatory approaches are inconsequential or unnecessary. It merely suggests the need to think beyond the voluntary versus binding, soft versus hard dichotomy and to expand, in a sense, the notion of co-regulation, which has focused primarily on the articulation of actors – e.g. business interests, NGOs and multilateral organizations – usually for the purpose of designing and implementing voluntary initiatives or public–private partnerships.

Articulating non-governmental systems of regulation

The first type of articulated regulation involves complementarities between different forms of private and non-governmental authority. O'Rourke and others have examined the need and scope for building complementarity between the different emerging systems of non-governmental labour regulation (O'Rourke 2003; Sabel et al. 2000). As noted above, some multistakeholder initiatives are more effective than others in relation to different regulatory functions. The notion of articulated regulation, then, relates partly to 'connecting these initiatives in some inter-operable way [that] might help to overcome the challenges of access, scope and credibility' (O'Rourke 2003).

Complementarity within non-governmental systems is particularly important in relation to trade unions and NGOs. Despite some progress in terms of dialogue and collaboration via certain multistakeholder and other initiatives, there is still considerable tension between some trade union organizations on the one side and NGOs that are working with companies and multistakeholder initiatives to promote labour standards and rights on the other. Much of this tension revolves around trade union concerns that many NGOs are largely unaccountable, are not legitimate representatives of workers, and that the CSR initiatives and processes they propose are largely detached from democratic processes and public policy, or deflect attention from fundamental issues such as the denial of labour rights in China and other countries (UNRISD 2004). Some NGOs, for their part, tend to regard trade union structures as ossified, corrupt and patriarchal. Certain multistakeholder initiatives such as the Worker Rights Consortium and the Clean Clothes Campaign have promoted more collaborative relationships and forms of participation.

One particular area where the complementarity and inter-operability of non-governmental systems needs to be strengthened relates to complaints procedures. In the debate about CSR and its capacity to regulate corporate behaviour, considerable attention has focused on developing standards and systems related to monitoring, verification and reporting. While this focus has played an important role in highlighting the limits of internal monitoring and the need for hard data, more systemic approaches and independent verification, the NGOs and companies involved face the somewhat daunting task of gathering information and checking on the implementation of numerous standards contained in codes of conduct and certification guidelines throughout vast corporate structures and ever-lengthening global supply chains. Given the scale and international reach of TNC activities, the costs involved, and the reliance on commercial auditing techniques and analytical frameworks that often ignore the root causes of non-compliance and fail to obtain reliable information from workers and managers, mainstream monitoring and reporting often simply scratches the surface (Maquila Solidarity Network 2005; O'Rourke 2000; Clean Clothes Campaign 2005). The cost and complexity of such 'extensive' approaches seriously compromise their feasibility and scaling-up.

A complementary regulatory arrangement involves strengthening more 'intensive' approaches involving various forms of complaints procedures or complaints-based systems of regulation. Rather than trying to span a broad spectrum of TNC activities, complaints procedures enable different types of stakeholders and entities to identify specific abuses or instances of malpractice. Numerous types of institutions can and do function on the basis of complaints procedures. Trades unions, for example, often take action when a company is in breach of a specific component of a collective bargaining agreement. Watchdog NGOs, ombudsman-type institutions, the judicial process, and the investigative media, also function on the basis of complaints procedures. In 2000, the OECD strengthened its Guidelines for Multinational Enterprises and national complaints procedures. Some of the non-governmental regulatory institutions, such as the Worker Rights Consortium and the Clean Clothes Campaign function wholly or partly on the basis of complaints procedures, and other multistakeholder initiatives, such as the Fair Labour Association, have adopted such processes. This approach is also envisaged in the draft UN Norms on the responsibilities of TNCs referred to above.

The methods, procedures and types of informants used may vary considerably. Whereas the Fair Labour Association (FLA), for example, works mainly with commercial auditing firms and managers, the WRC engages workers and local organizations. As noted above, each approach has its advantages and limitations, but they can be complementary. An evaluation of the involvement of both these schemes in investigating complaints at a Honduran factory owned by the Canadian company, Gildan Activewear, led the Maquila Solidarity Network to conclude that rather than seeing these two approaches as incompatible, they can be complementary and mutually reinforcing: 'This is not meant to suggest, however, that the best elements of each initiative should be incorporated into one institution, since it is the interaction between the two initiatives that often produces the positive outcomes' (Maquila Solidarity Network 2005: 12). It is this philosophy that to some extent lies behind the Joint Initiative on Corporate Accountability and Worker Rights, an initiative that aims to test a variety of approaches to the implementation of codes of conduct (Maquila Solidarity Network 2005).[7]

The confrontation–collaboration nexus

The notion of articulating different forms of non-governmental regulation can also be extended to the interface between formal non-governmental regulatory systems involving standard-setting and related operational activities, and the informal realm of social activism or 'street regulation'. The dynamism and effectiveness of particular CSR initiatives is often linked to this dual presence of 'collaboration' and 'confrontation' (Bendell and Murphy 2002; Utting 2005b). Whereas collaboration can serve to construct a roadmap for reform and institutionalize the reform process, confrontation is often crucial for generating the political will needed to change the status quo and keep the reform process 'honest'. Confrontational activism, including various types of protest, campaigns, watch-dog activities and so-called 'naming and shaming', remains a key driver of voluntary initiatives, despite the tendency of some CSR leaders and practitioners to argue that social militancy is a thing of the past and that stakeholder dialogue and partnerships are the key for advancing the CSR agenda. It is the co-existence of these two forms of civil society regulatory action that often accounts for the ratcheting-up and scaling-up of particular multistakeholder initiatives. Sustained 'anti-' movements, such as the anti-sweatshop and anti-logging campaigns, are particularly important in this regard, and partly explain the dynamism and uptake of schemes associated with the Fair Labour Association and the Forest Stewardship Council (Conroy 2002).

Voluntary and legalistic approaches

A third form of 'articulated regulation' refers to the arena where voluntary and legalistic approaches or public policy interact in a complementary or synergistic way (Gunningham and Sinclair 2002; UNRISD 2004; Utting 2002a; Ward 2003). Over and above the fact that CSR should, by definition, imply compliance with existing environmental, labour and human rights law, and involve going 'beyond compliance', articulation can manifest itself in numerous ways.

- So-called international soft law, which is the basis of many CSR standards, may be non-binding but it nevertheless carries moral authority, is applicable to a broad universe of agents (for example, all governments or corporations), and may encourage or require national governments to incorporate its provisions in legislation at the national level. This has occurred to some extent, for example, in the case of the international code of conduct related to the marketing of breastmilk substitutes.

- Hard law can oblige companies to adopt 'voluntary' approaches, for example, by requiring them to be more transparent and to report on their social or environmental performance, but not specifying what that performance should be. If performance standards are found to be low, then it is up to others such as civil society organizations, the media and public opinion to expose, 'name and shame' or otherwise bring pressure to bear on a company to improve its performance. Pollutant Release and Transfer Registers (PRTRs), which impose reporting obligations on companies producing toxic substances, now exist in certain countries, as well as internationally through the PRTR Protocol signed in 2003.
- Other laws, related, for example, to freedom of association and freedom of information, pave the way for CSR by creating an enabling institutional environment, which safeguards and facilitates the role of actors and organizations that can exert pressures on companies, such as trade unions, NGOs and the media. And laws on misrepresentation and false advertising frame voluntary reporting by companies (Ward 2003: 5).
- Forms of 'negotiated agreements', which are sometimes used in the field of waste management and others areas of environmental protection, establish legally grounded objectives or targets, and involve some element of sanction in cases of non-compliance, but they grant the companies involved the flexibility to decide how to comply in the most cost-effective way (Hanks 2002).
- The mere threat of mandatory regulation, at both national and international levels, has long been a crucial driver of voluntary CSR action and soft law. The voluntary guidelines for transnational corporations and international codes of conduct that were established in the 1970s emerged in a context where several developing country governments were calling for binding regulations on TNCs. More recently, the considerable impetus behind voluntary company triple-bottom-line reporting and revenue transparency in the United Kingdom, has occurred in a context where a broad-based coalition of actors has called for mandatory reporting.
- Litigation has important implications for CSR. Cases of 'foreign direct liability', for example, where parent companies are held legally accountable in their home countries for malpractice abroad, aim 'to generate legal precedents at the boundaries of CSR' (Ward 2003: 7).
- Public policy can promote voluntary initiatives through market-based incentives associated, for example, with taxation, subsidies and credit (Welford 2002). Indeed, the so-called corporate social welfare model that

emerged in East Asia in the decades that followed the Second World War – where many large corporations assumed limited but important welfare functions – was premised on a compromise where selected corporations received tangible economic benefits in return for corporate welfare provisioning.

- Stock market regulations can require all listed companies to adopt CSR standards. The listing of certain South African companies, for example, on the New York Stock Exchange appears to have prompted some improvements in corporate social and environmental performance in South Africa. Within the country itself, the Johannesburg Stock Exchange now requires listed companies to adhere to the King Report's Code of Corporate Practice and Conduct (Fig et al. 2003; ILO Socio-Economic Security Programme 2004).
- CSR standards may be incorporated into contracts of different types, for example, agreements related to international investment and trade (UNCTAD 2003) or contracts with CEOs, which specify the use of CSR indicators in performance reviews and the calculation of bonuses.[8]
- Voluntary initiatives that are derived from international law or are adopted by democratically-elected governments or inter-governmental processes are often considered to have greater legitimacy and carry more legal weight (see Bernstein and Cashore in this volume). This point is often emphasized by those in the legal community, as well as by some trade union organizations that are concerned about the increasing role of NGOs, which are considered to be largely unaccountable, in designing labour standards (UNRISD 2004).
- Voluntary schemes like the Global Compact may be weak in terms of compliance mechanisms and have sometimes been used to fend off legalistic approaches. On one level, however, they can be said to articulate voluntary and legalistic approaches given the fact that they not only promote principles derived from international law but also reinforce the notion that international human rights law applies not only to states but also to corporations.
- Articulation may be sequential, with voluntary initiatives paving the way for harder or legalistic initiatives once a particular standard gains broader 'cultural' acceptance, is internalized by business and other actors, and when coalitions of organizations and actors backing the ratcheting-up of standards or legalistic approaches expand, sometimes with the support of certain business interests. This is evident, for example, in the case of the Publish What You Pay Campaign and the emergence of a group of companies and business-interest organizations supporting the proposed UN Norms on the Responsibilities of TNCs and other Business Enterprises with Regard to Human Rights.
- Articulation applies more generally to the interface between CSR and public governance, and the need to recognize that voluntary approaches often

work best 'where government and the public sector is effective, predictable and clear, ... where citizens and workers are empowered and human rights are respected; and where principles and institutions of justice ... public participation and access to information are all recognized' (Halina Ward quoted in UNRISD 2004).

Policy coherence

The above forms of articulated regulation relate to approaches concerned explicitly with improving social, environmental and human rights aspects of company performance. The need to articulate regulatory systems is also apparent in another sense. Companies attempting to engage with the CSR agenda are typically enmeshed in two very different regulatory environments, one involving norms, rules and institutions that promote social and environmental protection; and another associated with a variety of incentives and pressures aimed at enhancing or securing conditions for profitability and growth through cost-reduction, de-regulation, and flexibilization. These two environments are in constant tension and, in some respects, are contradictory. This, of course, reflects the age-old tension between commodification, accumulation and efficiency, on the one hand, and social protection and equity, on the other hand, that has characterized development under capitalism. In certain historical contexts, however, as argued in the final section of this chapter, such contradictions have been managed through forms of articulated regulation that enable social and economic policies to be mutually reinforcing or at least less contradictory.

A fourth arena of articulated regulation, then, relates to the need for policies to work in tandem rather than against each other, or to constitute enabling rather than disabling environments for institutional reforms associated with the ratcheting-up and scaling up of CSR and corporate accountability. Such 'policy coherence' is required both at the micro level of the firm and the macro level of government and international policies. The ratcheting-up and scaling-up of CSR and corporate accountability policies and practices currently confront two fundamental contradictions. Firstly, TNC affiliates and suppliers in global value chains are often confronted by seemingly contradictory policies of parent companies or large buyers, which insist on higher environmental and labour standards and compliance with codes of conduct, on the one hand, but simultaneously impose tough contract conditions that squeeze margins and delivery schedules, which increase the intensity of labour and overtime, on the other hand. Secondly, government and international policy often talks the talk of social and sustainable development but walks the walk of macro-economic and other deregulatory policies that may inhibit growth, small enterprise development and infant industries, and result in the deterioration of labour standards and the environment, particularly in developing countries. While such contradictions are, to some extent, features of certain patterns of capitalist development, they can be modified and managed in ways that are less contradictory. In relation to the firm-level contradictions it is important, for example, for companies a) to get CSR out of the ghetto of an individual office or unit, or even the mindset of a particular CEO, and mainstream or internalize CSR culture and policies throughout the corporate structure; b) to introduce CSR criteria into incentive systems; and c) not simply to impose tougher CSR conditions on suppliers but share responsibility for the costs involved, and ensure that CSR initiatives translate into productivity gains (Zadek 2004). In relation to the macro contradictions, particularly important are policies, campaigns and laws related to rights-based approaches to development, social justice, tax justice, greater 'policy space' for developing countries, more equitable North–South trade relations, and the democratization of international institutions.

Understanding the potential and limits of progressive institutional reform

Why are we seeing an apparent ratcheting-up of standards, and regulatory authority being increasingly assumed by civil society organizations and multistakeholder entities? Are the limitations that characterize multistakeholder approaches and non-governmental regulatory systems likely to be overcome? And should we expect to see any significant progress on the CSR and corporate accountability fronts, in terms of these ad hoc initiatives and fledgling approaches becoming a more generalized feature or variant of stakeholder capitalism?

To answer these questions it is necessary to say something about the theory of institutional change and to weigh up the different factors and forces that shape institutional outcomes and trajectories of change. Of particular importance are elements and contexts associated with injustice or crisis, the role of 'agency' and organized interests, the influence of ideas and institutions, and the spaces and constraints associated with structural conditions.

Crisis and agency

A useful starting point is Polanyi's notion of the need for markets to be embedded in institutions that mitigate their negative social and environmental impacts, and his analysis of the 'double movement'. This suggested that the crude liberalization and excessive reliance on the self-regulating market that characterized late nineteenth century globalization, generated perverse social conditions and a social and political reaction that resulted in the re-embedding of markets in various institutional and political arrangements (Polanyi 1957). From this perspective, voluntary initiatives, corporate self-regulation and certain forms of non-governmental regulatory action can be seen as part and parcel of broader efforts to promote 'embedded liberalism'

(Ruggie 2003), or as important elements of a new social compact adapted to contemporary globalization (Hopkins 1999), where openness of markets is secured on the basis of a compromise involving CSR.

In fact CSR responds to a dual crisis. First it relates to a crisis of the dominant model of accumulation and social protection that characterized early and mid-twentieth century industrial capitalism, which is often referred to as Fordism (Jessop 1999; Lipietz 1992). Second it relates to the crisis of development that affects the global South, elements of which have been exacerbated or projected onto the world stage in the contemporary era of globalization.

In the 1980s and 1990s, a series of events and conditions contributed to the reality or perception that contemporary patterns of capitalist development and economic liberalization were fuelling crises of various sorts. These included signs of environmental crisis related to deforestation, pollution, global warming and ozone depletion; the human and developmental costs of structural adjustment programmes and 'the race to the bottom'; persistent mass poverty and the growing gap between rich and poor; the explicit character of corporate greed and conspicuous consumption; the growing imbalance between corporate rights and obligations; and a series of high profile cases involving corporate crime or abusive practices.[9]

New social movements and transnational activism focused the spotlight on global corporations and demanded institutional reforms. NGOs proliferated during these decades and an increasing number began to engage with CSR issues and companies themselves. These agents of change, however, assumed certain characteristics that shaped their approaches and the nature of their demands and proposals. Compared to corporatist entities such as trade unions, which had been one of the principal change agents of previous decades, NGOs were relatively weak and fragmented. Neither were they empowered through their relations with political parties, as the labour movement had been. In addition, the types of demands they put forward and their tactics were conditioned by the tendency for many NGOs to become more involved in service delivery, and consultative and commodified activities. There was, in fact, a blurring of the distinction between an important strand of 'civil society' and 'business'.

Certain strands of governance theory help to explain the evolving nature of attempts to bring big business under social control. Not only the perverse effects of commodification and economic liberalization but also the perceived or real limitations of government and intergovernmental regulation fuelled the search for 'third way' alternatives. Furthermore, globalization, ever-expanding value chains, increasing complexity, uncertainty and risk require institutions at multiple levels that can enhance systemic coordination and stability. Forms of multiplayered and multilayered governance, where different actors (private, civil society, governmental and inter-governmental) come together both on an organizational basis in networks, and on an ideological and ethical basis through shared values and agreed norms (Keohane and Nye 2002), appear to offer considerable potential in this regard. The political underpinnings of this approach have to do not only with the reality or threat of pressure 'from below' but also new configurations of power involving multiple actors at different levels (Held 2003).

The role of agency in shaping the CSR agenda relates, of course, as much to the political strategies of corporations and business organizations as it does to civil society actors. It was the large global brand name companies that were particularly susceptible to the above pressures, and they mobilized effectively to influence, if not lead, the CSR 'movement' (Utting 2005b) and to shape the agenda on their terms. This leadership role – and the shift from reactive or defensive posturing to proactive engagement, noted above – can be usefully explained in Gramscian terms (Levy and Newell 2002). Throughout much of the history of capitalism elites have attempted to rule through consensus or 'hegemony'. This involves not only accommodating certain oppositional demands but also exercising 'moral, cultural and intellectual leadership' (Utting 2002b). Such an approach is particularly obvious in the field of CSR and in relation to big business engagement with multistakeholder approaches and public–private partnerships. Through such arrangements big business has skillfully opened up or accessed another arena for shaping the public policy process (Richter 2001, 2003).

French regulation theory provides further insights into the capacity of capitalist elites and relations to adapt in socially-sensitive ways in order to secure conditions for ongoing and long-term accumulation. Crucial in this regard is the role of extra-economic factors (of the type typically associated with CSR), namely institutions, shared visions, agreed standards, networks, partnerships and new modes of calculation (Jessop 1999). Some argue that the inherent tendency for self-preservation or self-reproduction through adaptation is even more ingrained. So-called 'autopoietic' systems are said to adapt through a self-regulating mechanism, which ensures that they change largely on their own terms and resist external intervention (Jessop 1999).

Indeed, a major challenge to the corporate accountability agenda comes from certain organized business interests that have proved quite adept at mobilizing to resist certain efforts to strengthen the regulatory environment. This can be seen, for example, in the political backlash in the United States against attempts to reapply the Alien Torts Claims Act (ACTA)[10] (Taylor 2004). Or it can take the form of attempts to reassert the model of softer voluntary approaches and corporate self-regulation, albeit with some fine-tuning and compromises. In the realm of international policy making related to corporate regulation, the discourse and practice of voluntary initiatives is often used as a means of crowding out the consideration or adoption of other regulatory approaches.

There is nothing new about this situation. Voluntary approaches have long been a compromise solution for accommodating demands for tougher international regulation of business. During the 1970s, for example, there were increasing calls for a New International Economic Order (NIEO) and binding regulations on TNCs. Against this backdrop, the United Nations began drafting a comprehensive code of conduct for TNCs. The drafting process itself ran into opposition and was eventually scuppered but what did emerge was a series of international agreements in the shape and form of non-binding principles and guidelines for TNCs. These were adopted, for example, by the OECD in 1976 and the ILO in 1977, as well as in the 1980s, by United Nations agencies concerned with the marketing and use of specific products such as breast-milk substitutes, medicinal drugs and pesticides. More recently, the use of the soft to displace the hard was seen clearly at the World Summit for Sustainable Development in Johannesburg when business interests rallied against certain proposals for 'corporate accountability', arguing that their involvement in company reporting and public–private partnerships obviated the need for harder regulatory action. And even many of the partnership proposals that were announced at the Summit failed to materialize once the spotlight was lifted (Commission on Sustainable Development 2004).

The use of the 'soft' to fend off or dilute the 'hard' is evident not only in relation to legalistic approaches but even within the spectrum of voluntary initiatives. To the extent that 'multistakeholder initiatives' (MSIs) represent a hardening of approaches such as corporate self-regulation, business often opposes MSIs, arguing that self-regulation is sufficient to meet the challenge of improving company social and environmental performance. This tactic was apparent in consultations organized by the World Health Organization (WHO) and the International Business Leaders Forum, which attempted to convince leading food and beverage TNCs that multistakeholder approaches could be useful for addressing some of the serious health and nutrition problems linked to the mass consumption of many of their products.[11] The response of some of the business representatives was to argue against such approaches on the basis that they could deal with problems of concern to the WHO through self-regulatory approaches.[12] A paradoxical situation existed where even self-regulation was regarded by some participants as a fundamentally progressive step forward, given that the initial position of business had been to deny that their companies were implicated in the problematique of poor health and nutrition. By agreeing to self-regulation, companies were accepting some degree of responsibility.

A similar response is playing out in relation to the draft UN Norms on the Responsibilities of TNCs and Other Business Enterprises with Regard to Human Rights, referred to in section two.[13] The Norms attempt to address some of the weaknesses that characterize the Global Compact and voluntary initiatives more generally, namely picking and choosing among standards, weak compliance with agreed standards, and free-riders. The Norms pull together a wide range of standards that are derived from international law that applies to states, but which are commonly found in multistakeholder initiatives. The Norms state that all TNCs and related companies have an obligation to uphold such standards, and propose an implementation and monitoring mechanism. They push the envelope even further by stipulating 'adequate reparation' in cases of stakeholders affected by non-compliance.

These harder aspects were anathema to some business interests and governments, and the 2004 session of the UN Commission on Human Rights, which considered the Norms, not only reminded the Sub-Commission that the Norms had no legal status and that it was not to perform any monitoring function, but also that it had never been asked to draft any such norms in the first place.[14] One of the reasons put forward by opponents was that they were essentially unnecessary since voluntary instruments such as the Global Compact and the OECD Guidelines on Multinational Corporations already exist. This was the position, for example, of the International Chamber of Commerce. Other business actors within the CSR community have adopted more nuanced positions. At a multi-stakeholder consultation on the Norms, organized by the Office of the High Commissioner for Human Rights in 2004,[15] several representatives of TNCs and business-interest organizations accepted that there was a need for a 'Global Compact Plus', i.e. for some ratcheting-up of standards and compliance mechanisms through voluntary approaches, but that the 'harder' aspects of the Norms related to monitoring and redress were unacceptable or politically a non-starter. In 2005, the Commission on Human Rights passed a resolution calling on the UN Secretary-General to appoint a Special Representative on Business and Human Rights in order to identify and clarify standards, examine regulatory approaches and methodologies for impact assessment, and compile a compendium of best practices. The Special Representative's interim report of 2006, suggested that the way forward lay not with the Norms, which were dismissed as 'a distraction' but with 'principled pragmatism'. Such an approach would essentially continue the process of scaling-up and ratcheting-up existing voluntary initiatives, and expanding forms of 'collaborative governance' involving co-regulatory or multistakeholder initiatives, as well as some of the regulatory initiatives referred to above that operate at the interface of voluntary and legalistic approaches. Specific reference was made to such aspects as extending the extraterritorial application of some home countries' jurisdiction for the extreme human rights abuses committed by their firms abroad; best practice learning and capacity-building in developing countries; the development of effective impact assessment tools; and extending CSR and monitoring initiatives to state-owned enterprises.

Ideas and knowledge

Crisis, interest group conflicts and political manoeuvering do not in themselves necessarily explain why particular agendas and processes of institutional reform emerge. This depends also on other conditions and contexts related to the role of ideas, how knowledge becomes embedded, and the ways in which pre-existing institutions and structures shape the substance, scope and pace of reform.[16]

Concerning the role of ideas, certain terms, concepts and schools of thought have been up for grabs and have been quickly assimilated and disseminated by key actors that are shaping the CSR agenda. The speed and force with which these ideas have informed global discourse may say more about the consolidated and globalizing nature of so-called epistemic communities, i.e. the formal and informal networks through which ideas are disseminated and learning takes place, than it does about the inherent worth of the ideas themselves.

Particularly influential have been ideas and thinking associated with ecological modernization, new institutional economics (NIE) and innovative approaches to management. Ecological modernization highlighted the role of technological and managerial innovations in improving the efficiency of resource use; 'win–win', as opposed to zero-sum, scenarios; systems-based approaches, and the capacity of existing institutions to internalize care for the environment, without fundamental restructuring (Hajer 1995). NIE emphasized the need for institutions that can minimize transaction costs (Toye 1995). These include risks to corporate reputation and sales posed by activists and 'ethical consumers', or risks and uncertainty that derive from the rapidly changing geography and structures of production and exchange in the context of globalization. Formal and informal institutions are needed to minimize such risks and to reinforce corporate control over suppliers and other stakeholders associated with global value chains. Thinking related to the concept of social capital, which emphasizes the economic benefits derived from collaborative relations and trust, reinforced this approach. CSR, multistakeholder initiatives and public–private partnerships are particularly relevant in this regard (Utting 2000, 2002b).

From the field of management studies emerged various concepts that have influenced CSR policy and practice. The type of systems-based management approaches and the notion of responsiveness to selected stakeholders (e.g. customers) that underpinned the concept of total quality management[17] resonated with stakeholder theory. The latter questioned the notion that the social responsibility of an enterprise consisted solely of making money for its owners or shareholders. The critique that developed in the 1970s and 1980s emphasized the multiple responsibilities of companies beyond the purely economic, and the fact that sound or strategic management required responsiveness and accountability to a variety of stakeholders who affect, or are affected by, the operations of a company (Freeman 1984). Since the notion of 'responsibility' relates to the realm of ethics and principles, attention soon turned to the nuts and bolts of how to improve the quality of CSR actions or 'corporate social performance', which includes motivating principles, processes and observable outcomes (Hopkins 1999). Engagement with stakeholders was crucial not just for ethical reasons but for key aspects of management associated with organizational learning, knowledge management and various advantages that derive from networking (Ruggie 2001; Zadek 2001). The so-called business case for CSR was reinforced further with the theorization and popularization of 'win–win'. Applied initially to the arena of corporate environmental responsibility, the notion of win–win suggested that practices involving recycling, pollution control and the production of environmental goods and services could make sound business sense from the perspective of cost reduction and competitive advantage (Porter and van der Linde 1995).

While these ideas challenged some aspects of neoliberal and management orthodoxy that had disregarded the reality of market failure and the complex determinants of successful enterprise, they did not really question fundamentals to do with labour market flexibilization, structural adjustment, free trade and investment, state downsizing, and corporate-driven globalization. Indeed, many of the interests that support CSR – including not only business but also governments, international organizations and the growing number of NGO service providers, take as given several of the basic tenets or features of neoliberalism. The original statement by the Secretary-General of the United Nations at the World Economic Forum that established the Global Compact (Annan 1999), for example, called for a compact in which the United Nations would support the idea of an international trade and investment regime largely free of restrictions, in return for company action to adopt voluntary improvements in relation to labour, human rights and environmental standards. More recently, this vision has been reinforced by the United Nations Commission on the Private Sector and Development, which also calls on corporations to engage far more proactively with local communities and enterprises (UNDP Commission on the Private Sector and Development 2004).

The ideas taken up by the corporate accountability movement, however, were somewhat different. Two strands of thinking were particularly influential: rights-based approaches to development and anti- or alternative globalization. The former not only emphasized the recognition of human rights as an objective of development, but emphasized the key role of legal instruments at international, regional and national levels (ODI 1999). For some, rights-based approaches also included a strong political element, namely that of 'empowerment', or the notion that the recognition and realization of rights depended crucially on increasing the capacity of disadvantaged groups in society to exert claims on the powerful. Other challenges were posed by activists and scholars who were highly critical of dominant patterns of globalization and adhered to the slogan of the World Social Forum that 'A Better World is Possible'. Those calling for a more fundamental reshaping or rolling-back of globalization emphasized the need to reassert social control over corporations via civil society, social movements and the state; the downsizing or breakup of corporations; halting altogether certain economic activities that have perverse social and environmental impacts; redirecting state resources and creating a policy environment conducive to local development and small enterprises; subsidiarity; and collective property rights (Broad 2002).

Structural constraints and spaces

Civil society pressures, corporate political strategies and the role of ideas explain to a considerable extent the content and dynamics of the CSR and corporate accountability agendas and movements. Corporate engagement with the CSR agenda was relatively easy since it posed no fundamental threat to corporate interests or the dominant 'neoliberal' macro-economic regime. This agenda assumes that capitalism can largely reform itself through relatively minor adjustments to existing institutions.

Indeed, the pattern of institutional reform related to CSR is very much conditioned by a range of structural factors and contexts that work for and against CSR. The pressures on companies to prioritize 'business-as-usual' practices and shareholder interests over other stakeholder interests are extremely powerful (see Cutler in this volume), and they are institutionalized in legal and incentive structures, as well as in corporate or management culture. As noted above, this often results in onerous contract conditions and pressures on suppliers. Structural conditions associated with 'cheap consumerism' *à la* Walmart also restrict the scope for expanding so-called ethical consumer markets for socially- and environmentally produced products, and partly explain the stubbornness of fair trade and ethical investment markets to break out of their very niche status. Such structural constraints go some way to explaining the relatively weak uptake and implementation of many CSR initiatives, as well as the litany of cases or exposés of 'greenwash', 'bluewash' and malpractice involving so-called CSR companies, leaders and organizations.[18]

The problem, however, is not just that structural conditions impose limits on CSR, or that perversity and do-gooding coexist; it is also that the scaling-up of the CSR agenda or the process of embedding liberalism seems to be dwarfed by ongoing economic liberalization or 'disembedding' of the type exposed by Joseph Stiglitz in *The Roaring Nineties* (2004), theorized by Blyth in *Great Transformations* (Blyth 2002) and documented empirically by the ILO (ILO Socio-Economic Security Programme 2004). Yet the scale of this disembedding tends to be downplayed or wished away in mainstream CSR discourse, or it is assumed that the CSR snowball, as it gathers momentum, will eventually outstrip and overtake any disembedding process.

In practice, as noted above, we do see some ratcheting-up and scaling-up of voluntary CSR standards and implementation procedures. The question that needs to be asked, however, is how does this process fare in relation to counter-trends involving ratcheting-down, that is, with policies and processes associated with economic liberalization or 'disembedding' that can have perverse social, environmental and other developmental impacts. If one considers the pace and scale of certain policies and processes that characterize neoliberal reform, then one might be excused from concluding that any scaling-up or ratcheting-up of CSR pales in comparison. These include 'flexibilization' of labour markets and sub-contracting that often undermine labour standards and labour rights; permissive fiscal 'reform' and tax avoidance or evasion that reduce corporate taxation; the downsizing of state institutions and capacity; the so-called race to the bottom associated with certain patterns of FDI, and the cut and run tactics that accompanied the termination of the Multi-Fibre Arrangement in January 2005.

It would be wrong to assume, however, that basic structural contexts and trends associated with capitalism and corporate globalization make a nonsense of CSR, i.e. that the profit motive and shareholder interests are totally at odds with forms of 'do-gooding' that may detract from short-term shareholder returns, contradict the tendency to externalize costs, or actually increase costs. Whilst often overstated, there is some validity to the assertion, continually emphasized by CSR exponents and business leaders, that there is a business case for CSR and scope for 'win–win' opportunities related to improved social, labour and environmental performance, on the one hand, and competitive advantage, risk and reputation management, productivity gains related, for example, to employee motivation and reduced staff turnover, and even cost reduction through aspects such as eco-efficiency, on the other hand (Porter and van der Linde 1995; Holliday et al. 2002).

Just as important, is the fact that structural change partly explains the emergence and dynamism of CSR. Far from simply contradicting or constraining CSR, certain structural conditions that characterize contemporary capitalism and patterns of industrial organization actually suggest the need for institutional and management reforms of the type associated with CSR (Utting 2000). This is apparent in relation to intangible assets, global value chains, flexibilization, and the increasing number of factors and institutions that impact economic coordination systems.

Intangible assets such as brand names have increased dramatically in value. CSR is a crucial weapon to defend such brands against risks and to enhance brand value though improved company and product reputation and image (Jenkins 2002). Global value chains have lengthened and deepened through foreign direct investment, networking and sub-contracting. This expansion of relations with a broader range of enterprises is partly driven by the need for greater flexibility of production systems as companies seek to adjust quickly to rapid changes in consumer demand and new market opportunities. CSR institutions such as codes of conduct, certification and labelling can play an important role in the development of collaborative relations between the firms that make up a network or commodity chain. CSR has also become a key means of ensuring that the corporate centre in these systems controls the chain and links on the periphery of that chain, through, for example, the introduction of codes of conduct, certification and other requirements in supply chain management, or acquiring additional eyes and ears, not only through NGOs and auditing firms engaged in monitoring and certification, but also through the type of global framework agreements entered into with international trade union organizations (Utting 2002a).

Given the scale and complexity of those systems, TNCs, as central players, and other organized business interests must preoccupy themselves not only with the more immediate aspects of production, marketing, costs of production, prices and profits, but also with a multiplicity of other institutions that facilitate the coordination and smooth functioning of economic systems (Shafaeddin 2004) and reduce transaction costs. Such institutions include, for example, networking, various types of alliances, partnerships, trust, multi-stakeholder dialogue and so forth, i.e. precisely the types of institutions and relations that characterize and are promoted by CSR.

While structural arguments are often used to explain or refute the possibility of CSR, the above discussion suggests that the structural context and its relationship with CSR is far more complex, and is likely to vary in different industry and societal settings. While it does not constitute the straitjacket that some critics portray, it does constrain the room for manoeuver, but it can also facilitate some types of progressive institutional reform.

Future directions

Let us now return to the question of what we can expect in terms of any significant advance on the CSR and corporate accountability fronts, and the institutionalization of these approaches as core components of a more generalized model of 'stakeholder capitalism'. The analysis above suggests that their substance and trajectory are likely to vary depending on the company, sector, country and region, reflecting the specificities of structural, political and institutional conditions and contexts.

In general terms, however, despite some signs of a reaction to CSR,[19] we can probably expect more of the same in terms of gradual scaling-up and incremental ratcheting-up. Corporate bankruptcy scandals and more exposés of 'greenwash' and 'bluewash' have kept the perception and reality of crisis and the abuse of corporate power very much alive. This has served to sustain the pressures on global corporations to engage with the CSR agenda and for some hardening of softer approaches. Furthermore, the CSR service industry, which includes NGOs and multistakeholder initiatives, is expanding, and a growing body of governmental, regional and inter-governmental organizations are supporting such initiatives and approaches. Indeed, CSR has become an important feature of the 'good governance' and poverty reduction agendas associated with the so-called post-Washington Consensus. The learning processes and 'path dependency' that characterize the CSR experience also reinforce the tendency for incremental change, as does the fact that the ratcheting-up of CSR may be part and parcel of a political strategy to fend off harder approaches related to corporate accountability and law.

But it seems clear that any major advance would require a more conducive structural and political environment. This is apparent if we look at the conditions under which more socially-sensitive models of capitalism emerged historically. In the case of post-Second World War social democracy in Europe, the East Asian corporate social welfare model, and early twentieth century Fordism in the United States[20] different combinations of structural and political elements played a key role in improving corporate social performance, at least in relation to selected groups or stakeholders. Such elements included, for example, changes in patterns of industrial organization that required new labour relations; a 'proactive' state or bureaucracy; strong labour or other social movements, or periods of militant activism; organic links between social movements, citizens and political parties; corporatist and class compromises; and relatively high rates of economic growth. Also apparent is the degree of policy coherence, in the sense referred to above, where, to some extent, the macro policy environment reinforced, rather than contradicted, both state and corporate strategy concerned with social protection (Mkandawire 2004; Perret 2004). Such factors and contexts resulted in significant improvements in certain aspects of corporate social policy and performance.[21]

The contemporary structural, political and institutional backdrop to CSR and corporate accountability appears quite different. Dynamic nationalist development projects and visions, in which the state plays a leading role, are few and far between; in many countries levels of economic growth remain persistently low; and the balance of forces has shifted significantly in favour of big business, due in part to the weakening of labour movements. Civil society activism, including that connected with CSR, is often fragmented, short-lived and disconnected from political parties. Indeed, as mentioned above, mainstream CSR discourse, practice and activism can have the effect of marginalizing and undermining the role of key social actors and institutions, such as trades unions, political parties, governments and Southern-based interests, in relevant decision-making, consultative and implementation processes. And instead of being mutually reinforcing and synergistic, there are major tensions and contradictions between macro-economic policy and social and sustainable development, or between CSR and dominant consumption patterns and corporate strategies which are often more conducive to a 'race to the bottom' than to raising social and environmental standards.

The piecemeal nature of many CSR initiatives, and the focus on social and environmental protection, contrast with the emphasis on redistribution and a somewhat more equitable and systematic sharing of the benefits of growth and productivity that characterized earlier models of stakeholder capitalism. The experimental, ad hoc, and, often rhetorical nature of many CSR initiatives belies another important difference: under previous models, there emerged institutions that could sustain redistributive commitments (Mackintosh and Tibandebage 2004; Mkandawire 2004).

Globalization has clearly changed some of the rules of the game that govern institutional change, in particular the scope for regulating markets through national level interventions and politics, and the possibility that liberalism could be embedded on the basis of a narrow class compromise involving factions of capital and organized labour. Other levels of intervention (inter-national, regional and local), players and relationships have become more important, and the range of issues that need to be addressed is broader (Jessop 1999, 2001). But some of the features that explain the emergence of more socially-sensitive models of capitalism in previous historical periods remain as relevant today as they did in the past.

The challenge confronting the ratcheting-up and scaling-up of CSR is per-haps more substantive than political. Indeed, the strength of CSR, and the reason why it has been catapulted onto the world stage and into mainstream discourse and policy agendas, lies in the fact that it is being promoted by a broad coalition of social forces. It has brought together the reformist wings of two of the most significant 'movements' of modern times, namely certain actors associated with neoliberalism and a looser mélange of social forces and ideologies associated with 'sustainable development'. Politically, there-fore, the CSR 'movement' is rather strong. The inherent weakness of CSR resides in the fact that it is not only swimming against the strong current of neoliberal reform, but it attempts to modify relatively minor aspects of that reform project without seriously questioning its fundamentals. In this regard, the key challenge confronting the CSR agenda from the perspective of progressive institutional reform, relates to contradictions associated with this situation.

At best, CSR can contribute to raising awareness of certain social and environmental problems and serve to caution against blind faith in market forces. It can also reinforce some aspects of the normative culture and culture of compliance associated with rights-based approaches to development and governance. And by getting the ball rolling or pushing the envelope in terms of new issues, new business practices and institutions, it can create conditions related to organizational learning and path dependency that are conducive to the gradual scaling-up of CSR initiatives and the incremental hardening of softer regulatory approaches. At worst, CSR involves a transfer of regula-tory authority to largely unaccountable agents and renders more stable and palatable a model of capitalism that generates or reinforces widespread social exclusion, inequality and environmental degradation. The likelihood that this worst case scenario will materialize increases in contexts where the CSR agenda marginalizes issues of empowerment, redistribution, and the crucial role of public policy and trade unions in social protection and embedded liberalism. Such a scenario will also likely gain ground where neoliberal reform projects are being actively pursued, and where the proponents of CSR disregard the contradictory or perverse implications for economic and equitable development associated with certain approaches to CSR, not least the way it can reinforce the economic power and political influence in TNCs.

The corporate accountability movement generally pays more attention to these aspects and is, therefore, quite different. Indeed, one way of characterizing and distinguishing the CSR and corporate accountability agendas is in terms of how they relate to three of the principal reform agendas of the contemporary era, namely neoliberalism, embedded liberalism and progressive variants of 'alternative globalization'. The CSR agenda straddles both the neoliberal and embedded liberalism camps, and so is more palliative than transformative. The corporate accountability agenda also has one leg in the embedded liberalism camp, as is evident in the case of initiatives involving standard setting, code implementation, monitoring and certification – or ratcheted-up variants of CSR. But it has another leg grounded in the anti- or alternative globalization camp where issues of rights, redistribution, empowerment, compliance and redress assume centre stage. The key challenge confronting the corporate accountability movement may be more political than substantive. It will inevitably face considerable opposition and resistance from the powers that be and confront the difficult task of building the type of broad-based coalitions required to promote progressive institutional change. This requires not only forging links between campaigns and different types of activism – involving trade unions and NGOs, as well as Northern and Southern activists – but also reconnecting activism with democratic party politics and processes. It also requires confronting the difficult question of alliances and compromises involving business interests, and exploring more systematically the potential for complementary, synergistic and pluralistic approaches to regulation.

Notes

1. A slightly modified version of this paper has been published by the United Nations Research Institute for Social Development (UNRISD) (Utting 2005a). Petter Utting is Deputy Director and CSR Research Coordinator, UNRISD. The author would like to thank Kate Ives and Anita Tombez for research and editorial assistance, and Dara O'Rourke, Shahra Razavi, Jem Bendell, Thandika Mkandawire, Naren Prasad, Gabriele Köhler and Ann Zammit for their comments on an earlier draft, as well as Volker Rittberger, Lothar Reith and various other participants at the 2004 Tübingen conference, where some of these ideas were originally presented.

2. See Prahalad 2005; United Nations Commission on the Private Sector and Development 2004; World Commission on the Social Dimension of Globalization 2004; United Nations Millennium Project 2005.
3. While ISO 14001 certification continues to expand at a healthy rate, the rate of expansion is far less than that achieved for quality management certification under the ISO 9000 series. Whereas 66,000 entities obtained ISO 14001 certification during the scheme's first nine years of existence, the corresponding figure for ISO 9000 certification of approximately 340,000 facilities was five times greater (see ISO 2004).
4. Of this 9 per cent, two-thirds (6%) replied that 'change would have been difficult to implement without being a participant' while one-third (3%) replied that 'the change would not have happened without being a participant'.
5. This point was raised by Dwight Justice, ICFTU, at the UNRISD conference, 'Corporate Social Responsibility and Development: Towards a New Agenda?', 17–18 November 2003, Geneva.
6. See, for example, International Forum on Globalization (2002) and Broad (2002).
7. A pilot project is being implemented in Turkey, involving the CCC, the Ethical Trading Initiative (ETI), FLA, WRC, the Fair Wear Foundation (FWF) and Social Accountability International (SAI).
8. See, for example, the commentary on the Norwegian company, Statoil, in ILO Socio-Economic Security Programme 2004: 357.
9. These included, for example, the Union Carbide gas leak in Bhopal, India in 1984; the Exxon-Valdez oil tanker disaster in 1989; deforestation or forest degradation associated with farming and forestry systems linked to McDonalds, Mitsubishi and Aracruz; environmental and social impacts, and human rights abuses, linked to mining and oil companies like Rio Tinto and Shell; and sweatshop conditions in supply chains of Nike and other companies.
10. Through this law, that was passed in 1789, foreign nationals can bring a case to a US court for a civil wrong committed in violation of international law (Abrahams 2004).
11. For an analysis of such linkages, see WHO 2003.
12. The author participated in one of these consultations in 2003.
13. The 'Norms' were drafted by a working group of experts established in 1999 by the United Nations Sub-Commission on the Promotion and Protection of Human Rights, adopted in their draft form by the Sub-Commission in August 2003.
14. United Nations Economic and Social Council. 2004. Report to the Economic and Social Council of the Sixtieth Session of the Commission. UN Doc. E/CN.4/2004/L.11/Add.7, 22 April. United Nations, New York.
15. The meeting was attended by the author.
16. For an analysis of how modern capitalism has been shaped by the interplay of ideas, interests and institutions see Mark Blyth 2002. For a similar analysis related to corporate environmental responsibility see the work of David Levy et al., including Levy and Newell 2002; Levy and Kolk 2002.
17. For a discussion on the links and parallels between total quality management and CSR or 'total responsibility management', see Waddock and Bodwell 2002.
18. 'Greenwash' is defined in the Oxford dictionary as 'Disinformation disseminated by an organization so as to present an environmentally responsible image.' The term 'bluewash' was coined to refer to the process of image enhancement that

takes place when companies associate themselves with the United Nations (symbolized by its blue flag) (Bruno and Karliner 2000; CorpWatch 2000). In both cases, as Bruno and others point out, image enhancement often takes place against a backdrop where companies are doing little, if anything, to significantly change their relationship to society and the environment (Greer and Bruno 1996). Various types of award schemes, such as the Greenwash Awards, organized by CorpWatch, and the Public Eye Awards in Davos, organized by Swiss-based NGOs, identify the Global Compact and other companies that continue to act irresponsibly in relation to labour, environmental, human rights and fiscal practices (www.corpwatch.org, www.evb.ch).
19. Some suggest the need to jettison the CSR project, partly because of what are considered to be its flawed assumptions and negative impacts for individual firms in terms of cost, market access and competitiveness (Henderson 2001; *The Economist*, 22 January 2005), as well as the fact that the privatization of regulatory authority transfers responsibility to largely undemocratic or unaccountable private and non-governmental institutions. From a developmental perspective there are also concerns that CSR throws up barriers to trade and employment, and ultimately enhances the competitive advantage of big business.
20. The 'social sensitivity' of these models was, of course, restricted in terms of geography, sectors, firms and the types of social benefits involved. Typically, the environment (and future generations) were excluded and some of the costs of any social compromise were externalized or displaced to the developing world or unregulated arenas including the household and unpaid labour (Jessop 1999).
21. It should be noted that the social benefits that characterized these models were limited not only in type but also in terms of the groups that benefited. The so-called 'grand compromise' that characterized Fordism (Lipietz 1992), particularly in the United States, was a fairly narrow pact between specific sectors of business and labour. In the case of East Asia, such gains were primarily related to a small group of large corporations that needed to attract and retain skilled labour (Pempel 2002). Others groups or stakeholders, including those associated with the supply chain in developing countries, were often excluded.

References

Abrahams, D. (2004): *Regulating Corporations: a Resource Guide*. Geneva: UNRISD.
Annan, K. (1999): Secretary General Proposes Global Compact on Human Rights, Labour, Environment. UN Press Release No. SG/SM/6881/Rev.1*.
Bendell, J. (2004): Barricades and Boardrooms: a Contemporary History of the Corporate Accountability Movement. Programme on Technology, Business and Society, Paper No. 13. Geneva: UNRISD.
Bendell, J. and D. F. Murphy. (2002): Towards Civil Regulation: NGOs and the Politics of Corporate Environmentalism. In: Utting P. (ed.), *The Greening of Business in Developing Countries: Rhetoric, Reality and Prospects*. London: Zed Books.
Blyth, M. (2002): *Great Transformations: Economic Ideas and Institutional Change in the Twentieth Century*. Cambridge: Cambridge University Press.
Braithwaite, J. and P. Drahos. (2000): *Global Business Regulation*. Cambridge: Cambridge University Press.

Broad, R. (ed.). (2002): *Global Backlash: Citizen Initiatives for a Just World Economy*. New York: Rowman & Littlefield.

Broad, R. and J. Cavanagh. (1999): The Corporate Accountability Movement: Lessons and Opportunities. *The Fletcher Forum of World Affairs* 23(2): 151–69.

Bruno, K. and J. Karliner. (2000): *Tangled up in Blue: Corporate Partnerships at the United Nations*. Transnational Resource & Action Center (TRAC), San Francisco.

Clean Clothes Campaign. (2005): *Looking for a Quick Fix: How Weak Social Auditing is Keeping Workers in Sweatshops*. Amsterdam: Clean Clothes Campaign.

Commission on Sustainable Development. (2004): Partnerships for Sustainable Development: Report of the Secretary-General. New York: United Nations.

Conroy, M. (2002): Can Advocacy-led Certification Systems Transform Global Corporate Practices? In: Broad (ed.), op cit.

Corpwatch. (2000): Letters to Kofi Annan Blasting the Global Compact Corporations. www.corpwatch.org.

Cutler, A. C., V. Haufler and T. Porter (eds.). (1999): *Private Authority and International Affairs*. Albany, NY: SUNY Series in Global Politics. State University of New York.

The Economist (Special Edition) (2005): A Survey of Corporate Social Responsibility, 22 January: 3–18.

Fig, D., A. Bezuidenhout, R. Hamman and R. Omar. (2003): Reflections on Corporate Social and Environmental Responsibility in South Africa: an Overview. Presented to UNRISD Conference on Corporate Social Responsibility and Development: Towards a New Agenda? Geneva, 17–18 November 2003. Sociology of Work Unit, University of the Witwatersrand, Johannesburg.

Freeman, R. E. (1984): *Strategic Management: a Stakeholder Approach*. Boston: Pitman.

Greer, J. and K. Bruno. (1996): *Greenwash: the Reality behind Corporate Environmentalism*. Penang, Malaysia: Third World Network.

Gunningham, N. and D. Sinclair. (2002): *Leaders and Laggards: Next Generation Environmental Regulation*. Sheffield: Greenleaf.

Hajer, M. (1995): *The Politics of Environmental Discourse: Ecological Modernization and the Policy Process*. Oxford: Clarendon Press.

Hanks, J. (2002): Promoting Corporate Environmental Responsibility: What Role for 'Self-Regulatory' and 'Co-Regulatory' Policy Instruments in South Africa? In: Utting P. (ed.), *The Greening of Business in Developing Countries: Rhetoric, Reality and Prospects*. London: Zed Books.

Haufler, V. (2001): A Public Role for the Private Sector: Industry Self-Regulation in a Global Economy. Washington, DC: Carnegie Endowment for International Peace.

Held, D. (2003): From Executive to Cosmopolitan Multilateralism. In: Held D. and M. Koenig-Archibugi (eds.), *Taming Globalization: Frontiers of Governance*. Cambridge: Polity.

Henderson, D. (2001): Misguided Virtue: False Notions of Corporate Social Responsibility. London: Institute for Economic Affairs.

Holliday, C., S. Schmidheiny and P. Watts. (2002): *Walking the Talk: the Business Case for Sustainable Development*. Sheffield: Greenleaf Publishing.

Hopkins, M. (1999): *The Planetary Bargain: Corporate Social Responsibility Comes of Age*. London: Macmillan.

Huber, E. (2002): *Models of Capitalism: Lessons for Latin America*. University Park, PA: Pennsylvania State University Press.

ILO Socio-Economic Security Programme. (2004): Economic Security for a Better World. Geneva: ILO.

International Forum on Globalization. (2002): Alternatives to Economic Globalization: a Better World is Possible. San Francisco: Berrett-Koehler.

International Labour Office (ILO) (1999): Multinational Enterprises and Social Policy: Reflections on Twenty Years of the Tripartite Declaration. Geneva: ILO.

International Organization for Standardization (ISO) (2004): The ISO Survey of ISO 9001 and ISO 14001 Certificates – 2003. www.iso.org.

Jenkins, R. (2002): Corporate Codes of Conduct: Self-Regulation in a Global Economy. In: NGLS/UNRISD (eds.), *Voluntary Approaches to Corporate Responsibility: Readings and a Resource Guide*. NGLS Development Dossier. Geneva: United Nations.

Jessop, B. (1999): The Social Embeddedness of the Economy and Its Implications for Economic Governance (draft). Department of Sociology, Lancaster University. www.comp.lancaster.ac.uk/sociology/soc016rj.html, accessed on 25 February 2005.

Jessop, B. (2001): Capitalism, the Regulation Approach and Critical Realism. In: Brown A., S. Fleetwood and J. Roberts (eds.), *Critical Realism and Marxism*. London: Routledge. www.lancs.ac.uk/fss/sociology/papers/jessop-capitalism-regulation-realism.pdf, accessed on 25 February 2005.

Keohane, R. (2002): *Power and Governance in a Partially Globalized World*. London: Routledge.

Keohane, R. and J. Nye Jr. (2002): Governance in a Globalizing World. In: Keohane, op. cit.

Krut, R. and H. Gleckman. (1998): *ISO14001: a Missed Opportunity for Global Sustainable Industrial Development*. London: Earthscan.

Levy, D. and A. Kolk. (2002): Strategic Responses to Global Climate Change: Conflicting Pressures on Multinationals in the Oil Industry. *Business and Politics*, (4)3: 275–300.

Levy, D. and P. Newell. (2002): Business Strategy and International Environmental Governance: Toward a Neo-Gramscian Synthesis. *Global Environmental Politics*, 2(4), November: 84–101.

Lipietz, A. (1992): *Towards a New Economic Order: Postfordism, Ecology and Democracy*. Cambridge: Polity.

Mackintosh, M. and P. Tibandebage. (2004): Inequality and Redistribution in Health Care: Analytical Issues for Developmental Social Policy. In: Mkandawire T. (ed.), *Social Policy in a Development Context*. Basingstoke: Palgrave Macmillan.

Mkandawire, T. (2004): Social Policy in a Development Context: Introduction. In: Mkandawire T. (ed.), *Social Policy in a Development Context*. Basingstoke: Palgrave Macmillan.

Maquila Solidarity Network (MSN) (2005): Codes Memo, No. 18, Dec 2004/Jan 2005.

Murphy, D. F. and J. Bendell. (1997): *In the Company of Partners: Business, Environmental Groups and Sustainable Development Post-Rio*. Bristol: Policy Press.

Newell, P. (2002): From Responsibility to Citizenship: Corporate Accountability for Development. *IDS Bulletin* 33(2): 91–100.

O'Rourke, D. (2000): Monitoring the Monitors: a Critique of Pricewaterhouse Coopers (PwC) Labor Monitoring. Web.mit.edu/dorourke/www/index.html, accessed on 25 February 2005.

O'Rourke, D. (2003): Outsourcing Regulation: Analyzing Nongovernmental Systems of Labour Standards and Monitoring. *Policy Studies Journal* 31(1): 1–29.

Overseas Development Institute (ODI) (1999): What Can We Do with a Rights-Based Approach to Development? Briefing Paper, September. London: ODI.

Pempel, T. J. (2002): Labor Exclusion and Privatized Welfare: Two Keys to Asian Capitalist Development. In: Huber (ed.), *Models of Capitalism: Lessons for Latin America*. Pennsylvania State University Press.

Perret, B. (2004): Which French Third Way? Administrative and Social Empowerment: Lessons from the Second Left in Power. wanadoo.fr/bernard.perret/New-York%20Liberalism2004.htm, accessed on 7 February 2005.

Polanyi, K. (1957): *The Great Transformation: the Political and Economic Origins of Our Time*. Boston, MA: Beacon Press.

Porter, M. E. and C. van der Linde. (1995): Green and Competitive: Ending the Stalemate. *Harvard Business Review* September–October: 120–34.

Prahalad, C. K. (2005): *The Fortune at the Bottom of the Pyramid: Eradicating Poverty Through Profits*. Upper Saddle River, NJ: Wharton School Publishing.

Richter, J. (2001): *Holding Corporations Accountable: Corporate Conduct, International Codes, and Citizen Action*. London/New York: Zed Books.

Richter, J. (2003): Building on Quicksand: the Global Compact, Democratic Governance, and Nestlé. CETIM/IBFAN-GIFA/Berne Declaration, Geneva/Zurich.

Ruggie, J. G. (2001): global_governance.net: the Global Compact as Learning Network. *Global Governance* 7(4), October–December: 371–8.

Ruggie, J. (2003): Taking Embedded Liberalism Global: the Corporate Connection. In: Held D. and M. Koenig-Archibugi (eds.), *Taming Globalization: Frontiers of Governance*. Cambridge: Polity.

Sabel, C., D. O'Rourke and A. Fung. (2000): Ratcheting Labor Standards: Regulation for Continuous Improvement in the Global Workplace. Social Protection Discussion Paper No. 0011. Washington DC: World Bank.

Shafaeddin, S. M. (2004): *Who is the Master? Who is the Servant? Market or Government? An Alternative Approach: Towards a Coordination System*. Geneva: UNCTAD.

Stiglitz, J. E. (2004): *The Roaring Nineties: Why We're Paying the Price for the Greediest Decade in History*. London: Penguin.

SustainAbility. (2003): *The 21st Century NGO: in the Market for Change*. London: SustainAbility.

Taylor, M. (2004): Corporate Fallout Detectors and Fifth Amendment Capitalists: Corporate Complicity in Human Rights Abuse. In: UN Global Compact and Office of the High Commissioner for Human Rights, *Embedding Human Rights in Business Practice*. New York: UN Global Compact Office.

Toye, J. (1995): The New Institutional Economics and its Implications for Development Theory. In: Harris J., J. Hunter and C. M. Lewis (eds.), *The New Institutional Economics and Third World Development*. London: Routledge.

United Nations Economic and Social Council. (2004): Report to the Economic and Social Council of the Sixtieth Session of the Commission. UN Doc. E/CN.4/2004/L.11/Add.7, 22 April. New York: United Nations.

United Nations Commission on the Private Sector and Development. (2004): Unleashing Entrepreneurship: Making Business Work for the Poor. New York: United Nations Development Programme.

United Nations Conference on Trade and Development (UNCTAD) (2003): FDI Policies for Development: National and International Perspectives. Geneva: UNCTAD.

United Nations Millennium Project. (2005): Investing in Development: a Practical Plan to Achieve the Millennium Development Goals. New York: Earthscan/Millennium Project.

United Nations Research Institute for Social Development (UNRISD) (2004): Corporate Social Responsibility and Development: Towards a New Agenda? Conference

News, Report of the UNRISD Conference (Geneva, 17–18 November 2003). Geneva: UNRISD.

Utting, P. (2000): Business Responsibility for Sustainable Development. Occasional Paper No. 2. Geneva: UNRISD.

Utting, P. (2002a): Regulating Business through Multistakeholder Initiatives: a Preliminary Assessment. In: NGLS/UNRISD (eds.), *Voluntary Approaches to Corporate Responsibility: Readings and a Resource Guide*. NGLS Development Dossier. Geneva: United Nations.

Utting, P. (ed.) (2002b): *The Greening of Business in Developing Countries: Rhetoric, Reality and Prospects*. London: Zed Books.

Utting, P. (2004): Neue Ansätze zur Regulierung Transnationaler Unternehmen. Potenzial und Grenzen von Multistakeholder-Initiativen. In: Brühl T., H. Feldt, B. Hamm, H. Hummel, J. Martens (eds.), *Unternehmen in der Weltpolitik: Politiknetzwerke, Unternehmensregeln und die Zukunft des Multilateralismus*. Bonn: J. H. W. Dietz.

Utting, P. (2005a): Rethinking Business Regulation: From Self-regulation to Social Control. Programme Paper TBS 15. Geneva: UNRISD.

Utting, P. (2005b): Corporate Responsibility and the Movement of Business. *Development in Practice*, 15(3 and 4), June.

Waddock, S. and C. Bodwell. (2002): From TQM to TRM: Total Responsibility Management Approaches. *Journal of Corporate Citizenship* 7(Autumn): 113–26.

Ward, H. (2003): *Legal Issues in Corporate Citizenship*. Stockholm/London: Swedish Partnership for Global Responsibility/IIED.

Welford, R. (2002): Disturbing Development: Conflicts between Corporate Environmentalism, the International Economic Order and Sustainability. In: Utting P. (ed.), op. cit.

World Commission on the Social Dimension of Globalization (WCSDG) (2004): *A Fair Globalization: Creating Opportunities for All*. Geneva: International Labour Organization.

World Health Organization (WHO) (2003): *Diet, Nutrition and the Prevention of Chronic Diseases*. Report of a Joint WHO/FAO Expert Consultation. WHO Technical Report Series 916. Geneva: WHO.

Zadek, S. (2001): *The Civil Corporation: the New Economy of Corporate Citizenship*. London: Earthscan.

Zadek, S. (2004): The Path to Corporate Responsibility. *Harvard Business Review* December.

Abbreviations and acronyms

AA	AccountAbility
ACTA	Alien Torts Claims Act
AIDS	acquired immunodeficiency syndrome
CCC	Clean Clothes Campaign
CSR	corporate social responsibility
EITI	Extractive Industries Transparency Initiative
ETI	Ethical Trading Initiative
EU	European Union
FLA	Fair Labour Association

FWF	Fair Wear Foundation
HIV	human immunodeficiency virus
ICFTU	International Confederation of Free Trade Unions
ILO	International Labour Organization
IUF	International Union of Food and Allied Workers
ISO	International Organization for Standardization
MSIs	multistakeholder initiatives
NGOs	non-governmental organizations
NIE	new institutional economics
NIEO	New International Economic Order
OECD	Organization for Economic Cooperation and Development
PRTR	Pollutant Release and Transfer Register
SA	Social Accountability
SAI	Social Accountability International
TNCs	transnational corporations
UN	United Nations
UNCTAD	United Nations Conference on Trade and Development
UNRISD	United Nations Research Institute for Social Development
US	United States
WHO	World Health Organization
WRC	Worker Rights Consortium

10
The Two-Level Logic of Non-State Market Driven Global Governance

Steven Bernstein, Benjamin Cashore

The failure of governments and international institutions to effectively address significant global social and environmental problems has created a policy void that an array of voluntary, self-regulatory, shared governance and private arrangements are beginning to fill (Andrews 1998; Gunningham, Kagan and Thornton 2003; Harrison 1998; Howlett 2000; Rosenbaum 1995; Rosenau 2000; Ruggie 2004; Webb 2002). Despite increasing scholarly attention to these new policy arenas, most current research conflates these initiatives with what is arguably the most conceptually distinct and authoritative form of non-state global governance to arise in the last 50 years: non-state market driven (NSMD) governance systems (Cashore 2002). Their purpose is to develop socially and environmentally responsible practices in the marketplace by creating incentives and disincentives, through market supply chains, often through the use of a label that signals compliance to pre-established standards. Their distinctiveness is especially notable along two dimensions. First, they include governance institutions with decision-making and compliance mechanisms. Second, contrary to the vast majority of voluntary or self-regulatory initiatives, NSMD governance systems *reject* state sovereign authority, turning instead to markets (firms, consumers, as well as affected societal actors) for legitimacy to govern.

Leading transnational social and environmental organizations, including groups as diverse as the World Wide Fund for Nature (WWF), Greenpeace, and Oxfam, frustrated with both governmental inertia and perceived limitations of voluntary or corporate social responsibility initiatives, are increasingly attracted to the NSMD governance model because it aims to comprehensively address social and environmental problems governing a particular sector. NSMD governance must not, therefore, be confused with pilot projects or niche market labeling schemes that have little discernible influence on broad trends or social regulation.

One early indicator of their potential influence is their rapid spread. Buoyed by existing support of NSMD governance in the forest sector[1] – the vast majority of forest companies in Europe and North America now support some form of forest certification – NSMD governance systems have proliferated to address some of the most critically important problems facing the planet, including fisheries depletion, food production, mining, construction, rural and community poverty, inhumane working conditions and human rights abuses. While still at a nascent stage, their potential reach is undeniably significant: if successful in the current sectors being targeted, NSMD systems would regulate 20 percent of international trade.[2]

This potential stems from their explicit goal to transform the international political economy, and their premise that market-incentives are critical, but insufficient, first steps in a wider project to reorient social and business norms of acceptable and appropriate behaviour (Levi and Linton 2003: 419). For these reasons, we argue that NSMD governance systems are more likely than other non-state or hybrid governance systems to transform authority in the global marketplace. They operate in what John Ruggie (2004: 504) has labeled an emerging global public or social domain,[3] an 'increasingly institutionalized transnational arena of discourse, contestation, and action concerning the production of global public goods, involving private as well as public actors.' Here, publics increasingly express their demands to moderate the excesses of global liberalism and to 'embed' markets in broader societal goals, shifting the traditional site of such contestation and governance away solely from sovereign states and the interstate realm.

What makes NSMD systems a unique form of global governance? Will they be able to effectively address global policy problems where governments have not? How do these emergent market-driven systems gain governing authority and what is their transformative capacity? Given the nascent stage of NSMD, such questions are difficult to answer with empirical data only (since support is still emerging) but likewise timely. Now is the moment when scholarly work should aim to shed light on the mechanism and conditions under which they are most likely to gain authority and, ultimately, be effective.

To address these questions, we advance existing scholarship on legitimacy and NSMD systems, which has primarily focused on the domestic context, to generate hypotheses applicable to any scale of 'global governance.' Specifically, we expand the scope of empirical work to the full range of sectors in which NSMD systems vie for authority. This move allows us to comprehensibly probe important differences between NSMD systems and the proliferation of private authority and public-private partnerships. Second, we conceptualize how these market-based systems interact with *existing* globally entrenched norms and institutions. This move draws attention to a major constitutive basis of legitimacy that constrains and mediates the acceptance of NSMD systems, and which has been ignored in previous work that focused primarily on the motivations of non-governmental groups or firms to create or join such systems (Prakash 1999, 2000; Raines 2003; Rivera 2002; Sasser 2002).

Applying insights from constructivist scholarship in International Relations (IR), we argue that an analysis of the constitutive basis of global legitimacy is a critical, yet overlooked step, in understanding how the social structure of global authority – the rules, norms and institutions that define what appropriate authority is, where it is located, and on basis it can be justified – influences the emergence of NSMD systems. This global level is especially important because it captures legitimating dynamics in the emerging social domain where one might notice shifts in global authority and observe new forms of regulation of the global marketplace. To understand how NSMD systems' authority might ultimately gain widespread acceptance, it is necessary to examine the independent and intersecting effects of *both* firm choices within marketplace dynamics and these broader global dynamics.

Studying non-state governing systems poses several research challenges, especially because, as an emergent form of authority, their potentially transformative impacts have largely yet to occur. Thus, most of the growing literature on NSMD systems sidestep questions of legitimacy, focusing instead on their theoretical challenge to state authority and ideological underpinnings (Falkner 2003) or on firm choices to participate or not. Our theoretical departure is necessary because legitimacy – defined generally as the acceptance and justification of shared rule – is required for the transformation of authority. If NSMD systems are to realize their potential by moving beyond static systems in which firms and social actors constantly evaluate and re-evaluate whether to withdraw support based on short-term cost-benefit calculations, they must somehow become more deeply engrained as a legitimate form of authority. Identifying the conditions under which this can occur is the focus of our study.

Drawing very loosely on Putnam's metaphor on the interactions of domestic and international bargaining, we argue that NSMD legitimation dynamics interact at two 'levels': an 'internal' market-level that determines and influences how the sector-specific community interacts to grant authority to create policy; and an 'external' level, usually overlooked, comprising the broader set of institutions and norms that constrain and direct NSMD's institutional form and substance. Whereas Putnam focused on levels delineated by traditional state-centered governance, the two levels of NSMD global governance are non-territorial. The legitimacy dynamics thus cannot be easily extrapolated from existing comparative and International Relations (IR) scholarship, which largely assumes territorial-based bargaining.

This paper proceeds in five parts. First, we identify the rationale behind the emergence of NSMD global governance. Second, we review the proliferation of transnational NSMD governance systems over the last 10–15 years. Third, we identify key features that render 'governance' an accurate descriptor of NSMD systems. They serve to distinguish NSMD from traditional sovereign and public/private governance institutions on the one hand, and self-regulatory, voluntary, and information-based policy initiatives on the other. This section undertakes an overdue conceptual housekeeping to distinguish among the array of new governance arrangements and their implications for the configuration of authority in global governance. Fourth, drawing on these distinctions, we explain why legitimacy is central for explaining the success or failure of NSMD governance. Fifth, we identify two levels at which legitimacy must be achieved by NSMD systems and develop hypotheses about their direct and intersecting effects.

The rationale for non-state market driven global governance

The underlying rationale for NSMD global governance systems is as follows. Global liberalism effectively frees mobile multinational firms from inconvenient national regulation and similarly discourages countries desperate for foreign investment and income from trade from raising environmental, labour or other social standards (Braithwaite and Drohas 2000). The practices of multinational firms directly, or indirectly through perverse incentives to keep standards and costs low in their supply chains, are, according to this rationale, a primary culprit in the social dislocation and negative environmental consequences that accompany globalization. For these reasons, states and intergovernmental institutions have shown an inability or unwillingness to regulate firm activity in the global marketplace, rendering direct governance *through* the marketplace necessary. NSMD governance systems aim to *reverse* global liberalism's impact on policy and regulatory development by targeting large multinational companies with market incentives (price premiums, market access, 'social licences' to operate) or disincentives (boycott campaigns, shaming), which in turn should put pressure along the market's supply chain to encourage compliance to a governing system's rules and procedures.

Many non-governmental organizations (NGOs) view NSMD systems, if successful, as a way to hold firms accountable to the broader public for potentially negative social and environmental consequences of their activities in the global marketplace (Sasser 2002: 5). That is, they share with more radical groups a critique of economic globalization and neoliberalism as culprits in the inability or unwillingness of states to address serious ecological and social problems. However, instead of rejecting the market, NSMD supporters attempt to harness arenas of private authority to achieve their aims.

Recognition that the social domain is interwoven with global markets is imperative for any analysis of how NSMD governance systems gain authority; indeed, the goal of NSMD is to embed global markets in a social domain. The connection here builds on Ruggie's (1982) concept of 'embedded liberalism,' which extended to the international level Karl Polanyi's (1944) insight that market activity must, ultimately, be socially sustainable. Ruggie argued that post Second World War multilateral institutions served the dual purpose of sustaining and stabilizing international liberalism, while ensuring that the substance of the agreements reached rested on legitimate social bargains within leading states. They accomplished this in part with rules that supported liberal markets, but left room for domestic intervention and adjustment. Late twentieth century globalization, however, began to change that equation as liberalized transaction flows, economic integration and an ideology exalting self-regulating markets took hold. As Ruggie has put it:

> Embedded liberalism presupposed an *international* world. It presupposed the existence of *national* economies, engaged in external transactions, conducted at *arms length*, which governments could mediate at the *border* by tariffs and exchange rates, among other tools. The globalization of financial markets and production chains, however, challenges each of these premises and threatens to leave behind merely national social bargains. (Ruggie 2003: 94)

NSMD systems, if successful, could fill this governance gap by creating an arena in which markets would again be embedded within a social domain, but at the global level. For these reasons, NSMD systems must be classified according not only to their use of markets, but also to whether they contain purposeful social steering efforts. Systems that otherwise look like NSMD but work to limit, or ignore, social steering, are, as we show below, 'wolves in sheep's clothing', containing fundamentally different purposes and different legitimacy dynamics.

The rise of non-state market driven global governance

Beginning in the early 1990s, a number of NGOs, frustrated with their efforts to influence governmental or intergovernmental processes, began to develop their own sets of socially and environmentally responsible business practices (Table 10.1). They accredited firms who accepted these standards, often by creating an environmental 'label' that customers of products – whether manufacturers, retailers or end-users – could then require in their purchasing policies. The intention was to reward companies with an economic 'carrot' by providing recognition in the marketplace of their responsible business practices, with a corresponding promise of either market access and/or a price premium.[4]

Arguably the first full-fledged, globally focused NSMD system was the Forest Stewardship Council (FSC) certification programme (Cashore, Auld and Newsom 2004; Gereffi, Garcia-Johnson and Sasser 2001). Transnational environmental groups and their social allies created the FSC in 1993 following frustration over failed efforts to achieve a binding global forest convention. Its founders developed governing procedures to avoid what they saw as a key problem with state centred processes: business domination. Thus, the FSC

Table 10.1: Examples of NSMD governance certification systems

	Origin	Initiators	Policy problem	Market	Regulatory target	Tracking process?	Eco-label or logo
Fair Labour Association	2003*	Industry, Clinton administration	Sweat shops	Apparel, shoes	Producers	Yes	No (publishes reports on compliance)
Fair Trade Labelling Organization (FLO)	1997**	Array of NGO and consumer groups	Working conditions, rural poverty	Includes coffee, tea, cocoa, sugar, bananas, soccer balls	Primary and value added producers (e.g., sweat shops)	Yes	Label and Logo
Forest Stewardship Council	1993	Environmental groups, socially concerned retailers	Global forest deterioration	Forest products	Industrial forest companies and forest owners	Yes	Label and logo
International Federation of Organic Agriculture Movements (IFOAM)	1997***	Food growers	Food production (soil, water, human health)	Agricultural products	Farmers and processors	Yes	Logo
Marine Aquarium Council (MAC)	1998	Environmental groups, aquarium industry, public aquariums and hobbyist groups	Ecosystem fisheries management and fish handling	Marine aquarium trade	Producers and value added	Yes	Label

(Continued)

Table 10.1: Continued

	Origin	Initiators	Policy problem	Market	Regulatory target	Tracking process?	Eco-label or logo
Marine Stewardship Council	1996	Environmental groups and Unilever	Fisheries depletion	Fish sales	Fishers	Yes	Label and logo
Mining Certification Initiative	2001	World Wide Fund for Nature, Placer Dome	Natural resource destruction	Mining products	Mining companies	Emerging	Emergent
Programme for the Endorsement of Forest Certification (PEFC) (Umbrella for a number of national schemes)	2000	European forest owners association	Sustainable forestry	Forest products	Forest owners	Yes (in some countries)	Logo
Rainforest Alliance responsible coffee	2003	Rainforest Alliance	Environmental impacts of coffee harvesting	Coffee	Coffee harvesters	Yes	Label
Social Accountability International (SAI) (Originally CEPAA)	1997	Council on Economic Priorities Accreditation Agency (an NGO)	Workers rights, community involvement, water and waste	Range	Producers	Yes	Logo

Sustainable Agriculture Network (SAN)	1991	Rainforest Alliance	Social, labour and environmental	Agricultural products including bananas, coffee, cocoa, citrus, flowers and foliage	Farmers	Yes	Label
Sustainable Forestry Initiative (SFI)	1994*	American Forest & Paper Association	Sustaining forests	Forest products	Forest companies	Yes	Logo
Sustainable Tourism Council	2003****	Rainforest Alliance	Maintaining ecosystems structure and function	Tourism	Tourism operators	Emerging	Unifying

* Year converted itself from a self-regulation programme to certification system.

** FLO united 15 separate initiatives, the first of which was the 1988 Fair Trade Initiative based in Holland.

*** Founded in 1972, but gradually evolved to NSMD system. In 1997 established an arms-length body to accredit certifiers.

**** Effort to unify disparate eco-tourism programmes operating globally.

Sources: Primary research as well as Bartley (2003), Courville (2003), and Vallejo and Hauselmann (2004).

excludes governments from formally participating and, to ensure that business interests do not dominate, includes environmental, social and economic decision-making chambers, each with equal voting weight. The emphasis on greater participatory forms of governance is a key feature of these new systems in recognition of the need to build institutional arrangements that would respond to and adapt to what members of affected communities deem legitimate or appropriate. As a global system, the FSC created nine international principles and criteria (later expanded to ten) to guide the development of environmentally and socially appropriate standards in local settings around the world. The FSC accredits and requires auditors to certify companies who manage their operations according to FSC rules.

The FSC experiment strongly influenced the projects of environmental and social activists in other sectors, as well as how business adapted its existing corporate social responsibility initiatives. For example, groups working on consumer campaigns designed to ameliorate the poverty of coffee producers in developing countries and improve working conditions in textile factories created the Fair Trade Labelling Organization (FLO) programme, which institutionalized and formalized governing arrangements in previously fragmented and uncoordinated activities. The result was highly visible labels on companies that adhered to the FLO rules for their sector. FLO now covers a diverse range of international commodity products and specialized goods including coffee, tea, cocoa, sugar, bananas, rice, fresh fruit, juice, honey, vanilla, nuts, clothing, sporting goods, flowers, wine and diamonds. Similarly, Social Accountability International, which originated in governmental processes designed to address sweat shop labour, morphed into an NSMD arena of authority that now monitors individual companies according to specified social criteria, including child labour and worker safety (Bartley 2003; Courville 2003a).

The FSC-inspired approach subsequently spawned the Marine Stewardship Council (MSC) governing natural fisheries management, the Marine Aquarium Council (MAC), governing ecosystem fisheries management, the nascent Mining Certification Initiative (MCI) and the Sustainable Tourism Council, among others (see Table 10.1). In some sectors more than one NSMD option exists. These alternatives can be established by 'friendly' competitors, such as the Rainforest Alliance's coffee programme, which offers interested companies more relaxed standards than those developed through Fair Trade, while others arose from industry sources who, concerned about the prescriptive approach of socially and environmentally inspired systems, created competitors they hoped would gain recognition in the marketplace.

Nowhere is this competition fiercer than in forestry, where industry either transformed existing self-regulation programmes into NSMD systems or created new programmes to directly compete with the FSC. In an example of the former, the American Forest and Paper Association converted its voluntary code of practices programme, Sustainable Forestry Initiative (SFI), into one that developed 'on the ground' standards and a 'third' party auditing process to assess whether companies were in compliance. In the latter case, business initiated NSMD alternatives include the Canadian Standards Association SFM Programme, Indonesia's LEI Programme, the Finnish Forest Certification Programme, Brazil's CERFLOR certification programme, and Malaysia's Tropical Timber Council (MTTC) programme, all of which developed with the assistance of the very governmental agencies the FSC consciously excluded. Whereas the FSC emerged as a system of global governance, many FSC alternatives first emerged at the domestic level. However, their interest in competing as a 'legitimate' NSMD system in the global marketplace resulted in their swift initiation into the global arena, first by adapting their systems to transnational market requirements or, in the case of the Programme for Endorsement of Forest Certification (PEFC), by creating formal global institutions.[5]

As NSMD systems proliferate, countervailing coordinating efforts continue to be developed, both by social and environmental NGOs and business associations. Examples include the Rainforest Alliance's efforts to unify the hundreds of Sustainable Tourism programmes, many with nonexistent or superficial third-party auditing, by creating a single global governing structure. Efforts are also underway to create a 'Sustainable Coffee Partnership' umbrella to manage fair trade, shade grown, and the newly created Rainforest Alliance's sustainable coffee programme.[6] An even larger umbrella organization, ISEAL, has been created to develop agreement on 'best practices' for any NSMD system (Courville 2003b).

Umbrella approaches vary in terms of their requirements for individual programmes. Some, such as PEFC, leave so much discretion to the individual initiatives that it is difficult to ascertain what practices the umbrella organization will prohibit or permit.[7] Partly in response, social and environmental actors have established a new umbrella organization, the Ethical Certification and Labelling Space, to establish performance criteria for social responsibility in eco-labelling systems.[8] Its creation is, arguably, an attempt to create a 'super' system of governance systems to draw a clear distinction from industry alternatives.

Key features of non-state market driven (NSMD) governance

Building on the above review, and drawing on Cashore (2002) and Cashore, Auld and Newsom (2004), we identify six features of NSMD governance that distinguish it from state governance, public–private partnerships, as well as from forms of 'non-governance' such as self-regulation, voluntary codes of conduct and information disclosure approaches. These distinctions are crucial, as they point to the need for our exploration of legitimacy at 'two levels' that determine whether and how NSMD systems might achieve authority to govern. Each feature is discussed below, and the distinctions developed

Table 10.2: Alternative authorities in global governance

Features	Non-state market driven governance	Shared private/public governance	Traditional international governance
Location of authority	Diffuse: producers and consumers along the supply chain (audience/market players); non-state institution as location, interpreter, and implementer, of rules.	Some delegation possible (e.g., de facto granting authority to technical experts, or to shared public/private decision-making bodies for standard setting). Sovereign governments remain ultimate authority (explicit or implicit). Transfer of authority is rare.	Sovereign governments. Some delegation to institutions is possible. Transfer of authority is rare.
Source of authority	Shifting norms enabling markets, 'soft' global law and emerging norms in global social domain, shifting economic incentives, acceptance of programme by supply and demand side audiences.	State sovereignty and consent (deep structure of international system). Monopoly on legitimate use of force. Possibly legalization or constitutionalization.	State sovereignty and consent (deep structure of international system). Monopoly on legitimate use of force. Possibly legalization or constitutionalizaiton.
Role of governments	Interested players, (potential facilitator or debilitator).	Shares policy making authority.	Has policy making authority.

between NSMD and other forms of governance are summarized in Tables 10.2 and 10.3, following that discussion.

Absence of state authority

The most important feature of NSMD governance systems is that they eschew the sovereign authority of states. This crucial point highlights their distinctive identity within global governance and the limits of even the proliferating literature on 'governance without government' to address NSMD systems' legitimacy dynamics. Much of that literature continues to focus on inter *governmental* institutions, such as the United Nations and its affiliates, the World Trade Organization (WTO) and so on, or the broader 'regimes' in the issue areas they help manage. These organizations are never far removed from

Table 10.3: Non-state governance versus self-regulation and state-based non-governance

	NSMD governance	*Self regulation*	*State-based non-governance*
Who participates in rule making	Environmental and social interests/stakeholders participate with business interests	Business-led	NA
Rules – substantive	Non-discretionary	Discretionary-flexible	Complete discretion (Voluntary or Required reporting)
Rules – procedural	To facilitate implementation of substantive rules	End in itself (belief that procedural rules by themselves will result in decreased environmental impact)	To create learning environment
Policy scope	Broad (may include rules on secondary consequences of activities such as labour, indigenous rights, wide-ranging environmental impacts, etc.)	Narrower (management rules and continual improvement in practices)	Narrow (reporting of pollution)

governmental authority: states establish them, their rules generally apply to states, and their formal authority rests on state consent.

For similar reasons, public/private partnerships, which have proliferated as governments in both domestic and foreign policies seek to implement policy objectives in more efficient and effective ways (Börzel and Risse 2005; Salaman 2002), fall outside of the NSMD phenomenon. Here, governments and nongovernmental actors – be they firms, nongovernmental political or activist groups, individuals or groups of experts – jointly participate. Examples of such efforts range from governments contracting out to private companies the delivery of public services to partnerships in development projects. Yet public/private partnerships still rely on states for rule-making authority, serving to reinforce the role of the state, albeit a more fragmented one, rather than create new sources of authority. NSMD systems also fall outside the set of 'private authority' cases examined by Cutler, Haufler, and Porter (1999: 19), who assert that private international authority only exists when 'private sector actors' are 'empowered either explicitly or implicitly by governments and international organizations with the right to make decisions for others'.

When governments do play important roles in NSMD systems, they remain non-authoritative. For example, international development agencies in many countries have provided money and support for burgeoning systems in cases where sympathetic officials saw the potential of NSMD to accomplish goals they had been unable to achieve through regulatory processes in target countries. Similarly, intergovernmental institutions such as the International Tropical Timber Organization and the World Bank have provided intellectual and financial resources in cases where officials have seen compatible mandates with the NSMD model. Governmental agencies have also facilitated dialogue and deliberations over rule development for NSMD systems. Finally, governments may facilitate and support NSMD systems by virtue of their position in the supply chain – either as producers of products (in the case of government owned firms) or as purchasers of NSMD products when they require that suppliers conform to an NSMD governance system. As with any large organization, the choices of governments matter. However, their influence comes from the size and resources of government akin to a large multinational company, not because their sovereign authority forces compliance. These forms of governmental activity work to *support*, rather than *undermine*, NSMD systems as arenas of authority.

Some deviation from the ideal-type is also possible, where NSMD systems take on a more hybrid appearance, with governments playing a more direct role. Governments could, for example, require that their own producers, or imports to their country, conform to rules developed by an NSMD system. In such an instance, some of the actors in the sector would be operating under traditional state control. However, the question for analysis is whether states simply adopt the standard or bring rule-making back into the intergovernmental realm. In the former case, the authority for the rules still rests with the processes and substance of the NSMD system.[9] In the latter case, the legitimacy dynamics begin to look more like those in traditional sovereign state diplomacy and less like the model we present below. In the long run, some might hope states do step back in, using their power and authority to regulate in the social domain, but the very dynamics that precipitated the rise of NSMD systems have militated against states easily doing so. Nevertheless, the second of our 'two levels' of NSMD legitimating dynamics, reveals that NSMD governance systems necessarily interact with state authority – their rules must navigate within a broader global system of institutions and norms which is still largely state-based.

Institutionalized governance mechanisms

The corollary to the absence of sovereign state authority is that NSMD systems create governing systems – i.e., institutions designed to create and implement policy where actors and organizations participate in adaptive policy-making

deliberations. The most advanced systems have created sophisticated institutions for the participation of civil society and organized groups, even
including popular elections among members, and processes through which
policies adapt over time in response to learning, deliberation and conflict
among members of the community. Hence, the NSMD model constitutes *governance* because, if successful, it creates a reflex system of political authority
and steering, in which a community of actors purposely guide themselves in
an ongoing process towards collective goals or values (Rosenau 1995).[10] The
question for analysis, then, which we address below, is how, given the lack
of sovereign authority underpinning these efforts, NSMD systems become
recognized by members of a community so that decisions of the 'authority'
in question create obligations on members to submit to its rules or norms?

NSMD systems' well-developed governing institutions distinguish them
from eco-labelling, self-regulation, as well as voluntary codes of conduct
that do not attempt to institutionalize governing apparatuses. For example,
most eco-labelling programmes, once established, provide largely static
or unchangeable measures of environmental quality. Hence, labelling of
environmentally friendly detergents, while an important part of political
consumerism (Michelleti et al. 2003), does not create an adaptive arena
in which stakeholders and organized interests deliberate to create policy.
Similarly, corporate self-regulation initiatives create their own (usually voluntary or discretionary) rules and procedures to guide corporate behaviour.
While efforts may be undertaken to include the broader community, ultimate
authority over what to do, and how to do it, rests with the firm itself. Hence,
efforts by McDonald's, Home Depot, Ikea, Nike, or Wal-Mart to improve their
own corporate images (efforts that usually follow some kind of NGO targeting activity), fall outside of the NSMD governance phenomenon, and pose
quite different conceptual or theoretical challenges since legitimacy in these
cases must find a basis within the confines of the firm itself.

Likewise, widespread efforts by industry associations to create voluntary
codes of conduct, such as the chemical industry's voluntary Responsible Care
Programme, generally make no effort to build governing mechanisms beyond
the association itself (Gunningham, Grabosky, and Sinclair 1998: 137–266;
Prakash 2000). For example, Responsible Care, initiated following Union Carbide's Bhopal disaster in order to head off threats of governmental intervention, includes no formal role for social or environmental groups. Although
industry association programmes are a step beyond firm-level CSR initiatives, and must be perceived as appropriate by the community who authorize
them, that community is limited to industrial interests. Achieving legitimacy
within an 'internal' community follows a different logic than NSMD systems that require legitimacy within the broader social and environmental
community. Hence, although codes of conduct may be influential, they qualify as statements of principle rather than governance. The same applies to
NGOs that create their own sets of responsible standards that lack input from

other affected actors or communities, such as New York-based International Audubon Society's sustainable golf course programme or Green Globe 21.

For similar reasons activist campaigns that target a particular firm to change its practices are not, by themselves, examples of NSMD governance. To be sure, these activities may help, or hinder efforts to develop NSMD systems (Sasser et al. 2004), but by themselves do not constitute governance.

Market-based authority

Authority granted to NSMD systems emanates from the market. Producers and consumers along a supply chain grant authority as products move from extraction to end-users (in the case of commodities such as forest or agricultural products) or from service providers to consumers (in the case of services such as tourism). A system's governing institutions are 'empowered' ultimately by acceptance by these players, wherever they happen to reside in the global supply chain. The market logic requires that customers will demand products or services that adhere to the standards in the marketplace. Recognition of this feature further distinguishes NSMD governance from most prevailing forms of voluntary standards and self-regulation, where market benefits are only indirect and relatively abstract, i.e., where companies estimate that corporate social responsibility affords 'goodwill' with civil society that will improve their image and business. With NSMD systems, the particular product or service is necessarily 'tracked' along the supply chain so that further end users can purchase the certified product.

Policy arena is the social domain

The ultimate purpose of NSMD governance systems, or *raison d' être*, is to regulate the global social domain. This means that any analysis of how NSMD governance gains legitimacy must pay attention to whether and how they attempt to ameliorate global problems that, in their absence, firms would have no incentive to address. This feature distinguishes NSMD governance systems from new arenas of private authority or knowledge networks in which economic incentives for profit-maximizing firms inherently exist. For example, arenas of private authority designed to address business coordination problems, such as the standardization of electrical appliances (the reason the International Organization for Standardization (ISO) was originally created), accounting standards (International Accountings Standards Board and the International Federation of Accountants), or compatibility of new technologies (e.g., the International Technology Roadmap for Semiconductors), pose no puzzles as to why firms would comply (Porter 2004).

In contrast, NSMD systems impose social and environmental regulatory *burdens* on the companies who join them. This point cannot be overemphasized. What makes NSMD governance systems unique, and worthy of careful conceptual and empirical attention, is that their primary aim is to embed markets in broader societal needs. In this sense they are not only market driven, but also aim to reconfigure markets.

Stakeholders and broader civil society part of authority granting process

Recognition that NSMD systems use markets to steer business towards social purposes necessarily requires that attention be paid to the range of actors that make up the 'political community' of NSMD systems and the nature of their membership. Unlike the problem of legitimacy of nation-states, where community membership and obligation (of citizens) is essentially automatic, organizations or individuals who participate in NSMD governance decide *whether* to *join* and *withdraw*. As James Rosenau has noted, 'the essence of [new sites of authority] is that they derive their legitimacy from the voluntary and conditional participation of individuals who can revoke their consent at any time' (Rosenau 2003: 308). Citizens within nation-states, operating in systems in which power, authority and political community are largely fused, rarely evaluate whether to 'withdraw' and largely take as 'given' state authority (even if they evaluate particular laws or policies as inappropriate). The reverse is true with NSMD systems. If the organizations and actors who created them deem them as illegitimate, this is a death blow – as consent will be removed.

Hence, understanding how stakeholders grant legitimacy is crucial, and, as we show below, cannot, in most cases, be reduced solely to pragmatic calculations of economic benefits. While businesses must evaluate these systems as having some kind of economic benefit, the social and environmental interests that created these systems must maintain their support and perceive them as legitimate arenas of authority with which to address globally important problems.

Just who constitute the 'internal members' or stakeholders will vary according to the scheme. In the case of forestry, membership will include forest landowners and forest management companies, producers of forest products and purchasers of those products further down the supply chain, as well as retailers and consumers (Cashore, Auld and Newsom 2004; Sasser 2003). In the case of tourism, relevant audiences include tour operators, travel service providers, hotel and resort owners, as well as the workforce in the local communities that are the destinations of travellers, and travellers themselves. In the case of fair trade coffee, relevant audiences include coffee brokers, communities who subscribe to fair trade, coffee retailers and individual coffee consumers. In mining, it is the mining companies, the communities directly affected by their operations, and manufacturers who purchase mined resources and retailers who sell consumer mined products such as diamonds in high-priced specialty shops. Hence, audiences differ depending on the scheme, although wider audiences of potential consumers and global civil society overlap in many networks.

Enforcement mechanisms and mandatory requirements

A final characteristic of NSMD governance is the existence of mechanisms to verify compliance, including consequences for non-compliance. The most common mechanism is a third party audit in which auditors 'certify' the firm or producers as being in compliance with the rules, or identify improvements required for a successful audit. This distinction highlights a reliance on outside verification of rule compliance rather than self-reporting, and similarly addresses widespread concerns about 'empty promises' sometimes associated with industry self-regulation or even the inability or unwillingness of governments to effectively implement and monitor public policy.

This feature separates NSMD governance from a range of what otherwise seem to be similar approaches. For instance, the industrial association dominated Ethical Trading Initiative does not rely on independent third party certification that its members are following practices (Vallejo and Hauselman 2004). Likewise, Responsible Care does not require that members participate in the programme or undergo third party auditing (for these reasons existing accounts reveal significant gaps in the implementation of the US Chemical industry's own association's guidelines). However, as with the other five features of NSMD governance, organizations can evolve. For instance, for years the Fair Labour Association (FLA), spawned by the US Apparel Industry Partnership (with support from the Clinton Administration), lacked well developed mandatory standards to which companies were independently verified (Bartley 2003). However, in response to competition with Fair Trade, FLA introduced mandatory third party auditing towards specified standards (Göbel 2004: 51–2).

The enforcement feature distinguishes the NSMD phenomenon from corporate codes of conduct and information-based initiatives that have emanated from governmental, intergovernmental, and non-governmental sources. Because these efforts do not use state sovereign authority, but instead frequently rely on the state's ability to create networks in which civil society and corporate actors can interact, they look strikingly similar to NSMD governance with the crucial exception that no requirement exists to ensure successful 'on the ground' implementation of goals or principles.

A good example is the Global Compact, a UN sponsored set of ten principles in the area of human rights, environment, labour and anti-corruption. Although it fits with the NSMD focus on the social domain, and provides for an institutionalized system of policy making, it does not require that those who accept the principles be subject to independent verification or follow specified on-the-ground rules. Instead, firms sign up to implement very broad principles, which are based on existing multilateral declarations. Adherence to the principles is voluntary and the initiative is not designed to formally regulate participants' activities (Ruggie 2002, 2003, 2004). (However, there are signs that it is moving in the direction of an NSMD system, though gradually. It currently attempts to engage the wider community of stakeholders through the marketplace, and encourages self-monitoring and civil society groups to play a watchdog role. Its 'learning forum' also encourages identification and diffusion of best practices.)

Similarly, prominent intergovernmental initiatives to create voluntary codes of conduct fail to require adherence to rules. For example, The OECD's Guidelines for Multinational Enterprises (revised in 2000) is a non-binding agreement among states, not firms. While it encourages a wide range of good practices and establishes National Contact Points to promote them (Wilkie 2004), the standards are voluntary even for those firms that sign on, and there is no ongoing decision-making process apart from whatever national governments ultimately decide.[11]

The most prominent information mechanism, the Global Reporting Initiative, fits the same pattern. Highly touted as a mechanism to operationalize transparency and accountability for initiatives such as the OECD guidelines and Global Compact, it simply provides guidelines for organizations to report their pollution levels and other sustainability measures (Global Reporting Initiative 2005).

Lack of enforcement of mandatory standards and the absence of formal market mechanisms also excludes ISO's environmental management systems. These systems are commonly and improperly confused with NSMD systems because they have expanded to focus on issues in the social domain and companies who subscribe to ISO are audited for compliance to their procedures (Kollman and Prakash 2002). However, ISO standards are negotiated by a combination of industry and state delegates, with limited openness to participation from non-industry representatives. Moreover, ISO emphasizes the existence of 'management systems' and does not require *any* on the ground changes. Indeed, it is notable that when ISO expanded its focus to the social domain from strictly business coordination problems, which did create specific and mandatory 'on the ground approaches' associated with such things as developing manufacturing requirements for electrical appliances, it shifted its requirements to focus on procedures rather than on the ground behavioural changes (Clapp 1998, Cochoy 2003).

The two-level legitimacy logic of NSMD governance

If an institution is based around markets and their supply chains rather than territories, and if non-governmental groups successfully create transnational pressures that operate independently of states, then under what conditions can such governance systems gain sufficient legitimacy to be accepted as the proper guide to behaviour in the global marketplace and social domain? Here, we understand legitimacy as intimately tied to authority. In other words, our concern is very close to the traditional Weberian understanding of political legitimacy, with one important difference: we apply the concept outside the context of the nation-state, which was the political community that concerned Weber. Thus, legitimacy 'reflects a more general support for a regime [or governance institution], which makes subjects willing to substitute the regime's decisions for their own evaluation of a situation' (Bodansky 1999: 602).

We argue that answering the above question requires identifying legitimacy dynamics at two non-territorial levels: an 'internal' market-level that creates the logic through which NSMD systems gain direct authority to create policy; and an 'external' level comprising the broad set of institutions and norms that enable and constrain an NSMD's form and rules.

Legitimacy must be *actively* achieved at the first level, where support is highly dynamic and various agents work to achieve or fend off efforts to gain support in the marketplace. For the most part, the second level *structures* dynamics at the first level, by creating the conditions, constraints, and opportunities within which *agents* at the first level operate. Recognition of this second level may enhance agent-based efforts at the market level by opening them up to generalized norms in international law and politics, or to norms of participation and stakeholder involvement. The key feature of this second level is the 'social fitness', i.e. how close NSMD institutions are to already accepted norms and institutions permeating environmental, social and economic governance. Though less common, choices made in the formulation and operation of an NSMD system can also be a driver of change in the second level, when norms are contested. In these cases NSMD systems, to the extent that they 'fit' with one competing norm over another, may help 'tip the scales' in favour of one of those sets of norms, in effect transforming level two.

This idea of fitness draws on insights from sociological institutionalism and constructivist IR scholarship inspired by it. Both view legitimacy as embedded in social systems that provide a basis of appropriateness, or that make the purposes, goals or rationale of an institution understandable to the relevant audience in society (Bernstein 2001; Florini 1996; Suchman 1995; Weber 1994). In other words, that broader environment of institutional, cultural, societal and legal norms provides a rationale and justification for what an institution that operates within it is and does. Since there is some element of choice in designing NSMD systems, any thorough analysis must assess the tension between their *transformative* aspects and the requirement that they comply, or 'fit', with key structural features found at both levels.

Defining legitimacy

Drawing on the above discussion, we define legitimacy as present when a community recognizes a shared rule or institution as justified and appropriate. We purposely employ a broad definition rather than adding specific content to what legitimacy requires by definitional fiat. In some literature, legitimacy means that actors no longer question the practice, as it becomes such a routinized feature of daily life that no conscious 'evaluation' occurs (Suchman 1995). Other work emphasizes the evaluations that can occur when an entity is deemed to be consistent with existing norms about appropriate behaviour, form or function. Still others understand legitimacy as a normative concept, based on what is 'morally' appropriate or link legitimacy directly to issues of 'justice' and legitimate procedures (or what Franck (1990) calls generically 'right process'), although even this literature assumes that adherence to these normative criteria generates acceptance of the institution as authoritative. All of these understandings of legitimacy potentially matter and require attention. Our approach is to treat the problem as a matter of investigation, not definition. Thus we focus conceptual attention on how the two 'levels' determine and shape the process and content of legitimacy granting. This approach highlights that *criteria of legitimacy are contingent on historical understandings at play and the shared norms of the particular community or communities granting authority.*

The following two subsections identify the legitimacy dynamics at each level, as well as their interaction. Hypotheses generated from that analysis are listed following each discussion.

Level I: internal market-network level

The bulk of existing work on NSMD governance and legitimacy reveals an expected result – that for market-driven systems to work, profit-maximizing firms must evaluate them as providing an economic benefit. That is, firms are unlikely to sign on to voluntary initiatives that do not deliver price premiums, efficiency gains, niche markets or other economic benefits. Moreover, this empirical research suggests that firms are motivated in the short-term by either loss avoidance (i.e., threats of boycotts or decreased demand for non-certified products) or expected gains. However, existing literature misses what we argue is a more complex process at this level both in terms of a firm's initial evaluation of whether to join an NSMD scheme, and, once joined, whether to maintain membership.

Firm-level decisions to join: There are two reasons why pure cost–benefit analyses neither predict, nor completely explain, what choices firms might make. First, literature on firm-level greening reveals that in cases of high uncertainty, firms 'fall back' on preconceived notions of the world informed by entrenched norms – so much so that firms operating in the same region facing the same environmental pressures have been found to take very different decisions in regard to societal pressures over their environmental behaviour (Greening and Gray 1994; Prakash 2001). Second, different types of firms, across and within sectors, will make decisions based on different time horizons. For instance, Nike's copyright on its 'swoosh' means that it does not operate in a purely competitive market. It creates for itself an easy target for environmental activism (Klein 1999), but also corresponding leeway in how it responds to such pressures (Peretti 2003). Similarly, some businesses, especially those that are not publicly traded and have little debt, can 'afford', at least in the short turn, to be proactive in ways their competitors cannot, if they are similarly disposed to supporting NSMD-style solutions.

Firm-level decisions once joined: Decisions to sign on and become part of an NSMD system's political community, usually initially for pragmatic reasons, must be distinguished from decisions once they are a member. That is, NSMD governance systems create detailed rules to which its members are bound, but if participants do not perceive the systems as legitimate, they will either immediately withdraw their support, or, in the case of firms who reluctantly join because of coercive market pressure, will pursue *exit* strategies. However, the context of decision-making changes when institutions are viewed as legitimate. NSMD systems in which businesses are constantly pursuing exit strategies will be unsustainable because without legitimacy, they will be unable to perform their most important function: enabling adaptive learning processes that create substantive rules to which all members of the community must adhere. Put another way, once firms decide to join NSMD, their frames of reference for maintaining membership change as legitimacy-granting interacts with pragmatic evaluations.

Interactions of firms and social actors: The support from social and environmental groups that NSMD systems must maintain does not stem from business interests, but from the governance system's purpose in ameliorating a specific and substantive global problem. Findings on NSMD systems' active efforts to change market dynamics, reviewed above, show that while pragmatic considerations often drive firms, they make these decisions within a complex web of interaction with social and environmental groups, as well as with purchasers further down the supply chain who themselves are being converted to pro-NSMD purchasing policies. As a result, interaction and learning among members of a market network's political community are central for achieving legitimacy. Hence, to the degree that NSMD governance systems facilitate learning and overlapping goals of members, such as certainty in the global marketplace (Garcia-Johnson 2001) and protection of firms' reputations (Haufler 2001; Klein 1999), legitimacy is enhanced. It follows that *community building* is an important criteria in attempts to increase the authority of governance systems that link civil society and market actors in governing networks.

In turn, the ideas and norms promoted and held by civil society organizations are deeply shaped by the second or 'external' level, which includes not only substantive norms regarding values such as environmental integrity, but also procedural norms that in the contemporary period increasingly promote participation, access, deliberation and accountability to affected groups (i.e., democratic norms). Thus, procedures and structures that ensure stakeholder access and deliberation, and accountability to those affected by decisions, enhance legitimacy. The rationale for this argument is that lack of participation or accountability in rule-making, or lack of resources to enable participation, prevent a sense of 'ownership' among participants in the scheme, which can in turn influence perceptions of justice and fairness (de Azevedo 2004: 88–9; Raines 2003; Woods 1999). For example, Raines' (2003) study of perceptions of legitimacy of the ISO 14000 standards found a strong direct correlation among developing country delegates between involvement in the creation of the standards and their legitimacy. Such processes link decision-making and outcomes of a governance scheme to the communities that authorize it, and over which it is granted authority.

The above argument emerges specifically from attention to how legitimacy links to political community and power to generate political authority. Legitimacy can be nurtured in part by a common experience of the world inhabited by internal network actors and organizations (i.e., the world of the global marketplace), enhanced technologies and modalities of communication within their networks, and some degree of shared knowledge and normative frameworks.[12] In other words, to the degree these criteria are met, those communities meet minimal conditions enabling of political community. These conditions are more easily met in self-regulatory systems, with smaller, more homogenous memberships. This problem of political community poses a greater challenge for NSMD governance, which by design engages a wider array of stakeholders and audiences. Owing to differences in relevant audiences in terms of identities (producers, consumers, environmentalists), geographic location, or interests, consensus may be lacking on what constitutes either procedural or substantive legitimacy. For example, private market authorities and networks tend to share a focus on pragmatic and performance-oriented criteria of legitimacy according to standards developed by network members, driven by goals of efficiency and economic gain, but actors within an NSMD network may disagree on whether those or other performance criteria produce legitimacy or their relative importance compared to (or in conjunction with) deliberation or other procedural aspects of legitimacy.

Such dynamics and dilemmas are evident in the forest sector, where shared knowledge across different economic value holders was a key part of the FSC vision. However, such shared knowledge, largely owing to competition among systems and different visions, has not yet materialized. As a result, other arenas designed to promote learning and understanding, but which explicitly avoid efforts to devise policy standards, such as the Forest Dialogue, are attempting to fill this void in an effort to promote the NSMD idea across different value holders and competing governance systems.

The problem of community is particularly acute for firms and interest groups in developing countries, who may worry about 'eco-imperialism' and being disadvantaged by standards that make it relatively harder for their firms to compete in the global marketplace. In such cases, vulnerable firms may feel they have little choice but to participate, yet the social and economic consequences of doing so could undermine the scheme in the longer run, and in the shorter term make implementation less likely (Raines 2003). Without legitimacy, governance is unlikely to generate the market power required to back up implementation and compliance.

Some governance systems are also having difficulty designing structures that accomplish stakeholder involvement, but avoid capture by particular powerful interests. In other words, they generate power without legitimacy and thus undermine the authority of the institution. For example, the Marine Stewardship Council, following complaints of a 'democratic deficit' from its backers and NGOs at its inception in 1997, undertook a governance review with terms of reference that read in part, 'as the organization [MSC] progressively implemented the governance structure it became evident that it was cumbersome, expensive to operate, and leaves the MSC open to potential capture by particular interest groups or sectors' (Marine Stewardship Council 2001). The resultant overhaul focused on better ensuring openness, transparency and accountability to all stakeholders, but left ultimate decision-making to a board of trustees, which reflected a broad range of interests and technical expertise, rather than its stakeholder council, in order to avoid such a capture.

Likewise, for many NGOs, certification is not taken for granted as a panacea, but is seen as a dynamic, intense struggle to steer it towards its original aim. Sasser (2002), for example, found that most NGOs will not be ready to grant full legitimacy to non-state governance until the on the ground effects are shown to improve environmental or social integrity.

Below, we summarize the hypotheses generated by the above analysis of internal network dynamics (level one). We include hypotheses on firm and social actor choice, which concern both necessary (though not necessarily sufficient) conditions for the initial granting of legitimacy as well as the causal impact of legitimacy on firm and social actor behaviour. A third set of hypotheses addresses conditions under which an NSMD system gains authority to govern (is perceived as appropriate and justified) in the market sector in question.

Hypotheses for Legitimacy at Level One
I. Firm Choice to Support
  a. Decisions to join
      i. *Firms must evaluate that their participation will yield greater benefits than costs.*
        1. *The greater the behavioural changes required by an NSMD system, the less likely firms will support.*
        2. *The greater the market benefits, the more likely firms will support an NSMD system.*
  b. Firm behaviour once it joins
      i. *Without granting legitimacy, firms will be engaged in constant*

> *re-evaluation of support, making long-term support untenable, as firms constantly leave and join and/or pursue exit strategies.*
>
> ii. *When firms see NSMD as an appropriate arena of authority, 'day-to-day' evaluations will cease. Evaluations will focus on conflicts within the system rather than challenging the system as a whole.*

II. Social Actors' Choice to Support

   a. *Social and environmental actors grant support based on normative concerns about global social and environmental deterioration.*

   b. *Social actors will deem as illegitimate those systems that are perceived to entrench the breakdown of embedded liberalism.*

III. Conditions Under Which NSMD Systems will be Perceived as a Legitimate Governing Authority

   a. Interaction of social behaviour and firm behaviour

   > i. *Firms and social actors must **both** perceive NSMD systems to be legitimate forms of authority* (a conundrum since each may exert an opposite pressure on costs).
   >
   > ii. *The greater the range of members of the market-level political community, the more difficult it will be for NSMD systems to gain support.*
   >
   > iii. However, *if legitimacy is achieved, the greater the range of members, the greater the impact in addressing the environmental or social problem to which NSMD systems were created and the greater its legitimacy relative to systems with narrower ranges of members* (such as self-regulatory systems).

   b. Procedures of NSMD systems

   > i. *To the degree non-state governance systems facilitate learning and overlapping goals,* such as certainty in the global marketplace and protection of firms' reputations, *legitimacy is enhanced.*
   >
   > ii. *Procedures and structures that ensure stakeholder access and deliberation, and accountability to those affected by decisions, enhance legitimacy and effective outcomes.*
   >
   > iii. *To the degree non-state governance systems create appropriate adaptive mechanisms and policies in governing complex phenomena, legitimacy is increased.*

Level II: external level of norms and institutions

The 'external' or global level serves a dual function: it constitutes what qualifies as legitimate governance, thus provides enabling conditions and justifications for particular forms of governance, and it constrains or delimits the range of rules considered acceptable. This level is comprised of two components: formalized 'hard law' and an intersubjective set of norms and practices that permeate global governance.[13] The latter may include 'soft law'[14] as well as uncodified norms nonetheless understood to reflect shared beliefs about appropriate behaviour (Bernstein and Cashore 2004).

Our overarching hypothesis at this level is that legitimacy requires that the basic institutional elements of an NSMD system – its norms and rules – fit with existing sets of *institutionalized norms* already accepted as legitimate in the relevant issue areas. This argument stems from the recognition that rules and institutions compete for social fitness, which turns attention to the conditions for success in that competition. Thus, if a scheme is operating in the global marketplace, its rules and norms must fit with various sets of institutionalized global marketplace norms as well as political norms (such as not violating sovereignty), and emerging democratic, social, and environmental norms in the global social domain.

Given that the internal market-network level is fluid and sector specific, identifying the relevant aspects of the intersecting second level requires careful empirical analysis, since it corresponds with the non-territorial market structure or boundaries of the particular product or service in question. Thus, its norms may emanate from, or be institutionalized within, traditional national states, a regional trade bloc, or wider global society. While above all else this level directly taps into norms and institutions in an emerging global social domain, the public authority of sovereign states and international institutions also remain important components of this level for several reasons. First, sovereign states generate 'hard' international law that in itself is a source of legitimacy and illegitimacy, something reinforced by well institutionalized sovereignty norms at this level.[15] Second, states, with relatively few exceptions, continue to dominate regulation and patterns of economic development within their borders. Third, states remain major players in the facilitation and management of rules of global capitalism, individually and through international organizations.

We distinguish 'hard' law from 'softer' norms not because one is more binding – 'hard' law is mainly binding on states, which are not the primary targets of NSMD governance – but because they do not always develop in unison. For instance, the proliferation of norms emerging in the social domain (e.g., environment, human rights and labour) are often ahead of intergovernmental agreement. In such cases NSMD systems can benefit by tapping into these emerging norms more efficiently and swiftly than can governments. This ability facilitates the emergence of NSMD because these norms affect evaluations of actors at the first level. At the same time, if NSMD systems are insensitive to existing norms, it works against them. For example, in the forestry case, cross-national survey findings and interviews of non-industrial landowners in the United States, Germany, the UK, Canada and Sweden, found that their strong notions of private property rights and fierce feelings of independence militated against the legitimacy of

FSC *and* industry-created programmes because landowners deem any outside rules as largely inappropriate, although this resistance could be mitigated by attention to procedural legitimacy reinforced by norms at this level.

Procedural Legitimacy Norms and Democratization of Global Governance: There exists a general normative trend to democratize global governance. Examples range from demands for democratic reform and greater public accountability (whether to states and/or broader affected publics) of international institutions (Held and Koenig-Archibugi 2005; Payne and Samhut 2004) to the emergence of 'stakeholder democracy', which moves beyond mere participation to 'collaboration' and truer 'deliberation' among states, business and civil society (Bäckstrand and Saward 2004; Vallejo and Hauselman 2004). The latter idea most notably was a central theme of the 2002 World Summit on Sustainable Development (WSSD) and resonates especially with the NSMD governance form. Environmental institutions, norms, treaties and declaratory law have been particularly supportive of ongoing improvements in public participation and transparency. For example, Rio Declaration Principle 10 asserts that 'environmental issues are best handled with the participation of all concerned citizens, at the relevant level' and promotes access to information, participation in decision-making and access to judicial and administrative proceedings at the national level. These provisions are formally institutionalized most notably in the 1998 Aarhus Convention on Access to Information, Public Participation in Decision-making and Access to Justice in Environmental Matters, which came into force in 2001. Negotiated under the auspices of the UN Economic Commission for Europe, it includes provisions for transparency and participation at the international as well as national levels.

Our earlier discussion showed how these level-two norms have informed actor expectations at level one. Returning to the example of forest landowners, the same study that found resistance to certification, even by forest landowner association certification programmes, also found that suspicion of these programmes mitigated when landowners were specifically involved in the creation of rules and they deemed their participation as purely voluntary. The feelings of disenfranchisement by these forest owners illustrate that, since these governance systems involve firms and not countries, the question is not whether individual firm's needs are taken into account, as much as whether firms of different sizes (e.g., small and medium sized as well as large firms), or that face different social and ecological challenges, are represented. This poses a challenge for institutions with limited resources to assist firms that may feel disenfranchised or to ensure that all relevant stakeholders are represented.

Substantive Norms: The relevant normative environment for most cases of NSMD governance includes not only specific declarations or principles that might apply to the sector, product or process in question (for example, the Statement of Forest Principles or Convention on Biodiversity in the case of forestry), but also broadly accepted norms of global environmental, labour and human rights governance. These may be embodied in international treaties and declarations, as well as action programmes, statements of leaders, or, more broadly speaking, even emerging 'world society' (Meyer et al. 1997).

In the forestry area, for example, certification provided a way around the stalemate in international negotiations over a forest convention. It constituted a solution that bypassed thorny debates over sovereignty (because it targets firms, not states), but at the same time fit with wider environmental norms that had shifted to be more sympathetic to market mechanisms and international liberalism more broadly (Bernstein 2001). While the debate over the effectiveness of economic instruments versus bans or other compliance and control mechanisms in environmental policy continues (Esty and Chertow 1997; Gunningham and Sinclair 2002; Porter and van der Linde 1995), a strong policy consensus continues to favour market mechanisms and complementarities between environmental protection, economic growth and liberalized markets. Recent events reinforce this position, such as the 2002 WSSD, where public–private partnerships (type II outcomes) emerged as a dominant mechanism to implement sustainable development in the shadow of disappointing progress in most areas of inter-state cooperation. Initiatives such as the UN Global Compact serve to reinforce the normative understanding – be it empirically accurate or not – that working with the marketplace is the most appropriate way to address global environmental and social problems. These developments have created a supportive normative environment for NSMD governance.

Hence, when there is overlap between evolving norms and the values and understandings of relevant audiences at the internal market network level, legitimacy is further enhanced. Conversely, when norms are contested at the global level, such as those that emphasize biodiversity conservation or banning child labour, vis-à-vis those that emphasize liberalized trade and economic development opportunities, those promoting NSMD systems may actually be able to 'choose' one norm over the other, or reframe the issue in a way favourable to their preferred outcome. Thus, they potentially can influence the second level by 'tipping the scales' in favour of the NSMD norm.

Norm of Popular Sovereignty: The norm of popular sovereignty is also an important component of this level, i.e., the idea that citizens inside a territory are the only appropriate sources of authority to govern. Hence, a perception that a governing system is 'providing influence from outside' may evoke that norm, provoking resistance. Firms and wider publics may resent 'foreign' interference with domestic practices. Likewise a nationalist chill may militate against domestic firms supporting transnational governance systems that target domestic production. These concerns can be reinforced by producer and consumer communities that are still largely nationally based, generating corporate and consumer cultures (Pauly and Reich 1997). This can result, for example, in organized national resistance to a particular non-state governance scheme, or preferences for home-grown governance that reflects those cultures.

Many governance systems implicitly recognize the mediating role of national boundaries by granting national or regional bodies the right to develop domestically appropriate rules through consultation processes. This may create domestic within-network legitimacy dynamics. The two-level logic we have outlined should still apply in such cases, but sovereignty may affect the location of the relevant network, possibly limiting it to a particular state rather than operating globally.

However, we hypothesize that globalization can mitigate the normative impact of popular sovereignty: the higher the market pressure and greater the globalization of production the more likely that the power of advocacy and consumer pressures in the global market will overwhelm domestic corporate culture and popular sovereignty. This barrier to legitimacy for global NSMD systems may also be mitigated to the degree that the 'interference' is in line with wider norms that resonate with the political culture and identity of the national or local societies in question (Keck and Sikkink 1998).

Preliminary evidence in the forest sector supports this overall mitigating effect of globalization. For example, one comparative study found that commitments from retailers and purchasers of forest products were easier to obtain, and had more direct market impact, when those retailers and purchasers were *outside* of the domestic unit. German publishers paid much less attention to requiring that their domestic supply be FSC certified than their foreign supplies. They thereby avoided becoming embroiled in domestic debates about the supremacy of German forestry, and accusations of pandering to foreign demands. As a result, German publishers more greatly influenced legitimation struggles in British Columbia, Canada, an important foreign supplier, than at home (Cashore, Auld and Newsom 2004).

Hard Law and Formal Institutions: Even with a normative context broadly conducive to the acceptance of NSMD governance systems, they must be designed to avoid running foul of relevant international 'hard' law. Operating in the marketplace, international economic rules, especially the increasingly legalized rules under the WTO and regional trade agreements, provide an important potential constraint. At the same time, the broader neoliberal normative environment in which contemporary trade regimes sit provide enabling conditions for market-friendly systems such as NSMD governance, while specific liberalizing rules, which target state regulation, leave relatively more leeway for non-state governance. These two features of international trade law have worked in favour of the proliferation of non-state systems, and even their active financial support by some governments who view private systems as a way to pursue policy objectives without risking trade disputes (Bartley 2003: 447–51).

The multilateral institution most relevant to NSMD governance systems is the WTO, particularly the Agreement on Technical Barriers to Trade (TBT).

It covers labelling governance systems, including eco-labelling, and is binding on WTO members. Consistent with the norms that underpin the trade regime, the TBT aims primarily to ensure that technical regulations and standards do not 'create unnecessary obstacles to international trade' (preamble and Article 2.2). It permits national programmes and standards, including for environmental purposes, as long as they do not discriminate on the basis of national origin, are necessary for the stated objective, and are the least trade restrictive to achieve that objective (Article 2). In addition, the TBT states that recognized international standards (such as an ISO standard), or relevant parts of them 'shall' be used 'as a basis for their technical regulations' except when they would be inappropriate or ineffective for the 'legitimate' objectives covered by the TBT.[16]

The implications of these provisions for non-state market driven governance are uncertain for two main reasons.[17] First, whereas the TBT covers nongovernmental governance systems (Article 3), whether such a scheme would be recognized as an international standard is uncertain since the TBT only specifically refers to national standards. Nor is it clear what a transnational scheme's status would be if not recognized by states. Second, while the TBT recognizes labels that include production and processing methods (PPMs), it is silent on non-product related PPMs (i.e., life-cycle analysis that takes into account values or effects not directly related to production of products for export or import), which are often part of eco-labelling systems. Thus, any disputes would probably be decided based on GATT (1994) criteria, such as whether a label treated 'like' products dissimilarly, or whether a standard was a legitimate exception based on health and safety or environmental criteria. There have been a number of WTO cases touching on these issues, but none addressing non-governmental standards.

These issues and related concerns remain ongoing subjects of controversy within the WTO Committee on Trade and Environment (CTE) and TBT committee. Committee discussions suggest openness to eco-labelling in principle because it does not deny market access, but many developing countries continue to express concern that they could restrict sales. They also argue that such systems potentially violate sovereignty (especially in the case of non-product related PPMs) since they involve guidelines on practices within an exporting state, not just the nature of a product. Moreover, different countries may argue that they have different optimal levels of pollution and should not be subject to the same standard. This North–South divide shows little sign of easing (WTO 2000).

Where does all this leave non-state market driven governance systems? As private transnational voluntary governance systems operating in the marketplace, they are largely immune from WTO discipline, unless adopted by a government. Indeed, they ironically may have more success if governments or intergovernmental organizations do not adopt them as policy. For example, the International Labour Organization (ILO) considered, but rejected a Fair

Trade label owing to concerns it would be treated as a non-tariff trade barrier and contravene WTO rules (Bartley 2003: 15) and the World Bank is under fire for testing an assessment tool for certification because some parties view it as favouring one scheme (FSC) over another (e.g., PEFC). Still, most existing systems, by design, would not likely run foul of the TBT even when they include non-product related PPMs, since their criteria are generally consistent with equivalency of environmental measures in importing countries (i.e., different environmental goals apply to different countries), mutual recognition (i.e., if it qualifies in the exporting country, it should qualify in the importing country), as well as general WTO goals such as transparency (Hock 2001: 363–5). The success of NSMD systems has put more pressure on their proponents to directly engage with institutions such as the WTO, as well as continue their work in other forums to have their standards recognized as legitimate.

Hypotheses for Legitimacy at Level Two

I. Norms

    a. *If a scheme is operating in the global marketplace, its norms must fit with various sets of institutionalized global marketplace norms as well as political norms (such as not violating sovereignty).*

        i. *Overlap between these evolving norms and the values and understandings of relevant audiences at the network level increases legitimacy, disjunctures reduce legitimacy.*

    b. *Where norms are contested at the second level, NSMD systems can 'choose' which to support, which contributes to the institutionalization of the chosen norm at both levels.*

II. Formal Institutions

    NSMD systems must be designed to avoid running foul of relevant international 'hard' law.

III. Interaction Between Levels One and Two:

    a. *Norms at level two define appropriate instruments and modalities within networks (level one).*

    b. If subject to advocacy efforts to champion NSMD in a particular country, *the greater the targeted sector's market is globalized, the less likely that mitigating factors associated with the norm of popular sovereignty would disrupt legitimacy dynamics.*

        i. *The greater the transnational economic pressure applied, the less popular sovereignty norms constrain NSMD systems from gaining legitimacy.*

        ii. *The more an NSMD system is perceived by relevant audiences as addressing global problems and adhering to global norms where governments have failed to do so, the less popular sovereignty norms will constrain NSMD systems from gaining legitimacy.*

Conclusion

Whether non-state governance systems can successfully address major global environmental and social problems is one of the most important questions facing students of private authority. To address this question, we first distinguished the NSMD 'ideal type' from hybrid, public/private or self-regulation systems that are often symptoms of, rather than solutions to, the breakdown of embedded liberalism. This discussion highlighted that NSMD governance systems are far more ambitious than other systems focused on niche markets, which arguably do more to assuage the conscience of those purchasing eco-friendly products than to systematically address wider global problems. This ambition also carries the risk that if NSMD systems move beyond niche markets but fail to gain sectoral-wide acceptance, they could, perversely, segment responsible behaviour while maintaining a healthy market for firms practicing unbridled development.

Thus, the ability of NSMD systems to gain widespread support and become globally effective is not preordained. Indeed, the inductively developed hypotheses on legitimacy – the second step in our analysis – suggest considerable challenges at both 'levels' identified; especially considering the ultimate goal of NSMD governance is no less than transforming authority relationships in the global marketplace. Still, developing these hypotheses is a significant and necessary step forward from existing scholarship in identifying under what conditions such governance systems will be accepted as justified and appropriate guides to behaviour in the global marketplace and social domain.

Although our hypotheses will require testing to gain confidence in their accuracy, one major implication is worth highlighting: effective institutional design is essential. Systems must be designed to create a learning environment in which stakeholders can 'build community' that taps into shared understandings of legitimacy among participants.[18] These understandings in turn often stem from broader legitimating norms at the global level (our level two). We noted that community-building poses a much greater challenge for non-state governance systems than either self-regulation or technical knowledge networks. And whereas states face similar problems of building legitimacy across an array of interests and identities, their public policy processes institutionalize community building and learning through mechanisms such as elections, legislative committee hearings, public consultations and expert involvement. To the extent that NSMD systems develop comparable mechanisms, they too are more likely to gain legitimacy across an array of policy community members. Manipulation of markets will not succeed on its own in getting firms, consumers or other relevant audiences to accept these governance systems in the absence of attention to these underlying legitimacy dynamics.

There will also be critics who believe that any attempt to work directly with firms in governance will inevitably lead to watered down standards and compromised principles and that failed governmental efforts must be reinvigorated. For these reasons, NSMD systems ultimately must be assessed on whether they end up being another symptom of global liberalism's downward pressure on regulation, or whether they can build governing arrangements that fill the gap left by the breakdown of embedded liberalism. Filling this gap is also in the interest of the corporate sector if pressures continue to mount for global social regulation. Firms have a vested interest in the arguably more efficient, responsive and inclusionary NSMD model when the most likely legitimate alternative is a blunter governmental response, with potentially greater perverse impacts on economic activity.

Whether organizers and supporters of NSMD systems will make choices that result in broad-based support from civil society and consumers, and ultimately facilitate the development of standards that address real world problems, remains to be seen. We have attempted here to identify processes and conditions that strategic actors need to be aware of when making such decisions. In so doing, we drew attention to broader market legitimation dynamics, highlighting the need to move beyond the current fixation among researchers in this area on firm level cost/benefit calculations of whether to join. Any conclusions based solely on such analyses are incomplete, and potentially, premature – in effect, kneecapping expectations of NSMD systems before they have had time to develop into enduring and adaptable legitimate arenas of authority. As our empirical examples and analysis suggests, many NSMD arrangements are engaged in legitimating processes that include forums where stakeholders and targeted actors can discuss, argue, and deliberate on what standards *should* apply and how to achieve them, which in turn can transform the basis on which actor calculations are made. Just how these systems emerge and gain legitimacy should be of critical importance to anyone interested in whether the current trajectory of global capitalism can facilitate, rather than debilitate, efforts to ameliorate increasingly acute global social and environmental problems.

Acknowledgements

Portions of this chapter have appeared in: Steven Bernstein and Benjamin Cashore (2007): Can Non-State Global Governance be Legitimate? A Theoretical Framework. *Regulation and Governance* 1(4): 347–71. They are reproduced here with permission.

The authors thank John Braithwaite, Tim Bartley, Will Coleman, Claire Cutler, Radislov Dimitrov, Thorsten Göbel, Carmen Huckel, Erin Hannah, Stefan Kaufman, Volker Rittberger and participants in the Tübingen conference for their comments on previous versions of this chapter. We are grateful to Erin Hannah, Radhika Dave and Larissa Yocom for valuable research assistance. Steven Bernstein gratefully acknowledges funding for this project from the Social Sciences and Humanities Research Council of Canada. Benjamin Cashore thanks Graeme Auld, Deanna Newsom, Emily Noah, Aseem Prakash, Erika Sasser, Errol Meidinger, Fred Gale and James Lawson for their collaboration on related work that has pushed forward his thinking on these issues. He gratefully acknowledges support from the USDA's National Research Initiative, the Ford and Merck foundations, the Rockefeller Brothers Fund, and the Doris Duke Charitable trust.

Notes

1. For example, the estimated global market for Forest Stewardship Council (FSC) certified wood products exceeds \$5 billion. It currently certifies over 50 million hectares in over 62 countries (FSC 2005). Total coverage of this sector is much greater since other NSMD systems, discussed below, also certify forests.
2. Export data were derived from all products traded globally in the forest, marine resources, coffee, mining, textiles, clothing and tourism sectors, as measured by the World Trade Organization (WTO 2002) and the Food and Agriculture Organization (FAO 2003). These sectors account for about \$1,952 billion of trade earnings of a total of \$9,089 billion in earnings for total world trade of goods and services.
3. Ruggie (2003; 2004) has used the language of both 'social' and 'public' domain, apparently settling on the latter (2004: 504). We prefer 'social' domain because it not only can be distinguished from strictly marketplace activity and government (public) authority, but also because it points to its target: governing in the realm of human interests and values rather than, say, economic efficiency or national security as ends in themselves. See also Drache 2001.
4. While often referred to as 'certification systems' (Gerrefi, Garcia-Johnson and Sasser 2001), this term conflates other forms of authority with non-state or market driven governance. For similar reasons we do not address all of the initiatives identified by scholarly work on political consumerism (Micheletti, Føllesdal and Stolle 2003).
5. European Forest Owners originally created the PEFC as an 'umbrella' 'mutual recognition' programme for national initiatives developed to compete, or preempt, the FSC model in domestic settings.
6. Personal interviews and Vallejo and Hauselmann (2004).
7. We include systems here that originated as business self-regulation because a classification system should exist independent of how governance systems originated. Notably, however, such systems tend to begin with less well developed governance and fewer standards.
8. Personal communication, Michael Conroy. See also www.piec.org/ecl_space/
9. In practice, most NSMD systems, often for reasons of legitimacy, require adherence to domestic and international law as part of their systems (Courville 2003a: 281, 294).
10. Beyond that, the term governance is highly contested. Governance may be centralized or decentralized, hierarchical (as in the state) or non-hierarchical (as in

cooperative systems such as the sovereign state system), more or less formalized, with weak or strong enforcement, and so on.

11. Notably, the guidelines are part of a wider OECD instrument, the Declaration on International Investment and Multinational Enterprises, designed to create a level playing field in investment through such norms as national treatment and to promote investment liberalization. This suggests a continued imbalance between liberalization and social regulation in multilateral agreements which, as our earlier discussion of embedded liberalism suggested, created a demand for NSMD governance. The Declaration can be found at www.oecd.org/document/24/0,2340,en_2649_34889_1875736_1_1_1_1,00.html.
12. Porter's (2004) discussion on successful private and hybrid networks identifies some of these features.
13. We use the term global to differentiate this level from a strictly state-centric (international) focus, but recognize that marketplaces may not be truly global and global norms may not be universally accepted.
14. We understand 'soft' international law to mean largely declaratory or non-binding law, but with wide acceptance or agreement among states that frequently serves as a basis for future 'hard' law.
15. We specifically *do not* equate law and legitimacy, but still acknowledge that law is often an important source and indicator of legitimacy for a rule.
16. 'Legitimate' objectives explicitly mentioned include national security, prevention of deceptive standards, and protection of human health and safety, animal or plant life health, and the environment.
17. Space limitations prevent a full discussion, but see Chang 1997; Joshi 2004; Ward 1997.
18. In this regard the work of Sabatier and Jenkins-Smith (1993) is useful in addressing how 'secondary belief systems' (as opposed to 'core' values) about appropriate institutional design can be transformed when advocacy coalitions, bound by very different core values, participate in cross-coalition learning processes.

References

Andrews, R. (1998): Environmental Regulation and Business Self-Regulation. *Policy Sciences* 31 (September): 177–97.

Bäckstrand, K. and M. Saward (2004): Democratizing Global Environmental Governance? Stakeholder Democracy at the World Summit for Sustainable Development. Paper presented to the 5th Pan-European conference on International Relations. The Hague, September: 9–11.

Bartley, T. (2003): Certifying Forests and Factories: States, Social Movements, and the Rise of Private Regulation in the Apparel and Forest Products Fields. *Politics & Society* 31 (September): 433–64.

Bernstein, S. (2001): *The Compromise of Liberal Environmentalism*. New York: Columbia University Press.

Bernstein S. and B. Cashore (2004): Non-State Global Governance: is Forest Certification a Legitimate Alternative to a Global Forest Convention? In: Kirton J. and M. Trebilcock (eds.), *Hard Choices, Soft Law: Combining Trade, Environment, and Social Cohesion in Global Governance*. London: Ashgate Press: 33–63.

Bodansky, D. (1999): The Legitimacy of International Governance: a Coming Challenge for International Environmental Law? *American Journal of International Law* 93 (July): 596–624.

Börzel, T. A. and T. Risse (2005): Public–Private Partnerships: Effective and Legitimate Tools of Transnational Governance? In: Grande E. and W. P. Louis (eds.), *Complex Sovereignty: Reconstituting Political Authority in the 21st Century*. Toronto: University of Toronto Press: 195–216.

Braithwaite, J. and P. Drahos (2000): *Global Business Regulation*. Cambridge: Cambridge University Press.

Cashore, B. (2002): Legitimacy and the Privatization of Environmental Governance: How Non-State Market-Driven (NSMD) Governance Systems Gain Rule-Making Authority. *Governance* 14 (October): 502–29.

Cashore, B., G. Auld, and D. Newsom (2004): *Governing Through Markets: Forest Certification and the Emergence of Non-state Authority*. New Haven: Yale University Press.

Chang, Seung Wha. (1997): GATTing a Green Trade Barrier: Eco-Labelling and the WTO Agreement on Technical Barriers to Trade. *Journal of World Trade* 31 (February): 137–59.

Chertow, M. R. and D. C. Esty (eds.) (1997): *Thinking Ecologically: the Next Generation of Environmental Policy*. New Haven: Yale University Press.

Clapp, J. (1998): The Privatization of Global Environmental Governance: ISO 14000 and the Developing World. *Global Governance* 4 (August): 295–316.

Cochoy, F. (2003): The Industrial Roots of Contemporary Political Consumerism: the Case of the French Standardization Movement. In: Micheletti M., A. Føllesdal, and D. Stolle (eds.), *Politics, Products, and Markets: Exploring Political Consumerism Past and Present*. New Brunswick, NJ: Transaction Press: 145–60.

Courville, S. (2003a): Social Accountability Audits: Challenging or Defending Democratic Governance? *Law and Policy* 25 (July): 269–97.

Courville, S. (2003b): Understanding NGO-Based Social and Environmental Regulatory Systems: Why We Need New Models of Accountability. Paper read at 'Accountability in a Complex World: Conceptualizing Constitutional and Regulatory Efficacy in the Face of Globalization and Privatized Governance.' New York, March: 14–15.

de Azevedo, T. R. (2004): The Forest Stewardship Council: a Developing Country Perspective. In: Kirton J. and M. Trebilcock (eds.), *Hard Choices, Soft Law: Combining Trade, Environment, and Social Cohesion in Global Governance*. London: Ashgate Press: 65–94.

Cutler, C., V. Haufler, and T. Porter (1999): Private Authority and International Affairs. In: Cutler C., V. Haufler and T. Porter (eds.), *Private Authority in International Politics*. New York: SUNY Press: 3–28.

Drache, D. (ed.) (2001): *The Market or the Public Domain*. London: Routledge.

Falkner, R. (2003): Private Environmental Governance and International Relations: Exploring the Links. *Global Environmental Politics* 3 (May): 72–87.

FAO (2003): *Forest Products Statistical Data*. See: www.fao.org/forestry/en

Florini, A. (1996): The Evolution of International Norms. *International Studies Quarterly* 40 (September): 363–89.

FSC (2005): Estimated Size of FSC Global Market Revised to US$5 Billion. News Release. Document #: FSC-PUB-20-01-2005-04-22.

Garcia-Johnson, R. (2001): Certification Institutions in the Protection of the Environment: Exploring the Implications for Governance. Paper presented at the 23rd Annual Research Conference of the Association for Public Policy, Analysis, and Management. Washington DC, 1 November.

Gereffi, G., R. Garcia-Johnson and E. Sasser (2001): The NGO–Industrial Complex. *Foreign Policy* 125 (July/August): 56–65.

Global Reporting Initiative (2005): www.globalreporting.org.

Göbel, T. (2004): Does Monitoring Entail Legitimacy? MNCs, Monitoring Mechanisms, and Three Stories About the Legitimacy of Codes of Conduct. MA Thesis, University of Tübingen.

Greening, D. W., and B. Gray (1994): Testing a Model of Organizational Response to Social and Political Issues. *Academy of Management Journal* 37 (June): 467–98.

Gunningham, N., R. A. Kagan, and D. Thornton (2003): *Shades of Green: Business, Regulation, and Environment.* Stanford, CA: Stanford University Press.

Gunningham, N. and D. Sinclair (2002): *Leaders and Laggards: Next-Generation Environmental Regulation.* Sheffield: Greenleaf Publishing.

Gunningham, N., P. N. Grabosky, and D. Sinclair (1998): *Smart Regulation: Designing Environmental Policy.* Oxford: Clarendon Press.

Harrison, K. (1998): Talking with the Donkey: Cooperative Approaches to Environmental Protection. *Journal of Industrial Ecology* 2 (Summer): 51–72.

Haufler, V. (2001): *A Public Role for the Private Sector: Industry Self-Regulation in a Global Economy.* Washington DC: Carnegie Endowment for International Peace.

Held, D. and M. Koenig-Archibugi (eds.) (2005): *Global Governance and Public Accountability.* Oxford: Blackwell.

Hock, T. (2001): The Role of Eco-Labels in International Trade: Can Timber Certification be Implemented as a Means to Slowing Deforestation? *Colorado Journal of International Environmental Law and Policy* 12 (Summer): 347–65.

Howlett, M. (2000): Managing the 'Hollow State': Procedural Policy Instruments and Modern Governance. *Canadian Public Administration* 43 (Winter): 412–31.

Joshi, M. (2004): Are Eco-Labels Consistent with World Trade Organization Agreements? *Journal of World Trade* 38 (February): 69–92.

Keck, M. and K. Sikkink (1998): *Activists Beyond Borders: Transnational Issue Networks in International Politics.* New York: Cornell University Press.

Klein, N. (1999): *No Logo.* New York: Picador.

Kollman, K. and A. Prakash (2002): EMS-based Environmental Regimes as Club Goods: Examining Variations in Firm-level Adoption of ISO 14001 and EMAS in UKI, US, and Germany. *Policy Sciences* 35 (March): 43–67.

Levi, M. and A. Linton (2003): Fair Trade: a Cup at a Time? *Politics and Society* 31 (September): 407–32.

Marine Stewardship Council (2001): Conclusions of the MSC Governance Review. July (accessed August 2001, www.msc.org, but since removed from website).

Meyer, J. W. et al. (1997): World Society and the Nation-State. *American Journal of Sociology* 103 (July): 144–81.

Micheletti, M., A. Føllesdal, and D. Stolle (eds.) (2003): *Politics, Products, and Markets. Exploring Political Consumerism Past and Present.* New Brunswick, NJ: Transaction Press.

Pauly, L. W., and S. Reich (1997): National Structures and Multinational Corporate Behaviour: Enduring Differences in the Age of Globalization. *International Organization* 51 (Winter): 1–30.

Payne, R. A. and N. H. Samhat: *Democratizing Global Politics.* Albany, NY: SUNY Press.

Peretti, J. (with M. Micheletti) (2003): The Nike Sweatshop Email: Political Consumerism, Internet, and Culture Jamming. In: Micheletti M., A. Føllesdal, and D. Stolle (eds.), *Politics, Products, and Markets: Exploring Political Consumerism Past and Present.* New Brunswick, NJ: Transaction Press: 127–44.

Polanyi, K. (1944): *The Great Transformation.* Boston: Beacon Press.

Porter, M. E. and C. van der Linde (1995): Green and Competitive: Ending the Stalemate. *Harvard Business Review* 73 (September–October): 120–34.

Porter, T. (2004): Compromises of Embedded Knowledges: Standards, Codes and Technical Authority in Global Governance. In: Bernstein, S. and L.W. Pauly (eds.). Albany, NY: SUNY Press.

Prakash, A. (1999): A New-Institutional Perspective on ISO 14000 and Responsible Care. *Business Strategy and the Environment* 8 (November/December): 322–35.

Prakash, A. (2000): Responsible Care: an Assessment. *Business and Society* 39 (June): 183–209.

Prakash, A. (2001): Why do Firms Adopt 'Beyond-Compliance' Environmental Policies? *Business Strategy and the Environment* 10 (September/October): 286–99.

Raines, S. Summers (2003): Perceptions of Legitimacy in International Environmental Management Standards: the Participation Gap. *Global Environmental Politics* 3 (August): 47–73.

Rivera, J. (2002): Assessing a Voluntary Environmental Initiative in the Developing World: the Costa Rican Certification for Sustainable Tourism. *Policy Sciences* 35 (December): 333–60.

Rosenbaum, W. A. (1995): *Environmental Politics and Policy*. 3rd edn. Washington: CQ Press.

Rosenau, J. N. (1995): Governance in the Twenty-first Century. *Global Governance* 1 (January–April): 13–43.

Rosenau, J. N. (2003): *Distant Proximities: Dynamics Beyond Globalization*. Princeton: Princeton University Press.

Rosenau, P. Vaillancourt (eds.) (2000): Public–Private Policy Partnerships. Cambridge, MA: MIT Press.

Ruggie, J. G. (1982): International Regimes, Transactions and Change: Embedded Liberalism in the Postwar Economic Order. *International Organization* 36 (Spring): 379–415.

Ruggie, J. G. (2002): The Theory and Practice of Learning Networks: Corporate Social Responsibility and the Global Compact. *Journal of Corporate Citizenship* 5 (Spring): 27–36.

Ruggie, J. G. (2003): Taking Embedded Liberalism Global: the Corporate Connection. In: Held D. and M. Koenig-Archibugi (eds.), *Taming Globalization: Frontiers of Governance*. Cambridge: Polity: 93–129.

Ruggie, J. G. (2004): Reconstituting the Global Public Domain – Issues, Actors, and Practices. *European Journal of International Relations* 10 (December): 499–531.

Sabatier, P. and H. Jenkins-Smith (eds.) (1993): *Policy Learning and Policy Change: an Advocacy Coalition Approach*. Boulder, CO: Westview Press.

Salaman, L. M. (2002): Introduction. In: *The Tools of Government: a Guide to the New Governance*. New York: Oxford University Press: 1–47.

Sasser, E. (2002): The Certification Solution: NGO Promotion of Private, Voluntary Self-Regulation. Paper presented to the 74th Annual Meeting of the Canadian Political Science Association. Toronto, May: 29–31.

Sasser, E. (2003): Gaining Leverage: NGO Influence on Certification Institutions in the Forest Products Sector. In: Teeter L., B. Cashore and D. Zhang (eds.), *Forest Policy for Private Forestry*. Wallingford, UK: CAB International: 220–44.

Sasser, E. et al. (2004): Direct Targeting as an NGO Political Strategy: Examining Private Authority Regimes in the Forestry Sector. Paper presented to the Association of Public Policy Analysis and Management. Washington DC, Nov.

Suchman, M. C. (1995): Managing Legitimacy: Strategic and Institutional Approaches. *Academy of Management Review* 20 (July): 571–610.

Vallejo, N. and P. Hauselmann (2004): *Governance and Multistakeholder Processes.* New York: Sustainable Commodity Initiative, a Joint Venture of UNCTAD and IISD.

Ward, H. (1997): Trade and Environment Issues in Voluntary Eco-labelling and Life Cycle Analysis. *RECIEL* 6 (July): 139–47.

Webb, K. (ed.) (2002): *Voluntary Codes: Private Governance, the Public Interest and Innovation.* Ottawa: Carleton University Research Unit on Innovation, Science and the Environment.

Weber, S. (1994): Origins of the European Bank for Reconstruction and Development. *International Organization* 48 (Winter): 1–38.

Wilkie, C. (2004): Enhancing Global Governance: Corporate Social Responsibility International Trade and Investment Framework. In: Kirton J. and M. Trebilcock (eds.), *Hard Choices, Soft Law: Combining Trade, Environment, and Social Cohesion in Global Governance.* London: Ashgate Press: 297–329.

Woods, N. (1999): Good Governance in International Organizations. *Global Governance* 5 (January–March): 39–61.

WTO (2000): Committee Tackles Market Access Issues. *Trade and Environment Bulletin* 32 (17 March) available at www.wto.org/english/tratop_e/envir_e/te032_e.htm.

WTO (2002): *Statistics: International Trade Statistics 2002. Trade by Sector.* See: www.wto.org/english/res_e/statis_e/its2002_e/its02_bysector_e.htm

Conclusion: Authority Beside and Beyond the State

Volker Rittberger, Martin Nettesheim, Carmen Huckel, Thorsten Göbel

Introduction

Global economic integration is one of the most powerful forces shaping the contemporary international system. It has sparked processes of convergence in business and law as well as society and culture. It has also challenged established principles of the international order, created legal challenges and lacunae and is leading to new demands on states to fulfil functions previously outside of their jurisdictions. The role of the state to ensure the provision of public goods and achieve the goals of governance has become strained, and newly emerging policy issues are now increasingly dealt with by competing global, regional and national institutions.

Not surprisingly, current ideas and predictions for the future of the global political economy vary greatly in terms of the foreseen role of states, international institutions and non-state actors. Some observers see states as being weakened by rising non-state and supra-state actors such as transnational corporations, civil society organizations or international organizations. They fear that we are witnessing a retreat of the state, with state power being shifted from weak to strong states, upwards (to international institutions), sideways (from states to markets) (Strange 1996: 189; Stiles 2000), or that 'corporations rule the world' (Korten 2001). Others predict a strengthening of state power through engaging with non-state actors, interpreting recent attempts at the use of private authority and self-regulation as heavily reliant on the state in the final instance (Sending and Neumann 2006; Jordan, Wurzel et al. 2005). On both sides of the debate, there are varying views on the desirability, potential and problems of current trends. The contributions in this volume focus on how newly emerging institutions, actors, forms of regulation and concepts of legitimacy in the global political economy play out in broader debates about authority on the global level.

The purpose of this volume has been to analyse the changing patterns of authority in the global political economy with an in-depth look at new forms of regulation as well as at the non-state actors that are emerging as important participants in global governance institutions. Two main observations have provided the basis for this examination. First, regulation is increasingly being developed outside of the decision-making fora of states. This is most prominently taking place at the supranational level and within institutions that exercise authority beside and beyond the state. States appear to share decision-making authority with non-state actors, and must deal with increasingly complex global organizations. States are having to react to, and negotiate through, a new global political and legal environment. Private and market-driven regulation is also emerging as a realm where rules of conduct are formulated and applied independently of states or inter-state institutions. Second, the established ordering principles of public international law and international relations are being challenged by global norms and expectations demanding the better provision of global public goods and solutions to transnational problems. Where state capacity is waning, or political priorities are contested, new actors are exercising authority through new global institutions concentrating on issue-specific governance.

In this volume the chapters have brought together interrelated perspectives from political science studies on global governance and public international law. Within both these disciplines two themes: first, role of the state and, second, state relations with other actors, have come to play a critical role for studies dealing with new patterns of authority beside and beyond the state.

Looking at the emergence of new patterns of authority in the global political economy from the perspective of public international law, one cannot but discern a multifaceted picture with regard to the role of the state. An analytical approach will conclude that recent developments have already left deep imprints in the *theory* and *doctrine* of public international law, which is currently undergoing a fundamental transformation. It came into existence in the sixteenth and seventeenth centuries as a legal order *coordinating* the external acts of sovereign states. The system was founded on the notion of consensus and reciprocity, and the legitimacy of its norms relied on the affirmation of sovereign states: They had the freedom to accept or reject the binding quality of a norm, and the government of each state was perceived as legitimately representative of its citizens in the international forum. The methodology of this public international law quite naturally centred on the 'will of states'.

In the second half of the nineteenth century, new forms of international cooperation emerged. International organizations provided a forum in which nation-states could pursue common goals and aims. The structures and procedures of international organizations continued to be based on the principles of consensus and reciprocity. No state was obliged to participate, and no state was bound by the decisions of the international organization against its will. Since the early years of the second half of the twentieth century, two developments subjected the structures of public international law to fundamental changes: First, the institutional features of international organizations were hardened ('institutionalization'): In more and more cases, international organizations became enabled to adjust and update, to administer, to apply and to enforce the regulatory content of the treaties, on the basis of which they were constituted. Some of the institutions were entrusted with law-making authority; others had the power to – directly or indirectly – use coercion to bring a state in violation of its obligations into line. In other cases, international institutions were delegated the role of finding obligatory and binding settlements for disputes – thereby inevitably not only interpreting, but also adjusting and amending the substantive rules.

Second, the traditional structures of public international law have been gradually superseded and supplemented by yet a third layer. This layer comprises rules and norms that are aimed at the protection of certain substantive common goods: the protection of human rights, the protection of an unspoiled environment, the assistance to countries in their development process and the fight against poverty and lately also the concern for democracy. Here it is possible to speak about a *'materialization of public international law'* (Nettesheim 2002: 569). The substantive common goods or bads at which the attention of this new order is directed are partly genuinely *transnational* – in the sense that they would have cross-border effects (environmental pollution, state failure, etc.). In other instances, the rules relate to what one could call ethical standards of worldwide relevance. The increasing use of terms such as 'international community' indicates the depth of the redefinition of global public goods and of the responsibility of states. At the same time, the dimension of certain problems, such as transnational migration or environmental destruction, is growing; in more and more cases, they are of a truly global dimension (e.g. the depletion of the ocean resources). With the increasing porosity of national borders, increasing integration of markets, the growth of globally operating economic actors, and finally the emergence of a transnational civil society with global reach, the regulatory environment of public international law is quickly changing. Some of the changes are a consequence of the actions of states and international organizations, some of the alterations reflect the changed setting. The 'materialization' of public international law is not situated in a static environment. The relevant political and ethical standards are developing dynamically and with astonishing speed.

These developments described above link the public international law perspective with a political science perspective on changing patterns of authority that are being observed and analysed in global governance debates. The two previously mentioned themes 'role of the state' and 'its relations with other actors', provide ground for complementarity among the different perspectives offered by the disciplinary approaches of public international law and political science.

Seen from a global governance perspective, it is clear that, while states remain central actors in global politics, they increasingly interact with a widening array of other actors. The roles that states and these new actors play are, especially since the end of the cold war, in a state of flux, exacerbated by changing global conditions and the emergence of new transsovereign issues (Brühl/Rittberger 2001; Cusimano, Hensman et al. 2000). We notice, for example, an increasing number of organized non-state actors being involved in agenda-setting, decision-making, policy implementation and monitoring of activities in partnership with state actors (Risse 2002; Salamon 1995). Multi-state and for-profit actors, too, are changing in their role and function as providers of material and non-material resources for global governance, and are facing changing expectations. This rise in the number of actors, as well as their changing role and function, have sparked the need for, and an increase in, new forms of inter- and transnational institutions (Rosenau 2002). These institutions are necessary for tackling transsovereign problems and for contributing to public goods provision on a global scale, which none of the actors can accomplish or want to do effectively in their own capacity.

This evolving path of international institution-building goes hand in hand with changing rules of social order and expectations of cooperation amongst various agents from both the public and the private sector and has increasingly gained attention in studies into global governance, the latter defined as: 'The collective identification of high-potential approaches for solving common problems and the process of transforming them into binding rules of behaviour, monitoring behaviour and, if necessary, adjusting the rules to changes in external conditions' (Rittberger 2003: 181f; Rittberger 2004: 249).

Global governance clearly breaks with other major schools of thought in political science and public international law in the way the role of the state is addressed. Indeed, the short- and long-term future role of the state is arguably the most contested facet in globalization discourses. The exclusive authority of the state over a given, territorially determined community has been seen as one precondition for its internal and external sovereignty in the Westphalian system of international relations. The state has been understood as the organizational form with comparative advantages in terms of power, manifested in its ability to tax constituents and to wield the legal monopoly of physical force. However, in order to retain authority in its internal and external relations, states also have to fulfil governance functions such as rule of law, welfare, security, identity and channels of participation (Zürn 2001: 53). Only the effective fulfilment of these functions provides the legitimacy that authority is based on.

Globalization has challenged states' ability to be able to adequately perform these tasks. They have come under pressure from both internal and external sources. Increasingly interconnected economies, the rapid fluidity of ideas and cultures across borders, new modes of communication and cross-border identities undermine the authority of the state. This implies that multinational corporations and other non-state, i.e. civil society actors are becoming more important. In addition, interdependence and new transnational problems create the demand for new solutions that cannot be provided by states alone. The authority of the state is increasingly challenged and has been shifting to new actors and institutions that are in a better position to deal with these issues.

Summary

In this volume, we have taken an in-depth look at some of these newly emerging institutions of authority examining their form, consequences and potential. We have also concentrated on the provision of global public goods, reflecting on the limitations of, and new challenges for, the state and focused attention on new actors and the question of regulation. The chapters have also referred to the four different dimensions of global governance analysis that were laid out in-depth in the Introduction, namely demand, supply effect and design. We will now take a closer look at these four underlying themes of analysis and how they have been manifested with the five key substantive aspects of the volume, i.e. 1) the rise and 'constitution' of new institutions for governance in the global political economy; 2) the definition of (global) public goods, their (under-)supply, and their transformation into private goods (and vice versa); 3) the contribution of civil society organizations to global governance in general and to the provision of (global) public goods in particular; 4) business actors' contributions to global governance and to the provision of (global) public goods; and 5) the differences between various modes of regulation incorporated in new institutions for global governance.

Part 1

In terms of *demand*, there is agreement amongst the authors in the first part 'New Institutions for Global Governance' containing chapters by Volker Rittberger et al. and Jeffrey Dunoff, that the current system of global governance in the form of executive multilateralism is, in many ways, inadequate. Executive multilateralism refers to 'a decision making mode in which governmental representatives coordinate policies internationally, with little national parliamentary control and away from public scrutiny' (Zürn 2004: 264). Whether one takes examples from world trade, as does Dunoff, international and interregional conflict, or public health and corporate social responsibility, as does the chapter by Rittberger et al., all of the authors recognize a demand for new patterns of authority, including new roles played by states and non-state actors, such as civil society and business actors. This is due, first, to changes in the international system, such as the end of the cold war, the technological revolution in the field of communication, and the process of global economic liberalization and integration, both temporal and spatial, and, second, to the rise of new transsovereign problems, especially negative externalities arising from macro changes, such as the increasing depletion of environmental resources, transnational migration, new health pandemics or new security threats such as transnational terrorism.

However, in terms of *supply*, i.e. the extent to which new institutions for global governance have formed and gained influence, the chapters do differ in their arguments and conclusions. Rittberger et al. identify a definite trend towards more *inclusive institutions for global governance* encompassing state actors, international bureaucracies and non-state actors. They suggest that new inclusive institutions, such as the UN Global Compact or the Global Fund to Fight AIDS, Tuberculosis and Malaria, have the potential to close certain governance gaps in the current system of global governance. They thus offer refute to the claim that non-state actors can only play a complementary role to state-based institutions and that states are the only actors that can provide responsible governance even on the global level. For Dunoff, a trend towards the constitutionalization of public international law is observable but does not necessarily reflect a strengthening of the state. Rather, there is a centralization of authority within international organizations such as the WTO and an increase in the capacity of such organizations to act independently of member states. He also sees a diffusion of authority towards other international legal regimes and international organizations, such as the WHO or FAO whereas Rittberger et al. express scepticism in this regard with respect to the ILO.

In sum, the first two chapters address different approaches to the analysis of the *supply* of new institutions for global governance; first, inclusive institutions that integrate both public sector and private sector actors as members, and second, a strengthening of international organizations through their 'constitutionalization'. The two approaches explored by Rittberger et al. and Dunoff recognize that actors other than states (e.g. international organizations, civil society and business actors) contribute to both the *supply* of, and also the *demand* for, new institutions for global governance. While there is congruence in terms of the *demand* for new institutions, there is disagreement in terms of the *supply* dimension. Two camps can be identified, the first prioritizing states over non-state actors, and the second recognizing and integrating the potential of non-state actors' participation in new institutions for global governance. The contributions addressed in the book as a whole can all be located in either the first or the second camp. Indeed, the debate which has developed between the two first chapters sets the stage for the analyses and discussions presented in the remaining chapters.

Part 2

The contributions by Inge Kaul and Peter-Tobias Stoll that follow the (global) public goods approach in the second part 'Providing and Managing Global Public Goods' examine why new governing institutions for the provision of global public goods are needed, and which state or non-state actors are most suited to be part of these institutions. The authors highlight deficits in the provision of global public goods, explain why there is a mismatch between the demand for, and the supply of, public goods and argue that new institutions for global governance have the potential to alleviate this mismatch.

The *demand* for public goods varies across societies. Due to different preferences, not every actor values a good equally and derives the same utility from its consumption. Kaul suggests that, therefore, the traditional definition of public goods (following the logic of economics based on the properties of nonrivalry and nonexcludability) takes on a new quality in a global political economy, as globalness constitutes a special dimension of publicness. Thus it needs to be determined whether public goods are indeed *pure* public goods, or rather only *de facto* nonexclusive and available for all to consume in the sense that they are made public by deliberate public-policy choices.

Stoll addresses the under*supply* of global public goods. He argues that this under*supply* is due not only to a lack of provision of public goods by states and state based international institutions, but also to legal and political constraints, such as the assignment of intellectual property rights to business actors (cf. the WTO/TRIPS) and the privatization of public utilities (e.g. in the field of energy and water supply). Based on the assessment that states and international organizations can hardly cope with the rising demand for global public goods, he holds that it is necessary to explore the role of non-state actors in the provision of public goods with a view to enhancing it. By showing, for instance, that the protection of the environment cannot be sufficiently provided by state regulation alone, Stoll suggests that the provision of public goods requires the establishment of new governance institutions incorporating private sector actors. By allowing private actors to collect certain benefits from the commercial uses of public goods (e.g. genetic resources) or by establishing public–private partnerships to implement infrastructure projects, public goods provision can be improved.

According to Kaul, who emphasizes the importance of acknowledging that public goods are not always provided by the state alone, the provision of public goods should be opened for private contributions. In addition, she suggests that public goods provision could be improved by promoting global governance, with a voice for all relevant stakeholders and reduced information asymmetries. Yet, she acknowledges that states remain central actors in the provision and management of public goods. She also suggestes that states can fulfil their role best by moving towards the notion of responsible sovereignty, i.e. by internalizing negative cross-border spillovers and encouraging, where possible, positive spillovers.

The chapters by Kaul and Stoll show that states and state-based institutions, in the form of executive multilateralism, in many ways fail to provide the global public goods currently needed, resulting in a mismatch between the demand and the supply of these goods. They propose that effective alternatives to executive multilateralism will involve the provision of public goods, at least in part, through institutions incorporating non-state actors including business and civil society organizations.

Part 3

In terms of *supply,* Helmut Anheier and Nuno Themudo as well as Wolfgang Benedek in the part 'Civil Society and Global Governance' see NGOs as actors with the capacity and incentive to create or sustain new institutions for global governance. Anheier and Themudo claim that NGOs can play, and are playing, a significant role within global institutions. They analyse the growing visibility of NGOs in international relations and how this has presented them with new organizational challenges. They show that the salience of NGOs is increasing both in terms of numbers and in terms of revenue, and Benedek posits that global governance can no longer be imagined without the important role that they play. For example, in a number of cases NGOs have influenced international public opinion, one example being the rallies at the WTO Ministerial Conference in Seattle in 1999 where NGOs demonstrated their power to influence opinion and to prevent the successful completion of international negotiations.

Both chapters address different aspects of the institutional *design* of NGOs and how it affects their legitimacy and their capacity to shape institutions for, and processes of, global governance. Anheier's and Themudo's account finds that there are four different ways or, as they refer to them, 'expressions' through which NGOs can gain influence in global governance. First, through the 'new public management expression' NGOs are playing a role as service provider, often as sub-contractors of states or international organizations. This approach is replacing conventional development assistance policies of national and international donors. NGOs seek to capitalize on the comparative advantages of non-profit organizations through public–private partnerships, competitive bidding and sub-contracting under the general heading of privatization. Second, through the 'corporate expression' NGOs are adopting a corporate style based on cost efficiency. And they are even working together with corporations performing tasks previously undertaken by states. Third, through the 'social capital or self-organization expression' NGOs concentrate on building transnational relations and trust. This 'expression' is based on the positive and often indirect role of NGOs in facilitating and creating a sense of social inclusion that is seen as essential for the functioning of modern societies, both nationally and transnationally. Fourth and finally, through the 'activist expression' NGOs act as a source of dissent, challenge and innovation, as a countervailing force to governments and corporations. Here, NGOs take on the role of a 'watchdog' keeping both markets and states in check. In sum, the new public management and corporate 'expressions' put emphasis on organizational efficiency, whereas the social capital and activist 'expressions' emphasize internal democracy and member participation. Anheier and Themudo suggest that NGOs can reconcile conflicting sets of demands that arise from these different 'expressions' by choosing appropriate internal governance and management designs.

Taking Anheier's and Themudo's findings one step further, Benedek claims that, if NGOs want to maximize their influence in global governance, they also need to increase their organizational accountability and legitimacy. Benedek suggests that NGOs need to be (more) accountable to their members and supporters as well as to the public at large. This, in turn, will positively affect NGOs' legitimacy. There are two principal ways to increase the accountability of NGOs: either NGOs take steps to increase their accountability internally, e.g. through the disclosure of funding sources and more transparent decision-making processes; or, externally, by making use of the gatekeeper function of international organizations, which, by admitting NGOs into a consultative or other status with more participatory rights, exert a measure of quality control. Examples are the criteria laid down by ECOSOC and the WTO for NGO participation. Benedek concludes that, despite some disadvantages, the institutionalized participation of NGOs within international organizations can contribute to a strengthening of their legitimacy and vice versa and thereby provide more legitimacy for global governance as well.

These last two contributions move past a mere recognition of the roles that NGOs have played in international affairs. They point out that NGOs are in a position to strategically shape their future role in institutions for global governance by adopting certain strategies that are either service or advocacy oriented. Furthermore, they are not only able to steer the direction of their engagement in terms of what role they play, but also to enhance their influence within new institutions for global governance through increasing their accountability and legitimacy, either internally or externally or both.

Part 4

Claire Cutler and Virginia Haufler in the part 'Business in Global Governance' emphasize the strong empirical evidence that business actors are playing an increasingly important role in global governance. Cutler explores the idea of developing binding public international law applicable to business actors, while Haufler refers to the role that business actors have played in zones of conflict.

Haufler argues that the new role that business actors are taking on in zones of conflict, such as the promotion of human rights or the support for more transparent revenue-sharing with host country governments, has been facilitated by a variety of changes in the international system. These changes are reflected, first, in the changing nature of the state in the developing world, second, in the shift of the development paradigm from a state-centric, protectionist model to one based on liberalization, deregulation and privatization, third, by the possibility of humanitarian intervention, and, fourth, by the more prominent role of civil society advocacy groups in targeting corporations. Due to these changes in the international system, states and civil society actors have chosen to support a more active role of business actors that essentially delegates the handling of some security-related tasks in zones of conflict to private sector entities.

While Haufler takes an empirical-analytical approach, Cutler uses critical theory to give an account of the evolution of the public role of business actors from the dawn of the corporate age in the early twentieth century. She examines the idea of corporate social responsibility (CSR) as the normative foundation of an emerging role of business in a new 'public' sphere. By analysing the emerging global business civilization as a dimension of the expansion of 'private' authority in global governance, she asserts that conditions of late capitalism are reflected in the development of transnational corporate law. New 'privatized' institutions, such as the International Court of Arbitration of the International Chamber of Commerce, facilitate the mobility and expansion of capital and related patterns of flexible accumulation.

Disagreement arises between the contributors over the effects that the more prominent role of business actors in global governance can and will have. Haufler notes that even NGOs, which have previously focused on the negative impacts of businesses on zones of conflict, now emphasize the positive contributions that business actors *can* make in zones of conflict, e.g. by actively promoting and supporting revenue transparency of the host government and revenue sharing programme between central governments and regional or local administrations. By alluding to the fact that corporations can be caught between the norm of corporate social responsibility and the sovereign demands of the host state, Haufler points at the sometimes difficult and complex situations business actors find themselves in. Moreover, it has to be taken into account that the exact boundaries of legitimate and illegitimate action of corporations are difficult to define, and change with time and circumstance. By taking the oil sector as an example, she shows how leading states, international organizations and NGOs are promoting a more direct role for corporations in host country politics.

From a different perspective, Cutler argues that, because business actors are not yet subjects of public international law, institutions promoting CSR are of a self-regulatory nature and therefore favourable to corporate interests. To remedy this situation she supports the idea of developing binding international economic laws governing CSR. In addition, she maintains that the benefits of self-regulation, such as the reduction of transaction costs can all be reduced to the bottom line of increased profitability. Cutler concludes that the discourse of efficiency informing the CSR movement is problematic and that the CSR movement needs to be critically examined in terms of the interests it serves.

The contributions by Cutler and Haufler underline that business actors play an active role in global governance, complementing functions that have been traditionally reserved for the state. In certain instances, they cooperate directly with states, as in the case of trade disputes within the WTO dispute settlement mechanism. In other instances, states as well as civil society actors allow for more authority to be transferred to business actors by supporting an active role of business in zones of conflict. Cutler takes a more critical point of view and refers to the disadvantages of a more prominent role of business actors. She warns that the dominance of the 'efficiency principle' that drives business actors may not always serve the public interest.

Part 5

In the part 'Regulation in Global Governance' Peter Utting as well as Benjamin Cashore and Steven Bernstein focus on the *design* of new transnational governance institutions, members of which include business, NGOs and sometimes states and international organizations. Cashore and Bernstein claim that non-state market-driven institutions, for example the Forest Stewardship Council, in which the state is not involved or does not play a decisive role, are a new way for addressing global challenges. In contrast, Utting suggests that purely non-state market-driven institutions are insufficient for effectively establishing rules and standards and ensuring compliance on a global scale. Instead, he pleads for more accountable institutions that include at least some elements of compulsory state-regulation.

Cashore and Bernstein show that there are non-state market-driven institutions that encourage socially and environmentally responsible practices in the global marketplace and that these institutions and resulting practices have proliferated over the last decade. The key design characteristics of non-state market-driven institutions are the absence of state-centred public authority, an institutionalized system of societal input and policy adaptation, a central role for the market, a policy focus on social domains, legitimacy granted through stakeholders including civil society groups and, last but not least, the monitoring of compliance with the rules of the institution through non-state verification procedures. Since these non-state market-driven institutions lack the traditional enforcement capacities of the state, Cashore and Bernstein suggest that their authority rests on their ability to gain and project legitimacy. Non-state market-driven institutions gain legitimacy in two ways: first, by fulfiling the expectations of primary stakeholders within the market-centred network of those directly affected by the rules of the institution, and, second, by adopting rules that correspond with existing international norms. Cashore and Bernstein hypothesize that the more a market is globalized, the less likely it is that national factors, such as the structure of domestic markets or national corporate and consumer culture, have an influence on legitimacy dynamics associated with non-state market-driven governance.

Utting analyses the recent shift towards non-state and co-regulatory institutions for CSR. In contrast to Cashore and Bernstein, his chapter highlights the limitations of both corporate self-regulation and what he terms co-regulation. Utting presents a 'corporate accountability' approach to overcoming the limitations inherent in current regulation, such as the multitude of CSR standards and the difficulties of their implementation, as was also addressed by Cutler. The author suggests that 'corporate accountability' implies a nuanced but nevertheless renewed and strengthened role for the state and international organizations, which is reflected in more compulsory elements in new institutions for global governance, such as monitoring, verification, and eventually reparation payments, envisioned, for instance, in the 2003 UN Draft Norms on the Responsibilities of Transnational Corporations and other Business Enterprises with regard to Human Rights (Weissbrodt and Kruger 2003).

However, the debate between self-regulation versus state or co-regulation is, in his view, misleading. For him, an interface between these forms of regulation would be a more fruitful approach to designing future institutions for global governance. He therefore puts particular emphasis on business regulation via various forms of institutional design and 'articulated regulation'. He identifies four forms: 1) Complementarity between different non-state market-driven institutions, i.e. complementary and mutually reinforcing institutions should be connected in some inter-operable way, as e.g. in the attempt to unite several complementary institutions in the textile sector (Fair Labour Association; Workers Rights Consortium; Ethical Trading Initiative; Social Accountability International; Clean Clothes Campaign; and Fair Wear Foundation) in a 'Joint Initiative on Corporate Accountability and Workers' Rights'; 2) the interface between confrontational and more cooperative forms of civil society activism, i.e. recognizing that the co-existence of these two forms of activism often accounts for the ratcheting-up and scaling-up of self-regulation and co-regulation; 3) increased interactions, not confrontation, between self-regulatory and state-backed legal approaches to regulation in global governance; and 4) greater policy coherence at both the micro-level of the corporation and the macro-level of states and international organizations.

In order to have a functioning global system that ensures compliance with institutionalized norms and rules, the authors discuss alternative designs to state regulation of markets. Their chapters show that there are at least two other forms of regulation, including, first, non-state market-driven regulation, and second, co-regulation which incorporates both elements of self-regulation and a degree of state and international organization involvement.

In conclusion

The realm of changing patterns of authority in the global political economy provides for plentiful room for differing approaches and fruitful debate. No other issue sets a greater division within globalization debates than the discussion about the future role of the state. Even in a multilayered and multipillared system of global governance, the state still emerges as a next to indispensable participant in the policy-making cycle. Nevertheless, it is widely accepted that current patterns of governance must be further developed. The intellectual and political challenge is to devise institutions for global governance which combine effectiveness of policy-making with standards of accountability and legitimacy.

It is important to take a critical view of the varying extent to which debates on global governance and public international law approach changing patterns of authority and the changing role of the state, both in view of current empirical realities and potential normative challenges. The contributions in this volume recognize this importance and offer substantial material for further analysis and reflection. While states will maintain their role and function as a cornerstone of the international system, it is observed that the number and the influence of global governance institutions, both intergovernmental and more inclusive in design, will continue to rise, and the decision-making authority of these organs will increase. The impacts of regulations stemming from these institutions will also grow, in sheer quantity as well as in quality.

Therefore, on the one hand, more knowledge and research is required about these institutions, their origin, their effects, as well as if, and how, such effects can be attributed to the work of the institutions. Since the ultimate goal of global governance institutions is not merely to function well, but to bring about change in some social condition, measuring the actual beneficial change or its absence is a high-stakes activity for any institution. Institutions for global governance cannot be judged as successful unless they actually deliver on their problem-solving goals.

On the other hand, the quest for legitimacy to exercise such authority will also gain significance. This is of special importance because increased authority of institutions of global governance often leads to a size versus participation paradox. In small institutions, the avenues through which citizens or civil society organizations are able to participate in decision-making are relatively open and easily negotiable, but their external problem-solving impact is limited. Larger more complex institutions have the potential for greater external impact, but can offer only limited opportunities for participation.

More research on these issues, more scholarly exchange and a combination of different perspectives from the fields of public international law and political science studies on global governance should be the aim. This volume has set a starting point in this regard, and we hope that, following our precedent, the issues and themes examined here will be further explored in future work on the changing patterns of authority in a global political economy.

References

Brühl, Tanja and Volker Rittberger (2001): From International to Global Governance: Actors, Collective Decision-making, and the United Nations in the World of the

Twenty-First Century. In: Rittberger, Volker (ed.): *Global Governance and the United Nations System*. Tokyo/New York: United Nations University Press: 1–47.

Cusimano, Maryann K., Mark Hensman and Leslie Rodrigues (2000): Private-Sector Transsovereign Actors – MNCs and NGOs. In: Cusimano, Maryann K. (ed.): *Beyond Sovereignty: Issues for a Global Agenda*. Boston: Bedford/St. Martin's: 253–82.

Jordan, Andrew, Rüdiger Wurzel and Anthony Zito (2005): The Rise of 'New' Policy Instruments in Comparative Perspective: Has Governance Eclipsed Government? In: *Political Studies* 53 (3): 477–96.

Korten, David C. (2001): *When Corporations Rule the World*. Bloomfield, CT: Kumarian Press.

Nettesheim, Martin (2002): Das kommunitaere Voelkerrecht. In: *Juristenzeitung* 57 (12): 569–78.

Risse, Thomas (2002): Transnational Actors and World Politics. In: Carlsnaes, Walter, Thomas Risse and Beth A. Simmons (eds.): *Handbook of International Relations*. London: Sage: 255–74.

Rittberger, Volker (2003): Weltregieren: Was kann es leisten? Was muss es leisten? In: Küng, Hans and Dieter Senghaas (eds.): *Friedenspolitik: Ethische Grundlagen Internationaler Beziehungen*. Muich/Zürich: Piper: 177–208.

Rittberger, Volker (2004): Weltregieren zwischen Anarchie und Hierarchie. In: Rittberger, Volker (ed.): *Weltpolitik heute. Grundlagen und Perspektiven*. Baden-Baden: Nomos: 245–70.

Rosenau, James (2002): NGOs and Fragmented Authority in Globalizing Space. In: Ferguson, Yale and R. Berry Jones (eds.): *Political Space: Frontiers of Change and Governance in a Globalizing World*. Albany: State University of New York Press: 261–79.

Sending, Ole Jacob and Iver B. Neumann (2006): Governance to Governmentality: Analyzing NGOs, States, and Power. In: *International Studies Quarterly* 50 (3): 651–72.

Salamon, Lester M. (1995): *Partners in Public Service*. Baltimore, MD: The Johns Hopkins University Press.

Stiles, Kendall (2000): Grassroots Empowerment: States, Non-State Actors and Global Policy Formulation. In: Higgot, Richard, Geoffrey Underhill and Andreas Bieler (eds.): *Non-State Actors and Authority in the Global System*, London: Routledge, 33–47.

Strange, Susan (1996): *The Retreat of the State: the Diffusion of Power in the World Economy*. Cambridge: Cambridge University Press.

Weissbrodt, David and Muria Kruger (2003): Norms on the Responsibilities of Transnational Corporations and Other Business Enterprises with Regard to Human Rights. In: *American Journal of International Law* 97 (4): 901–22.

Zürn, Michael (2001): Political Systems in the Postnational Constellation: Societal Denationalization and Multilevel Governance. In: Rittberger, Volker (ed.): *Global Governance and the United Nations System*. Tokyo/New York: United Nations University Press: 48–87.

Zürn, Michael (2004): Global Governance and Legitimacy Problems. In: *Government and Opposition* 39 (2): 260–87.

Index